AF880594

Springer Proceedings in Business and Economics

Springer Proceedings in Business and Economics brings the most current research presented at conferences and workshops to a global readership. The series features volumes (in electronic and print formats) of selected contributions from conferences in all areas of economics, business, management, and finance. In addition to an overall evaluation by the publisher of the topical interest, scientific quality, and timeliness of each volume, each contribution is refereed to standards comparable to those of leading journals, resulting in authoritative contributions to the respective fields. Springer's production and distribution infrastructure ensures rapid publication and wide circulation of the latest developments in the most compelling and promising areas of research today.

The editorial development of volumes may be managed using Springer's innovative Online Conference Service (OCS), a proven online manuscript management and review system. This system is designed to ensure an efficient timeline for your publication, making Springer Proceedings in Business and Economics the premier series to publish your workshop or conference volume.

More information about this series at https://link.springer.com/bookseries/11960

Arti Chandani · Rajiv Divekar · J. K. Nayak
Editors

Achieving $5 Trillion Economy of India

Proceedings of 11th Annual International Research Conference of Symbiosis Institute of Management Studies

Springer

Editors
Arti Chandani
Symbiosis Institute of Management Studies
Symbiosis International (Deemed University)
Pune, Maharashtra, India

Rajiv Divekar
Director, Symbiosis Institute of Management Studies
Symbiosis International (Deemed University)
Pune, Maharashtra, India

J. K. Nayak
Department of Management Studies
Indian Institute of Technology Roorkee
Roorkee, Uttarakhand, India

ISSN 2198-7246 ISSN 2198-7254 (electronic)
Springer Proceedings in Business and Economics
ISBN 978-981-16-7817-2 ISBN 978-981-16-7818-9 (eBook)
https://doi.org/10.1007/978-981-16-7818-9

© The Editor(s) (if applicable) and The Author(s), under exclusive license to Springer Nature Singapore Pte Ltd. 2022
This work is subject to copyright. All rights are solely and exclusively licensed by the Publisher, whether the whole or part of the material is concerned, specifically the rights of translation, reprinting, reuse of illustrations, recitation, broadcasting, reproduction on microfilms or in any other physical way, and transmission or information storage and retrieval, electronic adaptation, computer software, or by similar or dissimilar methodology now known or hereafter developed.
The use of general descriptive names, registered names, trademarks, service marks, etc. in this publication does not imply, even in the absence of a specific statement, that such names are exempt from the relevant protective laws and regulations and therefore free for general use.
The publisher, the authors and the editors are safe to assume that the advice and information in this book are believed to be true and accurate at the date of publication. Neither the publisher nor the authors or the editors give a warranty, expressed or implied, with respect to the material contained herein or for any errors or omissions that may have been made. The publisher remains neutral with regard to jurisdictional claims in published maps and institutional affiliations.

This Springer imprint is published by the registered company Springer Nature Singapore Pte Ltd.
The registered company address is: 152 Beach Road, #21-01/04 Gateway East, Singapore 189721, Singapore

Contents

About the Editors

Dr Arti Chandani is presently working with Symbiosis institute of Management Studies, Pune as Associate Professor. Dr. Arti Chandani has more than 23 years of experience in Teaching and research. She has published more than 50 papers in journals. She is the guest editor for special issue of journal, "International Journal of Public Sector Performance Management" and "International Journal of Business and Globalisation" which are being published by InderScience. She is also the Member of Editorial Board of International Journal of Digital Accounting Research (SCOPUS Indexed).

She has been awarded Best teacher by National Foundation for Entrepreneurship Development (NFED), Chennai in September, 2003. She has also received awarded for Best Teacher in Financial Management by Dainik Bhaskar National Education Leadership awards in October, 2013. She has been invited to deliver session by Department of Economics, Bangalore University, Bangalore. She was also invited to deliver a talk "Union Budget 2021- Suggestion" by EGROW foundations, Delhi on 25 Dec., 2020. She has also received many best papers award for the papers presented in various international conferences. In addition to this, she has also received 5 more best paper awards. She has been part of the organizing committee of International conference, Organised by NFED, Coimbatore- ICCRESMA for year 2020. She is also the Reviewer of International Journal of Innovation Science, International Journal of Emerging markets, Journal of Indian Business Research, Reviewer of "Information Resource Management Journal" of IGI Global along with other journals. She has also completed online courses from NPTEL in the area of research and training. She has also completed FDP from IIM-Kolkatta.

She is also the editor of the SIMS Annual International Research Conference: Unleashing the research journey. She is the conference convener of SIMSARC, since 2013, which is annual International research conference of Symbiosis Institute of Management Studies.

Brig (Dr.) Rajiv Divekar is the Director of Symbiosis Institute of Management Studies for the last 12 years. SIMS is amongst the top ranked B-schools in India which is over 27 years old.

Prior to this he was Head of Faculty Strategic and Operational Studies at Army War College and Faculty member in Defence Strategic Studies at Defence Services Staff College, Wellington. He has done his PhD from Symbiosis International University. He is a M. Phil from D A V V University and MSc from Madras University. A Gold medallist in BE (civil), he has done his MBA specializing in Human Resource Management. He has rich experience of strategy, planning, logistics and human resource management based on his service with multinational teams as part of United Nations Force in both Somalia and Lebanon. He has served in Kargil and Leh on the LoC where he was responsible for the Logistics and Supply Chain Management for soldiers located on posts at 17,000–22,000 feet in the Siachen Glacier.

He has a large number of research publications in National & International Journals & also in Scopus listed Journals. He is also a reviewer for a journal which is indexed in SCOPUS.

Under his leadership and guidance, SIMS has been organising an Annual International Research Conference for last 11 years. He teaches Strategy, Human Resource and Leadership to MBA students and has been invited to deliver talks at various organisations and institutes as also to deliver key note address in conferences.

He is a recipient of many awards in the field of education. He has been awarded "The Rashtriya Vidya Gaurav Gold Medal" by the Indian Solidarity Council, the "Rajiv Gandhi Education Excellence Award" by International Institute of Education and Management and the "Education Leadership Award" by Education Leadership Awards, Dubai.

Dr Jogendra Kumar Nayak is an Associate professor at IIT Roorkee. His area of research interests includes B2B marketing, Pricing, Tourism marketing. He teaches Marketing Research, Marketing Management and B2B Marketing to the students of MBA and B.Tech courses. He is currently deputed as a Professor-In-Charge of Training & Placement Department in DOMS (Department of Management Studies)-IIT Roorkee. In the year 2017 he was awarded as an 'Expert Member of Standing Committee on Research Methodology' by Ministry of Home Affairs, Govt. of India, also as a 'Reviewer for the Executive Government agency, Poland' by National Science Centre and in the year 2018 as a member, Board of studies and advisory board member of Abdul Kalam Technical University.

He did his PhD from VGSOM, IIT-Kharagpur in the field of marketing in 2012 and MBA from Bharti Vidyapeeth's IMED, Pune University in 2001 and a Civil Engineering graduate from Utkal University.

His major Research project includes a study on the handicraft industries: Empowering the artisans funded by ICSSR and Marketing Practices in Handicraft sector in Uttarakhand, funded by IIT. Some of his consulting assignments entailed working on projects like "Traidcraft-Study the Potential of Handloom sector in Orissa", and "European Union-Capacity building of Small and Medium Industries in Orissa".

He is also an active member of American Marketing Association, Member of System Dynamics Society and Eastern Asian society of transportation studies. He holds lifetime membership of the Indian Economic Association as well as the Indian Society for Technical Education.

In addition to his remarkable contribution and achievements in the field of Marketing, he has published close to 40 research papers with reputed journals from the publishing houses of Elsevier, Sage, Springer and Taylor & Francis. More than 50% of his papers are in FT-50, A* and A rated journals. He is also an author of an informative textbook on "Retail Management" publicized by Cengage Publications in the year 2016. He has NPTEL online courses on Marketing research and International business.

Factors Affecting the Growing Economic Inequality: An Empirical Study with Reference to BRICS Countries

Monika Mathur and Vaishali Jain

Abstract Economic inequality refers to the uneven distribution of earnings and opportunity between various groups in society and is a point of major concern in almost all the nations in the world. This study aims to analyse the effect of various factors over the increasing inequality in BRICS nations. The study takes into consideration factors like trade openness, credit, net foreign assets and health and tries to assess their impact as a driving force behind the increasing inequality in these countries. The augmented Dickey–Fuller test for stationarity has been applied followed by multiple regression. To explore causality, Granger causality test is applied. All the models are tested for autocorrelation using the Breusch–Godfrey Lagrange Multiplier test. Wald test is applied to examine the significance of independent variables. The study provides statistical evidence about the positive and negative effects of trade openness, healthcare finance, net foreign assets and healthcare expenditure on income inequality in BRICS nations. Findings may help to work intensively on the relevant causes of inequality for these five countries. This paper will add to the already present literature on inequality which is one of the important problems of the countries across the world.

Keywords Inequality · Income distribution · Economic growth · BRICS economies

1 Introduction

With increasing global growth and per capita income, the issue of increasing inequality is becoming equally important for the world. As per the World Bank

M. Mathur
Manipal University Jaipur, Jaipur, India
e-mail: monika.mathur@jaipur.manipal.edu

V. Jain (✉)
Christ (Deemed University), Lavasa, Pune, India
e-mail: vaishali.jain@christuniversity.in

© The Author(s), under exclusive license to Springer Nature Singapore Pte Ltd. 2022
A. Chandani et al. (eds.), *Achieving $5 Trillion Economy of India*, Springer Proceedings in Business and Economics, https://doi.org/10.1007/978-981-16-7818-9_1

Inequality report of 2019, India has 55% of the income share owned by top 10% population, while this is 41% for China, 55.6% for Brazil, 45.5% for Russian Federation and 65.1% in South Africa (World Inequality Database, 2018).

A recent study among others by (Assouad et al., 2018) has argued that there is extreme level of inequality present in India, Brazil, South Africa and the Middle East, with top ten per cent income shares above 50% of national income comparable to their counterparts in rich countries. They also argue that historical segregation and economic policies have been responsible for such extreme inequality in these nations. As BRICS nations symbolize economies of the developing world, a study of factors having an impact on inequality will help in understanding and designing better policies. The study of inequality in these countries become more important as they habitat 41% of total world population (United Nations, 2019). Although, as a result of high rate of economic growth, the population below poverty line has gone down (however, the exact percentage is debatable in the research community), the standards of living of the people have improved tremendously. Question of increasing inequality should be equally important to address as it has been strongly argued by (Weisskopf, 2011). He explains that various types of inequalities, i.e. class inequalities, group inequalities, post-reform consumption inequalities and like are increasing the gains to rich. Study of inequality literature unanimously argues that inequality has adverse impact on poverty reduction, growth and sustainability of economy. Growth scenarios in these five nations changed from the decade of 1990, and thus, study of driving forces of inequality and their relative intensity in these nations is important in last 25 years. In last two decades, these countries have acquired a prominent position in the world economy, and thus, BRICS nations have been selected for this study. A discussion of major determinants of inequality in these countries may result into better policy decisions in this direction.

India started liberalizing its economy from late 1980s and made several changes in its economic policies in 1991 onwards to make Indian economy a more open one. The focus of economic policies in this period moved from state intervention and central planning for more justifiable distribution to the LPG policies commonly known together as economic reforms. Indian economy has witnessed a high rate of growth in GDP since then. In Brazil too, GDP started registering speedy growth from late 1980s onwards. With economic reforms in China starting from late 1970s, the growth rate picked up in the subsequent years. In China, Gini index started rising from 1980s, and the then moderately unequal country became one of the highly unequal countries in terms of wealth and income. Russian Federation has seen radical economic changes in the decade of 1990 after switching to market economy. Thus, this study tries to estimate factors driving inequality of income in these emerging countries.

2 Review of Literature

A vast amount of literature is available on the topic of income inequality. This paper tries to study multiple factors responsible for increasing income and wealth inequalities in five fastest growing economies of the world. The review undertaken in this study is based on factors which have been studied with respect to causation of inequality. A detailed review of factors that have been responsible for increasing inequality in various countries, especially the BRICS nations have been considered for the study. This paper takes into consideration within country inequality in BRICS nations and does not present a comparative study of them. It analyses the relative intensity of various components which have been responsible for rising income inequalities in these countries. A study of BRICS nations and the challenges faced by them on inequality by (Ivnis, 2013) highlights the socio-economic factors as one of the prominent for widening inequality. A study on BRICS by (Younsi & Bechtini, 2018) evaluates the relationship between economic growth, financial development and income inequality and concludes that financial growth is one reason for increasing inequality; however, inflation and income inequality has a bidirectional relationship. (Barlow et al., 2009) also study the impact of globalization, internal reforms and private effects on inequality. (Goesling, 2005) studies that over a period significance between nations inequalities has reduced and within nation inequality has become prominent to study and understand. It has been established by various researchers including (Papanek & Kyn, 1986) and (Barro, 2000) that echelon of economic growth does not clarify the variations in inequality or their across different countries. He strongly argues that the relationship between rates of economic growth and investment and income inequality is negligible. (Gregorio & Lee, 2007) contend that other than direct effects, inequality also has indirect effects on the growth as it has a bearing on other factors of growth as well. (Barro, 2008) further affirms this by studying relationship between health and income inequality and male upper-level school attainment.

An in-depth study of inequality across the globe has been done and published by Thomas Piketty. His analysis of India from 1922 to 2014 concludes that since the beginning of income tax in India in 1922, the share of top 1% of national income holders has been the highest at present (Chancel & Piketty, 2019). They argue that in the period of 1980–2014, the bottom 0.1% of the people held share of national income and wealth more than the bottom 50% of the people. (Piketty & Qian, 2009) further study the income tax reforms in China and India and argue that over this period Chinese income tax revenue has grown as a percentage of GDP due to reforms and economic growth, but despite growth and reforms in India, the ratio of income tax revenue to GDP remains constant due to exemption policy adopted.

A study made by (Huagun & Haynes, 2011) studies that the causal factor for increasing regional disparity in China has been due to non-compensation in terms of employment opportunities in other sectors resulting from economic growth and loss of jobs in agricultural sector. Another study by (Jian et al., 1996) analyses real income inequality in Chinese provinces and concludes that during the period of 1966–1978, real incomes started converging although after 1990, the divergence in the real income started at a much faster rate due to rapid growth rate of coastal provinces in comparison with interior provinces.

While (Kiyoto, 2012) studies the ambiguous effect of international trade on income inequality through the multiple-cone neoclassical growth model. He argues that labour surplus countries can see a rise in income inequality based on his results. (Sun & Heshmati, 2010) study the impact of openness in international trade on China's growth and concluded that eastern region of China has witnessed a robust growth, while Central and Westerns China has lagged in growth. (Edwards, 1997) in a cross-country analysis suggests that trade openness and increasing inequality cannot be linked together evidently in developing countries (Alsamawi et al., 2014) found that inequality-intensive commodities like agricultural and electronic goods produced in developing countries and their trade with developed countries have also resulted in inequality. He further argues that consumption of such commodities has been responsible for increasing within country inequality as well.

(Juo, 2016) studies the effect of informal employment on income distribution in urban China and concludes that the higher section of the urban economy contributes more towards income inequality in the country. In fact, findings of a study made for OECD countries reveal that differences in wages and salaries are one of the primary causes of increasing inequalities between rich and poor countries and that technological progress has been more beneficial to skilled workers (Foster et al., 2011). While studying the poverty reduction in India across the states post-1990 period, (Datt & Ravallion, 2002) study that the rural–urban gap in reduction of poverty ratio has been expanding. In fact, findings of (Rey, 2001) based on study made in USA focus on strong positive association between degree of regional autocorrelation and measures of inequality.

(Fasianos et al., 2017) studied an asymmetric association between income inequality and the household debt in USA. They argued that falling trends in inequality does not affect household debt. (Berisha & Meszaros, 2018) also studied household debt as one of the components for increasing inequalities and concluded that rising income inequality may result in economic contraction.

Economic reforms in India and China have included financial sector reforms as well which aimed to promote economic growth with financial inclusiveness. While a study by (Claessens & Perotti, 2007) suggests that financial development can bring down income inequality, liberalization in financial sector, if unguarded for, may lead to increased inequalities. A study made by (Ang, 2010) explores the case of India and concludes that lesser grown financial system and mechanisms affect poor more adversely than rich and therefore developed financial system is necessary for increasing equality. Another study of OECD countries by (Tridico, 2018) reveals that financialization, a deepening of labour flexibility, the weakening of trade unions act as primary factors for inequality in these nations. A study of financial development in reducing inequality by (Seven & Coskun, 2016) suggests that although financial development helps in growth, it does not necessarily decrease the poverty ratio in low income countries. Study of inequality of a sample of advanced and developing countries with the perspective of knowledge and use of financial markets by (Prete, 2018) concludes that more economic literacy and knowledge lead to lesser growth of inequality. (Sebastian & Sebastian, 2016) used credit to GDP ratio to measure financial development suggesting that financial development increases income inequality.

Access to health is one of the major determinants and consequences of inequalities of opportunities. A study of BRICS nations made by (Mújica et al., 2014) analyses that although there is increasing prosperity and improvement in health standards in these nations, sharp inequalities in health are present within and between BRICS countries. A study of impact of privatization on economic growth and income inequality in 82 countries for a period of 11 years (1991–2002) finds that privatization does not have a significant negative impact, while good governance definitely had positive effects on economy (Adams & Mengistu, 2008).

(Bumann & Lensink, 2016) explored the relationship between income inequality and liberalization of capital account. They measured financial depth in terms of ratio of private credit to GDP and found that financial liberalization helps reduce income inequality if the financial depth is high, i.e. when the ratio of private credit to GDP is equal to or greater than 25%.

(Haan & Sturm, 2017) examined the relationship between income inequality, financial liberalization, financial development and banking crisis for 121 countries. They concluded that though all the three factors have an unfavourable effect on income inequality, financial development has a moderating impact on the relationship between financial liberalization and income inequality.

Growth in the world today has been information and technology-based which has given wings to the idea of globalization as well. Undoubtedly in India and China too, the growth has been based on technology and Internet. Rise in income and wealth inequalities is also attributed to growth of information technology as argued by (Pohjola, 2002). (Jaumotte et al., 2013) examined the effect of technology, trade and financial globalization on income inequality for fifty-one countries for a period of 23 years and concluded that in most of the countries they studied, inequality has increased in the upper part. They also found that while increase in trade leads to lower income inequality, increased financial globalization results in increased income inequality. Among other factors, skill premium earned by human capital has been termed as one critical factor determining increasing inequality by (Zhuang et al., 2014). The study strongly contends that higher level of wages earned by skilled human capital is one of the major driving forces of inequality. Technological change has favoured skilled labour more than unskilled one in terms of incomes. Their study also holds regional inequality in India and People's Republic of China as one of the major inequality determinants. Spatial inequality measured by two components, i.e. rural–urban inequality and interregional, has been argued as one more reason for inequality in Asian countries. Study by (Wang et al., 2014) discusses the rural–urban inequality and inter-household inequality. It further argues that Hukou system has resulted into labour immobility from less grown rural areas to more developed urban area, which has led to increasing inequality. While the study talked about other factors as well, but the areas remain unexplored. So, the factors like trade openness, financial sector growth, net foreign assets and healthcare expenditure have been explored in the present study. Various studies related to the inequality in different sectors like or amounting to the extent have been made in India and China (Borooa et al., 2015; Cain et al., 2010; Kumar et al., 2016), but after reviewing the literature, study related to the aforementioned three factors in context of five BRICS countries was not found explicitly. Therefore, this present study adds to the already existing literature of inequality and its determinants from the period of 2000–2016 in Brazil, China, India, Russian Federation and South Africa.

The above review of literature shows that though there are many studies conducted on the factors affecting the increasing inequality yet there is a paucity of literature focusing on India and China with respect to the factors affecting the inequality.

3 Research Objectives

Based on the research gap, the study puts forth the following objectives:

(1) To study the impact of trade openness on income inequality.
(2) To study the impact of healthcare expenditure on income inequality.
(3) To study the impact of domestic financial sector development on income inequality.
(4) To study the impact of net foreign assets on income inequality.

Scope of the study is limited to the economic inequality in BRICS nations, i.e. Brazil, China, India, Russian Federation and South Africa.

4 Data Description

The present study explores the relationship of trade openness, credit, net foreign assets, healthcare finance, household expenses on health and capital health expenditure on the economic inequality with reference to Brazil, China, India, Russian Federation and South Africa. Trade openness is defined as the ratio of sum of exports and imports to GDP. Credit is defined as the ratio of private credit to GDP. Net foreign assets are defined as the ratio of net foreign assets to GDP. Healthcare finance is measured as the ratio of government schemes and compulsory contributory healthcare financing schemes to current health expenditure. Household expenses on health are defined as household out-of-pocket payment towards health expenditure as a percentage of current health expenditure. Capital health expenditure is measured as a percentage of current health expenditure.

For the purpose of study, the data is collected for a period of 16 years from year 2000–2015. Since latest data for all the variables is not available, we have taken data till 2015 only.

The data for inequality, i.e. the percentage of population having top 10% and bottom 10% share in income, has been taken from world inequality database. Source of data for domestic credit to private sector and GDP ratio, net foreign assets to GDP ratio, health expenditure (all the variables) and trade openness is taken from World Bank Database.

5 Research Methodology

For the purpose of analysis, data is first tested through the augmented Dickey–Fuller test (ADF test) to check for stationarity, and then, a multiple regression is applied to check the effect of trade openness, private credit, healthcare finance, household expenses on health and capital health expenditure on the economic inequality. Further, to explore the nature of causality, Granger causality test (Engle & Granger, 1987) is also used. All the models are checked for autocorrelation using the LM test of (Breusch, 1978) and (Godfrey, 1978). Wald test is applied to test the significance of explanatory variables. Data is analysed using EViews 10.

5.1 *Test for Stationarity*

A series is considered stationary when it is a stochastic process with a constant mean, variance and auto-covariance with change in time. A stationary series is reflective of the previous behaviour of the series to future. This implies that if a shock appears in a stationary series, its effect will gradually become weak. In other words, the effect of the shock at time $t + 1$ will be weaker than that of t and will further decrease from $t + 1$ to $t + 2$ and so on and so forth.

In order to examine whether each time series contains a unit root or it is stationary, the study uses the most widely used stationarity test namely augmented Dickey–Fuller test or ADF test (Dickey & Fuller, 1979). The null hypothesis of non-stationarity is checked against the alternate hypothesis of stationarity in the ADF test (Dickey & Fuller, 1979).

5.2 *Granger Causality*

Causative association between a set of two variables can be detected using the Granger causality test (Engle & Granger, 1987). An independent variable (X) is said to Granger cause the dependent variable (Y), if the prediction error of dependent variable (Y) is condensed by using lagged values of independent and dependent variable. For the purpose of this study, Granger causality is tested using the below mentioned equation:

$$\Delta \mathrm{I}_\tau = \varphi_{10} + \sum_{i=1}^{p} \varphi_{11i} \Delta I_{t-i} + \sum_{i=1}^{p} \varphi_{12i} \Delta T_{t-i} + \sum_{i=1}^{p} \varphi_{13i} \Delta F_{t-i} + \sum_{i=1}^{p} \varphi_{14i} \Delta \mathbf{NFA}_{t-i} + \sum_{i=1}^{p} \varphi_{15i} \Delta \mathbf{HCF}_{t-i} + \sum_{i=1}^{p} \varphi_{16i} \Delta \mathbf{HP}_{t-i} + \sum_{i=1}^{p} \varphi_{17i} \Delta \mathbf{CHE}_{t-i} + u_{1t} \quad (1)$$

Here, φ's denotes the parameters that are to be estimated, u_t's denotes the error terms, and ε_{t-1} is denoting the error correction term (ECT). Significance of short-run causality is indicated by the F statistics on the lagged explanatory variables of ECM. Lag length is selected using the Schwarz criterion (SIC) and Akaike info criterion (AIC). The null hypothesis of no causality in Eq. (1) is H_O: $\varphi_{12i} = \varphi_{13i} = \varphi_{14i} = \varphi_{15i} = \varphi_{16i} = \varphi_{17i} = 0$ against H_1: $\varphi_{12i} \neq \varphi_{13i} \neq \varphi_{14i} \neq \varphi_{15i} \neq \varphi_{16i} \neq \varphi_{17i} \neq 0$.

While Breusch–Godfrey Serial Correlation LM Test is used to check the presence/absence of autocorrelation in all the models, recursive estimates of CUSUM test are applied to check the stability of the models. All the models were free from serial correlation and were found to be stable at 5% level of significance.

6 Empirical Results

In the first step, descriptive statistics are calculated for all variables-dependent and independent. Results of descriptive statistics are displayed in Tables 1, 2, 3, 4 and 5 for India, China, Brazil, Russian Federation and South Africa, respectively. Subsequent to this, after checking the data for stationarity using augmented Dickey–Fuller (ADF) test, five regression models are run where inequality is the dependent variable, while trade openness, domestic credit, net foreign assets, expense on healthcare finance, household payments for health care and capital health expenditure are the independent variables for Brazil, China, India, Russian Federation and South Africa, respectively. Regression results are tested for autocorrelation using Breusch–Godfrey

Table 1 Descriptive statistics (India)

Statistics	Inequality	Trade	Credit	NFA	HCF	HP	CHE
Mean	28.864	43.357	43.372	16.361	22.878	69.273	4.928
Median	28.175	46.375	46.876	16.457	22.341	69.982	4.982
Max	38.199	55.793	52.385	21.821	28.021	74.106	7.576
Min	19.426	26.274	28.339	8.576	19.633	62.224	2.960
SD	6.7301	10.157	9.111	3.551	2.580	3.986	1.499
Skewness	0.1023	−0.4732	−0.5634	−0.649	0.582	−0.436	0.148
Kurtosis	1.5417	1.9038	1.7146	3.255	2.270	1.799	1.933

Source Own calculations by author(s)

Table 2 Descriptive statistics (China)

Statistics	Inequality	Trade	Credit	NFA	HCF	HP	CHE
Mean	61.878	50.083	121.242	41.754	41.676	49.535	7.426
Median	61.601	48.498	120.694	45.413	41.774	49.329	7.545
Max	78.563	64.478	152.551	56.127	60.181	64.191	11.550
Min	41.255	38.527	101.917	20.043	21.975	35.089	1.574
SD	11.244	8.6954	13.419	11.994	13.700	10.463	2.712
Skewness	−0.2602	0.3173	0.683	−0.519	−0.071	0.014	−0.561
Kurtosis	2.0841	1.7980	3.004	1.935	1.468	1.386	2.523

Source Own calculations by author(s)

Table 3 Descriptive statistics (Brazil)

Statistics	Inequality	Trade	Credit	NFA	HCF	HP	CHE
Mean	147.478	25.890	45.826	7.334	38.263	39.079	6.715
Median	145.290	26.042	45.782	9.686	39.071	38.368	7.836
Max	171.688	29.678	66.829	18.168	44.458	47.807	10.500
Min	123.386	22.106	27.686	−3.703	25.381	30.502	3.107
SD	13.061	2.098	14.982	6.285	5.440	5.718	2.703
Skewness	0.137	−0.231	0.157	−0.303	−0.714	−0.096	−0.134
Kurtosis	2.506	2.409	1.457	2.064	2.958	1.554	1.381

Table 4 Descriptive statistics (Russian Federation)

Statistics	Inequality	Trade	Credit	NFA	HCF	HP	CHE
Mean	199.506	52.658	36.588	25.759	60.897	33.463	4.035
Median	197.913	51.706	41.554	25.567	61.730	33.398	3.799
Max	291.353	61.111	55.946	39.765	63.707	38.646	8.039
Min	133.692	46.193	16.838	11.701	58.041	30.792	1.215
SD	48.029	5.034	12.879	8.134	1.940	2.195	2.402
Skewness	0.634	0.319	−0.163	−0.189	−0.426	0.708	0.266
Kurtosis	2.527	1.677	1.788	2.182	1.659	3.006	1.501

Serial Correlation LM Test, stability using the recursive estimates of CUSUM test, and finally, Wald test is applied to check the significance of independent variables. Results of LM test and Wald test as reported in Tables 6 and 7, respectively, show that the model is free from serial correlation and all the independent variables are significant contributors to the dependent variable.

Regression results as presented in Table 8 show the impact of independent variables over the dependent variable. The results envisage that **in India**, a unit increase in the ratio of private credit to GDP, healthcare finance and household out-of-pocket

Table 5 Descriptive statistics (South Africa)

Statistics	Inequality	Trade	Credit	NFA	HCF	HP	CHE
Mean	72.621	59.315	141.109	13.120	47.299	10.526	2.642
Median	48.455	60.113	145.941	14.344	50.530	10.139	2.901
Max	151.062	72.865	160.125	19.393	54.972	14.335	3.364
Min	34.135	51.078	110.718	2.742	33.439	7.699	1.405
SD	46.559	5.842	13.915	4.478	7.836	2.431	0.621
Skewness	0.935	0.507	−0.924	−0.802	−0.728	0.276	−0.590
Kurtosis	2.063	3.031	3.092	3.050	1.966	1.518	2.131

Table 6 Results of autocorrelation (Breusch-Godfrey serial correlation LM test)

Model	F-value	Obs R square
F_{ineq}(Ineq/Trade, Credit, NFA, HCF, HP, CHE) for India	1.189558 (0.3592)	4.058577 (0.1314)
F_{ineq}(Ineq/Trade, Credit, NFA, HCF, HP, CHE) for China	1.037567 (0.4030)	3.658583 (0.1605)
F_{ineq}(Ineq/Trade, Credit, NFA, HCF, HP, CHE) for Brazil	5.763861 (0.0601)	9.865277 (0.0672)
F_{ineq}(Ineq/Trade, Credit, NFA, HCF, HP, CHE) for Russian Federation	1.72817 (0.1104)	11.72207 (0.1028)
F_{ineq}(Ineq/Trade, Credit, NFA, HCF, HP, CHE) for South Africa	0.079044 (0.9249)	0.385076 (0.8249)

Source Own calculations by author(s) p values in ()

Table 7 Results of wald test

Model	F-value	Chi square
F_{ineq}(Ineq/Trade, Credit, NFA, HCF, HP, CHE) for India	144.9221 (0.0000)	869.5325 (0.0000)
F_{ineq}(Ineq/Trade, Credit, NFA, HCF, HP, CHE) for China	15.92990 (0.0002)	95.57940 (0.0000)
F_{ineq}(Ineq/Trade, Credit, NFA, HCF, HP, CHE) for Brazil	14.03555 (0.0007)	84.21330 (0.0000)
F_{ineq}(Ineq/Trade, Credit, NFA, HCF, HP, CHE) for Russian Federation	11.506673 (0.02884)	19.040039 (0.01713)
F_{ineq}(Ineq/Trade, Credit, NFA, HCF, HP, CHE) for South Africa	7.242796 (0.0067)	43.45677 (0.0000)

Source Own calculations by author(s) p values in ()

Table 8 Regression results

Independent variable	Inequality in India	Inequality in China	Inequality in Brazil	Inequality in Russian Federation	Inequality in South Africa
Intercept	20.47173 [0.645148] (0.5394)	−63.57762 [−0.630691] (0.5439)	512.3010 [2.839454] (0.0218)	264.6961 [0.109454] (0.9155)	247.9905 [0.849587] (0.4203)
Credit	−0.045484 [−0.184783] (0.8586)	0.238074 [0.748876] (0.4730)	−0.794330 [−1.937138] (0.0887)	−4.718153 [−1.032961] (0.3318)	0.718818 [0.708629] (0.4987)
Trade	0.008935 [0.119080] (0.9086)	0.178964 [0.854044] (0.4152)	−1.825350 [−2.260357] (0.0537)	−0.411907 [−0.032754] (0.9747)	1.654383 [1.120579] (0.2950)
NFA	0.011643 [0.065132] (0.9499)	0.394158 [0.881852] (0.4008)	2.012691 [2.371345] (0.0452)	2.815060 [0.632936] (0.5444)	2.012698 [0.620233] (0.5524)
HCF	−0.309016 [−0.723201] (0.4930)	1.138212 [1.116066] (0.2933)	−2.194610 [−1.196632] (0.2657)	−2.708968 [−0.119822] (0.9076)	−1.218591 [−0.199556] (0.8468)
HP	−0.187716 [−0.603122] (0.5654)	0.689100 [0.612169] (0.5556)	−4.707428 [−1.908237] (0.0928)	6.653836 [0.373158] (0.7187)	−19.43865 [−1.385705] (0.2032)
CHE	0.201841 [0.221572] (0.8310)	−1.406919 [−0.619987] (0.5506)	−4.168379 [−1.904178] (0.0934)	−0.267389 [−0.027612] (0.9786)	−52.64915 [−2.553827] (0.0340)
Adjusted R^2	0.253661	0.856568	0.848178	0.178406	0.727927

Source Own calculations by author(s), *t* values in [], *p* values in ()

expenses helps reduce the income inequality by 0.045484 units, 0.309016 units and 0.187716 units, respectively. On the contrary, a unit increase in the trade, net foreign assets to GDP ratio and capital health expenditure leads to an increase of 0.008935 units, 0.011643 units and 0.201841 units in income inequality, respectively. This indicates that an increase in the share of private credit, healthcare financing and household expenses on health has a favourable impact on income inequality whereas an increase in trade, net foreign assets and capital health expenditure has an adverse impact on income inequality in India. This relationship between the variables can be expressed in the form of following equation:

$$\mathbf{Ineq\_}\boldsymbol{IN} = \mathbf{20.47173 - 0.045484\ Credit + 0.008935\ Trade} \\ \mathbf{+0.011643\ NFA - 0.309016\ HCF - 0.187716\ HP + 0.201841\ CHE} \quad (2)$$

With respect to **China**, the results show that while a unit increase in private credit to GDP ratio, trade, net foreign assets to GDP ratio, healthcare finance and household out-of-pocket expenses leads to an increase in income inequality by 0.238074 units,

0.178964 units, 0.394158 units, 1.138212 units and 0.689100 units, respectively. On the contrary, a unit increase in capital health expenditure results in a 1.406919-unit decrease in income inequality. These findings envisage that while increase in private credit to GDP ratio, trade, net foreign assets, healthcare financing and household out-of-pocket expenses has an adverse impact on income inequality, increased capital expenditure on health has a favourable impact on income inequality in China. Following expression sums up the above findings:

$$\mathbf{Ineq\_}\boldsymbol{CN} = -\,\mathbf{63.57762 + 0.238074\ Credit + 0.178964\ Trade} \\ \mathbf{+0.394158\ NFA + 1.138212\ HCF + 0.689100\ HP - 1.406919\ CHE} \tag{3}$$

Regression results for **Brazil** show that every one-unit increase in private credit to GDP, trade, healthcare finance, household out-of-pocket expenditure and capital expenditure on health leads to lower the income inequality by 0.794330 unit, 1.825350 unit, 2.194610 unit, 4.707428 units and 4.168379 units, respectively. Whereas, with every one-unit increase in net foreign assets, income inequality increases by 2.012691 units. In short, while the share of private sector credit, trade, healthcare finance, household expenditure and capital health expenditure has a favourable impact on lowering the income inequality, net foreign assets have an adverse effect on reducing it. Following expression presents the above relationship:

$$\mathbf{Ineq\_}\boldsymbol{B} = \mathbf{512.3010 - 0.794330\ Credit - 1.825350\ Trade} \\ \mathbf{+2.012691\ NFA - 2.194610\ HCF - 4.707428\ HP - 4.168379\ CHE} \tag{4}$$

Regression results for **Russian Federation** show that while a unit increase in private credit to GDP, trade openness, healthcare financing and capital health expenditure leads to lowering the income inequality by 4.718153 units, 0.411907 units, 2.708968 units and 0.267389 units, respectively, a unit increase in net foreign assets and household expenses leads to a rise in income inequality by 2.815060 units and 6.653836 units, respectively. This implies that while private credit, trade openness, healthcare financing and capital health expenditure have a favourable impact on lowering the income inequality, net foreign assets and household expenses have an adverse effect on lowering this inequality. This relationship can be expressed in the form of following equation:

$$\mathbf{Ineq\_}\boldsymbol{RF} = \mathbf{264.6961 - 4.718153\ Credit - 0.411907\ Trade} \\ \mathbf{+2.815060\ NFA - 2.708968\ HCF + 6.653836\ HP - 0.267389\ CHE} \tag{5}$$

Regression results for **South Africa** show an increase of 0.718818 units, 1.654383 units and 2.012698 units in income inequality with a unit change in private credit to GDP, trade openness and net foreign assets, respectively. On the contrary, a

Table 9 Results of granger causality test

Dependent variable	Trade	Credit	NFA	HCF	HP	CHE
Δ_{Ineq}. India	1.29979 (0.3192)	3.30668 (0.0838)	3.03793 (0.0981)	0.45321 (0.6493)	0.61479 (0.5620)	1.99247 (0.1921)
Δ_{Ineq}. China	5.81405 (0.0239)	4.43646 (0.0456)	5.40184 (0.0288)	3.63024 (0.0698)	3.16744 (0.0909)	7.54863 (0.0119)
Δ_{Ineq}. Brazil	0.84671 (0.4639)	2.65370 (0.1306)	0.79353 (0.4849)	1.33750 (0.3154)	1.08158 (0.3839)	1.89043 (0.2126)
Δ_{Ineq}. Russian Federation	1.26622 (0.3328)	0.74316 (0.5058)	1.59808 (0.2607)	3.06953 (0.1025)	0.48726 (0.6314)	0.63805 (0.5532)
$\Delta_{\text{Ineq.}}$ South Africa	0.06149 (0.9408)	0.11288 (0.8947)	1.66780 (0.2481)	1.10216 (0.3778)	66.2016 (1.E-05)	0.64053 (0.5520)

Source Own calculations by author(s) *p* values in ()

unit increase in healthcare financing, household expenditure on health and capital health expenditure results in lowering the income inequality by 1.218591 units, 19.43865 units and 52.64915 units, respectively. This implies that while private credit, trade openness and net foreign assets have an unfavourable effect on lowering the income inequality in South Africa, expenditure on healthcare financing, household expenses on health and capital health expenditure have a favourable contribution towards lowering the income inequality. The following equation expresses the above relationship:

$$\mathbf{Ineq\_}\boldsymbol{SA} = \mathbf{247.9905 + 0.718818\ Credit + 1.654383\ Trade} \\ \mathbf{+2.012698\ NFA - 1.218591\ HCF - 19.43865\ HP - 52.64915\ CHE} \quad (6)$$

Post the regression analysis, data is tested for causality using the Granger causality test. Results of Granger causality are presented in Table 9 which envisages that though there is no statistical evidence of causative association of trade openness, private credit and healthcare expenses with inequality in Brazil, China, India, Russian Federation and South Africa, net foreign assets have a significant causal association with inequality only in Brazil. This is consistent with the available literature as well which says that it is difficult to establish a causative association between the variables under study. **(Piketty & Zucman, Capital is back: Wealth–Income Ratios in Rich Countries 1700–2010, 2014; Piketty & Qian, Income Inequality and Progressive Income Taxation in China and India, 1986–2015, 2009; Sebastian & Sebastian, 2016).**

7 Discussion

BRICS economies form the major share of fastest growing economies of the world and are crucial in development of the world. Inequality in these countries affects approximately 41% of the global population. The factors that have been studied across the globe which have contributed in increasing inequality are many, but in these emerging economies, the openness in terms of globalization increased during and post-1990s, and thus, it has been one of the factors which needs to be studied in detail. BRICS nations had focused on the growth of their financial market and strengthening its structure as the number of financial institutions, instruments and tools has grown over a period. Asymmetric expenditure on health care requirements and inaccessibility to health care is also one of the important socio-economic determinants which have been responsible for pushing people below the poverty line. For example, in India, approximately 70% and in China, approx. 65%, health care needs are fulfilled through out-of-pocket expenditure. The same holds for countries like Brazil, Russian Federation, and South Africa.

This study focusses on the extent to which the above five variables have been responsible for increasing income inequalities in BRICS nations (Brazil, China, India, Russian Federation and South Africa). It is a pertinent aspect of economy to check that when financialization in the economy rises, does it lead to deepening inequality? Studies in OECD and other developed countries have shown a direct relationship between increasing financial growth and rising inequality. Some of the researchers have also argued that intensification of labour flexibility has resulted in labour becoming more vulnerable having an adverse impact on equality. It reflects an ironical situation as a few studies show that even if financial growth has been taking place, its skewed in developing countries, and on the other hand, the study of developed countries shows increased financialization resulting to increasing inequality. Study of Brazil, China, India, Russian Federation and South Africa, in this paper, tries to analyse this situation, and based on findings, it can be observed that as there is increasing financial growth in these countries, there has been a some positive effect on reducing inequality. As per a recent report of World Health Organization, out-of-pocket expenditure in South East Asian countries is declining, but share of public spending is very low in these countries especially the middle income countries (Xu et al., 2018). This is one of the important social indicators of inequality in any economy. Thus, this paper analysed the variables like household out-of-pocket payment towards health expenditure as a ratio of current health expenditure and capital health expenditure as a percentage of current health expenditure. The findings suggest that out-of-pocket expenditure on health has been responsible for decreasing inequality in India, Brazil, Russian Federation and South Africa. Although the results show that this feature has been statistically insignificant. Various researchers have studied inequality in access to health care, but it is also one of the major reasons for increasing inequality. Access to health care requires intensive studies by researchers not only in terms of physical availability and financial accessibility but also quality of care.

Most of BRICS nations have witnessed economic reforms/openness from late 1980s and prominently from 1990s. The reforms have been in terms of opening of the economies for movement of goods and services, capital and labour across the borders. The process of globalization has resulted into rising growth rates for them, but at the same time, the Gini coefficients for all these countries remain high. There have been several studies related to impact of globalization on India and China, and the findings have been positive as well negative on sectoral basis. Studies by (Kanbur, 2014) also reveal that openness has made nations' economies more volatile and instable which affects inequality and poverty in its own way. He concludes that in last 30 years global integration has led to rising inequalities (of various types) both in developing as well as developed countries. (Alvaredo et al., 2013) argue that share of top income earners has increased over last 20 years in India and China as compared to European countries. Thus, present study provides with some analyses of the area which reveals that trade openness had adverse effect on income equality in emerging BRICS economies except South Africa. This calls for better governance to provide the benefits of trade openness to all the sections of the society. Studies by (Lim & McNelis, 2016) suggest mixed results for effect of trade and financial openness on improving Gini outcomes and also suggest that these changes depend upon the stages of economic development. Study of 51 countries for impact of trade and financial openness reveals that while trade globalization is associated with reduced inequality, financial globalization is related to increasing inequality (Jaumotte et al., 2013). This study also shows mixed results for trade openness on inequality amongst five nations, and it suggests that India, China, and South Africa have had a positive impact in reducing inequality. However, results show that financial assets have a positive impact in reducing inequality in all five nations.

8 Conclusion

The present study is an attempt to study the effect of trade openness, credit, net foreign assets, healthcare finance, household expenses on health and capital health expenditure on the economic inequality in Brazil, China, India, Russian Federation and South Africa. The study envisages the favourable impact of increase in the share of private credit, healthcare financing and household expenses on health over income inequality and unfavourable impact of increase in trade, net foreign assets and capital health expenditure over income inequality in India; favourable impact of capital health expenditure and unfavourable impact of increase in the share of private credit, increase in trade, increase in net foreign assets, increase in healthcare financing and household expenses on health over income inequality in China. In Brazil, increase in net foreign assets has an unfavourable impact on lowering income inequality, while there is a favourable impact of increase in the share of private credit, increase in trade, healthcare financing, household expenses on health and capital health expenditure over income inequality. In Russian Federation, private credit, trade openness, healthcare financing and capital health expenditure have a favourable impact on lowering the income inequality, whereas net foreign assets and household expenses have an adverse effect on lowering this inequality. While private credit, trade openness and net foreign assets have an unfavourable effect on lowering the income inequality in South Africa, expenditure on healthcare financing, household expenses on health and capital health expenditure have a favourable contribution towards lowering the income inequality. These results implicitly mean that policymaking in Brazil needs to focus more on increasing private credit, trade openness and health care. It also needs to focus on introducing new reforms for its foreign assets and related policies to narrow the gap between different income groups. China's economy needs to prioritize on availability of private sector credit to more inclusive population and benefits of capital expenditure in healthcare sector to be more widespread. China needs to introduce reforms in the sector of finance, trade and health care as all these are leading to an increased inequality in China. India needs to focus more on reducing out-of-pocket household expenditure on health and reforms in globalized policies to bring inclusive growth in the country. Russian Federation needs to focus on policy decisions pertaining to easy availability of private credit and increased healthcare financing and also introduce new measures to reduce the adverse effect of its foreign assets along with steps to reduce household expenditure on health. Last but not the least, South Africa needs to focus on increasing the expenditure in the sector of health and formulate policies to reduce the adverse impact of growing private credit, trade openness and foreign assets. In nutshell, BRICS nations shall implement policy decisions which help in reducing the skewness in financial availability, healthcare accessibility and more inclusively share the fruits of trade openness with all sectors of the economy.

Although all BRICS nations fall into the category of emerging economies, we need to look at many aspects of inequality and explore the factors affecting the same. Although all BRICS nations fall into the category of emerging economies, we need to look many aspects of inequality and reason out the factors responsible. But it cannot be denied that the five variables considered above are important to be considered as determining factors of inequality.

These conclusions can be summarized in following table.

Table 10 Summary of conclusions

Variable	Brazil	China	India	Russian Federation	South Africa
Credit	Favorable	Unfavorable	Favorable	Favorable	Unfavorable
Trade	Favorable	Unfavorable	Unfavorable	Favorable	Unfavorable
NFA	Unfavorable	Unfavorable	Unfavorable	Unfavorable	Unfavorable
HCF	Favorable	Unfavorable	Favorable	Favorable	Favorable
HP	Favorable	Unfavorable	Favorable	Unfavorable	Favorable
CHE	Favorable	Favorable	Unfavorable	Favorable	Favorable

9 Scope of Future Research

Macroeconomic factors like share of ICT capital in the capital block, net international investment position, skill premium, access to education and government spending can be studied for these five countries to have a comprehensive view of the issue.

References

Adams, S. & Mengistu, B. (2008). Privatization, governance and economic development in developing countries. *Journal of Developing Societies,* 415–438

Alsamawi, A., et al. (2014). The inequality footprints of nations: A novel approach to quantitative accounting of income inequality. *PLOS One,* 1–11

Alvaredo, F., Atkinson, A. B., Piketty, T. & Saez, E. (2013). The top 1% in international and historical perspective. *Journal of Economic Perspectives,* 3–20

Ang, J. B. (2010). Finance and inequality: The case of India. *Southern Economic Journal,* 738–761

Assouad, L., Chancel, L. & Morgan, M. (2018). Extreme inequality: Evidence from Brazil, India,the Middle East and South Africa. *AEA Papers and Proceedings,* 119–123

Barlow, D., Grimalda, G. & Meschi, E. (2009). Globalisation versus internal reforms as factors of inequality in transition economies. *International Review of Applied Economics,* 265–287

Barro, R. J. (2000). Inequality and growth in a panel of countries. *Journal of Economic Growth,* 5–32

Barro, R. J. (2008). Inequality and growth revisited. *ADB Working Paper Series on Regional Economic Integration*

Berisha, E. & Meszaros, J. (2018). Household debt, expected economic conditions, and income inequality. *International Journal of Finance and Economics,* 283–295

Borooa, V. K., Gustafsson, B. & Shi, L. (2015). China and India: Income inequality and poverty north and south of the Himalayas. *Journal of Asian Economics,* 797–817

Breusch, T. (1978). Testing for autocorrelation in dynamic linear models. *Australian Economic Papers, 17,* 334–355.

Bumann, S. & Lensink, R. (2016). Capital account liberalization and income inequality. *Journal of International Money and Finance, 61,* 143–162

Cain, J. S., Hasan, R., Magsombol, R. & Tandon, A. (2010). Accounting for inequality in India: Evidence from household expenditures. *World Development,* 282–297

Chancel, L. & Piketty, T. (2019). Indian income inequality, 1922–2015: From British Raj to Billionaire Raj? *Review of Income and Wealth,* 1–30

Claessens, S. & Perotti, E. (2007). Finance and inequality: Channels and evidence. *Journal of Comparative Economics,* 748–773

Datt, G. & Ravallion, M. (2002). Is India's economic growth leaving the poor behind? *Journal of Economic Perspectives,* 89–108

Dickey, D. A., & Fuller, W. A. (1979). Distribution of the estimates for autoregressive time series with a unit root. *Journal of American Statistical Association, 74,* 427–431.

Edwards, S. (1997). Trade policy, growth, and income distribution. *The American Economic Review,* 205–210

Engle, R. F. & Granger, C. W. J. (1987). Co-integration and error correction: Representation, estimation, and testing. *Econometrica, 55*(2), 251–276

Fasianos, A., Raza, H. & Kinsella, S. (2017). Exploring the link between household debt and income inequality: An asymmetric approach. *Applied Economics Letters*

Foster, M., Chen, W. H. & llenanozal, A. (2011). *Divided We Stand: Why Inequality Keeps Rising,* s.l.: OECD.org.

Godfrey, L. (1978). Testing against general autoregressive and moving average error models when the regressors include lagged dependent variables. *Econometrica, 46*, 1293–1301.
Goesling, B. (2005). Changing income inequalities within and between nations: New evidence. *American Sociological Review*, 745–761
Gregorio, J. D. & Lee, J. W. (2007). Growth and adjustment in East Asia and Latin America. *Economia*, 69–134
Haan, J. d. & Sturm, J.-E. (2017). Finance and income inequality: A review and new evidence. *European Journal of Political Economy, 50*, 171–195
Huagun, L. & Haynes, K. E. (2011). Economic structure and regional disparity in China: Beyond the kuznets transition. *International Regional Science Review*, 157–190
Ivnis, C. (2013). Inequality matters: BRICS inequalities fact sheet. *Oxfam Policy and Practice: Climate Change and Resilience*, 39–50
Jaumotte, F., Lall, S. & Papageorgiou, C. (2013). Rising income inequality: Technology, or trade and financial globalization? *IMF Economic Review*, 271–309
Jaumotte, F., Lall, S. & Papageorgiou, C. (2013). Rising income inequality: Technology, or trade and financial globalization? *IMF Economic Review, 61*(2), 271–309
Jian, T., Sachs, J. D. & Warner, A. M. (1996). Trends in regional inequality in China. *China Economic Review*, 1–21
Juo, H. (2016). How does informal employment impact income inequality? *Applied Economics Letters*, 1117–1120
Kanbur, R. (2014). Globalization and inequality.In *Handbook of Income Distribution*
Kiyoto, K. (2012). Trade liberalization, economic growth, and income distribution in a multiple-cone neoclassical growth model. *Oxford Economic Papers*, 655
Kumar, K., et al. (2016). Association between wealth and health among older adults in rural China and India. *The Journal of Economics of Ageing*, 43–52
Lim, G. C. & McNelis, P. D. (2016). Income growth and inequality: The threshold effects of trade and financial openness. *Economic Modelling*, 403–412
Mújica, O. J., et al. (2014). Socioeconomic inequalities and mortality trends in BRICS, 1990–2010. *Bulletin of the World Health Organization*, 405–412
Papanek, G. & Kyn, O. (1986). The effect on income distribution of development, the growth rate and economic strategy. *Journal of Development Economics*, 55–65
Piketty, T. & Qian, N. (2009). Income inequality and progressive income taxation in China and India, 1986–2015. *American Economic Journal: Applied Economics*, 53–63
Piketty, T. & Zucman, G. (2014). Capital is back : Wealth—income ratios in rich countries 1700–2010. *Quarterly Journal of Economics*, 1255–1310
Pohjola, M. (2002). The new economy: Facts, impacts and policies. *Information Economics and Policy*, 133–144
Prete, A. L. (2018). Inequality and the finance you know: Does economic literacy matter? *Economia Politica*, 183–205
Rey, S. J. (2001). Spatial analysis of regional income inequality, Urbana: Department of geography san diego state university and regional economics applications laboratory university of illinois
Sebastian, J. & Sebastian, W. (2016). Financial development and income inequality: A panel data approach. *Empirical Economics*, 291–314
Seven, U. & Coskun, Y. (2016). Does financial development reduce income inequality and poverty? Evidence from emerging countries. *Emerging Markets Review*, 34–63
Sun, P. & Heshmati, A. (2010). International trade and its effects on economic growth in China. *IDEAS Working Paper Series from RePEc; St. Louis*
Tridico, P. (2018). The determinants of income inequality in OECD countries. *Cambridge Journal of Economics*, 1009–1042
United Nations, D. o. E. a. S. A. P. D. (2019). *World Population Prospects 2019*. [Online]. Available at: https://population.un.org/wpp/
Wang, C., Wan, G. & Yang, D. (2014). Income inequality in the people's republic of China: Trends, determinants and proposed remedies. *Journal of Economic Surveys*, 686–708

Weisskopf, T. E. (2011). *Why Worry about Inequality in the Booming Indian Economy?* New Delhi: Economic & Political Weekly

World Inequality Database. (2018). *World Inequality Report 2018,* s.l.: World Inequality Lab

Xu, K., et al. (2018). *Public spending on health: A closer look at global trends.* World Health Organization.

Younsi, M. & Bechtini, M. (2018). Economic growth, financial development and income inequality in BRICS countries: Evidence from panel granger causality tests. *Munich Personal RePEc Archive*

Zhuang, J., Kanbur, R. & Rhee, C. (2014). What drives Asia's rising inequality. In: *Inequality in Asia and the Pacific: Trends, drivers, and policy implications* (pp. 37–57). London & New York: Asian Development Bank and Routledge

Prospects of FDI-Driven R&D—A Comparison Between Indian and Foreign Pharmaceutical Firms

J. C. Sharmiladevi

Abstract It is now an acknowledged and well-researched fact that foreign direct investment facilitates and enhances development of underdeveloped and developing economies. Multinational companies have also understood that with FDI, they can do more business than any other form of internationalization. India has proved to be as one of the attractive destinations for research and development (R&D). R&D FDI in India is increasing, but, at the same time, this increase is not matching with core R&D activities. Non-core R&D activates dominate 50% inflow of R&D, as most of these activities get tax concession from the government. R&D FDI is mainly made to take benefits, tax concessions from the government, which dilutes the desired benefits and spillover effects of FDI. An attempt is made in this chapter to check whether the foreign companies are going in tune with Indian companies in creating more R&D. Data is taken from pharmaceuticals companies, where the R&D intensity is very high. R&D and innovative potentials of foreign and Indian companies are compared from their balance sheet data. Results indicate that Indian owned companies are investing more towards R&D, than foreign owned companies, which is a highly encouraging phenomenon considering the current demand for innovation .

Keywords Research and development · Multinational corporations · Indian companies and foreign direct investment

1 Introduction

In recent time, researchers who are undertaking studies in international businesses have given significant place to the role played by foreign direct investment (FDI) in enhancing the productivity of domestic firms in domestic markets (Zhang et al., 2010). Research and development (R&D) is the core component for economic growth, which leads to innovation and innovation in turn leads to economic growth.

J. C. Sharmiladevi (✉)
Symbiosis Centre for Management Studies, Symbiosis International (Deemed University), Pune, Maharashtra, India
e-mail: sharmiladei@scmspune.ac.in

© The Author(s), under exclusive license to Springer Nature Singapore Pte Ltd. 2022
A. Chandani et al. (eds.), *Achieving $5 Trillion Economy of India*, Springer Proceedings in Business and Economics, https://doi.org/10.1007/978-981-16-7818-9_2

R&D allows scientists, technologists, researchers to develop new methods, techniques and create knowledge which enhances the quality and quantity of output. In the current period, firms depend largely on other external sources for enhancing the technical and innovative advantages, which necessitates the need to collaborate more with suppliers, contractors, competitors, universities and institutions (Kedia and Jain, 2013). To remain in the limelight, multination corporations (MNCs) adopt global strategies for their R&D activities. Technological and R&D alliances have become strategic needs for MNCs currently (Cassiman & Veugelers, 2006). Many MNCs locate their production facilities abroad through their subsidiaries and collaborations with local companies, mainly to cater to the local demands, taste and locally sourced materials. R&D facilities need to be created to make modifications and fit to the needs of the products and technologies (Mrinalini & Sandhya, 2013). Competitiveness or the competitive power is now no longer determined by factor-endowments and resources but by R&D and innovations (Erdal & Göçer, 2015).

Research and development is a learning process and takes place in different forms like reverse engineering, learning by doing, using, observing and sharing with others. For developing countries, promoting indigenous research and development is one of ways available for bridging the technology gap with developed countries. Adoption of foreign technology is an important channel for diffusion of technology in a host country, which has drawn attention of many policy makers in developing countries. In this context, many countries strive to attract more FDI through MNCs in the hope that they will act as a significant channel for transfer and spillover of technology.

As the international competition is highly dynamic, it is essential for countries and firms to develop new technologies and products to sustain. In this juncture, it has become essential for developing countries to have domestic firms with ability to design and produce high-tech products and qualified workforce, establishing production facilities to host countries by means of foreign direct investment (FDI) inflows (Erdal & Göçer, 2015). With this backdrop, the motivation for this student is to examine and analyse the potentials of Indian owned companies with foreign owned companies in terms of their total income and expenditure, research and development expenditure. The objective of this study is to identify, whether the Indian owned companies are doing better with their foreign counters parts in terms of R&D. This can be analysed in various manners; in this study, the researcher has analysed some of the vital annual financials like total income, total expenditure, expenditure on research and development for the top five Indian and foreign companies.

2 Review of Literature

As early in 1970s, R&D activities were undertaken by MNCs in foreign locations (Mansfield et al., 1979; Ronstadt, 1978). One-half and one-seventh respectively of the industrial R&D performed in Canada and UK and Germany were undertaken in US-based firms (Mansfield et al., 1979). Swedish-based MNCs located their R&D activities in other developed countries, to leverage upon the man power and infrastructure (Mrinalini et al., 2012).

Table 1 Organization/categorization of R&D activities

Mode	R&D organizations in MNCs	Activities
1	Central for global	Technology development in home country for global markets which are centralized
2	Local for local	Technology development for local markets which are decentralized
3	Local link	Specific technology development at particular locations for global markets
4	Globally linked	Technology development through cooperation in R&D in different countries for global markets

Source Bartlett and Ghosal (2013)

Most of the MNCs look in for strategic alliances with firms located in developed countries, despite the fact that developing countries like China and India have become Asia's hot spots of MNC R&D activities and facilities (Sun et al., 2006). Four modes of R&D organizations in MNCs have been identified by Bartlett and Ghosal (Table 1).

Ronstadt's pioneering studies on technological activities within American MNCs indicate four different R&D activities: technology transfer, indigenous technology, global technology and corporate technology. In another effort, Kuemmerle categorized global R&D activities into two groups: home-base-exploiting R&D that aims at exploiting firm-specific capabilities in manufacturing and marketing, and home-base-augmenting R&D undertaken to acquire new knowledge and capabilities.

Recently, Sun classified MNC R&D as strategic and tactical, on the basis of their importance. Strategic R&D occupies importance for the global markets of MNCs' in the long-run. Tactical R&D is significant for local markets in the short term. Both are different with respect to the nature and extent of activities, requirements for quality of labour force, communication channels, differences in markets, commitment and control from hierarchy to their locations in host countries (Sun et al., 2006).

A 1% increase in FDI inflows is leading to 0.38% and 0.13% increase in R&D investment for domestic and foreign firms, respectively. FDI positively influences a firms possibility and tendency in R&D besides inducing the host participants to pursue R&D activities irrespective of whether they are from a local or a foreign firm (Khachoo & Sharma, 2017). FDI in India has resulted in a reduction in R&D by manufacturing firms for short time period between 1994 to 1996, but it did not have any significant effect in the second half of the economic reform period from 1999 to 2001 (Kathuria, 2008).

Innovations and technology development are usually expected to take place in MNEs from developed countries (Castellani & Zanfei, 2013), which goes in tune with product life cycle hypothesis of Raymond Vernon (Vernon, 1966), and it is further explained with economies of scale associated which are the result of R&D, learning outcomes, economies of agglomeration, access to a rich and growing market (De Beule & Somers, 2010).

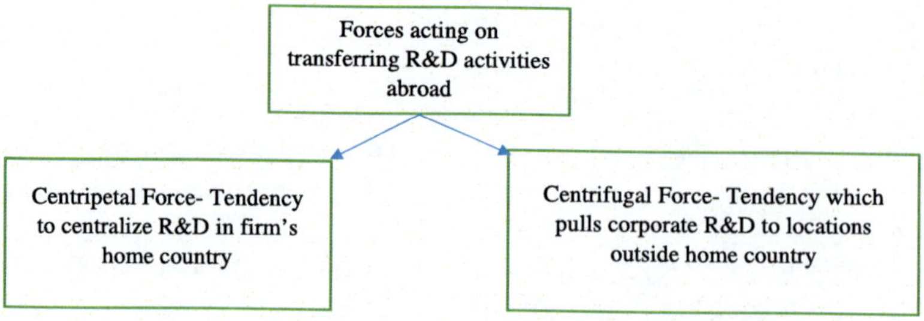

Fig. 1 Forces acting on transferring R&D activities. *Source* De Beule and Somers (2010)

There exists a link between foreign ownership, innovative behaviour and performances of enterprises. Membership in an MNE group, helps companies to overcome financial, technological, market and organizational obstacles. In such incidences the nationality of parent companies have less significance in relation to their innovative behaviours and performances (Dachs & Ebersberger, 2009).

In terms of transferring R&D activities abroad, two forces act upon namely centripetal and centrifugal forces. Centripetal forces are the one which supports centralized R&D in the firm's home country and centrifugal forces are the one which pulls corporate R&D activities to different locations outside of home country (De Beule & Somers, 2010) (Fig. 1).

From starting of 1960s, MNEs conducted R&D activities outside of their home countries mainly to support the manufacturing activities of their local subsidiaries. Such R&D activities are sometimes also used to for product adoption and local technology development for meeting market demands (Doh, 2005). This strategy is termed as asset exploiting, home-base exploiting or competence exploiting investment activities. Asset-exploiting strategies are associated keeping with the view that the MNEs function as a means to exploit firm-specific advantages in foreign markets (Dunning, 1998). Subsidiaries supports the exploitation of R&D activities by adapting technologies, products and processes to local needs, end user tastes and regulations (Dachs & Ebersberger, 2009). Study conducted by Sun (Sun et al., 2006) indicates that majority of foreign R&D in China is adaptive as well as tactical in nature and serves the Chinese market effectively; at the same time, strategic foreign R&D also exists, and they are engaged in projects for Chinese as well as global markets and they also conduct long-term original research.

Studies conducted on overseas R&D expenditure of US-based manufacturing MNEs indicate that too much attention given to MNE affiliates as technology creators is often not benefitting the host country economy. As the intercountry difference in R&D intensity is fundamentally determined by domestic market size and overall R&D capability, the impact of domestic market orientation of affiliates on R&D propensity varies depending on a particular countries' stage of global economic integration (Athukorala & Archanun, 2013).

3 Research and Development in India

In India, the R&D contributions come from private and public sources. Private R&D comes from large companies in specific industry sectors like pharmaceuticals and electronics; public R&D comes from government exploration in defence, atomic energy, space technology and agriculture. The pie-chart shows how the R&D spending in India is broken up in terms of the spenders, and non-private R&D takes the cake at 62% with the private sector and the industry contributing the balance.

According to a survey conducted by the Department of Science and Technology (DST), India, stands fourth among other countries in terms of the R&D spending as a percentage of gross domestic product. But the disturbing fact is the percentage remains same from 1996 to 2015. Table 2 indicates the R&D as percentage of gross domestic product in 1996 and 2015 for four countries. More than 80% of R&D spending are met by some of the public sector and government agencies like Defence Research and Development Organization (DRDO), Indian Space Research Organization (ISRO), Indian Council of Agriculture Research (ICAR), Department of Atomic Energy, Central Scientific and Industrial Research (CSIR), etc.

In Table 3, a comparison is made between per capita R&D among ten countries.

Table 2 R&D as percentage of gross domestic product

Country	R&D as % of GDP 1996	R&D as % of GDP 2015
China	0.56	2.07
Denmark	1.80	3.01
Germany	2.13	2.88
India	0.63	0.63

Source Department of science and technology, Government of India

Table 3 R&D expenditure per capita and gross domestic product for selected countries

S. no.	Countries	Per capita R&D
1	Denmark	1870.3
2	Sweden	1860.4
3	Israel	1572.1
4	USA	1430.5
5	UK	790.2
6	China	154.7
7	Brazil	131.5
8	Argentina	78.2
9	South Africa	55
10	India	10.8

Source UNESCO

Table 4 National expenditure on R&D in relation to GDP

Year	R&D as % of GDP*	R&D as % of GDP (year on year growth) **
2005–2006 (series 2004–2005)	0.81	–
2006–2007	0.80	−0.01
2007–2008	0.79	−0.01
2008–2009	0.84	−0.05
2009–2010	0.82	−0.02
2010–2011	0.77	−0.05
2011–2012 (series 2011–2012)	0.76	−0.01
2012–2013	0.74	−0.02
2013–2014	0.71	−0.03
2014–2015	0.69	−0.02

Source * Department of science and technology, ** author's own

It is understood well that the R&D per capita is extremely poor for India when compared with its competing countries like China, Brazil or Argentina.

An analysis of Table 4 indicates that there is no significant increase in the national expenditure on R&D from 1995–1995 (0.61) to 2014–2015 (0.69), which gives an indication of the inclinations of the government towards this sector. Governments hand holding is needed in order to enhance the investment and expenditure on R&D. The trend line shown in Fig. 2 indicates that the R&D expenditure is not consistently increasing. It was the highest in 2008 and 2009, after which it is not able to revive and continues to fall down (Fig. 3).

4 The Indian Pharmaceutical Industry

The Indian pharma industry (IPI) is world's third largest in terms of volume and supplies nearly 50% of world demand for vaccines, generic medicines, contributing to health care by manufacturing high-quality, cost-efficient medicines to Indian as well as to global market, with dominant local brands and intense competition among the foreign players. IPI along with government and other stake holders is responsible for increasing drug penetration rate to more than 50%, making India Polio-free, bringing down treatment costs of life-threatening diseases like Chronic Myeloid Leukaemia and Hepatitis C, to less than five per cent of its original cost.

The IPI is ranked third in terms of volume and tenth in value, having many unique characters 70–80% if retail market is dominated by branded generics, as early investors domestic firms dominates in formulation development, low price driven by intense competition, all of which presents their own opportunities and challenges (McKinsey & Company, 2015). IPI has contributed to India's economic growth by providing direct and indirect employment to over 2.7 million people in high-skill areas like R&D and manufacturing. The industry generates over USD 11 billion of

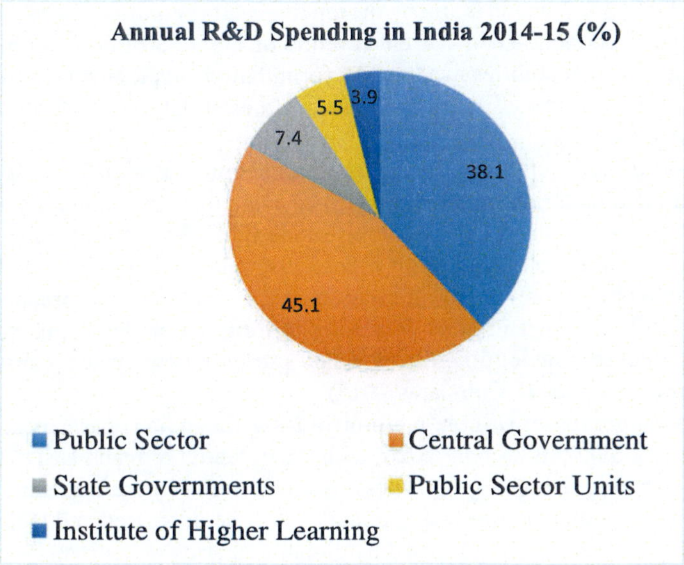

Fig. 2 System of splitting annual R&D in India (%). *Source* Department of Science and Technology, Government of India

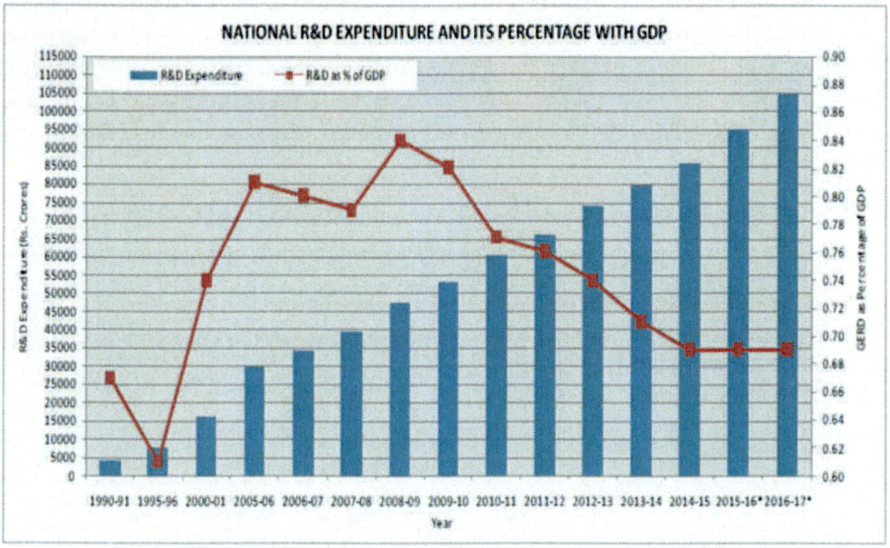

Fig. 3 National R&D expenditure and its percentage with gross domestic product

trade surplus every year and is among the top five sectors contributing to the reduction of India's trade deficit. Their current revenue of USD 38 billion can be attributed to its world class capabilities in areas like formulation development, entrepreneurial ability of firms and the vision of the industry to establish India's footprint in large international markets.

Some of the key features of the industry include produced different dosage forms with good manufacturing practices (GMP) certification, the second highest number of United States Food and Drug Administration (USFDA) approved facilities, 40% less labour costs. IPI is ranked third in terms of volume and tenth in value, having many unique characters 70–80% if retail market is dominated by branded generics, as early investors domestic firms dominates in formulation development, low price driven by intense competition, all of which presents their own opportunities and challenges (McKinsey & Company, 2015).

From a market size of USD 12.6 billion in 2009, the Indian pharmaceutical market will grow to USD 55 billion by 2020, with the potential to reach USD 70 billion in an aggressive growth scenario. In a pessimistic scenario characterized by regulatory controls and economic slowdown, the market will be depressed and (Fig. 4).

Growth of IPI is largely governed by global scenarios rather than domestic business environment. As it is a highly knowledge-based industry, technology becomes outdated fast, and the process of innovation is highly expensive and runs for long duration. So the demand for technology is met by resources rich western world (Lalitha, 2002). IPI faced highest drop in its growth trend from 17.2% in the pre-reform period to 1% in post-reform period (1990–1991 to 2003–2004), which is mainly attributed to lack of investment in R&D in the wake of high competition in the 1990's (Mehta, 2011). Most of the investments made in IPI is undertaken in reverse engineering rather than developing new products (Lalitha, 2002) which can be a reason for this drop (Fig. 5).

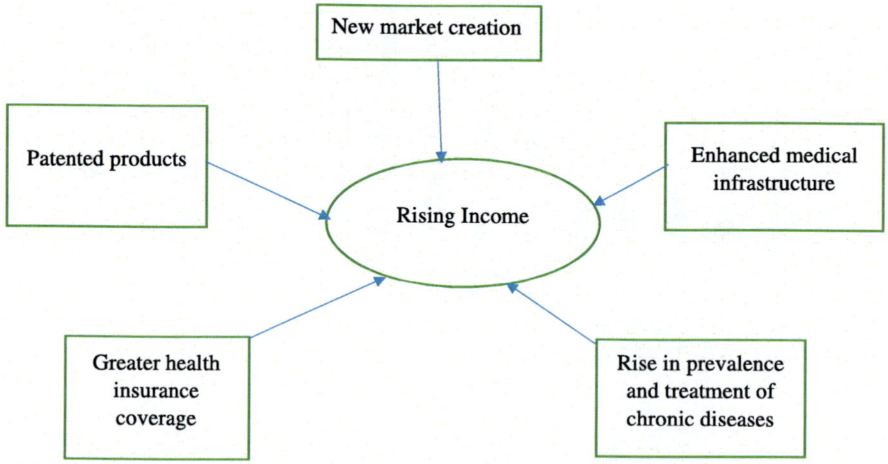

Fig. 4 Reasons for rising income in IPI. *Source* McKinsey and Company (2015)

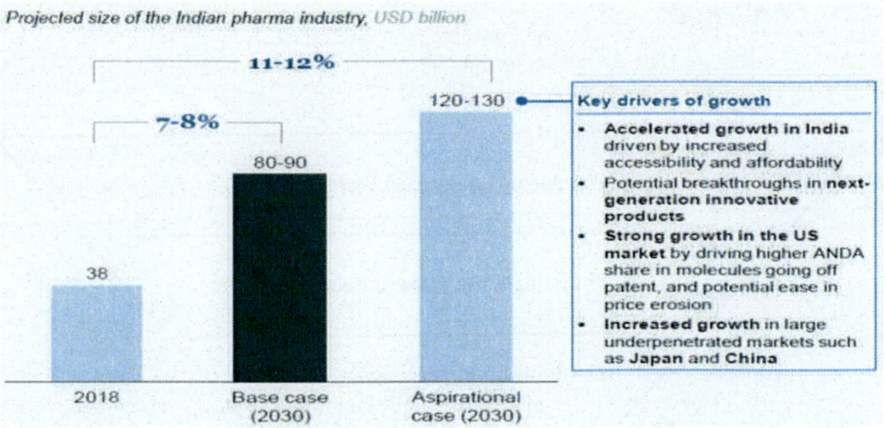

Fig. 5 Projected size of IPI by 2030. *Source* Alliance (2019)

The IPI is poised for growth with current rates of 7–8% compounded average growth rate (CAGR), with annual revenues expected to grow up to 80–90 billion USD by 2030 (Alliance, 2019).

4.1 Opportunities

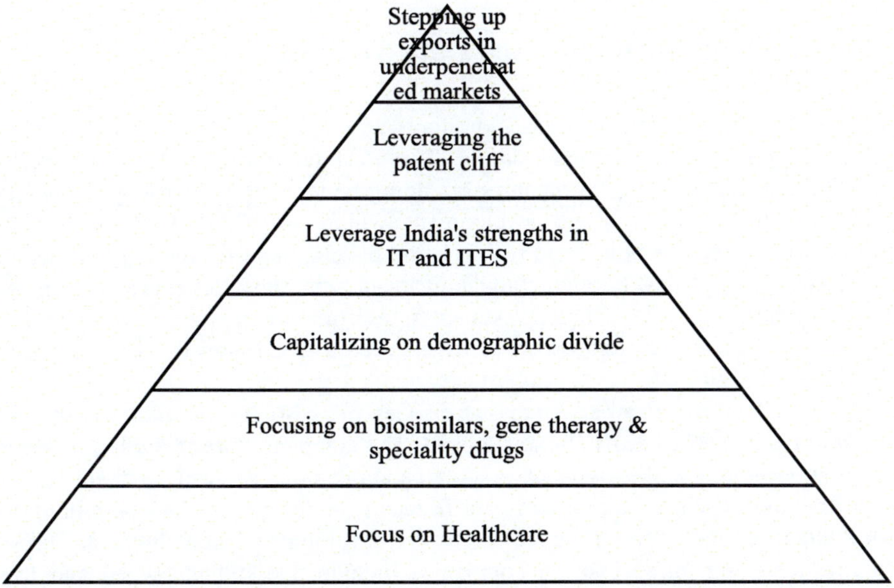

4.2 Challenges

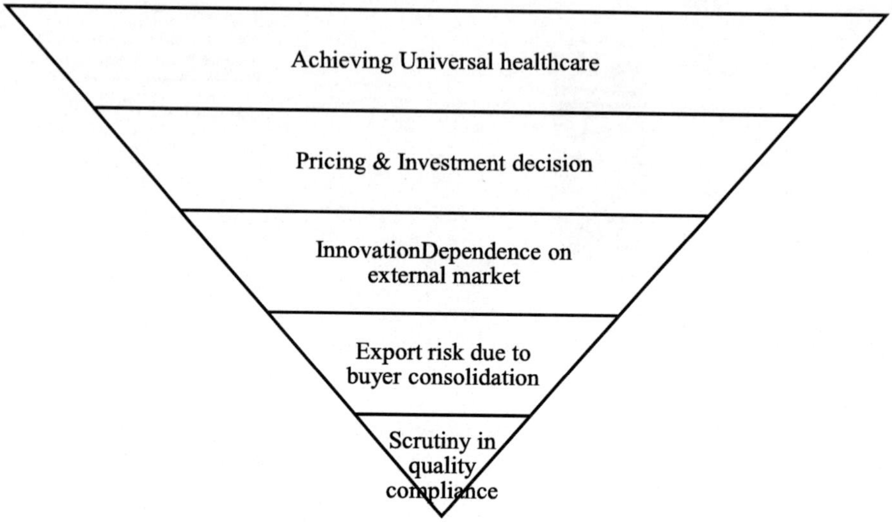

The IPI with all its merits and limitations holds to be a good case to study as it is highly driven by investment and innovation—both coming from MNCs in the form of FDI primarily, and this justifies the reason for choosing this industry among others.

5 Methodology Adopted and Data Analysis

This study is an applied research and adopts an empirical research design, using longitudinal data from secondary source. The objective of this study is to identify, whether the Indian owned companies are doing better with their foreign counters parts in terms of research and development, which is analysed with the help of total expenditure, expenditure on research and development for the top five Indian and foreign companies. Foreign companies mean here, those pharmaceutical firms receiving more than 10% of their investment funds from foreign sources and operating either as associates, subsidiaries or branches in India. The routes for receiving such funds are through FDI.

Data is taken from Prowess database from Centre for Monitoring Indian Economy (CMIE) from 2009 to 2018 non-annualized. The companies are identified in terms of their ranking on the basis of market capitalization, as well as their operation in India. Their balance sheet data is taken for ten years, data pertaining to total income, total expenditure, research and development expenditure are taken for the ten companies. The ten companies include five Indian owned and five foreign owned companies. Indian companies are Cipla, Lupin, Sun Pharmaceuticals, Reddy's laboratories, Aurobhindo pharma. Foreign companies include Pfizer, Glaxo Smith Kline Becham\Smithkline Beecham, Proctor and Gamble health, Sanofi and Zydus. Due to non-availability of adequate data, two companies from the list were dropped—Reddy's laboratories and Zydus.

Firstly, research and development expenditure as a percentage of total expenditure is calculated by the researcher in order to understand the importance; individual companies are giving towards R&D. Table 5 indicates the details pertaining to total income, total expenditure, research and development expenditure as captured from their respective company balance sheets. The calculation is shown in Table 5, which indicates that the Indian owned companies average expenditure on research and development as a percentage of total expenditure is very high when compared with any of the foreign counterparts. Lupin laboratories stand first with an R&D spending of 16.5%, followed by Sun pharmaceuticals at 9.02%. Cipla's figure is at 7.07% and Aurobhindo pharma spends 5%. While the figures for Indian owned companies are encouraging but from the table, it indicates that the foreign owned companies average expenditure on research and development as a percentage of total expenditure is very less. Pfizer-1.51%, P&G health-1.07%, Sanofi-0.45%, GSK/SKB-0.23%.

Secondly, one sample t test is used to test whether the sample mean is different from the population mean. As the researcher is not aware of the population mean, calculation of one sample t test is more meaningful than undertaking z test. One sample t test is separately done for Indian owned and foreign owned companies and their hypothesis are as follows. This t test is conducted for the variable total income and research and development expenditure.

H_0: Sample mean is not the same as the population mean.
H_1: Sample mean is same as the population mean.

If the significance (p-value) is less than 0.05 (95%), we reject the null hypotheses and accept the alternate hypothesis.

Thirdly, regression coefficient is calculated taking total income as an independent variable and research and development expenditure as a dependent variable. This exercise is also calculated separately for Indian and foreign companies. If the regression square value is high crossing 0.60, then it is an indication that the dependent variable is significantly influencing independent variable that is total income.

In Fig. 6, it indicates that the expenditure on R&D is ranging high for Indian companies and the four foreign companies Pfizer, GSK, P&G and Sanofi is having a lowest range of averages for R&D as a percentage of total expenditure.

One sample t test is undertaken for to know whether or not the sample mean is different from population mean for the variables average total income and average research and development expenditure. Results of the one sample t test indicates that the sample mean is the same as the population mean; as the significance value is 0.002 which is less than 0.5, we reject the null hypothesis that the sample mean is same as the population mean in terms of the average total income for Indian companies (Tables 6 and 7).

Table 5 .

Name of company	Details: Mar 2009–Mar 2018: Non-annualized: Rs. million	2009	2010	2011	2012	2013	2014	2015	2016	2017	2018	Averages
Aurobhindo Pharma Ltd	Total income	30,248.30	34,404.20	42,870.00	43,977.90	55,960.10	73,443.30	83,120.60	95,116.70	99,171.60	103,838.00	66,215.07
	Total expenses	29,252.30	30,621.40	38,295.80	43,505.30	52,211.00	62,079.90	69,548.00	80,265.60	81,790.80	89,052.10	57,662.22
	R&D expenses (capital and current account)	1032.30	1,014.80	1,757.20	1989.00	2333.40	2708.00	3598.80	4425.60	5904.00	6491.40	3125.45
	R&D expenditure as % of total expenditure	3.528953	3.314022	4.588493	4.571857	4.469173	4.36212	5.174556	5.513695	7.218416	7.289441	5.00
Cipla Ltd	Total income	53,768.60	58,604.00	64,903.70	72,230.30	85,237.10	98,363.00	103,726.30	123,980.20	111,123.90	117,797.40	88,973.45
	Total expenses	47,136.00	50,441.00	56,686.90	60,878.30	73,073.50	86,060.80	95,405.90	107,073.70	100,811.80	105,232.70	78,280.06
	R&D expenses (capital and current account)	2515.00	2,626.80	2,848.50	3238.30	4251.40	5175.10	8441.40	10,353.40	10,305.60	9802.20	5955.77
	R&D expenditure as % of total expenditure	5.335625	5.207668	5.02497	5.319301	5.817978	6.013307	8.84788	9.669415	10.22261	9.314785	7.07
Sun Pharmacheuticals	Total income	41,140.60	26,813.20	33,752.50	44,467.10	27,892.60	31,736.70	84,865.20	81,800.10	84,829.00	92,257.50	54,955.45
	Total expenses	28,725.50	18,135.80	19,894.60	28,293.30	22,832.40	60,167.20	96,425.40	92,819.00	86,736.00	95,610.80	54,964
	R&D expenses (capital and current account)	1511.00	1436.70	1,592.00	2184.00	3102.20	4223.90	9092.30	8293.90	10,430.70	9,852.00	5171.87

(continued)

Table 5 (continued)

Name of company	Details: Mar 2009–Mar 2018: Non-annualized: Rs. million	2009	2010	2011	2012	2013	2014	2015	2016	2017	2018	Averages
	R&D expenditure as % of total expenditure	5.260135	7.9219	8.002171	7.719142	13.58683	7.02027	9.429362	8.935563	12.0258	10.30428	9.02
Lupin laboratories	Total income	30,295.60	37,529.40	45,563.40	54,556.40	72,077.20	94,751.80	100,675.60	115,520.90	129,305.40	102,430.60	78,270.63
	Total expenses	26,380.50	31,020.30	37,468.70	47,838.00	61,297.30	71,967.50	78,410.10	88,939.40	99,744.70	88,137.30	63,120.38
	R&D expenses (capital and current account)	2,669.10	4,251.10	5,475.60	6161.60	7988.40	9929.20	11,961.90	18,145.10	29,245.00	19,865.50	11,569.25
	R&D expenditure as % of total expenditure	10.1177	13.70425	14.6138	12.88014	13.03222	13.79678	15.25556	20.40164	29.31985	22.53927	16.56
Pfizer	Total income	10,691.90	9456.10	13,913.50	12,262.50	16,186.00	12,743.40	19,980.40	21,906.30	22,735.20	20,944.80	16,082.01
	Total expenses	7930.50	7988.20	11,971.60	10,601.20	11,180.70	10,506.40	19,800.60	18,337.60	19,525.00	17,069.00	13,491.08
	R&D expenses (capital and current account)	283.5	292.7	106.7	64.7	175.8	148.2	174	205.4	275		172.6
	R&D expenditure as % of total expenditure	3.574806	3.664155	0.891276	0.610308	1.572352	1.410569	0.878761	1.120103	1.408451		1.51
GSK/SKB	Total income	20,706.10	21,160.80	23,551.00	26,489.40	29,397.60	28,951.40	36,502.40	29,644.70	31,147.00	29,672.00	27,722.24
	Total expenses	14,963.50	16,362.10	18,116.00	22,744.30	23,099.20	24,440.00	31,799.80	27,344.30	26,984.20	26,731.50	23,258.49

(continued)

Table 5 (continued)

Name of company	Details: Mar 2009–Mar 2018: Non-annualized: Rs. million	2009	2010	2011	2012	2013	2014	2015	2016	2017	2018	Averages
	R&D expenses (capital and current account)	126.8	80.2	54.4	38.7	24.6	27.5	21.9	20	19	22.5	43.56
	R&D expenditure as % of total expenditure	0.847395	0.490157	0.300287	0.170153	0.106497	0.11252	0.068868	0.073141	0.070412	0.08417	0.23
P&G health	Total income	5255.60	5624.50	6,291.90	7277.00	8475.40	9182.10	9973.00	10,546.90	11,681.70	22,413.60	9672.17
	Total expenses	4571.00	4957.80	6,054.60	6458.10	8208.10	8910.20	9453.60	9773.40	10,719.70	14,061.10	8316.76
	R&D expenses (capital and current account)	20.4	28.5	33.9	64.2	90.3	112.3	125.1	156.2	175.7	171.2	97.78
	R&D expenditure as % of total expenditure	0.446292	0.574852	0.559905	0.9941	1.100133	1.260353	1.323305	1.598216	1.639038	1.217543	1.07
Sanofi	Total income	11,666.30	14,070.70	14,858.10	17,370.20	20,165.30	22,730.50	25,464.10	26,042.00	25,901.00	28,611.00	20,687.92
	Total expenses	10,322.60	11,902.10	13,047.40	15,692.90	17,608.20	21,604.40	21,885.00	23,352.00	21,664.00	25,410.00	18,248.86
	R&D expenses (capital and current account)	132.3	55.2	67.4	41.7	60.7	40.3	54	98	88.5	117	75.51
	R&D expenditure as % of total expenditure	1.281654	0.463784	0.516578	0.265725	0.344726	0.186536	0.246744	0.419664	0.408512	0.460449	0.45

Source Authors own calculations

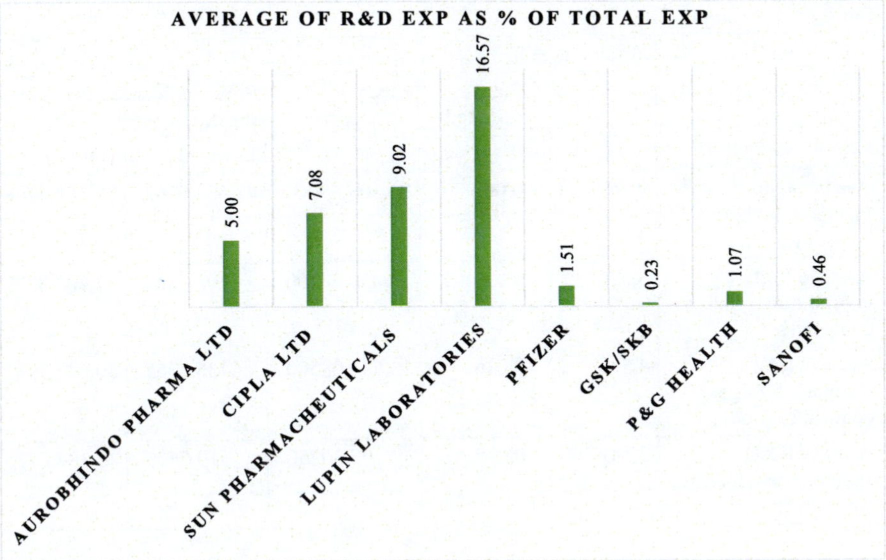

Fig. 6 Average of research and development expenditure as percentage of total expenditure. *Source* Authors own calculations

Table 6 One-sample statistics

Variables tested	No.	Mean	Std. deviation	Std. error mean
Average total income—Indian companies	4	72,103.6500	14,734.96897	7367.48449
Average R&D expenditure—Indian companies	4	6455.5850	3611.88354	1805.94177
Average total income—foreign companies	4	18,541.0850	7607.17229	3803.58615
Average R&D expenditure——foreign companies	4	97.3625	54.87287	27.43644

Results of the one sample *t* test conducted for average R&D expenditure indicate that the sample mean is the same as the population mean; as the significance value is 0.037 which is less than 0.5, we reject the null hypothesis that the sample mean is same as the population mean in terms of the average R&D expenditure for Indian companies. In the case of foreign companies also the results are identical, in terms of average total income and R&D expenditure, the null hypothesis is rejected as the significance is 0.016 and 0.038 which is less than 0.05. Here also, the null hypothesis is rejected, and alternate hypothesis is accepted indicated that the sample means are same or identical with the population mean.

Table 7 One-sample test

	Test value = 0					
	t	df	Sig. (2-tailed)	Mean difference	95% confidence interval of the difference	
					Lower	Upper
Average total income—Indian companies	9.787	3	0.002	72,103.65000	48,657.0262	95,550.2738
Average R&D expenditure—Indian companies	3.575	3	0.037	6455.58500	708.2723	12,202.8977
Average total income—foreign companies	4.875	3	0.016	18,541.08500	6436.3763	30,645.7937
Average R&D expenditure—foreign companies	3.549	3	0.038	97.36250	10.0475	184.6775

Simple linear regression is run, taking average total income as the independent variable and average R&D expenditure as the dependent variable. Regression is separately run for Indian companies and foreign companies (Tables 8 and 9).

Results of the regression analysis indicate that the *R* square value is very low to the tune of 0.164 indicating that only 16.4% of the total changes happening in the independent variable that is total income is explained by R&D expenditure in the case of Indian companies (Tables 10 and 11)

Results of the regression analysis indicate that the *R* square value is low to the tune of 0.339 indicating that only 33.9% of the total changes happening in the independent variable that is total income is explained by R&D expenditure in the case of foreign companies. This is an improvisation when compared with the Indian companies.

6 Discussions and Conclusions

The objective of this study is to identify, whether the Indian owned companies are doing better with their foreign counters parts in terms of research and development. Although a case-based analysis might give a better result, here the research is undertaken taking the balance sheet data for ten years for eight companies (four Indian and four foreign owned companies). Results of the *t* test strongly support that the sample companies studied are similar to the population. It is understood from Table 5 that the averages of research and development expenditure as a percentage of total expenditure are higher in the case of Indian companies when compared to foreign owned companies. This means Indian pharmaceutical companies are investing more towards their R&D, than the foreign owned companies, which is a highly encouraging

Table 8 Regression coefficients

Model	R	R square	Adjusted R square	Std. error of the estimate	Change statistics					Durbin-Watson
					R square change	F change	df1	df2	Sig. F change	
1	0.405[a]	0.164	−0.253	4043.82118	0.164	0.393	1	2	0.595	0.725

a. Predictors: (Constant), average total income

b. Dependent variable: Average R&D expenditure

Table 9 ANOVA

ANOVA[a]						
Model		Sum of squares	df	Mean square	*F*	Sig.
1	Regression	6,432,128.638	1	6,432,128.638	0.393	0.595[b]
	Residual	32,704,979.448	2	16,352,489.724		
	Total	39,137,108.086	3			

a. Dependent variable: Average R&D expenditure—Indian companies

b. Predictors: (Constant), average total income—Indian companies

phenomenon considering the current demand for innovation-driven development. At the same time, it is quite peculiar to see the phenomenon as indicated in regression results; in both Indian and foreign companies, the research and development expenditure is less significantly powerful in explaining the total income, as the *R* square is less to the tune of 0.164 (16.4%) and 0.339 (33.9%). This is an indication that the income is determined more by factors apart from research and development. In other words, the role played by R&D is less significant in determining profits. This phenomenon is more strongly visible in the case of Indian companies.

In case of foreign companies, this aspect is already identified in literatures by Dachs and Ebersberger, Sun et al. as MNEs usually locate their research centres in their respective home countries (Dachs & Ebersberger, 2009) as they want to protect trade secrets. In some cases, this phenomenon of the MNCs will also help them in maintaining their quality standards and benchmarking to an extent in the international arena, taking into considerations their specific requirements towards patents, intellectual property rights and local content requirements. This factor very well goes with the literatures (Sun et al., 2006) which support the fact that big companies and MNEs from countries like China and India are now investing more in R&D as the future for their expansion and survival, which also results in their own individual development.

At a time when the international community is looking into factors like innovation, specialization and sustainability, research must occupy the prime spot and should act as the direct determinant of incomes. But, the flip side of the IPI is still the industry is driven more by factors other than research, innovation and development. Market forces strongly determine the survival and profits, rather than innovation and research, which means, IPI are still depending upon demand conditions and other related market forces to make profit rather than aiming to enhance their income through R&D indigenization.

It is also understood that transition economies like India are struggling in the international arena to create patents, intellectual property rights, as the amount of investment undertaken towards research and development is extremely less. Most of the investments in R&D in India currently is undertaken by various governmental agencies—a trend which needs to change. This phenomenon is also witnessing change,

Table 10 Modal summary

Model	R	R square	Adjusted R square	Std. error of the estimate	Change statistics					Durbin-Watson
					R square change	F change	df1	df2	Sig. F change	
1	0.583[a]	0.339	0.009	54.62090	0.339	1.028	1	2	0.417	1.251

a. Predictors: (constant), average total income—foreign companies

b. Dependent variable: average R&D expenditure—foreign companies

Table 11 ANOVA

ANOVA[a]						
Model		Sum of squares	df	Mean square	F	Sig.
1	Regression	3066.212	1	3066.212	1.028	0.417[b]
	Residual	5966.885	2	2983.442		
	Total	9033.096	3			

a. Dependent variable: average R&D expenditure—foreign companies

b. Predictors: (constant), average total income—foreign companies

but this change is very slow. With the kind of development plans, the current government is planning; it is extremely essential to undertake more investment by individual enterprises to support the objectives of the government of achieving more development, which incidentally will also enhance the development of individual companies.

This study is one of the first of its kind to check the potentials of pharmaceutical companies—both Indian and foreign in terms of their research and development expenditures. An understanding of the significance of R&D and its potentials will help the IPI to stand firmly in the international arena in the near future. As the developed west is getting stagnant, it is time for the developing east to take charge of the situation to go head strong in creating a stable future.

References

Alliance, I. P. (2019). *The Indian pharmaceutical industry-the* way *forward Contents*

Athukorala, P. and Archanun, K. (2013). Multinational enterprises and the globalization of R&D: A study of US-based firms. In *Multinational Enterprises in Asian Development*. https://doi.org/10.4337/9781847204103.00014

Bartlett, C. A. and Ghosal, S. (2013). Managing the global firm. In C. A. Bartlett, Y. Doz, & G. Hedlund (Eds.), *Managing the global firm* (pp. 27–5836–27–5836). Routledge. https://doi.org/10.5860/choice.27-5836

Cassiman, B., & Veugelers, R. (2006). In search of complementarity in innovation strategy: Internal R&D and external knowledge acquisition. *Management Science, 52*(1), 68–82. https://doi.org/10.1287/mnsc.1050.0470

Castellani, D. and Zanfei, A. (2013). *Multinational firms, innovation and productivity*. MA, USA: Edward Elgar, Cheltenham, UK Northamption. https://doi.org/10.4337/9781847201591

Dachs, B., & Ebersberger, B. (2009). Does foreign ownership matter for the innovative activities of enterprises? *International Economics and Economic Policy, 6*(1), 41–57. https://doi.org/10.1007/s10368-009-0126-3

De Beule, F. and Somers, D. (2010). The impact of international R&D on home-country R&D for Indian multinationals. *Transnational Corporations, 24*(1), 27–55. Available at: https://unctad.org/en/PublicationChapters/diaeia2017d2a3_en.pdf (Accessed: 24 July 2019)

Doh, J. P. (2005). Offshore outsourcing: Implications for international business and strategic management theory and practice. *Journal of Management Studies, 42*(3), 695–704. https://doi.org/10.1111/j.1467-6486.2005.00515.x

Dunning, J. H. (1998). Location and the multinational enterprise: A neglected factor? Location and the multinational enterprise: A neglected factor? *Journal of International Business Studies, 29*(1), 45–66. https://doi.org/10.1057/palgrave.jibs.8490024

Erdal, L., & Göçer, İ. (2015). The effects of foreign direct investment on R&D and innovations: Panel data analysis for developing Asian countries. *Procedia—Social and Behavioral Sciences, 195*, 749–758. https://doi.org/10.1016/j.sbspro.2015.06.469

Kathuria, V. (2008). The impact of FDI inflows on R&D investment by medium-and-high-tech firms in India in the post-reform period. *Transnational Corporations, 17*(2), 45+. Available at: https://unctad.org/en/Docs/diaeia20082a3_en.pdf (Accessed: 3 June 2019).

Kedia, B. L. and Jain, S. C. (2013) *Restoring America's global competitiveness through innovation*

Khachoo, Q., & Sharma, R. (2017). Relative institutional quality and FDI inflows in ASEAN countries. *International Journal of Emerging Markets, 44*(3), 427–446. https://doi.org/10.1108/JES-10-2015-0188

Lalitha, N. (2002). *Indian pharmaceutical industry in WTO regime: A SWOT analysis, economic and political weekly*

Mansfield, E., Teece, D. and Romeo, A. (1979). Overseas research and development by US-based firms. *Economica, 46*(182), 187–196. Available at: https://www.jstor.org/stable/pdf/2553190.pdf?refreqid=excelsior%3Ab9c72e1b2ad732ce58e2ccf213130b85 (Accessed: 9 July 2019)

McKinsey & Company. (2015). India pharma 2020: Propelling access and acceptance, realising true potential.

Mehta, S. (2011). *Economic reforms, technological intensity and industrial development in India, Economic and Political Weekly*. Available at: https://about.jstor.org/terms (Accessed: 18 October 2019)

Mrinalini, N., Nath, P. and Sandhya, G. D. (2012). R&D strategies of MNCs in India: Isolation or integration? *Economic and Political Weekly, XLVII*(13), 73–78. Available at: https://www.jstor.org/stable/pdf/23214713.pdf?ab_segments=0%2Fdefault-2%2Fcontrol&refreqid=search%3Ae9440a39997cc6c0a0b9bca51b2f1012 (Accessed: 6 July 2019)

Mrinalini, N. and Sandhya, G. D. (2013). *Foreign direct investment in R&D in India †, CURRENT SCIENCE*. Available at: https://www.currentscience.ac.in/Volumes/105/06/0767.pdf (Accessed: 3 June 2019)

Ronstadt, R. (1978). *Research and development abroad by U. S. multinationals* (Vol. 20(1), pp. 7–9). New York: Praeger, The International Executive, John Wiley & Sons, Ltd. https://doi.org/10.1002/tie.5060200105

Sun, Y., Du, D. and Huang, L. (2006). Foreign R&D in developing countries: Empirical evidence from. *China Review*. Available at: https://about.jstor.org/terms (Accessed: 6 July 2019)

Vernon, R. (1966). International investment and international trade in the product cycle. *The Quarterly Journal of Economics, 80*(2), 190. https://doi.org/10.2307/1880689

Zhang, Y. et al. (2010). FDI Spillovers in an emerging market: The role of foreign firms country origin diversity and domestic firms absorptive capacity. *Strategic Management Journal, 31*(9), 969–989. https://doi.org/10.1002/smj.856

AI as a Tool in Internal Communication to Reduce Employee Attrition Rate in India

G. Nikita and Sai Nethra Velicheti

Abstract As employees are representatives of their business to the outside world, a structured communication strategy can bridge the knowledge gap and create an informed workforce. This research takes into account the role of artificial intelligence in internal communication that delves into the benefits that arise when employees are fully involved in the organisation's ethos, values and functioning (Aristotle and Smith in Prior analytics. Hackett Pub. Co., Indianapolis, 1989). The objective of this research is to understand the role of AI in increasing employee engagement; application of AI in tandem with work stress for employees; ease of AI usage with respect to up-skilling/cross-skilling, switching organisations, etc. The methodology implemented is a mixed method approach. The primary data collection consisted of a pilot study through a structured questionnaire among 60 working professionals that includes 50 employees and ten industry experts as respondents for the quantitative study. For qualitative study, in-depth interviews with five industry experts included two corporate communication professionals, two human resources professionals and one person working for artificial intelligence. The timeline for this research was across three months, i.e., December 2018–February 2019, and the sample size of 60 people was selected purposively.

Keywords Artificial intelligence · Attrition · Employee engagement · Internal communication · Corporate communication · India

This paper is a revised and expanded version of a paper entitled "AI as a tool in internal communication to reduce employee attrition rate in India" presented at Symbiosis Institute of Management Studies Annual Research Conference, Pune, 16–18 December 2019.

G. Nikita (✉) · S. N. Velicheti
Symbiosis School of Media and Communication, Symbiosis International (Deemed University), Bengaluru, India
e-mail: nikita.g@ssmc.edu.in

S. N. Velicheti
e-mail: sai.nethra@ssmc.edu.in

© The Author(s), under exclusive license to Springer Nature Singapore Pte Ltd. 2022
A. Chandani et al. (eds.), *Achieving $5 Trillion Economy of India*, Springer Proceedings in Business and Economics, https://doi.org/10.1007/978-981-16-7818-9_3

1 Introduction

Communication drives relationships and frames the behaviour of people at a workplace. It plays a significant role in improving the effectiveness of an organisation. Many organisations use strategic external communication for their customers, clients, stakeholders, etc., that brings marketing and communication specialists into play. There are many practices focused towards external communication, whereas it is also important to strengthen an organisation from within in order to achieve expected outcomes. An effective internal communication strategy can create a better workforce and transparency at work. Communication is often underrated as a function; however, among various functions of an organisation, communication should be given utmost importance as all the other management functions can be achieved only through effective communication. The exchange of ideas, information and views in and outside an organisation is termed as organisational communication. It includes individual and mass communication too. Organisational communication may also be described as the flow of communication between the various groups and units in an organisation. There are three forms of organisational communication—internal operational communication, external operational communication and personal communication.

Internal operational communication is the umbrella term for the communication that takes place in order to accomplish the day-to-day operations in an organisation. The key consumers and contributors of this type of communication are the employees of the organisation. This form of communication may be oral (face-to-face conversations, telephonic conversations, meetings, town halls, speech, etc.) and written (e-mails, reports, newsletters, Websites, memos, instructions, intranet, blogs, instant chats). Internal communication takes place in various directions depending on the flow of information such as horizontal and vertical communication. Vertical communication takes place from superiors to subordinates (downward communication) and from subordinates to superiors (upward communication). Horizontal communication, on the other hand, is the information exchange that takes place between peers and colleagues in the organisation. They may be working at the same level in the company and may involve people from different organisational units/departments. External operational communication is the communication with external groups that are not a part of the organisational framework. These groups include clients, customers, stakeholders, suppliers, government agencies, regulatory bodies and authority, local community, special interest groups and the general public.

In an organisational environment, communication takes place across various levels and different kinds of communication exist. In a corporate setting, communication takes place across various genres: marketing communication, management communication and organisational communication. Marketing communication includes the communication that goes hand in hand with sales of goods and services. Advertising, sales promotional activities, etc., are a part of marketing communication efforts, whereas management communication is the bridge between the line managers and staff. It includes the day-to-day communication mostly done by the human resources department of the organisation. Organisational communication includes the internal and external communication that takes place and also includes areas such as investor relations, stakeholder relations, and corporate communication. While marketing communication and management communication are mostly function-specific, organisational communication is something that is applied across the organisation at various levels and across departments. It is a niche function and is performed by the corporate communications department of the organisation.

Internal communication was initially identified under the human resource management or an extension for staff communication or employee relations or even industrial relations. The functioning of this department has changed overtime, this has also led to the advent of change communication as a major aspect of internal communication. The evolution of internal communication has been divided into three phases of development. They are:

1. industrial relations during the pre-1960s
2. realistic journalism during the mid-1960s to 1980s
3. marketing from the late 1980s till now.

The present stage of development involved a strategic approach to aid the management and form business-oriented attitude. The business case study for internal communication (Cowan, 2014) discusses the three key features as sources of performance improvement with respect to time. The highest preference being focus on employees, followed by improving products, services and cost cutting, draws the attention to structure better communication for employees and focus on communication within the organisation to maximise performance of an organisation. Although communication is required of all the managers, the reality in terms of what is delivered on a day-to-day basis is completely different. Internal communication needs to be planned, coordinated and linked to business strategy, and hence, a specialist in this field comes into play. Internal stakeholders play a major role in information flow, and this demand focuses on proper dissemination of message based on style, timing, targeting and content of communication. The desired outcome is not just employee relations, but the way employees perform to better organisation performance.

Retaining employees today has become even more important than in the past. Over the years, the focus of most organisations has moved to its employees in addition to profits and business. Richard Branson had once said, "Clients do not come first. Employees come first. If you take care of your employees, they will take care of the clients". It is also believed that the cost of retaining an employee is much less compared to recruiting new hires. Attrition is the switching of employees from one organisation to another due to several reasons like lack of motivation, lack of growth opportunities, unfavourable organisational culture, etc. However, an environment where employees are encouraged to participate in building the organisation and include them as part of the bigger aspect of the organisation, they feel engaged and thus instilling a sense of belonging for the company. Therefore, employee engagement and advocacy matter in retaining employees over a period of time and hence reduce the attrition rates. The technological boom across industries has enabled a better work culture for employees, in spite of which there has been considerable attrition in organisations. According to Mercer's survey, 54% of Indians are seriously considering leaving their jobs and the figure rises to 66% in the age group 16–24 (Vorhauser-Smith, 2020). However, technology has an important role to play in engaging employees enough to retain them and make them feel motivated.

Internal communication is the communication that takes place within an organisation, across hierarchies to ensure everyone is on the same page. It is an important factor as it helps employees stay abreast with the activities of their organisation and drives employees towards organisational goals. A well-planned internal communication is an essential part of any organisation, and lack of proper communication with the employees can lead to lack of understanding of objectives, vision and mission of the organisation; lack of direction due to decreased understanding of the goal towards which they are working; inability to perform individual tasks wherein the highest quality is possible; lack of perception of consumer requirements and the challenges of competition; strained or deficient relations with immediate superiors; misunderstandings between different departments resulting in criticisms of one another; inability to pass on information to subordinates and insufficient assessment of quality and perfection. Lack of proper internal communication would lead to employees feeling left out and uninformed, leading to a feeling of being less engaged and dissatisfied, which may result in attrition.

The existence of an internal communication policy can decrease the feeling of uncertainty among employees in an organisation and help in motivating them to achieve a common goal, which is the core purpose of any organisation. Internal communication may be viewed as a two-pronged approach, i.e., as means of communication that connects people as well as a strategic tool for better teamwork in the organisation. Studies have concluded that there is a link between information and profitability and that communication was one of the most effective means for change in attitudes. Internal communication should be considered in all its factors: the source of information, the information itself, means and mediums used, recipients, the purpose of the message and the style of language used; efficiency by learning level is correlated with the quantity and quality of the information; the circulation of information is instrumental in the creation of bonds between people and cooperation among them in the workplace; information skewed is a source of contempt for the receivers and produces negative effects. One such research aimed at determining the role of effective communication in retention and motivation of employees establishes a workforce that understands the importance of effective communication to feel motivated and considers it as "a vital source of affiliation with the organisation and retention" (Ashfaq et al., 2012). Hence, communication should not only be viewed in its strategic dimension, but rather, it should be seen as an essential component that helps in the creation of synergy among the employees of the organisation, through a policy in internal communication.

The prospect of rhetoric' is also known as Becker mosaic model by Sam Becker. The models state that the classic models of communication are not very useful in this contemporary communication. There are multiple origins for messages which make the communication process dynamic. In an organisation, a varied set of channels are required at every level of the organisation that is suitable for each department.

As humans can themselves act as constraints, there must be an authentic source of communication. This model complements the study of internal communication that talks about the flow of information in an organisation. The information cascade is unlike the classical model of communication that is linear; the model supports the fact that contemporary communication is a dynamic process. The randomness of the process from origin of message till the receiver is all a nonlinear process. The communication is three dimensional, and the receiver ignores certain information and only consumes the message that is relevant to them. One of the drawbacks of this model is that it cannot define the environment and social aspects in the process of communication. The fourth dimension of internal corporate communication has been defined on various parameters such as understanding, awareness, belongingness and commitment of employees. These aspects can be used to evaluate the effectiveness of internal communication tools in organisations. Two major aspects to be included as a part of this framework are "corporate message' and 'credibility of source". The corporate message can be analysed based on content, context and structure of the message, whereas the credibility of the source can be studied based on the Becker's mosaic model of communication proposed by Sam Becker in The Prospect of Rhetoric to understand the dynamic process of communication. This model reduces the limitations of linear model of communication and stressed on four components of communication:

1. empty cells that are the unavailable message or source
2. vertical layers which as the sets of similar messages
3. cells that are either message or source based on the channel of communication
4. receivers going through the cells in a loop every time.

This research aims to explore the role of artificial intelligence (AI) as a tool in internal communication within an organisation to help reduce attrition by taking certain repetitive tasks from the human resources and corporate communications teams, thereby giving them more time to strategise and work with employees of their organisation. This extra time on their hands would help them engage with the employees better, know what they want and hence cater to their needs better. The study also attempts to understand if AI can totally replace human skill sets by taking over only the tasks that human resource professionals and corporate communication professionals find repetitive and not the entire workload of the said teams. In spite of its versatility in operations, it is to be noted that AI has its limitations.

2 Review of Literature

Effective internal communication of organisations affects the ability of strategic managers to engage employees and achieve objectives. A proposed theory with the potential to improve practices can help enhance internal communication. It is important to identify gaps in the academic literature and address calls for discussion and definition of internal communication, for theory on its mandates, scope and focus and to counteract the tendency to treat employees as a uni-dimensional "single public". To address these gaps, internal communication is defined and positioned within the corporate communication school of thought. The internal communication matrix could be used to supplement other forms of internal situational analysis and as an analytical tool which may be applied to the strategic analysis, planning and evaluation of internal communication (Jackson, 2014).

Internal communication is also based on intangible resources rather than organisational boundaries. The resource-based theory of the company, the constructivist theory of communication and the situational theory of publics complement the study of internal communication. Developing a resource model (RM) of internal communication based on interactive processes is aimed at creating two catalytic resources for organising: knowledge and allegiance. This model captures the concept of internal communication prevailing in business, based on interviews with ten internal communication managers in Italian companies. Intangible resources, such as knowledge and employee attitudes, contribute to the company's success. Promoting an active communication behaviours among employees improves the overall performance of an organisation (Mazzei, 2010). Despite the intranet preferred over the Internet, there is a gamut of grapevine communication which is controlled by organisations through formal meets and sending hard copies of newsletter to employee's residential address. This also helps in creating a positive impact on the employee's family members as well as uplifts the morale of the employee. Internal communication must be structured well catering to all the internal stakeholder's right from senior managers to front line staff (Argenti, 2013).

Neves (1998) considers internal communication as one of the most important components of integrated communication and shall transmit the messages according to the strategies defined by the human resources area and determine strategies for how and when to get messages to the internal public knowledge. The following few steps can ensure that everyone in the organisation is on the same page:

1. Invite teams to collaborate on creating content.
2. Make the content easily accessible to everyone.
3. Bimonthly meetings with team leads.
4. Remind employees that you are sharing this information with them because it is not just about having the right content; it is about having the right content at the right time.

Brito (2018) defined real employee engagement as a result of various factors such as positive employee experience, continuous interactions, success recognition, clear idea and purpose of task. There are various studies in the field of employee engagement, whereas one such study by Brito (2018) captures employee experience as one of the major factors for a good employee experience.

• Purpose • Positive experiences • Celebrating success openly • Ongoing interaction • Real employee engagement.

Ms. Rachel Miller, Director at All Things IC Limited, is an independent practitioner who helps companies and communications professionals improve their internal communication. In one of her presentations, she suggests four enablers for employee engagement success. They are:

1. Strong strategic narrative—it is suggested that visible, empowering leadership from the top management provides a strong strategic narrative about the organisation.
2. Engaging managers—Managers who focus on their people and give them scope treat their employees as individuals and coach and stretch them are another factor that the practitioner points towards success of employee engagement.
3. Employee voice—Throughout, the organisation would mean feedback from the employees is of importance.
4. Organisational integrity—Integrity is when you do what is right even when no one is looking.

2.1 Attrition

The biggest challenge that organisations face today is not attracting talent but retaining it. Companies are constantly under pressure to either cater to the ever-changing needs of the employees or lose them to competitors. According to KPMG Report 2018–19 in India's Annual Compensation Trends Survey (KPMG's Annual Compensation Trends Survey 2018–19, 2019), the average annual voluntary attrition across sectors in India is 13.1%, in which the highest voluntary attrition rate has been reported in the retail sector is 18.5%, while the lowest which has been reported by the automobile industry has been 6.6%. The survey analysed and brought together findings from 272 companies across 18 sectors. Analysing annual reports of three top IT firms in India from 2013 to 2017, one can see that there have been changes in the levels of attrition in these companies over the said period.

With global players entering the Indian market, the available talent pool has a huge range of options and some of these multinationals too are facing issues in retaining talent in their organisations. A recent survey by Glassdoor in 2016 confirms that benefits and perks play a major role when deciding whether to pursue a job. A few instances where companies are listening and have implemented the same are as follows:

- Netflix announced that it added unlimited employee maternity and paternity leave for the first year after a child's birth or adoption.
- Airbnb gives employees an annual stipend of US$2000 to travel anywhere in the world.
- Asana employees have access to executive and life-coaching services outside of the company.
- Zillow allows employees who are travelling to ship their breast milk home for free.

While there may be many reasons for attrition, the top three reasons, according to the KPMG report 2018–19, are as below:

- better career opportunities (31.0%)
- better pay elsewhere (25.2%)
- personal reasons—marriage, health, children, relocation, etc. (17.4%).

The stakeholder theory of organisation and business ethics addresses morals and values of organisations that are directly related to corporate social responsibility. The stakeholder theory seeks to define normative theory of stakeholder identification that is examined and classified for descriptive theory of stakeholder salience. Freeman's strategic management: a stakeholder approach is widely cited in the field as being the foundation to stakeholder theory that develops an approach for strategic management, corporate planning, organisational theory, system theory and corporate social responsibility.

The employee lifecycle model is a method used to visualise how an employee engages with their organisation. The relationship with the organisations can be understood with a framework that provides engagement strategy at every level. According to the employee lifecycle model, an employee goes through five stages while being associated with an organisation. They are—recruitment, onboarding, development, retention and exit or separation. An organisation could be excellent with its recruitment strategy but might not necessarily be good with holding on with their employees for a long time, resulting in an increase in attrition rates. The model is designed to build a good employee experience at across stages of an employee's lifecycle with their firms. The five stages can be described as follows:

1. Recruitment: it is all about finding each position within the organisation that can be visualised as a classic marketing funnel to attract potential candidates.
2. Onboarding: The second stage of this process involves immersing the new hired employees into the organisational culture and helps them understand the company's expectations consisting of employee's performance as well as social aspects at the workplace.
3. Development: This begins from the day an employee is hired. The process helps in building confidence and trust for the organisation by investing in learning opportunities for nurturing the skills of the workforce.
4. Retention: It is a crucial stage of employee lifecycle model. It begins with hiring the right person for the right task and creating transparency to listen and help employees to reduce retention or employee turnout.
5. Exit or saturation: The final stage of employee lifecycle is when the employee decides to leave the organisation. The reasons could be personal, retirement, new job or any other situation, but when other employees experience sadness and uncertainty, it is important to ensure that the separation is smooth and less stressful for the existing employees.

Today, the firms are striving to create positive employee experience and believe that successful businesses are always built on successful staff. Business now looks at developing their business as well as their staff in parallel. A focus on building positive employee experience helps in turn to improve customer experiences and retention of staff. Hence, employee experience has now become a core goal in internal communication. Employee engagement on the other hand gradually deteriorated due to complex workplaces, virtual presence, technology, dispersed staff, culture and other challenges. Employee experience thus fills the gap to overcome such drawbacks by skill development, non-traditional office environment and collaborations for better employee communication. In the age of digital disruption, the convergence of media, the usage of the Internet has turned into mobile phones. This innovation has helped companies to create mobile applications to engage employees and bring together dispersed staff at different geographical areas to become more global. Corporate apps have now become a commonplace to strengthen employee communication, engagement and loyalty.

Communication with key stakeholders is a most involved function in internal communication, and understanding the views and expectations of how an organisation should interact with its environment is a very crucial study. The two major focus areas are, on the one hand, communicating what the organisation does for sustainability and, on the other hand, advising organisations on how to increase credentials and earn the licence to operate. It is commitment of organisations of different stakeholders as government agencies, non-governmental organisations, employees, investors, investment firms and the general public who demand and seek information regarding company policy and governance, environmental issues, social programmes and involvement with the community. Major focus by corporate communication is to strategise CSR communication. Stakeholder's involvement and engagement is secured when tools are involved and informed. Consumers on the other hand want companies to behave ethical and responsible. The need is to assist if the company operations meet consumer standards both creating engagement and reporting help in toying innovative techniques and tools for stakeholder engagement and confidence.

One of the major aspects to tap in internal communication is the integrated solutions to communicate with employees and use of different media and tools of communication and penetrate the message into the minds of internal stakeholders. A repetitive approach to message and strategically sending messages to employees can enable better recall and informed workforce, especially when there is an overload of information and clutter for employees to manage and remember information flowing from the organisation. An integrated approach to communicate with the internal publics can be done effectively by stitching different media together to give a more focused perception about the organisation. If a company has proven track record of community engagement and partnership, the public is willing to forgive and forget and provide an opportunity to the company to start afresh.

2.2 *Technological Trends in Internal Communication*

Innovations and evolutions are a constant in the current age. Organisations are no exception to change as it seems to be the only thing that is constant. Internal communication professionals, like others, need to stay on top of these changes to ensure they are not left behind and also to ensure that their organisation does not become obsolete. Some of the trends predicted to be a part of organisations are:

- Digital dexterity: The ability and desire to exploit existing and emerging technologies for better business outcomes (Zamolo, 2018).
- Harmonious digital workplace: Emphasis on mobility and limiting the noise between digital workplaces to better support activity-based working (Zamolo, 2018).
- Embrace AI: AI would play a key role in boosting operational communication and employee experience (Zamolo, 2018).
- Mobile apps/corporate mobile apps: These apps would offer a modern and convenient window into the organisation. They would help strengthen employee communication, engagement and loyalty (Zamolo, 2018).

These are just some of the technological trends that would play a role in internal communication within organisations. However, the adoption of newer technologies would occur only if there are proper training facilities to help employees catch up with the trends; otherwise, adoption of these trends would only be a waste of monetary resources.

2.3 Theoretical Framework

Although there is no overall grand theory for internal communication, the systems theory can be relevant. A system can be described as "any set of interrelated elements that form a unified or complex whole" (Barker & Angelopulo, 2006). This can be associated with the employees in an organisation, and hence, we can consider a systems view while dealing with organisational relationships. The theory can be understood in a better way by taking the example of living organisms that need air, water, food and sunlight for survival. Of all the theories, the technology acceptance model (TAM) is considered the most commonly used theory for discerning an individual's acceptance of technology and information systems. It was adapted from the theory of reasoned action (Ajzen & Fishbein, 1980) and assumes that an individual's acceptance of information systems is based on two major factors: perceived usefulness (PU) and perceived ease of use (PEOU). "Perceived usefulness is defined as the potential user's subjective likelihood that the use of a certain system (e.g., single platform e-payment system) will improve his/her action. Perceived ease of use (PEOU) refers to the degree to which the potential user expects the target system to be effortless" (Lai, 2017). Relationship management theory originates from the general principles of public relations which highlight management of relationships as the core task of public relations (Barker & Angelopulo, 2006). The foundation of this theory focuses on the management of relationships between the public and organisations in a way that would benefit both the parties.

2.4 *Research Objective*

The objective of this study is to explore whether the use of AI in internal communication in an organisation would help the corporate communication and human resources departments to engage employees better by reducing their workload and help them focus on areas of their interest, thereby reducing attrition. Hence, the study focuses on:

1. The role of AI in increasing employee engagement within organisations.
2. Understanding application of AI in tandem with work stress for human resource and corporate communication employees.
3. Ease of AI usage with respect to. up-skilling/cross-skilling, switching organisations, etc.

2.5 *Research Questions*

Based on the review of literature done to identify theories that impacted the concept, the study draws an assumption or hypothesis. Data from industry professionals and employees were collected to add credibility to the research, followed by analysis of the data and conclusion. The research questions for the study are as follows:

1. Does involving AI for internal communication increases the engagement of the employee within the organisation?
2. What are the ways in which application of AI eases out the job stress for an employee of the human resources and internal communication team? Would he/she feel better off with or without AI in her/his work palette?
3. If AI eases the job of the internal communicator and human resources team member, would he/she want to switch or stay in the organisation, in addition to up-skilling or cross-skilling oneself?

3 Methodology

This section details out various steps adopted to conduct the research to identify key insights. The details include the area of study, research design, methodology used in conducting the research, sample size, sampling techniques used, participants in research and data collection method. The broad area chosen for this research is AI in communication, which has been narrowed down to one of the functions of corporate communication, i.e. internal communication. To understand how AI would help internal communication to reduce attrition in organisations, this research explores disciplines like human resources and employee engagement, as an overlap between corporate communications and human resources that had been found during preliminary research on the topic. The research further explores the contribution of participation marketing in improving employee advocacy, which leads to improved employee engagement.

3.1 Research Design

The methodology implemented was a mixed method approach of both qualitative and quantitative research methodologies. Primary data collection consisted of a basic pilot study done through questionnaire survey among a target audience of 60 professionals which included 50 employees and ten industry experts and in-depth interviews with five industry experts in the field of AI, corporate communication and human resource department. The industry professionals consisted of two corporate communication professionals, two human resource professionals and one person who were into AI. The employees were from diverse sectors including advisory services, analytics, automobile, banking and finance, communication, construction, e-commerce, education, engineering, FMCG, IT and technology, oil and natural gas and shipping. Hence, the sample size was 60 people, selected purposively. The questionnaire consisted of broad questions related to the topic of research, and the interview questions were comparatively specific in nature, based on responses in the questionnaire. Secondary sources of data collection included previous research papers and studies, annual reports, the Internet, and books on the subject. The timeline of research has been three months, i.e. December 2018 to February 2019.

4 Data Analysis

The study has incorporated a mixed method research. The quantitative study was based on a structured questionnaire; each was circulated on Google Forms to 60 professionals (50 employees and ten industry experts) to gather their opinions on the topic. The employees were from diverse sectors including advisory services, analytics, automobile, banking and finance, communication, construction, e-commerce, education, engineering, FMCG, IT and technology, oil and natural gas and shipping. As a part of qualitative study, in-depth interviews were conducted with five industry experts to gain a better understanding of their perspective on the topic. The industry professionals consisted of two corporate communication professionals, two human resources professionals and one person who were into AI. Data obtained from both the groups have been analysed in this section.

4.1 Sampling Framework

Of the 50 participants for the questionnaire survey, 56% (28 respondents) were male and 42% (21 respondents) were female, while the remaining 2% (1 respondent) did not want to mention their gender. The majority of the respondents were in the age group of 27–28 years (22.2% of the respondents which consisted of ten respondents each in the age bracket). Also, there were five respondents (11.1%) whose age was 30 years and three respondents (6.7%) who were 23 years old. This has helped garner insights on the opinions of the young working professionals. The experience spanned from 0.9 to 34 years in the industry. The majority (10%) of the respondents were in the industry for a period of either 1 or 6 years (five respondents each, and majority of them were either from the communication or IT/technology industry). Four respondents (8% each of the sample) were part of the industry for 4, 5, 7 or 10 years, and the majority of these worked in the IT/technology sectors, with banking and finance and communication sectors. This diversity helps in understanding what the young workforce thinks of the topic and also provides an insight into the thoughts of personnel with varied experience levels in the industry.

4.2 Insights and Analysis from Responses to Employees' Survey

For the question about recollection of any employee surveys conducted in the organisation, 38% (19 respondents) did not have an idea about the surveys, while a close 34% (17 respondents) had come across surveys conducted by the organisation. Out of the remaining respondents, 16% (eight respondents) seem to be unsure about the surveys conducted. However, 10% (five respondents) recollect specific surveys that were conducted by the organisation. Firstly, the facts gathered show that the *recall of surveys conducted is generally low*, and the internal communication and human resource departments should take measures to improve it.

Secondly, 58% of the respondents (29 respondents) affirmed to recollecting incidents where the organisation celebrated the achievements of its employees, while only 20% (ten respondents) could not recollect the same. Hence, it can be noted that *appreciation of employees for the work done does not go unnoticed by them.* Some of the incidents mentioned were the completion of a decade of business centre incorporation, which implies that the success was attributed to the employees; celebration of personal and professional accomplishments, including birthdays; getting coverage for the client, good media relations, handling events, etc.; for maintaining quality standards, celebration of completion of year anniversary with the organisation (rewarding and recognising loyalty to the organisation), spotlight awards and cheers for peers (recognition of work well done); rewards and recognition programmes, long-term service to the organisation and performance awards. These statistics imply that *employees appreciate it when organisations recognise their contributions and reward* them accordingly. This helps them engage better with the organisation.

- Twenty-three respondents agree that they are always informed about the organisational goals being met, while 16 strongly agree to the statement, 9 are neutral in their opinion and 2 disagree.
- Nineteen agree that surveys are conducted to find out how leadership and employees understand each other, while 14 strongly agree to the statement, 9 are neutral in their opinion, 7 disagree and 1 strongly disagree.
- Eighteen respondents strongly agree that communication between leadership and employees can be said to be two-way communication; while 17 agree, 8 are neutral in their opinion, while 6 disagree and 1 strongly disagree.
- Twenty respondents agree that the organisation celebrates its success with the employees, while 13 strongly agree. Thirteen are neutral in their opinion, while 3 disagree and 1 strongly disagree—16 respondents agree that their job inspires them, while 11 strongly agree to the same. Fourteen are neutral in their opinion, while 7 disagree and 2 strongly disagree.

These sets of questions helped gauge the employees' opinions on a variety of questions pertaining to the organisation, their work-life, and the kind of engagement achieved by various levels of communication with the employees. Most respondents agreed to be well-informed and motivated.

When asked about the usage of AI in their organisation, 42% (21 respondents) affirmed its usage, while 30% (15 respondents) said their organisation does not use AI. Twenty-eight percentage (14 respondents) were unsure of the usage of AI in their organisation.

On being asked about the type of tasks that they would like AI to take up, manual mundane tasks, repetitive tasks, voice assistant, tasks that reduce manual work and time, costing related work, analysis, Excel sheet work, communication, recruitment, skill mapping, employee performance, feedback and reports collection, administrative and facilities management, appraisal and documentation were the most common areas that employees wanted AI to take over.

The response to employees staying engaged to continue working for the current organisation, 26 respondents answered in the affirmative, while the remaining 24 answered in the negative. The reasons for continuing in the organisation included getting challenging work; being recognised for the work done, work-life balance, scope to learn and explore, good peer support, good treatment by management, great work culture, adherence to organisational goals, adoption of new technologies, growth opportunities, and feeling valued by the organisation. On the other hand, reasons for leaving were mostly about recognition; compensation and salary issues, office politics, ill-recognition of talent, repetitive work and lack of appreciation.

Some of the recommendations by employees to their current organisation in order to retain talent were keeping employees well-informed, salary hike, treating humans and technology at par with each other instead of just relying on technology, encouraging the employees, rewarding them properly and proper resource utilisation, better appraisal, 'listen' to employees, not just "hear", using young talent under the guidance of seniors, trainings and seminars, proper work-life balance, appreciation and better compensation, transparent communication, adopting newer technologies, more interaction between employees and management, better treatment of employees by immediate bosses and senior management, more perks, engaging work, profit sharing, proper delegation of work and reduction in power distance.

4.3 Insights and Analysis from Responses to Industry Experts' Questionnaire

Of the ten participants for the industry expert questionnaire, 70% (seven respondents) were male and 30% (three respondents) were female. The majority of the respondents were 30 years old (three respondents). Also, there was one respondent each for the age of 24, 29, 34, 37 and 63 years old (five respondents). Two respondents chose not to reveal their age, leading to just eight responses for the question. The experience spanned from 3 to 39 years in the industry. The majority (20%) of the respondents were in the industry for a period of four years (two respondents each, and they were from the communication industry). The remaining had 3, 7, 8, 9, 10, 13, 15 and 39 years of experience each, and they are from the IT/technology, communication and automobile sectors. This diversity helps in understanding what the young workforce thinks of the topic, and also provides an insight into the thoughts of personnel with varied experience levels in the industry, across various sectors of operation. The main channel of internal communication in the organisations is e-mail (used in all the ten organisations), closely followed by internal social networking channels (eight organisations) and in-person presentations like town halls, live forums and meetings (eight organisations). Newsletters are used by seven organisations, while videos and intranet each are used by six organisations to update their employees. Five organisations use their Website for communication. Four each out of the ten organisations use blogs, wall messaging, displays and banners, screens and screensavers, while podcasts and microsites are each used by three organisations in the list. Chabot and podcasts each are used by two organisations for communication. One of the organisations uses interactive walls in addition to other channels of internal communication, while another organisation uses an internal magazine that doubles up as a blog, internal social media and a microsite with the other channels of internal communication.

- Seventy percentage of the organisations (seven firms) used games/activities like fun Friday, fun-on-the-floor and rewards and recognition programmes to engage employees. Sixty percentage of the organisations' (six firms) employee engagement plans included outings and monetary benefits. None of the organisations have implemented all the options listed, as the programmes are tailor-made according to the industry and its need. One of the organisations does not indulge in any of the employee engagement programmes.

- Sixty percentage of the organisations (6 firms out of 10) gauge employee engagement/satisfaction through attitude surveys/feedback surveys, while the remaining 40% did not.
- Only 30% (three firms) used AI in their organisational operations, while the remaining 70% did not use AI.
- Ten percentage of the organisations (one firm) use AI in internal communication. The majority 90% of organisations (nine firms) do not use AI in internal communication.
- Sixty percentage of the industry experts (six respondents) feel that AI would help reduce their work pressure, while 30% (three respondents) feel AI would make no difference in their work pressure levels. Ten percentage (one respondent) were not sure whether AI would reduce their work pressure or not.
- Ninety percentage of the industry experts (nine respondents) agreed that they would prefer a job role where AI would take up mundane tasks, allowing them to take over other challenging tasks including those that involved emotional dealing. Ten percentage (one respondent) felt they would not prefer such a role.
- Ninety percentage of the experts (nine respondents) do not feel threatened by AI taking over their job, while 10% of them (one respondent) feels threatened about it.

If AI is presumably used in organisations, the preferred tasks for it would be all the mundane, repetitive manual tasks, e-mailers and other internal communication activities with all possible pre-fed answers, employee surveys, tracking papers, operations, research; market analysis, study of market trends, resume screening, collection of candidate data for recruitment, scheduling meetings, revising pay scales, handling increments and promotions, etc. On being asked about the usage of extra time provided by AI taking care of mundane tasks and whether they would continue in the same organisation or switch, *70% (seven respondents) of the industry experts said they would up-skill or cross-skill and continue in the current organisation.* Twenty percentage (two respondents) wanted to up-skill or cross-skill and leave the organisation. Ten percentage (one respondent) expressed interest in strategising and continuing in the same organisation. It was observed that they feel AI in internal communication would reduce attrition by improving employee engagement and 7 of the experts agreed with the statement that it would give the professionals time to strategise and come up with proactive initiatives to engage the employees. One of the respondents negated the statement, while 2 of them were not sure but said that AI in internal communication may reduce attrition by engaging employees, but there has to be an emotional connect with the employees as well, which can be brought by the human resource/corporate communication professionals.

4.4 Insights from Industry Expert Interviews

A seasoned veteran with 39 years of experience in the communications industry says that AI will help in reducing boring, mundane activities and raise motivational levels of employees. He/she will be able to raise the bar and contribute more meaningfully to the organisation. This in turn will reduce attrition. He also recommended that appropriate software tools have to be brought in to successfully implement AI and reap the benefits. People should be trained to use these tools and refresher courses conducted whenever upgrades or technological advances take place. On being asked whether he feels threatened by AI taking over his job, generally, he replied in the negative. Further, he opined "artificial intelligence will only help improve efficiency and accuracy in operations. It will also give insights into the future". Some of the thoughts on AI reducing work pressure, he said "may not reduce work pressure. But it will enhance knowledge and make the worker more efficient and smarter". He was affirmative when asked if he would prefer a job role where AI does the mundane tasks, letting him handle more challenging tasks and other tasks which require human emotions. He added, "Absolutely. That is the purpose of developing AI solutions". "All routine operations tasks like employee grades, pay scales, increments and promotions, etc." was his response when asked about the kind of tasks that he would want AI to take over. "Yes. AI will help in reducing boring, mundane activities and raise motivational levels of employees. He/she will be able to raise the bar and contribute more meaningfully to the organisation. This in turn will reduce attrition".

Another communications professional with seven years of experience says, "Few industries would need AI in internal communication, whereas a few will still be going strong with the traditional techniques. But yes, if an organisation has that kind of money and workforce, AI will play a pivotal role in reducing the attrition rates!".

One of the communications professionals with ten years of experience quotes, "The importance of employee engagement can't be overstated as employee engagement strategies have been proven to reduce staff turnover, improve productivity and efficiency. However, face-to-face engagement definitely is a better way to keep the workforce motivated. AI won't touch the emotional chords. Employee engagement has to be both rational and emotional".

An expert with more than four years of experience in AI, machine language, blockchain, human resource and a tech enthusiast says, "It's difficult to comprehend the effect of AI in reducing employee stress and attrition because the role of AI and machine learning hasn't reached that point in its lifecycle where it delivers relief". He added "My recommendation is that whist AI can be recommended to handle mundane and cumbersome tasks, its role in processing intent has been lost due to the inability to fully comprehend the required output. Because some jobs were never A + B = C".

Some of the takeaway from R professional with 15 years of experience highlighted by the quotes—"Yes, with AI taking over operational burden it gives more time to connect on employee pulse to work on some proactive initiatives" and "AI is definitely a boon and will be the future. It is not about taking over jobs, it will only help elevate the current jobs through re-skilling and becoming relevant to the times".

The overall sentiment of the industry experts on the topic is that AI is very nascent at this point in time in the industry, and its application would help them handle the mundane and routine tasks. However, *3 out of the 5 experts feel that when it comes to interaction with humans, AI may not be of much help*. Hence, they suggest that that aspect should be handled by humans, that is, by the corporate communication or internal communication specialists. Most experts foresee AI playing an important role in internal communication in the near future (in the next 3–5 years as per one of the experts), but the tasks would majorly be restricted to *mundane day-to-day tasks mentioned by experts as media tracking, social listening, preparing reports, analysis,* etc. *Experts point out that the extra time that gets saved by AI doing all the mundane tasks could be used to strategise and devise ways to engage the employees better, which would help make them feel valued and retain them in the organisation.*

5 Conclusions and Limitations

The findings of the research on the topic "AI as a tool in internal communication to reduce employee attrition rate in India" was intended to explore how the inclusion of AI could affect internal communicators' work and whether it would help address the issue of attrition in organisations today. It started with the assumption that AI would help reduce the workload of internal communicators and human resources professionals and would help them focus on employees better, thereby helping them devise strategies to reduce attrition. The research was done using a mixed method approach in which a questionnaire was circulated to 60 professionals to gather their opinions on the topic. The sample included employees and industry experts from diverse sectors as a part of the quantitative study of the research. In-depth interviews were conducted with five industry experts in corporate communications department, human resource department and expert working for AI for internal communication to gain a better understanding of their perspective on the topic, as a qualitative part of this research.

On reviewing literature available on the topic, and from the insights gathered from industry professionals through interactions with them, it can be concluded that AI would help in reducing the workload of the corporate communication and human resources professionals by helping reduce the mundane and repetitive tasks done by them, thereby helping them use the extra time available to concentrate better on their employees which may help make them feel valued and reduce attrition. Also, industry experts interviewed during the research process preferred to up-skill or cross-skill themselves in the extra time gained due to AI intervention in their job and chose to stay in the current organisation. Employees and industry experts have similar views on the role of AI in internal communication, wherein work stress would get reduced considerably due to reduction in redundant tasks, thereby improving motivation levels among the staff. As a result, the employees would feel encouraged to carry out activities that would help them stay engaged with the organisation and relevant to the industry, by getting extra time on their hands.

However, a major insight gathered from the research states that *AI cannot completely take over the functions of the corporate communications and human resources team when it comes to emotionally supporting the employees.* Humans would still be needed in those functions to cater to the employees' emotional needs and to ensure their emotional well-being. Hence, it can be concluded that, in addition to the implementation of AI in internal communications within organisations, human support is required to ensure the reduction in attrition. Thus, when AI and humans work hand-in-hand, there are better chances at reduction of attrition in organisations.

The limitations to the study were the gatekeepers to information in organisations, the hesitation of employees to talk about their organisation and its practices and the lack of subject matter experts on AI and its implementation in the country. The study has majorly taken into account the private sector in the country. Future research can be extended to see whether AI in the public sector would help it function effectively and efficiently, while also studying the attrition rates in the sector (whether or not there is an issue of attrition in the public sector in India). Since, attrition is a major concern in many organisations, there could be various factors affecting the mindset of employees, one such factor is building strategy to create transparency at workforce. A deeper understanding about adoption of the latest technology in the sector may also be included in the study.

References

Ajzen, I., & Fishbein, M. (1980). *Understanding attitudes and predicting social behavior*. Prentice-Hall.

Argenti, P. (2013). *Corporate communication.* The McGraw Hill Companies.

Aristotle, & Smith, R. (1989). *Prior analytics.* Hackett Pub. Co.

Ashfaq, M., Rehman, K. U., Safwan, N., & Humayoun, A. (2012). Role of effective communication in retention and motivation of employees. *International conference on arts, behavioral sciences and economics issues.*

Barker, R., & Angelopulo, G. (2006). *Integrated organisational communication.* Juta Legal and Academic Publishers.

Brito, M. (2018). Employee advocacy builds an entire workforce of brand advocates. In Brito, M. (Ed.), *Participation marketing—Unleashing employees to participate and become brand storytellers* (p. 3). Kogan Page Limited.

Cowan, D. (2014). *Strategic internal communication.* Kogan Page.

Jackson, P. R. (2014). Rethinking internal communication: A stakeholder approach. *Corporate Communication: An International Journal, 12*(2), 177–198.

KPMG's Annual Compensation Trends Survey 2018–19. (2019). [online] https://home.kpmg/in/en/home/insights/2018/04/kpmg-annual-trend-survey.html. Accessed October 31, 2019.

Lai, P. (2017). The literature review of technology adoption models and theories for the novelty technology. *JISTEM—Journal of Information Systems and Technology Management, 14*(1), 21–38.

Mazzei, A. (2010). Promoting active communication. *Corporate Communications, 15*(3), 221–234.

Neves, R. (1998). *Corporate image: How organizations (and people) can protect and take advantage of your best assets.*
Vorhauser-Smith, S. (2020). *How to stop employee turnover in India.* Forbes [online]. https://www.forbes.com/sites/sylviavorhausersmith/2012/07/02/how-to-stop-employee-turnover-in-india/?sh=3b79ad014817. Accessed January 19, 2019.
Zamolo, A. (2018). *Beekeeper blog* [online]. https://blog.beekeeper.io/internal-communication-trends/. Accessed February 2019.

G. Nikita is an academician and researcher in the area of corporate communication and advertising. She holds a Master's in Mass Communication and Journalism from The English and Foreign Language University and specialises with PG Diploma in Public Relations and Advertising from Indian Institute of Mass Communication. She has worked in the academia teaching students at the graduate level and has also worked as a writer and verbal trainer. She is a UGC-NET qualified and currently pursuing her Ph.D. in Internal Communication under the Faculty of Media and Communication of Symbiosis International (Deemed University). She has a passion for public speaking and has won various awards. Her research interests are in the areas of corporate communication, advertising and communication studies.

Sai Nethra Velicheti is Engineer and ex-IT professional whose love for writing led her to pursue her MBA in Public Relations. Being enthusiastic about corporate communications in general, and internal communication in particular, she keeps updating herself on these areas, in addition to managing a toddler and pursuing her passion for photography while taking a sabbatical from full time work.

World Income Classification and Emissions: A Study of the Relationship Using Machine Learning Techniques

Karthikeyan Chandramohan and Ramasamy Murugesan

Abstract Using classification and clustering on cross-sectional data for 185 countries, this study explores if the level of emissions in a country is a determinant of the income class of a country. This study also tests the presence of EKC relationship between emissions and income across the countries. Income classification and emission data of countries obtained from World Bank has been used. The results, which can have a variety of policy implications, reveal: (1) clustering based on CO_2 emissions alone has a considerable overlap with income classification, (2) CO_2 emission per capita alone predicts the income class of a country and (3) presence of EKC relationship between CO_2 emissions and income.

Keywords Emissions · Income classification · EKC · Logit · Probit · Clustering · Regression

JEL Classification O13 · Q56

1 Introduction

Emissions can be described as gases and particles put into the air from various sources. These emissions can be detrimental to the planet. Those gases that absorb radiation in the atmosphere, hence leading to global warming, are known as greenhouse gases. These greenhouse gases are measured in order to conduct climate science and formulate climate policy. CO_2, methane and nitrous oxide are the three greenhouse gases that are of primary concern. Air pollution occurs if these gases are excessively present. Pollution and economic growth share a more complex relationship which is different from the traditional view in which the former is the by-product of the latter. This

K. Chandramohan (✉) · R. Murugesan
Department of Humanities and Social Sciences, National Institute of Technology, Tiruchirappalli 620015, India
e-mail: 409116003@nitt.edu

R. Murugesan
e-mail: rmurugan@nitt.edu

© The Author(s), under exclusive license to Springer Nature Singapore Pte Ltd. 2022
A. Chandani et al. (eds.), *Achieving $5 Trillion Economy of India*, Springer Proceedings in Business and Economics, https://doi.org/10.1007/978-981-16-7818-9_4

view is backed by a growing body of empirical evidence (Paudel & Schafer, 2009; Paudel et al., 2011). The need for a sustainable development model has brought a greater emphasis to investigate this relationship extensively.

The early stages of development of a country lead to environmental degradation due to air pollution, deforestation, water contamination and several other factors. The pace at which environmental degradation happens slows as the level of income of the economy increases. The environmental quality starts to improve beyond a certain level of income. Societies adopt newer and newer technologies in order to conserve scarce resources (Grossman & Krueger, 1995). The relationship between environment quality and per capita income has been investigated in many studies. Studies have examined the direction of causality between income level and environmental quality with mixed results (Coondoo & Dinda, 2002). These studies have often investigated the relationship between CO_2 emissions and income per capita. These studies have often modelled the emissions based on income per capita (Mardani et al., 2018). Many studies test for the presence of EKC between CO_2 emissions per capita and income per capita. Studies arrive at a threshold income per capita, based on the emissions and other macroeconomic variables used to study the relationship, after which CO_2 emissions per capita will start declining. The income class to which the country belongs can be inferred from this per capita income. CO_2 emission per capita is highest at this income.

There are very few studies that investigate the relationship between income class and emissions. This study investigates the relationship between the GNI per capita and emissions. This study uses World Bank's Atlas method of classification of countries into high, upper middle, lower middle and low income class based on income per capita. Cross-sectional analysis of emissions and income class of a country will reveal if there is any relationship between them. It should also reveal which emission is strongly related to income. Any discrepancy between the income class and income class obtained from emissions is analysed further. This study also tests the EKC hypothesis for the emission that is a good predictor of the income class. These findings should serve as input for policy decisions where one country can adopt technology from another in order to reduce emissions.

2 Literature Review

2.1 Income Classification

Income distribution, as compared to income classification, has been analysed in the literature to a large extent. This has been analysed using different statistical techniques. Literature talks of income distribution at the intranational, international and global level (Heshmati, 2006). There are many methods to analyse income distribution, one of which is to use mean income per capita along with Gini coefficient. Income distribution across the world has been studied in the context of human capital, production and finance. Basco and Mestieri (2019) find that unbundling of production has been found to exacerbate inequality both in terms of welfare and income. De Haan and Sturm (2017) find that financial liberalization has an impact on inequality and is conditioned by financial development. Coady and Dizioli (2018) find a very strong positive and stable relationship between inequality in years of schooling and income inequality. This relationship is very prominent in emerging and developing countries.

Income classification has largely been used in literature as a method for describing the data. It has been used extensively in the health sciences to describe the occurrence of some ailment in different income classes. This study tries to explore if income classification can act as an important macroeconomic variable that can be predicted from emissions. The World Bank classifies the countries into high, upper middle, lower middle and low income economies based on the Atlas method. This classification dates back to the 1970s. GNI per capita is used to classify the countries into these categories. This ensures that all countries, having lesser GNI, get a better consideration in the classification. The setting of clearly defined categories of per capita classification is not completely scientific nor is it completely arbitrary (World Bank, 1999). This calculation of GNI per capita itself has been questioned based on theoretical grounds (Kenny, 2011; Sumner, 2012). Income classification has been criticized for its use outside the World Bank context (Fantom & Serajuddin, 2016). Alonso-Rodríguez (2001) investigates the relationship between world income classification and human development indicators using logistic regression. They find that public expenditure on education expressed as percentage of GDP is a good predictor of the income class. The relationship between income classification and emissions has not been investigated much in the literature.

2.2 *Greenhouse Gas Emissions and EKC Hypothesis*

Carbon dioxide is the main greenhouse gas. Combustion of fuels (coal, natural gas and oil) is the primary human activity that adds to the already existing level of carbon dioxide in the atmosphere. The literature on CO_2 emissions is very extensive (Mardani et al., 2018). The relationship between CO_2 emissions and economic growth has been investigated along with macroeconomic variables like electricity consumption (Chaabouni et al., 2016), energy consumption (Sharma, 2011), energy intensity (De Bruyn et al., 1998), tourism economics (Dogan et al., 2015), population (Lee et al., 2010), renewable energy (Menyah & Wolde-Rufael, 2010) and financial investment (Bekhet et al., 2017). This relationship has been investigated using ARDL, GMM, Granger Causality as well as artificial neural networks. The relationship between economic growth and CO_2 emissions has been investigated in many studies as an inverted U-shaped curve (Riti et al., 2017). This curve is similar in shape to the income—inequality curve of Kuznets (1955) and is known as the Environmental Kuznets Curve (EKC). This curve has been investigated by many researches using different methods and different types of data. Income has been modelled as a predictor of the quality of environment. This relationship has been modelled with emissions as the dependent variable using time series as well as panel data with varied power of income for an economy or a group of economies (Shahbaz & Sinha, 2019). CO_2 is the base with which other greenhouse gases are compared to determine their environmental impact. The emissions of other greenhouse gases are converted to CO_2 equivalent in order to make comparisons possible.

Methane is the second major greenhouse gas that is emitted from human activities. Methane is emitted from raising natural livestock, natural wetlands as well as leakages in natural gas systems. The lifetime of methane in the atmosphere is shorter than that of CO_2. Methane is 30 times more potent as a heat trapping gas than CO_2 (Princeton University, March 27, 2014). Benavides et al. (2017) found an EKC relationship between methane emissions and GDP per capita in Austria. According to their calculations, methane emission per capita will go on increasing till the per capita income reaches $150,037.38 after which they will start decreasing. Roca et al. (2001) found that economic growth and methane emissions increase together.

Nitrous oxide is the next largest greenhouse gas. It stays for a longer duration in the atmosphere before it gets recycled. Agriculture, fuel combustion, wastewater management and industrial processes increase the amount of N_2O in the atmosphere. Seldon and Song (1994) find a U-shaped relationship between oxides of nitrogen and per capita GDP. Zambrano and Fernandez (2017) found the presence of EKC for nitrous oxide in Germany using an ARDL model. They find that beyond per capita income of $27,880 the nitrous oxide emissions per capita start decreasing. Magnani (2001) estimated that industrial nitrous oxide emissions start declining between $9000 and $12,000 for a panel of 152 countries. The study used cross-sectional data for the year 1975.

The use of time series or panel data for testing the EKC hypothesis is often cited in the literature. There are very few studies that use cross-sectional data to investigate the relationship between other emissions and income per capita. Carson et al. (1997) find the presence of EKC relationship using cross-sectional data for the year 1990 of 50 states in the US for seven types of air emissions. They use a simple sign test to investigate the relationship. The air emissions that they study are greenhouse gases, air toxics, carbon monoxide (CO), nitrogen oxides (NO_x), sulphur dioxide (SO_2), volatile organic carbon (VOC), and particulate matter less than ten microns in diameter (PM10).

Hypothesis about why EKC is inverted U shaped can be classified into two scenarios. (1) Firms adapt to market or regulation changes by employing better technologies, (2) residents object to the presence of polluting firms. The first scenario comes about as a result of changes in consumption and production leading to lower levels of pollution per unit (Pfaff et al., 2004; Selden & Song, 1994). The second scenario is due to the demand for higher environmental quality in a locality. This could lead to pollution processes being pushed to low income areas (Arrow et al., 1995; Suri & Chapman, 1998). Keene and Deller (2015) state that EKC is an inductive theory and obtained from empirical observations. It does not originate from a stylized theoretical framework.

The literature that investigates the relationship between each of the top three greenhouse gases and income per capita usually does not analyse all the three greenhouse gases in a single study. This study explores if these variables show any significant relationship with GNI per capita. This study uses income classification as the predicted variable and emissions as the predictor variable. There are very few studies that use cross-sectional data. The use of clustering and classification techniques to investigate this relationship is also scarce in the literature (Mardani et al., 2018). This study also analyses countries that have been misclassified. The EKC hypothesis is also tested for the emission that is a good predictor of the income class in order to see if the misclassification can be explained. The usage of GNI per capita to test the EKC hypothesis is also not cited much in the literature.

3 Objectives

This study aims to:

- Find the relationship between income classification and different emissions
- Explore if different emissions can be used to determine the income class of a country
- Identify differences between the income class as per Atlas method and the income class based on emissions obtained using machine learning techniques
- Test the presence of EKC hypothesis between income per capita and emissions

4 Methodology

4.1 Data Description

There are a total of 202 countries in the year 2012 for which macroeconomic data is available in World Bank database. Table 1 gives the income classification as per GNI per capita calculated using Atlas method.

The World Bank's classification of economies was used to construct two binary variables: $cls1 = 1$ if the economy falls in high income group, $cls1 = 0$ if economy falls in non-high income group (this includes upper middle, lower middle and low

Table 1 Atlas method of income classification

Income class	GNI per capita range ($)
Low	<1035
Lower middle	1036 to 4085
Upper middle	4086 to 12,615
High	>12,615

income groups), *cls2* = *1* if the economy falls in high or upper middle income group, *cls2* = *0* if the economy falls in lower middle or low income group. The indicators of the emissions in the environment that are used in this study are:

(i) CO_2 per capita
(ii) Methane per capita
(iii) Nitrous oxide per capitaa

They are expressed in metric tons per capita. The data for methane emissions and nitrous oxide emissions is also calculated on per capita basis using population number derived by dividing total CO_2 emissions by CO_2 emissions per capita.

4.2 Cluster Analysis

Clustering is an unsupervised learning algorithm which tries to discover hidden patterns in data (Hair et al., 2013). This study employs the K-means clustering technique to check if income classification and emissions classification yield similar results. The clustering of countries based on CO_2, methane and nitrous oxide emissions is performed. The data has not been scaled when using a single emission, but has been scaled when using multiple emissions. Suppose there are *n* observations of the variables $y_1, y_2, \ldots, y_p$ then the clusters are formed such that

$$1/n \sum_{i=1}^{n} [\min_{j} (y_i - m_j)^2] \tag{1}$$

is minimized. $(y_i - m_j)^2$ represents the squared Euclidean distance. The centroid of the *j*th cluster is represented by m_j. The number of clusters in this is fixed to 2 in order to compare income classification and classification obtained using emissions.

4.3 Classification Techniques

This study uses both logit and probit models with *cls1* and *cls2* as the dependent variable. These variables are dichotomous that can take the value of 0 or 1. These models calculate the conditional probability as a nonlinear function of the independent variable. Amemiya (1981) asserts that "*One of the most important developments in econometrics in the past ten years has occurred in the area of qualitative response models, also known as quantal, categorical or discrete models*". These models are used in many different fields such as biometrics, marketing, finance and statistics. These models involve estimation of coefficients using maximum likelihood technique. A logit and probit model is analysed for each combination of income class and emissions.

4.3.1 Logit Model

The probability distribution of the income classification is modelled using a logistic probability distribution. This can be written as:

$$Pr(cls1 = 1|\text{Emissions}) = \frac{1}{1 + \mathrm{e}^{-Z}} \tag{2}$$

$$Pr(cls2 = 1|\text{Emissions}) = \frac{1}{1 + \mathrm{e}^{-Z}} \tag{3}$$

$$Z = \beta_1 + \beta_2 * (\text{Emissions Variables}) \tag{4}$$

Equation 2 is used to classify based on high or non-high income while Eq. 3 is used to classify into high or upper middle income and lower middle or low income.

4.3.2 Probit Model

The probability distribution of the income classification is modelled using a normal cumulative distribution function (NCDF). This can be written as:

$$Pr(cls1 = 1|\text{Emissions}) = F(\beta_1 + \beta_2 * (\text{Emissions Variables})) \tag{5}$$

$$Pr(cls2 = 1|\text{Emissions}) = F(\beta_1 + \beta_2 * (\text{Emissions Variables})) \tag{6}$$

$$F(\beta_1 + \beta_2 * (\text{Emissions Variables})) = \frac{1}{\sqrt{2\pi}} \int_{-\infty}^{\beta_1 + \beta_2 * (\text{Emissions Variables})} \mathrm{e}^{-z^2/2} \mathrm{d}z \tag{7}$$

Equation 5 is used to classify based on high or non-high income while Eq. 6 is used to classify into high or upper middle income and lower middle or low income.

4.4 *Testing the EKC Hypothesis Using Multiple Regression*

The following is a simple model to verify EKC hypothesis

$$E = \beta_0 + \beta_1 Y + \beta_2 (Y)^2 + \beta_3 (Y)^3 + \mathrm{e} \tag{8}$$

where E is emissions per capita; Y, the GNI per capita. The type of relationship between the two variables can be inferred from the coefficients β_1, β_2 and β_3 (Dinda, 2004).

(i) $\beta_1 = 0$, $\beta_2 = 0$ and $\beta_3 = 0$ then there is no relationship
(ii) An inverted U-shaped relationship (EKC) if $\beta_1 > 0$, $\beta_2 < 0$ and $\beta_3 = 0$
(iii) A U-shaped relationship if $\beta_1 < 0$, $\beta_2 > 0$ and $\beta_3 = 0$
(iv) A N-shaped relationship if $\beta_1 > 0$, $\beta_2 < 0$ and $\beta_3 > 0$

If EKC relationship holds, then the turning point is calculated as

$$\text{GNI Per Capita Turning point} = -\beta_1/2\beta_2 \tag{9}$$

If the relationship is N shaped, then there will be two turnaround points given by

$$\text{GNI Per Capita Turning Points} = \frac{\left(-\beta_2 \pm \sqrt{\beta_2^2 - 3\beta_1\beta_3}\right)}{3\beta_3} \tag{10}$$

5 Results

The analysis was carried out using R and E views software. These applications have all the necessary packages for running a qualitative response model. Data was collected for all the 202 countries, for the year 2012, from World Bank database. 185 countries have all the necessary data.

The summary statistics for GNI per capita and emissions are shown in Table 2. Table 3 gives the tabulation of the variables *cls1* and *cls2*.

The countries in high income category range from Bermuda with a per capita income of 106,080 to Hungary with a per capita income of 12,910 while the countries in non-high income range from Venezuela with a per capita income of 12,480 to Burundi with a per capita income of 260. Tunisia with a per capita income of 4090 is the last country in the high or upper middle income class while Marshall Islands with

Table 2 Descriptive statistics of the variables

	GNI per capita[a]	CO_2 emissions per capita[b]	Methane emissions per capita[b]	Nitrous oxide emissions per capita[b]
Min	260	0.030	0.011	0.001
1st quartile	1720	0.752	0.552	0.198
Median	5510	2.488	0.855	0.366
Mean	13,893	4.572	1.474	0.632
3rd quartile	14,100	6.066	1.566	0.588
Max	106,080	37.78	19.04	22.368

[a]Dollars
[b]Metric tons per capita

Table 3 Statistics for *cls1* and *cls2*

Class	Frequency	Percentage	Cumulative percentage
cls1 = *1*	55	29.73	29.73
cls1 = *0*	130	70.27	100
cls2 = *1*	105	56.76	56.76
cls2 = *0*	80	43.24	100

a per capita income of 3980 is the first country in the lower middle to low income class.

5.1 Cluster Analysis

K-means clustering using the different emissions per capita is carried out in order to analyse which clustering is closely related to grouping based on income.

Table 4 shows that clustering using only CO_2 emissions per capita yielded results closer to income classification. Cluster 1 comprises of 165 countries. There are 40 high income countries in this cluster. Cluster 2 comprises of 15 high income and 5 non-high income countries.

Table 5 lists the high income countries that belong to cluster 1. These high income countries have lesser emissions as compared to the high income countries in cluster 2. The GNI per capita in this table has a range from 12,910 for Hungary to 106,080 for Bahamas. There are 26 high income European countries in this cluster.

Table 6 gives the details of the means of the clusters formed by using methane emissions per capita. This classification yielded 129 countries of non-high income and 52 countries of high income falling into cluster 1 while only four countries, Brunei, Central African Republic, Qatar and Trinidad and Tobago are in cluster 2. The values of the centroids of each of the clusters are vastly different.

Table 7 gives the details of the means of the clusters formed by using nitrous oxide emissions per capita. Central African Republic is the only country in cluster 2. Clustering using this technique has very little resemblance to income classification.

K-means clustering with two clusters considering methane emissions per capita and CO_2 emissions per capita for determining the members resulted in the mean values for the clusters as shown in Table 8. The emissions have been normalized before clustering.

Cluster 1 comprises of 165 countries. There are 39 high income countries in this cluster. Cluster 2 comprises of 16 high income and 4 non-high income countries. The

Table 4 Cluster means based on CO_2 emissions per capita

Cluster no.	1	2
CO2 emissions per capita	2.90706	18.30837

Table 5 List of high income countries that have lower CO_2 emissions

Country name	GNI per capita	Country name	GNI per capita
Austria	50,060	Italy	36,000
Bahamas, The	23,580	Japan	49,480
Barbados	15,960	Korea, Rep	24,550
Belgium	47,190	Latvia	13,790
Bermuda	106,080	Lithuania	14,100
Chile	14,410	Macao SAR, China	61,410
Croatia	13,460	Malta	21,650
Cyprus	28,950	Netherlands	52,500
Czech Republic	19,350	New Zealand	36,720
Denmark	61,650	Poland	13,300
Equatorial Guinea	13,760	Portugal	21,150
Finland	48,670	Singapore	51,110
France	43,020	Slovak Republic	17,550
Germany	46,710	Slovenia	23,130
Greece	23,500	Spain	29,760
Hong Kong SAR	36,340	St. Kitts and Nevis	13,710
Hungary	12,910	Sweden	58,150
Iceland	40,750	Switzerland	84,880
Ireland	41,660	United Kingdom	41,200
Israel	32,180	Uruguay	13,910

Table 6 Cluster means based on methane emissions per capita

Cluster no.	1	2
Methane emissions per capita	1.178915	14.867887

Table 7 Cluster means based on nitrous oxide emissions per capita

Cluster no.	1	2
Methane emissions per capita	0.5140818	22.3687291

Table 8 Cluster means based on emissions per capita

Cluster no.	CO_2 emissions per capita	Methane emissions per capita
1	3.0	0.97
2	17.49	5.65

clusters formed with two emissions yield the same results as that when only CO_2 emissions is used.

5.2 Logit and Probit Models

Table 9 gives the logit and probit models based on different variables.

Table 10 gives the estimated coefficients, the *p*-values of these coefficients and the McFadden R^2. The statistics of interest are the *p*-values and McFadden R^2.

It is observed from the results that 1ALog, 1Blog, 1AProb and 1BProb models satisfy all the necessary conditions for a good fit. This leads us to the conclusion that there is a strong relationship between CO_2 emissions per capita and income classification. The analysis from model 1ALog finds that if the CO_2 emission per capita is more than 6.73, then there is more than 50 per cent probability that the country is a high income country. The classification of countries based on this is shown in Table 11. There are 42 countries that have emissions more than this; out

Table 9 Model sets

Model	Equation
1ALog	$Pr(cls1 = 1 \mid CO_2$ Emissions per capita$) = \emptyset(\beta_1 + \beta_2*(CO_2$ Emissions per capita$))$
1Blog	$Pr(cls2 = 1 \mid CO_2$ Emissions per capita$) = \emptyset(\beta_1 + \beta_2*(CO_2$ Emissions per capita$))$
1AProb	$Pr(cls1 = 1 \mid CO_2$ Emissions per capita$) = \varphi(\beta_1 + \beta_2*(CO_2$ Emissions per capita$))$
1BProb	$Pr(cls2 = 1 \mid CO_2$ Emissions per capita$) = \varphi(\beta_1 + \beta_2*(CO_2$ Emissions per capita$))$
2ALog	$Pr(cls1 = 1 \mid$ Methane Emissions per capita$) = \emptyset(\beta_1 + \beta_2*($Methane Emissions per capita$))$
2Blog	$Pr(cls2 = 1 \mid$ Methane Emissions per capita$) = \emptyset(\beta_1 + \beta_2*($Methane Emissions per capita$))$
2AProb	$Pr(cls1 = 1 \mid$ Methane Emissions per capita$) = \varphi(\beta_1 + \beta_2*($Methane Emissions per capita$))$
2BProb	$Pr(cls2 = 1 \mid$ Methane Emissions per capita$) = \varphi(\beta_1 + \beta_2*($Methane Emissions per capita$))$
3ALog	$Pr(cls1 = 1 \mid$ Nitrous Oxide Emissions per capita$) = \emptyset(\beta_1 + \beta_2*($Nitrous Oxide Emissions per capita$))$
3Blog	$Pr(cls2 = 1 \mid$ Nitrous Oxide Emissions per capita$) = \emptyset(\beta_1 + \beta_2*($Nitrous Oxide Emissions per capita$))$
3AProb	$Pr(cls1 = 1 \mid$ Nitrous Oxide Emissions per capita$) = \varphi(\beta_1 + \beta_2*($Nitrous Oxide Emissions per capita$))$
3BProb	$Pr(cls2 = 1 \mid$ Nitrous Oxide Emissions per capita$) = \varphi(\beta_1 + \beta_2*($Nitrous Oxide Emissions per capita$))$

Table 10 Model results

Model	$Pr(y = 1 \mid x)$	McFadden R-squared
1ALog	− 2.80 + 0.42 * CO_2 Emissions per capita P(0.00) (0.00)	0.364
1Blog	− 1.98 + 0.86 * CO_2Emissions per capita P(0.00) (0.00)	0.438
1AProb	− 1.64 + 0.23 * CO_2 Emissions per capita P(0.00) (0.00)	0.366
1BProb	− 0.89 + 0.34 * CO_2 Emissions per capita P(0.00) (0.00)	0.376
2ALog	− 1.24 + 0.26 * Methane Emissions per capita P(0.00) (0.02)	0.04
2Blog	0.05 + 0.16 * Methane Emissions per capita P(0.79) (0.12)	0.02
2AProb	− 0.72 + 0.12 * Methane Emissions per capita P(0.00) (0.00)	0.04
2BProb	0.06 + 0.07 * Methane Emissions per capita P(0.57) (0.08)	0.01
3ALog	− 0.86 − 0.01 * Nitrous Oxide Emissions per capita P(0.00) (0.91)	0.00
3Blog	0.33 − 0.10 * Nitrous Oxide Emissions per capita P(0.04) (0.40)	0.00
3AProb	− 0.53 − 0.00 * Nitrous Oxide Emissions per capita P(0.00) (0.91)	0.00
3BProb	0.21 − 0.06 * Nitrous Oxide Emissions per capita P(0.04) (0.38)	0.00

Table 11 Logit model classification into high or non-high income with probability >0.5

CO_2 emissions per capita	High income	Non-high income
More than 6.73	32	10
Less than 6.73	23	120

of this 32 are high income countries. There are 23 high income countries that have emissions lesser than this. The model has misclassified some countries but overall the model seems to be good.

The analysis from 1Blog finds that if the CO_2 emission per capita is more than 2.37, then there is more than 50 per cent probability that the country is high or upper middle income country. The classification of countries based on this is shown in Table 12. There are 95 countries that have emissions more than this, out of which 88 are high-upper middle income countries with 52 high income countries. There are 17 high or upper middle income countries with three high income countries that have emissions lower than this.

Table 12 Logit model classification into high-upper middle income with probability >0.5

CO_2 emissions per capita	High-upper middle income	Lower middle-low income
More than 2.37	88	7
Less than 2.37	17	73

Table 13 Probit model classification into High income with probability >0.5

CO_2 emissions per capita	High income	Non-high income
More than 7.14	29	9
Less than 7.14	26	121

Table 14 Probit model classification into high-upper middle income with probability >0.5

CO_2 emissions per capita	High-upper middle income	Lower middle-low income
More than 2.66	84	5
Less than 2.66	21	75

The analysis from model 1AProb find that if the CO_2 emissions per capita is more than 7.14 then there is more than 50% probability that the country is a high income country. The classification of countries based on this is shown in Table 13. There are 38 countries that have emissions more than this, out if this 29 are high income countries. There are 26 high income countries that have emissions less than this. The model has also misclassified some countries.

The analysis from 1BProb finds that if the CO_2 emission per capita is more than 2.66, then there is more than 50% probability that the country is high or upper middle income country. The classification of countries based on this is shown in Table 14. There are 89 countries that have emissions more than this value out of which 84 are high-upper middle income countries with 52 high income countries. There are 21 high or upper middle income countries with three high income countries that have emissions less than this.

The model based on high or upper middle income seems to have a slightly better fit for the data. This could be on account of some high income countries having low emissions. One can see from the results that a number of high income countries whose probability of belonging to the high income class is less than 50 per cent based on CO_2 emissions.

The models 2Alog and 2Aprob analyse the relationship between methane emissions and income classification into high and non-high. The *p*-values of the coefficients obtained in 2Alog and 2AProb are significant but the McFadden R^2 is very low suggesting that there may be some variables that have to be added. 2Blog and 2BProb models based on high-upper middle and lower middle-low income classification did not yield significant coefficients.

Table 15 Composite model

Model	$Pr(y = 1\|x)$
Logit	−2.78 − 0.02 ∗ Methane Emissions per capita + 0.42 ∗ CO_2Emissions per capita P (0.00) (0.87) (0.00) **McFadden R^2 – 0.36**
Probit	−1.62 − 0.02 ∗ Methane Emissions per capita + 0.23 ∗ CO_2Emissions per capita P (0.00) (0.81) (0.00) **McFadden R^2 – 0.36**

The *p*-values of the coefficients in the models (3 Series) that study the relationship between nitrous oxide emissions and income class are insignificant. Nitrous oxide is not a predictor of income class.

A composite model having the independent variables as CO_2 emissions per capita and methane emissions per capita that estimate the income class, the dependent variable, is formulated. Table 15 gives the relevant statistics for the composite model. The coefficient of methane emissions per capita is statistically insignificant and does not improve models 1Alog and 1Aprob.

Findings also suggest that logit and probit models can be used interchangeably. They do not seem to show significantly different results.

5.3 Testing the EKC Hypothesis Using Multiple Regression

Some high income countries have been clustered with countries that have low CO_2 emissions. Classification techniques also show that there are some high income countries with low CO_2 emissions. Multiple regression is used to check if clustering based on emissions and prediction of income class based on emissions can be explained in any other mathematical form.

The results of a simple EKC specification are shown in Table 16. The cubic term has been removed as the presence of the term resulted in high multicollinearity.

The coefficient for GNI per capita is positive and GNI per capita squared is negative. The *p*-values for the coefficients are statistically significant. The *R* square value is 0.41 but one can make inferences about the relationship from the regression. EKC relationship exists between CO_2 emissions per capita and GNI per capita. The

Table 16 EKC output for CO_2 emissions

Regressor	Coefficient	*p*-value
Intercept	0.98	0.00
GNI per capita	3.81e−04	0.00
GNI per capita square	−2.92e−09	0.00
Adjusted R^2	0.40	
DW statistic	2.08	
F Stat	43.3	

income turning point comes out to be 65,240 Dollars. This income falls in the high income class.

6 Conclusion and Scope of Future Research

This study starts by first clustering the countries based on their emissions per capita. Classification techniques are then used to check if income class can be predicted from emissions. Different models are analysed to determine the classification that best represents the data. This is different from the typical EKC specification where in emission per capita is the dependent variable and income per capita is the independent variable. EKC hypothesis is then checked for the emission that is a good predictor of the income class.

The findings from the study indicate that CO_2 emission per capita is a significant determinant of the income class of a country. The countries that have higher CO_2 emissions per capita are majorly the high or the upper middle income countries. Cluster analysis has also validated this fact to a large extent. There are some high income and some non-high income countries that are grouped differently as compared to the other members of their respective group. There are many high income European countries that have lower CO_2 emissions per capita. Logit and probit models confirm the fact that CO_2 emission per capita is a good predictor of the income class. The classification based on high-upper middle income and lower middle-low income best fits the data that is used.

The other greenhouse gases namely methane and nitrous oxide do not seem to be related strongly to income per capita. These variables do not provide any additional benefit when used along with CO_2 emissions to determine the relationship with income. There are a few countries that stand out from the rest as far as these emissions are concerned.

The study finds the presence of EKC relationship between CO_2 emissions and income per capita. This study is consistent with many other studies done for a country or a group of countries. The use of regression on cross-sectional data for validating this relationship is limited in literature. An analysis of the reasons for the presence of EKC in cross-sectional data may lead to a better understanding of this relationship. The findings suggest that there may be a bidirectional relationship between income per capita and CO_2 emissions per capita.

This study being exploratory in nature serves as a starting point for other studies. Studies on methane and nitrous oxide emissions are limited in the literature. One of the classification models resulted in significant coefficients for methane emissions. An investigation into the cause for high methane emissions in some of the countries can bring to light interesting facts about the relationship of methane with other macroeconomic variables. The relationship between CO_2 emissions, income and other macroeconomic variables can also be investigated further using machine learning techniques. The EKC relationship as analysed in this study can be improved further by the addition of other macroeconomic variables. The high income countries that have brought their emissions in control can act as role models for other countries. The role of policy in bringing down the emissions can be investigated further.

References

Alonso-Rodríguez, A. (2001). Logistic regression and world income distribution. *International Advances in Economic Research, 7*(2), 231–242.

Amemiya, T. (1981). Qualitative response models: A survey. *Journal of Economic Literature, 19*(4), 1483–1536.

Arrow, K., Bolin, B., Costanza, R., Dasgupta, P., Folke, C., Holling, C. S., Jansson, B. O., Levin, S., Maler, K. G., Perrings, C., & Pimentel, D. (1995). Economic growth, carrying capacity and the environment. *Science, 268*, 520–521.

Basco, S., & Mestieri, M. (2019). The world income distribution: The effects of international unbundling of production. *Journal of Economic Growth, 24*(2), 189–221.

Bekhet, H. A., Matar, A., & Yasmin, T. (2017). CO_2 emissions, energy consumption, economic growth, and financial development in GCC countries: Dynamic simultaneous equation models. *Renewable and Sustainable Energy Reviews, 70*, 117–132.

Benavides, M., Ovalle, K., Torres, C., & Vinces, T. (2017). Economic growth, renewable energy and methane emissions: is there an environmental Kuznets Curve in Austria? *International Journal of Energy Economics and Policy, 7*(1), 259–267.

Carson, R. T., Jeon, Y., & McCubbin, D. R. (1997). The relationship between air pollution emissions and income: US data. *Environment and Development Economics, 2*(4), 433–450.

Chaabouni, S., Zghidi, N., & Ben Mbarek, M. (2016). On the causal dynamics between CO_2 emissions, health expenditures and economic growth. *Sustainable Cities and Society, 22*, 184–191.

Coady, D., & Dizioli, A. (2018). Income inequality and education revisited: Persistence, endogeneity and heterogeneity. *Applied Economics, 50*(25), 2747–2761.

Coondoo, D., & Dinda, S. (2002). Causality between income and emission: A country group-specific econometric analysis. *Ecological Economics, 40*(3), 351–367.

De Bruyn, S. M., van den Bergh, J. C., & Opschoor, J. B. (1998). Economic growth and emissions: Reconsidering the empirical basis of environmental Kuznets curves. *Ecological Economics, 25*, 161–175.

De Haan, J., & Sturm, J. E. (2017). Finance and income inequality: A review and new evidence. *European Journal of Political Economy, 50*, 171–195.

Dinda, S. (2004). Environmental Kuznets Curve hypothesis: A survey. *Ecological Economics, 49*, 431–455.

Dogan, E., Seker, F., Bulbul, S. (2015). Investigating the impacts of energy consumption, real GDP, tourism and trade on CO_2 emissions by accounting for cross-sectional dependence: a panel study of OECD countries. *Current Issues in Tourism* 1–19.

Fantom, N., & Serajuddin, U. (2016). *The World Bank's classification of countries by income*. The World Bank.

Grossman, G. M., & Krueger, A. B. (1995). Economic growth and the environment. *The Quarterly Journal of Economics, 110*(2), 353–377.

Hair, J. F., Black, W. C., Babin, B. J., & Anderson, R. E. (2013). *Multivariate data analysis: Pearson new international edition*. Pearson Higher Ed.

Heshmati, A. (2006). The world distribution of income and income inequality: A review of the economics literature. *Journal of World-Systems Research, 12*(1), 61–107.

Keene, A., & Deller, S. C. (2015). Evidence of the environmental Kuznets' curve among US counties and the impact of social capital. *International Regional Science Review, 38*(4), 358–387.

Kenny, C. (2011). What does it mean to be low income? http://www.cgdev.org/blog/whatdoes-it-mean-be-low-income

Kuznets, S. (1955). Economic growth and income inequality. *The American Economic Review., 45*(1), 1–28.

Lee, C.-C., Chiu, Y.-B., & Sun, C.-H. (2010). The environmental Kuznets curve hypothesis for water pollution: Do regions matter? *Energy Policy, 38*, 12–23.

Magnani, E. (2001). The environmental Kuznets Curve: Development path or policy result? *Environmental Modelling & Software, 16*(2), 157–165.

Mardani, A., Streimikiene, D., Cavallaro, F., Loganathan, N., & Khoshnoudi, M. (2018). Carbon dioxide (CO_2) emissions and economic growth: A systematic review of two decades of research from 1995 to 2017. *Science of the Total Environment, 349*, 31–49.

Menyah, K., & Wolde-Rufael, Y. (2010). CO_2 emissions, nuclear energy, renewable energy and economic growth in the US. *Energy Policy, 38*, 2911–2915.

Paudel, K. P., Poudel, B. N., Bhandari, D., & Johnson, T. G. (2011). Examining the role of social capital in environmental Kuznets Curve estimation. *Global Journal of Environmental Science and Technology, 1*, 16.

Paudel, K. P., & Schafer, M. J. (2009). The environmental Kuznets Curve under a new framework: The role of social capital in water pollution. *Environmental and Resource Economics, 42*, 265–278.

Pfaff, A. S. P., Chaudhuri, S., & Nye, H. I. M. (2004). Household production and environmental Kuznets Curves. *Environmental and Resource Economics, 27*, 187–200.

Princeton University. (2014, March 27). A more potent greenhouse gas than carbon dioxide, methane emissions will leap as Earth warms. *Science Daily*. Retrieved February 11, 2019 from www.sciencedaily.com/releases/2014/03/140327111724.htm

Riti, J. S., Song, D., Shu, Y., & Kamah, M. (2017). Decoupling CO2 emission and economic growth in China: Is there consistency in estimation results in analyzing environmental Kuznets curve? *Journal of Cleaner Production, 166*, 1448–1461.

Roca, J., Padilla, E., Farré, M., & Galletto, V. (2001). Economic growth and atmospheric pollution in Spain: Discussing the environmental Kuznets curve hypothesis. *Ecological Economics, 39*(1), 85–99.

Selden, T. M., & Song, D. (1994). Environmental quality and development: Is there a Kuznets curve for air pollution emissions? *Journal of Environmental Economics and Management, 27*(2), 147–162.

Shahbaz, M., & Sinha, A. (2019). Environmental Kuznets curve for CO_2 emissions: A literature survey. *Journal of Economic Studies, 46*(1), 106–168.

Sharma, S. S. (2011). Determinants of carbon dioxide emissions: Empirical evidence from 69 countries. *Applied Energy, 88*, 376–382.

Sumner, A. (2012). Where do the poor live? *World Development, 40*(5), 865–877.

Suri, V., & Chapman, D. (1998). Economic growth, trade and energy: Implications for the environmental Kuznets Curve. *Ecological Economics, 25*, 195–208.

World Bank. (1999). *World Development Indicators*. World Bank.

Zambrano-Monserrate, M. A., & Fernandez, M. A. (2017, May). An environmental Kuznets curve for N_2O emissions in Germany: An ARDL approach. In *Natural Resources Forum* (Vol. 41, No. 2, pp. 119–127). Blackwell Publishing Ltd.

Impact of Soft Skills Training on Knowledge and Work Performance of Employees in Service Organizations

Sanjay K. Deshpande and M. M. Munshi

Abstract Soft skills have become inevitable for employees to effectively perform their jobs in the services sector. A growing body of research shows that soft skills can indeed be effectively taught (Bush in Media's planet eLearn newsletter, 2012). The effectiveness of soft skills training on the employees is measured using Kirk Patrick's model of training evaluation to study whether soft skills training imparted to the employees of the service sector can enhance employee knowledge and impact the dimensions of employee work performance. The result of this research study revealed that soft skill training was successful in enhancing employee knowledge and does the impact the employee work performance. This research study has provided insights about the impact of soft skills training on work performance of employees of the service sector and has contributed to the body of knowledge through the suggested training model and pedagogical tools for imparting soft skills.

Keywords Soft skills training · Training effectiveness · Training evaluation · Kirk Patrick model · Employee work performance · Employee knowledge · Services organizations

1 Introduction

In the current business scenario, role of soft skills in ensuring professional success and longevity of employees has assumed a higher importance than ever before. A research study by Watts and Watts in 2008s the above-mentioned point by stating that hard skills contribute to only 15% of one's success, while the remaining 85% is contributed by soft skills. Ever since the term *soft skills* was used for the first time in 1972, during CONARC conference in the USA, the importance of soft skills at the workplace has leapfrogged to an unprecedented level owing to changing customer orientation, preferences and loyalty, new business models. It has become inevitable for employees to possess high quotient of soft skills besides education qualification, professional certification and requisite domain knowledge to succeed in the current

S. K. Deshpande (✉) · M. M. Munshi
VTU, Belagavi, Karnataka, India

© The Author(s), under exclusive license to Springer Nature Singapore Pte Ltd. 2022

A. Chandani et al. (eds.), *Achieving $5 Trillion Economy of India*, Springer Proceedings in Business and Economics, https://doi.org/10.1007/978-981-16-7818-9_5

competitive era. Without being equipped with soft skills, it has become extremely difficult for employees to tread the professional path that was once chosen with relative comfort in the bygone days. With a significant rise in different types of services offered through online and offline platforms and ever-increasing customer expectations of better quality of services, the pressure on organization and employees to cater to customer demands is only mounting.

In today's competitive environment, soft skills enable employees to discharge a better performance on the expected lines and thereby reduce the gap between expected and offered services. Considering the universal fact that every individual is different, employees vary in their skills, competencies and behavior employee, and hence, work performance is not equitable, Therefore, soft skills training acts a key moderator and enabler to augment employee work performance. However, it is unwise to assume that every soft skills training program is effective and brings about the desired success. Rising training cost, lack of time, cut-throat competition have had a profound impact on training practices and resources of organizations. Hereafter, it is imperious that organizations assess the effectiveness of their training programs using the yardsticks like return on investment (ROI), return to learning (ROL) and many others too. Training evaluation enables the organizations to custom make the content, methods, training calendar, frequency, trainers, training budget as deemed necessary.

1.1 Objectives of the Research Study

(i) To determine if soft skills training can enhance employee knowledge.
(ii) To determine the impact of soft skill training on employee work performance.

1.2 Conceptual Framework of the Study

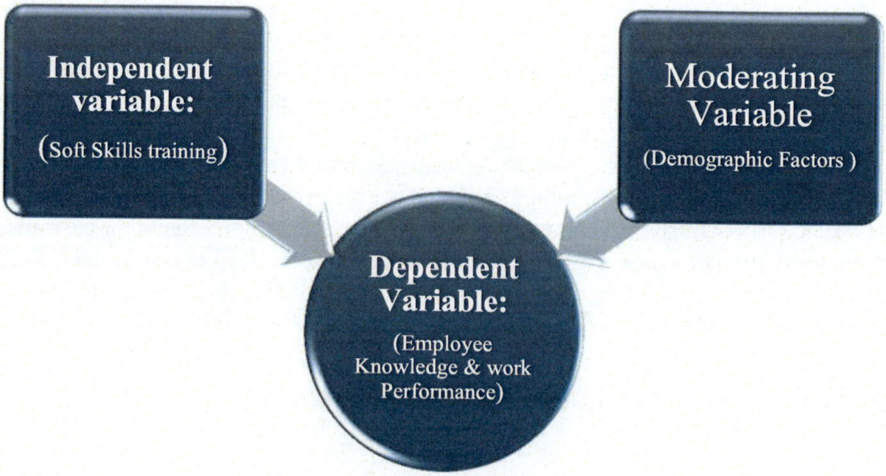

1.3 Brief History of Services Sector

It is worthwhile recalling that human beings have been treading on this Earth since 2,50,000 years. Service activities of many types have been essential aspects of the evolution of human culture and civilization. Long before the twentieth century, many scholars directed their attention to the service economy. Services are performed for people and by the people, which means that service activities are embedded in the five social institutions that sociologists describe as fundamental to the human civilization, family, education, government, economy, and religion (Poponoe, 1980). The Latin root of service is "servus," which means "slave, servant or serf". Services involve human relationships, and interactions, from long services, are performed within the context of human evolution. Clark (1940) a British and Australian economist was the first to show the impact of services on GNP, and he was also the pioneer to start studies on analyzing national economies using GNP as a tool.

Fig. 1 First era of services marketing. *Source* Raymond *P* Fisk Model

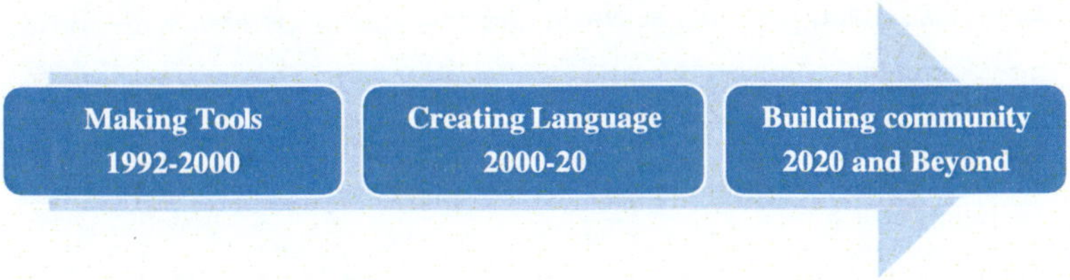

Fig. 2 Second era of services marketing

Table 1 Describes stages of different stages first era in the evolution of services marketing

Crawling stage	This stage was characterized by services marketing emerging as a distinct field; this was akin to amphibians crawling out of a swamp. Academic researchers witnessed the emergence of new species called services Marketing
Scurrying stage	This stage was characterized by the struggle of services marketing to stand on its own merit; many academic scholars published articles and research views on it. The first-ever book titled Services Marketing was published by Prof Lovelock from Harvard
Walking stage	This stage pertained about steps taken by services marketing to walk. During this stage, perhaps the most notable achievement was the development of *SERVQUAL—A* scale for measuring service quality

Source Raymond *P* Fisk Model (1993)

Table 2 Describes stages of different stages second era in the evolution of services marketing

Making tools stage	This stage was characterized by a congregation of research scholars from different fields and making technological improvements and sophistication in order to provide better services to customers
Creating language	This stage was characterized by developing common platforms like service centers, theaters and also a common language to sell services in an efficient way
Building community	This stage represents a futuristic appeal of services marketing; it aims to bring service sellers and buyers in a virtual community beyond physical market places

Source Raymond *P* Fisk Model (1993)

1.4 About Indian Services Sector

India's dominant services sector is known as the growth engine of the economy evident by the fact that it contributes about 57.3% to Indian gross value added, i.e., GVA (IBEF report), besides attracting a significant foreign direct investment (FDI) of 68.62 US billion dollars which accounts to INR 313,538,000 (at 71 Indian rupees per dollar) from 2000 to 2018 (IBEF report), the service sector employs 33% of India's employed population (Mehrotra-IL0 2019). India's services sector covers a vast variety of activities like trade, building and restaurants, transport, storage and communication, banking and finance, insurance, property, business services, community, social and personal services and services associated with construction.

1.5 Background to the Research Problem

A microscopic number of researchers have experimented at knowledge level of Kirk Patrick's training evaluation model. There is not much credible evidence on the measurement of results, viz. return on learning (ROL) Hence, a detailed research needs to be undertaken in this regard, the present literature survey did not provide ample insight about any significant study which has investigated the impact of soft skills training on the performance of employees in the service sector. *Hence "Impact of soft skills training on the knowledge and work performance of the employees of the service sector in general and Belagavi city of Karnataka state, India, in particular, remains to be known."* As such, this research study is taken up for purpose of the above-mentioned research problem. This empirically investigates the impact of soft skills training on the knowledge and work performance of employees in the service sector. The study focuses on the employees working in the service organizations in Karnataka state in general and Belagavi city in particular.

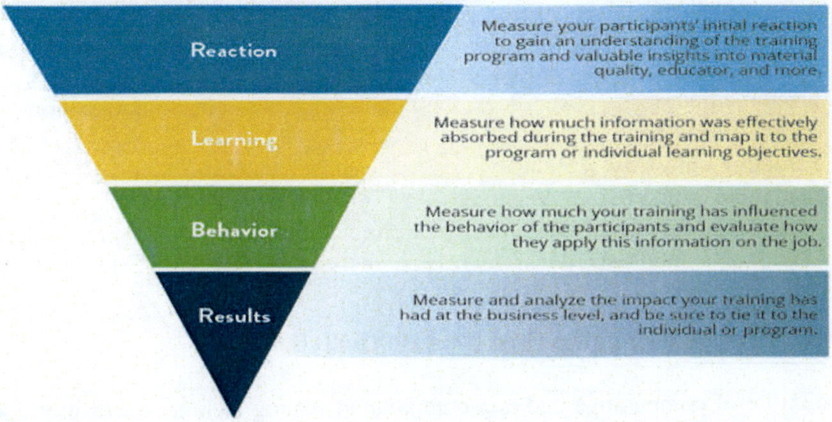

Fig. 3 Kirk Patrick training evaluation model. *Source* Linked learning blog by Paul Petrone

1.6 Scope of the Study

The study is conducted on the employees working in the service organizations of Belagavi city of Karnataka. Service organizations considered for the research include.

(a) Star hotels
(b) Telecommunication outlets
(c) Banks
(d) Insurance
(e) Organized large retail
(f) Post office
(g) Health care—hospital.

1.7 Model for Training Evaluation

See Fig. 3.

1.8 Research Methodology

This research study is descriptive in nature, and it is a quantitative study which aims to find out whether "*soft skill training*" "can change employee behavior and impact their performance." Questionnaires were administered on the employees of banks working in the city of Belagavi.

- Sampling method: cluster sampling
- Sample size: 600
- Sampling frame: Employees of service organizations such as banks (public and private), insurance-based organizations (public and private), large organized retailed stores, post offices, star hotels, hospitals, telecommunication-based organizations, etc.
- Sampling unit: City of Belagavi
- Statistical tool: SPSS 22 Version.
- Statistical tests used: Cronbach's alpha validity test, descriptive statistics, Wilcoxon signed ranked test, regression analysis.

1.8.1 Scaling Techniques Used for Data Collection

A mixture of comparative and non-comparative scaling technique was used in the questionnaire. Variables which are perception based were measured on 5-point Likert's scales with endpoints of "strongly disagree" and "strongly agree". Primary data was collected using a survey research method. Employees of the services sector (respondents) were asked to rate the extent to which they agree or disagree with their reaction to the training program. Respondents were asked to rate the extent to which they agree or disagree with statements that reflect the degree of change in knowledge and results when compared between before and after the training program.

1.8.2 Data Collection Instrument

A data collection instrument (questionnaire) was constructed and employed to measure the impact of a soft skills training program on the work performance of employees of service firms. Data collection instrument was constructed on the lines of Kirkpatrick training evaluation model referring to the contents mentioned in the book "*Kirkpatrick's levels of Training Evaluation*" authored by James Patrick, published by ATD press, Oct 2016. This data collection instrument (Questionnaire) had two sections in it, namely Section A and Section B. Section A is meant for extracting demographic data, and Section B is meant to extract employee opinion based on the components of Kirkpatrick's training evaluation model. Section B contained 31 items under 4 heads, namely *Reaction, Learning, Behavior and Results.* Reaction as a head contains 6 items on a non-comparative scale, and other 3 heads Learning, Knowledge, Results contain 25 items on comparative scale, i.e., before and after the soft skills training program.

1.8.3 Sample Size Calculation

Since the population for this research study was unknown, the minimum sample size estimated using the formula of Cochran (1977), discussed in his book '*Sampling Techniques*' was used.

Table 3 The stages of arriving at a sample size

No. of questionnaires distributed	1000
No. of filled questionnaires received back	734 (73.4%)
No. of the erroneous questionnaires	130
No. of questionnaires excluded for rounding off	04
No of questionnaires (samples used for data analysis)	600

$$\boldsymbol{n}_0 = \frac{\boldsymbol{z}^2 \times \boldsymbol{p}(1-\boldsymbol{p})}{\boldsymbol{e}^2}$$

The following values can be used for estimating the sample size:

$\boldsymbol{n}_0$ The sample size needed for a research study.
z^2 95% confidence level (The value of $(1 - \alpha)$ in standard normal distribution z-table, which is 1.96 for 95%).
$\boldsymbol{p}$ 50% variability of the population (which is maximum).
$\boldsymbol{e}$ 5% margin of error which is 0.05.

$$\boldsymbol{n}_0 = \frac{(1.96)^2 \times 0.5(1-0.5)}{(0.05)^2} = 384.16$$

As calculated and determined by the above-mentioned formula (Cochran's formula), minimum sample size of 384 and more can be used for the study. Though the minimum sample for the study was determined as 384, the researcher invested more efforts to make the study more comprehensive; hence, 600 samples were used for data analysis. About 1000 questionnaires were distributed in all, 734 respondents participated in the survey in the study, about 130 of questionnaires were erroneous in nature (half filled, wrongly filled), and eventually, 600 of them were selected for data analysis, (4 of them were excluded for the purpose of rounding off to 600, and since a sample of 600 is larger than the minimum sample of 384, discarding 04 was feasible). The response rate of this survey was 73.4% (734), and error rate from filled questionnaires was 17% (130) (Table 3).

2 Review of Literature

2.1 Soft Skills and Work Performance

Chaudhry and Abid (2011) conducted a study on employees in privately owned organizations to find whether their soft skills predicted their performance. Correlation and regression analysis were the statistical tools used for analysis. The results revealed that the soft skills scores of employees predicted their performance scores in organizations. They also recommended considering the component of soft skills of employees to take decisions pertaining to selection, retention, promotion, and transfer. Learning soft skills improves employees communication with others, improves relationships, enhances integrity, condenses stress levels, cultivates learning from mistakes, lessens power games at work, enhances empathy, administrates change more assertively, gets value and admiration from others, increases imagination and creativeness, and improves job and career prospects, thus empowers and motivates the individuals to perform better at the workplace.

Khokhar and Kush (2009) studied work performance of two different sets of employees one with high soft skills and others with low soft skills. For this study, 20 male employees were taken from a company who was having a graduation degree in engineering and a master's degree in management. This study was done in Uttarakhand state, India. The 20 samples comprised of two sets. One set (10 samples) that scored high soft skills and the other set (10 samples) that scored low soft skills. The work performances of these two sets of samples were measured. Later, the independent sample *t* tests were done to examine the mean difference between these two sets of samples. The results revealed that high soft skills people have good quality of work performance, ability to get along with others, ability to work without supervision, capacity on work, quantity on work, speed on the job, care in handling the company, ability to handle different jobs, dependability, initiative on the job, planning ability, attendance and punctuality, and of course the overall work performance. They have suggested that strengthening the soft skills s of the employees will foster the service orientation of employees in the organizations.

2.2 *Soft Skills Training and Work Performance*

Dr. Rajshekhar (2019) in a research study titled "*Teaching Soft skills: A Necessity In Modern Era*" said soft skills are inevitable and should be taught in schools, colleges, and organizations in view of rising demand for these skills, Furthermore, soft skills should also be taught to promote happy living besides for career development and reinforcing moral standards. Young graduates and employees fail to utilize the opportunities across India, and because of lack of soft skills, soft skills help employees to progress to higher positions, and when soft skills are imparted through training, the benefits are enormous; hence, training becomes extremely necessary.

Sahoo et al. (2017) in a research study titled "*Outcomes of Training and Development Measures in Public Sector Banks of India*" mentioned that investment in HR development initiatives like training, skill up-gradation, and other employee development programs will improve individual performance and organizational effectiveness. Investing in an employee is not the same as investing in equipment or machinery. Learning of soft and technical skills is necessary for building a career.

Properly designed and well executed of training programs aid in building competence and confidence among the employees and thereby accomplish an organizational goal.

Kaur (2016) studied the influence of training interventions on employee productivity and found that productivity in the service sector was significantly and positively influenced by various aspects of training and development programs including soft skills training; hence, soft skills training is an important activity of business organizations to enhance employee productivity.

According to Dr. Wushe et al. (2014) in a research titled "*Humanizing Leadership—The Effect of Business Soft Skills on Service Delivery in the Hospitality Industry*," delivering quality service through professional business soft skills to customers is a must for success and survival in today's competitive business environment. Hence, companies are now forced to invest more and more on soft skills training in order to groom their employees to present themselves in a better manner and improve their performance.

Dr. Elnaga and Imran (2013) in their research study titled "*The Effect of Training on Employee Performance*," mentioned that soft skills training is necessary to increase productivity, and also to motivate and inspire workers to perform jobs more effectively, they further said training makes the employees more capable by sharpening their decision making, problem-solving skills, and thinking ability. Training is provided to employees to help them perform their current and future jobs as per the standards and expectations of the organizations.

Truitt (2011)in a study titled "*The Effect of Training and Development on Employee Attitude as it relates to Training and Work Proficiency*" found that positive training paved for positive work efficiency; the study said 80% of trainees who attended training and had a positive experience.

In a research study titled "*Overqualified and under experienced—Turning graduates into hospitality managers*" by Raybould and Wilkins (2005), it was ascertained that many employees who join professional service organizations have insufficient knowledge about soft skills, since the academic knowledge and grades they took from their colleges and universities do not correspond to actual business needs, making it compulsory of almost all the service-based organizations to impart soft skills training to meet the business needs of service sector.

2.3 *Need for Evaluating Training Program*

Kamat (2019) in an article titled "*Measure the Effectiveness of Corporate Training*" mentions that the investment in training and development in increasing across the globe and is growing incrementally by 14% every year in the USA as per training industry magazine. However, results and efficiency of past training act as critical indicators for future training. With the rising focus on continuous learning and development of employees, organizations have realized the need to measure the effectiveness and the ROL of such training initiatives using reliable and appropriate methods.

Huka, Njehia and KariukiMbugua (2015) in a research study titled "*Business Training Evaluation: Application and Effects on Trainee Competencies*" mention that training evaluation basically aims to answer three critical questions: whether the training was successfully conducted, whether the immediate objectives of training are met, and whether it has resulted in any changes terms of improved competencies and subsequent performance of the trainees.

Mohamed and Alias (2012) in a research study titled "*Evaluating the Effectiveness of a Training Program Using the Four Level Kirkpatrick Model in the Banking Sector in Malaysia*" mention that it is necessary to evaluate every training program as investments on training are not worthwhile without doing evaluation, and effective evaluation should be well-planned and reliable. Therefore, organizations are required to collect study and analyze the data obtained from the training evaluation to upgrade the present training programs, if necessary, rather than just for training evaluation purposes.

Gordon (1991) in a research study titled "*Measuring goodness of training*" mentioned that to know the benefits accrued or will accrue evaluation of training becomes necessary, the problem of evaluation, however, has got snakier, as the amount of common ground for framing a discussion about goodness.

2.4 Construct Validity for Dimensions of Work Performance

Koopmans et al. (2012) categorized employee work performance into task performance, contextual and adaptive performance. Task performance refers to the proficiency with which an employee performs core duties or central job tasks. Contextual performance refers to employee behaviors needed to support organizational culture or environment made up by social and psychological factors and perform job tasks in the said environment. Adaptive performance refers to an employee's proficiency in being flexible to adapt to changes in work roles and responsibilities, work expectations, and work environment.

For the purpose of this research, based on the review of literature, the authors have developed the dimensions of work performance as under.

3 Research Questions and Hypothesis

Research Question 1: Whether the soft skills training program is effective in enhancing knowledge of employees of the service sector.
Research Question 2: Whether softs skills training has an impact on employee's work performance.

Hypothesis 1: Soft skill training is effective in enhancing employee knowledge
Hypothesis 2: Soft skill training has an impact on employee work performance

4 Analysis and Findings

4.1 Plan for Data Analysis

Research question 1 is addressed by hypothesis (H_1): *soft skill training is effective in enhancing employee knowledge* **[*Knowledge refers to acquiring new information in general and about pertaining to the job gaining clarity of expectations of the job and objectives of Soft Skills training to gain future success* (Patrick, 2016)].**

Here soft skill training is the independent variable and work performance is the dependent variable. Wilcoxon signed ranked test (also called paired ranked test, Wilcoxon T-test), a nonparametric test, is used to know the knowledge level before and after training method; as the data collected is perceptual in nature, the sample is drawn from sample population; a t *test is not used since the sample size is large (n = 600). The second section titled Learning of Part B of the questionnaire contains seven items (questions) about knowledge; the data is collected in a comparative way using Likert scale. Each item is tested in a comparative way (before and after the training program).*

Research question 2 is addressed by (H2): *Soft skills training has an impact on employee work performance* (Referring to Table 4 dimensions of work performance included work compliance and quality, personal motivation, confidence and determination to work decision making, conflict management, time management, error-free work, problem-solving, job satisfaction and self-value, independent working, clarity in communication).

For the purpose of testing this hypothesis, multi-regression analysis test is used impact. In the present study, multiple regression analysis was used to ascertain the impact of independent variable, i.e., soft skills training which includes data about (a) training infrastructure and environment (b) contents of training (c) presentation style (d) organization and dependent variable (employee work performance). Here, independent data (soft skills training) is a grouped variable and was correlated with

Table 4 Dimensions for measuring work performance

Work compliance and quality
Personal motivation
Confidence and determination to work
Decision making
conflict management
Time management
Error-free work
Problem-solving
Job satisfaction and self-value
Independent working (working with little or no supervision)
Clarity in communication

each dependent variable; i.e., dimensions of employee work performance and overall variance were tested.

4.2 *Data Analysis*

4.2.1 Showing Sample Distribution Among Different Clusters

See Fig. 4.

Cluster	No of respondents
Star Hotel	60
Telecommunication	64
Bank	160
Insurance	110
Retail	79
Post office	60
Health care – Hospital	67
Total	**600**

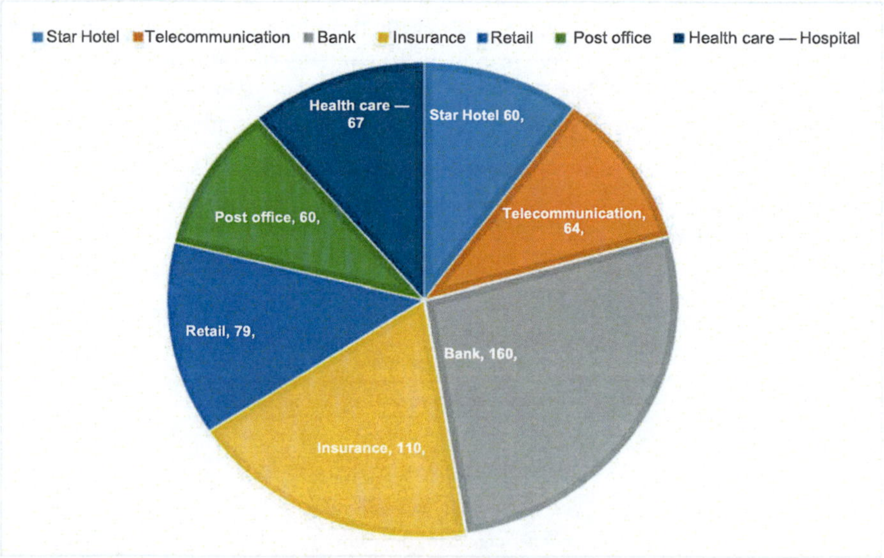

Fig. 4 Distribution of respondents among different clusters

Table 5 Cronbach's Alpha values for the dimensions of questionnaire

Name of the dimension	No. of items	Cronbach's alpha (α)
Reaction	6	0.834
Learning	7	0.947
Knowledge	8	0.967
Results	10	0.971

Reaction, Learning, Behavior, and Results are the components of Kirk Patrick's training evaluation model and have been used as dimensions in the questionnaire, since this research study is based on the lines of Kirk Patrick model.

4.2.2 Reliability Analysis Items in the Questionnaire

Interpretation: *Cronbach's coefficient alpha* is a popular test of inter-item consistency and reliability (Cronbach, 1946). As per the guidelines are given by Nunnally (1978) for analyzing Cronbach's alpha, the values between 0.5 and 0.6 for exploratory research can be considered. Cronbach's alpha for all the dimensions are above 0.6; hence, the reliability exists among all the dimensions in the measurement scale (Referring to Table 5).

> ***Hypothesis 1o: Soft skill training is not effective in enhancing employee knowledge***
> ***Hypothesis 1a: Soft skill training is effective in enhancing employee knowledge***

Objective: The objective of testing this hypothesis is to determine whether there is any change in employees' knowledge before and after the training program, and this helps in understanding if the soft skills training was effective in enhancing in employee knowledge. Here, employee knowledge is the dependent variable and soft skills training is an independent variable. Wilcoxon signed ranked test (also called paired ranked test, Wilcoxon T-test), a nonparametric test, was used to test the change in knowledge level before and after training. Each item is tested in a comparative way (before and after the training program). As the data collected was collected on a comparative scale and was perceptual in nature.

Interpretation: Table 6 represents *p-values* of test results of enhancing employee knowledge (before and after the training program), and Wilcoxon ranked sign test results are mentioned in Table 7.

Inference: Referring to Table 7, alternate hypothesis (H1a), i.e., *soft skill training, is effective in enhancing employee. Knowledge is accepted,* since in all the cases *(P-value <0.005) at 95% confidence level.* Hence, it is clear that soft skills training is effective in enhancing employee knowledge.

> ***H2o: Soft Skills training has no impact on employee work performance***
> ***H2a: Soft skills training has an impact on employee work performance***

Table 6 Results of Wilcoxon ranked *T* test to ascertain the change in employee knowledge

BT Before training	I have acquired information and knowledge that is new to me	Knowledge/information-acquired met the expectation and is applicable to the job	I believe that the needed soft skills, knowledge have been imparted	The training content and information will be helpful for my future success
AT After training	I have acquired information and knowledge that is new to me	Knowledge/information-acquired met the expectation and is applicable to the job	I believe that the needed soft skills, knowledge have been imparted	The training content and information will be helpful for my future success
Z	−20.221b	−20.018b	−19.641b	−19.531b
Asymp. Sig. (2-tailed)	0.000	0.000	0.000	0.000
BT Before training	Attitude has undergone a change in accordance with job requirements		I am clear about what is expected of me on the job	I understood the objectives of this training program
AT After training	Attitude has undergone a change in accordance with job requirements		I am clear about what is expected of me on the job	I understood the objectives of this training program
Z	−19.468b		−19.798b	−19.604b
Asymp. Sig. (2-tailed)	0.000		0.000	0.000

Table 7 *P*-values of Wilcoxon ranked *T* test of all items of knowledge

Details	*P*-value
1. I have acquired information and knowledge that is new to me (BT and AT)	000
2. Knowledge/information-acquired met the expectation and is applicable to the job (BT and AT)	000
3. I believe that the needed soft skills, knowledge have been imparted (BT and AT)	000
4. The training content and information will be helpful for my future success (BT and AT)	000
5. Attitude has undergone a change in accordance with job requirements (BT and AT)	000
6. I am clear about what is expected of me on the job (BT and AT)	000
7. I understood the objectives of this training program (BT and AT)	000

BT Before training, *AT* After training

Objective: The objective of this hypothesis is to know whether soft skills training causes any variance on employee work performance. Regression analysis was conducted to determine the impact of the independent variable (soft skills training) on dependent variable (work performance). Data for the dependent variable and the independent variable was collected on a continuous and comparative scale.

Interpretation: Multiple regression analysis was conducted to determine how soft skills training was related and caused variance to employee work performance. This overall regression model produced an R^2 of .232 which means that the soft skills explained an overall 23.2% of variance on the dependent variable employee work performance. The overall model was significant, F (1, 599) = 180.9, $p < 0.005$, and it accounted for 23.2% of the variance. The results indicated that overall soft skills training ($\beta = 0.482$, $p < 0.05$) had a statistically significant relationship with employee work performance. The strength of relationships (beta scores) indicated that soft skills training ($\beta = 0.482$) had a greater positive relationship with employee work performance.

Inference: Referring to Table 8

- *Alternate hypothesis H_6 is accepted, as P (0.000) < 0.005; hence, soft skills training has an impact on dimensions of employee work performance.*
- *Soft skills training showed a variance of 23.2% (R^2 value) on employee work performance.*

Table 8 Results of multiple regression analysis between soft skills training and employee work performance

Model summary

Model	*R*	*R*-square	Adjusted *R*-square	Std. error of the estimate
1	0.482[a]	0.232	0.231	3.64766

ANOVA[b]

Model		Sum of squares	*df*	Mean square	*F*	Sig
1	Regression	2407.880	1	2407.880	180.970	0.000[b]
	Residual	7956.654	598	13.305		
	Total	10,364.534	599			

Coefficients

Model		Unstandardized coefficients	Standardized coefficients	*t*	Sig	
		B	Std. error	Beta		
1	(Constant)	20.636	1.005		20.539	0.000
	Soft skills training	0.671	0.050	0.482	13.452	0.000

[a]Predictors: (Constant), soft skills training
[b]Dependent variable: work performance

5 Conclusion

This research study concludes by mentioning that, soft skills training is effective in enhancing employee knowledge, the study further claims that soft skills training caused a variance of 23% to employee work performance (Referring to Table 8), Which means soft skill training was instrumental in enhancing employee work performance by 23%, hence the second hypothesis stands accepted and proved.

6 Implications of the Study

There is a strong need to shed the old belief that training is a cost-centric approach, since the findings of this study claim that soft skills training provides significant benefits by enhancing employee performance. Hence, soft skills training should be made an integral part of the training agenda without any ignorance in service organizations.

7 Scope for Further Research

- Comparing key performance areas (KPA), key result areas (KRA) and feedback can better measure employee performance sought by customers to know if employee performance is on expected lines. *Anderson's value of learning model* can be used for research endeavor since its focus is on the evaluation of congruence between the learning program's/training goals and the strategic goals of the organization.
- Since the workforce in any organization is a blend of people coming from diversified backgrounds, it may be interesting to ascertain if background of the employees influences the efficiency of the training programs conducted. The study can focus on finding out if there education and cultural backgrounds unable or enable them to acquire the information, knowledge imparted during the training program.

8 Suggested Training Model for Developing Soft Skills

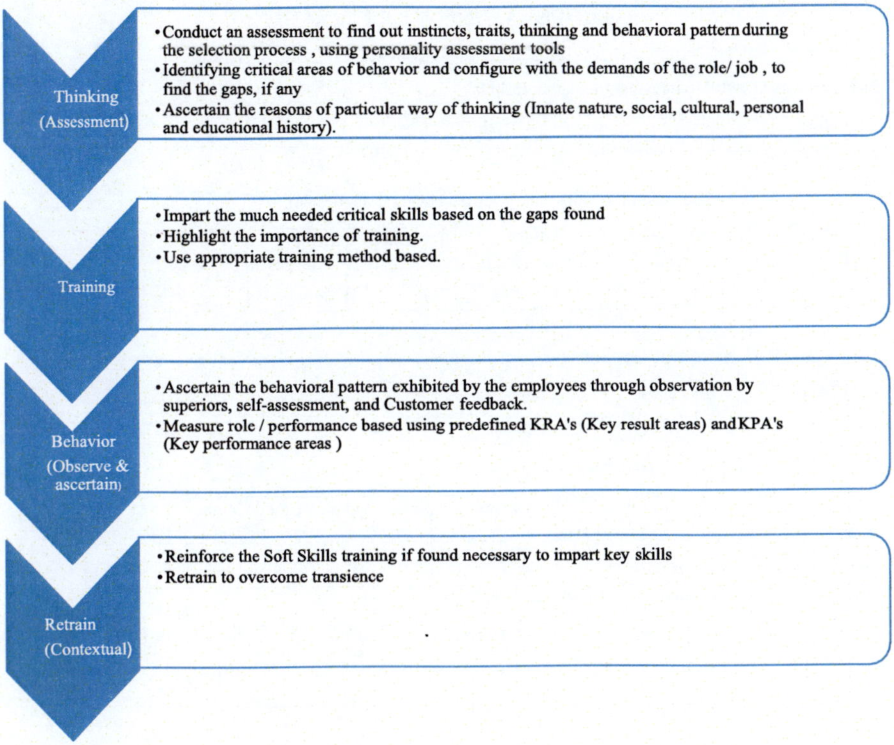

Data Collection Instrument Questionnaire

SECTION – A - GENERAL INFORMATION

1.1 Your Name (Optional):____________________1.2 Designation: ____________________

1.3 Have you attended training program on Soft skills

Yes		No	

1.4 Type of service organization you work with (Tick whichever is applicable).

Hotel	Telecommunication	Bank	Insurance	Retail	IT	Healthcare

1.5 Gender: (Tick whichever is applicable)

Male		Female	

1.6 Age: (Tick whichever is applicable)

20-25 Years	25-30 Years	30-35 Years	35-40 Years	40-45 Years	>45 Years

1.7 Educational qualification: (Tick whichever is applicable).

PUC	Diploma	Degree	PG

1.8 Your position in the organization. (Tick whichever is applicable).

Operational	Middle Level	Top Level

1.9 Your experience in this organization. (Tick whichever is applicable).

Below 5 Years	5-10 Years	10-15 Years	Above 15 Years

1.10 What type of Soft skills was imparted during the training you may tick more than one

Interpersonal skills like self-confidence, motivation, self-improvement	
Leadership and teamwork based	

Specific Skills- Time management, Negotiation, Decision making, Problem Solving, and other skills	
Attitude, Ethics, Etiquette based	
Communication skills- Written, Oral, listening, Reading	
Handling Stress and Criticism	
Any other	

SECTION B - BASED ON KIRK PATRICK MODEL

1. Reaction (Reaction of the trainees towards the trainer, training content and method)

5- Strongly Agree, 4-Agree, 3- Neither Agree nor Disagree, 2-Disagree, 1- Strongly Disagree

Si. No	SELF-ASSESSMENT OF TRAINEES REACTION TO INSTRUCTOR, MATERIAL, CONTENT	Rating (Tick whichever is applicable)				
1	Venue and arrangements for the training were good & acceptable	1	2	3	4	5
2	Contents of training were suited to my level of knowledge and skills and to th job requirements					
3	The presentation style of the facilitator contributed to learning and can be recommended to colleagues					
4	Training methods used have influenced me to be more attentive and engaged throughout the training					
5	Trainer/ facilitator encouraged participation					
6	Do you really feel the need for soft skill training to mould the employees and help them fit into job requirements					

2. Learning (Information, Knowledge acquired by trainees post-training program)

5- Strongly Agree, 4-Agree, 3- Neither Agree nor Disagree, 2-Disagree, 1- Strongly Disagree

BEFORE TRAINING					SELF-ASSESSMENT OF KNOWLEDGE AND SKILLS LEARNT RELATED TO JOB/ ROLE	AFTER TRAINING				
1	2	3	4	5	I have acquired information and knowledge that is new to me	1	2	3	4	5
1	2	3	4	5	Knowledge / Information acquired met the expectation and is applicable to the job	1	2	3	4	5
1	2	3	4	5	I believe that the needed Soft skills , knowledge have been imparted	1	2	3	4	5

1	2	3	4	5	The training content and information will be helpful for my future success.	1	2	3	4	5
1	2	3	4	5	Attitude has undergone a change in accordance to job requirements	1	2	3	4	5
1	2	3	4	5	I am clear about what is expected of me on the job	1	2	3	4	5
1	2	3	4	5	I understood the objectives of this training program	1	2	3	4	5

3. Behaviour (Behaviour of the trainees on the job, towards peers, post-training program)

5- Strongly Agree, 4-Agree, 3- Neither Agree nor Disagree, 2-Disagree, 1- Strongly Disagree

Before Training					Self-assessment of Behavioural ASPECTS	After Training				
1	2	3	4	5	Soft skill training had the potential to bring positive change in my behaviour	1	2	3	4	5
1	2	3	4	5	Change in behavior sustained over a period of time and helped me work better	1	2	3	4	5
1	2	3	4	5	I felt there is a noticeable and measurable change in the activity and performance of my role	1	2	3	4	5
1	2	3	4	5	I I have received support and encouragement for applying my learning to my job.	1	2	3	4	5
1	2	3	4	5	Soft skill training helped me to gain the required behavioural abilities	1	2	3	4	5
1	2	3	4	5	A system of accountability helps me to apply what I learnt.	1	2	3	4	5
1	2	3	4	5	Incentives encourage me to apply what I learnt	1	2	3	4	5

4. Result (End results, benefits accrued to the trainee after the training program)

5- Strongly Agree, 4-Agree, 3- Neither Agree nor Disagree, 2-Disagree, 1- Strongly Disagree

Before Training					Self-assessment of Knowledge and Skills Related to JOB/ ROLE	After Training				
1	2	3	4	5	My compliance and quality of work has increased	1	2	3	4	5
1	2	3	4	5	My personal motivation, confidence and determination to work has increased	1	2	3	4	5
1	2	3	4	5	I am able to take better decisions and thereby improve productivity (Decision Making)	1	2	3	4	5

1	2	3	4	5	My conflicts with co-workers have reduced	1	2	3	4	5
1	2	3	4	5	My time management skills and have been honed	1	2	3	4	5
1	2	3	4	5	I am able to work efficiency as error rates have decreased	1	2	3	4	5
1	2	3	4	5	My problem solving ability has increased	1	2	3	4	5
1	2	3	4	5	I have felt greater job satisfaction and also feel self-valued	1	2	3	4	5
1	2	3	4	5	I am able to work independently with little or no supervision	1	2	3	4	5
1	2	3	4	5	I am able to communicate and express ideas, suggestions, and inputs with more clarity to clients. (Clarity in Communication)	1	2	3	4	5

Suggestions: if any other types of training can be given to enhance the skill base and capacity of staff, is so mention.

References

Bush, C. E. (2012). The case for soft skills training, spring 2012 Edition of *Monarch Media's Planet eLearn Newsletter*.

Clark, C. (1940). The conditions of economic progress. London: Macmillan.

Chaudhry, A., & Abid, U. (2011). An investigation of the relationship between employees' emotional intelligence and performance. *African Journal of Business Management., 5*(9), 3556–3562.

Cochran, W. G. (1977). *Sampling techniques* (3d ed). New York: Wiley.

Elnaga, A., & Imran, A. (2013). The effect of training on employee performance. *European Journal of Business and Management, 5*(4), 137–147.

Fisk, R. P., Brown, S. W., & Bitner, M. J. (1993). Tracking the evolution of the services marketing literature. *Journal of Retailing, 69*(1), 61–85.

Grande, T., Wilcoxon (1956). Siegel (1945) sample Wilcoxon non parametric hypothesis test. *Six Sigma Study Guide.*

Gordon, J. (1991). Measuring the "goodness" of training. *ERIC, V* (28), 28th ser, 19–25.

Huka, G. S., Njehia, B., & KariukiMbugua, Z. (2015). Business training evaluation: application and effects on trainee competencies. *IOSR Journal of Business and Management (IOSR-JBM), 17*(1), 60–72.

Ibrahim, R., Boerhannoeddin, A., & Bakare, K. K. (2017). The effect of soft skills and training methodology on employee performance. *European Journal of Training and Development, 41*(4), 388–406.

Importance of Soft Skills for Professionals in the Digital World—BW Education. India Services Sector.

Judge, T. A., Thoresen, C. J., Bono, J. E., & Patton, G. K. (2001). The job satisfaction–job performance relationship: A qualitative and quantitative review. *Psychological Bulletin, 127*(3), 376–407.

Kamat, A. (2019). Measure the effectiveness of corporate training. *AJMR.*

Kaur, J. (2016). Impact of training and development programmes on the productivity of employees in the Banks. *Journal of Strategic Human Resource Management, 5*(1).
Khokhar, C. P., & Kush, T. (2009). Emotional intelligence and work performance among executives. *Europe's Journal of Psychology, 5*(1).
Koopmans, L., Bernaards, C., Hildebrandt, V., Van Buuren, S., Van Der Beek, A. J., & De Vet Henrica, C. W. (2015). Development of an individual work performance questionnaire. *International Journal of Productivity and Performance Management, 62*(1), 6–28.
Mehrotra, S. (2019). Informal employment trends in the Indian economy: persistent informality, but growing positive development. ILO (working paper).
Mohamed, R., & Alias, A. A. (2012). Evaluating the effectiveness of a training program using the four level Kirkpatrick Model in the Banking Sector in Malaysia.
Njehia, B. K., Guyo, S. H., & Mbugua, Z. K. (2015). Business training evaluation: application and effects on trainee competencies 120 (in e-proof pdf).
Nunnally, J. C. (1978). *Psychometric theory* (2nd ed.). New York: McGraw-Hill.
Patrick, J., Team, Wrote, M., Wrote, A., & Wrote, B. T. (2016). Kirkpatrick's four-level training evaluation model: analyzing training effectiveness. *Kirkpatrick's Training Evaluation Model*
Petrone, P. (2017). The best way to use the Kirkpatrick Model.
Rajshekhar, G. (2019). Multiculturalism in Indian English literature. *International Journal on Studies in English Language and Literature, 7*(3), 109–117.
Raybould, M., & Wilkins, H. (2005). Over qualified and under experienced—Turning graduates into hospitality managers. *International Journal of Contemporary Hospitality Management, 17*(3), 203–216.
Sahoo, K. K., Sahoo, C. K., & Tripathy, S. K. (2017). Outcomes of training and development measures in public sector banks of India: An overview. *Productivity, 57*(4).
Services (Rep.). (2019). IBEF.
Truitt, D. L. (2011). The effect of training and development on employee attitude as it relates to training and work proficiency. *SAGE Journals,* 1–13.
Wushe, T. (2014). Humanising leadership-The effect of business soft skills on service delivery in the hospitality industry in Harare, Zimbabwe. *International Journal of Social Sciences and Humanities Invention, 1*(8).

Are Recreational Activities Really Recreational at the Workplace?

Mahavadi Dhanshyam

Abstract The RoI of the human capital—the most important asset of organizations—depends primarily on the life quality of the individuals, represented by their performance levels, motivation towards work, and work-life balance. The advancement of fast and competitive business world accompanies increased working hours, which stress the employees further. To remain competitive, companies try to maximize the productivity of employees through recreational and wellness programs, which require high initial investment and significant costs to maintain. Thus, it is essential to assess their adequacy, effectiveness, and their actual role in the life quality of employees. Extant literature focuses on positive effects of the recreational programs, but the actual benefits accrued to the final customers (employees) remain doubtful. Through this study on Indian IT industry, the author assesses the effectiveness of these programs using four indicators. The results expose the inadequacies, emphasizing the need for flexible approach in designing such programs.

Keywords Recreational facilities · Employee wellness · Stress · Work-life balance · Effectiveness · Performance index · Life quality index · Motivation index

1 Introduction

Organizations throughout the world strive hard to develop their human capital—the most volatile of their assets. The amount and quality of work the employees put in are important determinants of the organizational success. Maintenance and improvement of this high-quality work are related to employees' satisfaction with their work and their social life within the workspace.

With organizations becoming flat and leaner, and demanding multitaskers, the job descriptions of employees have become very fluid, their scope wider, and their targets increasingly more and more challenging in most of the organizations. The pressure

M. Dhanshyam (✉)
Indian Institute of Management, Lucknow 226013, India
e-mail: fpm19017@iiml.ac.in

© The Author(s), under exclusive license to Springer Nature Singapore Pte Ltd. 2022
A. Chandani et al. (eds.), *Achieving $5 Trillion Economy of India*, Springer Proceedings in Business and Economics, https://doi.org/10.1007/978-981-16-7818-9_6

to achieve targets at workplace affects their work-life balance, making many professionals vulnerable to stress. Many organizations worldwide have tried to address this issue by making it mandatory in their policies to implement recreational activities at the workplace many times in a year. The labor laws and guidelines in many nations also mandate public limited companies to adhere to some minimum provisions related to employee morale and wellness.

Literature and practice-based evidence at different types of organizations worldwide stress the importance of recreational activities at workplaces. Recreational activities help in improving productivity of employees by refreshing their brains, helping them unlock their creative self to think out-of-the-box, revitalizing their bodies, and improving focus. Wellness programs aid in creating lighter work environment by creating a fun corner, thus helping in keeping the work stress levels low and employee morale high. A well-crafted and maintained recreational area is an easy gateway to encourage informal socializing which strengthens teamwork and collaborative efforts. It facilitates cross-team and inter-departmental knowledge exchange, a prerequisite for organizational learning. Well-organized recreational programs imbibe positive work culture in the organizations by lessening power distance and increasing approachability. This has an overall positive impact on organization performance through improvement of individual employee performance and team performance.

The advantages of recreational activities are numerous, and there is little doubt about their impact on the organization's performance. But, as most of the policies that are drafted at the higher management level get diluted when implemented at lower level of the organization, recreational activities may also face the same fate. Implementing recreational activities at different organizational levels productively is one of the most critical challenges that organizations face today. Most of the organizations, especially in India, organize recreational activities probably just for the sake of complying with HR policies. Employees seemingly do not participate very actively in the recreational activities conducted at their office/organization. Apparently, the perception of employees toward recreational activities is also very casual in nature.

All the above-mentioned points kindle an important question of '*Whether these recreational activities are at all beneficial for organization's productivity/output?*'.

This paper attempts to delve deep into the nature of recreational activities prevalent in Indian IT organizations and to seek a plausible answer for this question. The findings try to uncover the harsh reality that there exists a significant gap between '*what is*' and '*what it is aimed at*' at many major organizations. Given the huge investments incurred in provision of these activities, the research findings leave the practitioners with a food-for-thought on their present policies. For the aspiring researchers, the gap between aspirations and reality provides huge scope for understanding the organizational practice and develop innovative research questions for testing. For policymakers, the findings help fine-tune their guidelines to ensure overall human index development of their nations.

2 Literature Review and Background

Yang et al. (2009) demonstrate the relationship between quality of life and occupational stress among teachers in China. They find that teachers in China suffer with lower health status than the rest of their population, which is mostly due to the strain posed by their occupation and absence of any means to dilute or divert it. Tuisku and Houni (2015) assert cultural leisure activities as a source of well-being and coping with the stress of employees. Their experience of cultural activities in Finnish workplaces reveals that community participation is more effective than individual activities, and that they result in relaxation and psychological detachment from strain. Van den Brande et al. (2016) suggest wishful thinking, emotional coping, recreation, social support, and suppression as tools to suppress workplace bullying and the resulting stress. Okechukwu et al. (2019) assessed the effect of work stress on staff performance in the Nigerian banking sector and suggested that creation of time for rest and recreational activities as well as vacation packages are essential to break their monotony and revitalize them.

Gungaphul et al. (2012) have stressed the importance of promotion of leisure and recreation in the workplace with some focus on the recent trends in workplace recreation. Modern organizations are increasingly realizing the value of employee health, well-being personal and professional growth, and their linkage to the wellness programs. The advantages like increased productivity, enhanced work-life balance, platform to socialize, improved motivation, and betterment of professional behavior of the employees provided by the recreational activities are driving the organizations to invest heavily and encourage the employees to take active part in the same. Lacanienta et al. (2018) observed that leisure at workplace (LAW) can provide added value to the workplace by facilitating personal expressiveness, resilience, and organizational identification. Ledikwe et al. (2017) highlighted that ensuring the well-being of healthcare workers is critical in reaching international health goals, and demonstrated the method and effect of implementation of a National Workplace Wellness Program for health workers in Botswana.

Candice et al. (2012), through their case study, have examined a workplace recreation-based program using a social and ecological approach to wellness. The study highlights leadership, social support, and bonding as the primary benefits of the workplace recreation, even while the constraints related to job responsibilities, returning to work after perspiring, and limitations of physical space act as challenges in actual implementation of the recreational activities. They have established that the recreational activities improve the degree of identification of ownership that the individuals feel. Kukk et al. (2016) suggested leisure and recreation at workplace as an opportunity to result in positive integration of ethnic groups and refresh the employees.

In a detailed study conducted on the effects of workplace recreation on employee performance at Kenya Utalii College, Mokaya and Gitari (2012) discovered that the major reasons for engaging in workplace recreation were relaxation of mind, stress reduction, confidence building, and improvement of health of employees. They have found a positive correlation between the recreational facilities at workplace and the employee performance variables like job satisfaction, quality of service and customer satisfaction, and enhanced productivity. Most employees view recreational activities as intrinsic reward mechanism, wherein staff parties serve as a platform to obtain informal feedback on the employee performance and for recognizing one's achievements and gaining cognizance of their shortcomings, thus helping them meet their social needs that are otherwise constrained by the hectic schedules. By offering recreational facilities to employees, organizations boost the productivity of employees by meeting their physical and psychological needs, which in turn reduces their absenteeism, sick leaves, and medical costs, and acquire returns in the form of reduced turnover, improved working hours, and greater productivity. They further recommend that in order to achieve the desired results and performance, however, the recreational activities have to be carefully designed considering the different tastes, genders, age, and other cultural factors of the demographics. Kerner et al. (2017) found a negative correlation between leisure-time physical activity and absenteeism at work, showing that it improved availability and profitability of organizations.

Realizing that physical inactivity is the fourth most leading reason for deaths globally (Kohl et al., 2012) and that inactivity increases the risk on non-communicable diseases like cardiovascular disorders and diabetes. Amber and Mayer (2016), have conducted a research on the faculty and staff of a small private university located in the Pacific Northwest of the USA, with the hypotheses that workplace and environmental settings have a positive effect on health status, promote increased quality of life, reduce stress, and improve overall employee satisfaction. To this effect, Kohl et al. (2012) call for a systematic approach for capacity and infrastructure to design creative work environments. Harju et al. (2014) identified different causes of job boredom and found that it increased the likelihood of employees' turnover, absenteeism and early retirement intentions, poor health, poor workability, and stress symptoms. Morrison and MacKinnon (2008) have defined essentials for workplace wellness programs that include stakeholder engagement, employee participation and involvement, positive organizational culture, ability to reduce direct medical economic expenses resulting out of stress, and effects on humanistic outcomes. Amber and Mayer (2016) have found that workplace recreation has contributed to changing social norms at the university by developing a culture of health and wellness. They have addressed the primary problems of identification of indicators of work-related quality of life, identification of the recreation needs of the faculty and the staff, and identification of current trends for the usage of available recreational facilities. They found that the participants of the wellness program felt very healthy and full of energy. However, while around 75% of the participants had planned to use the recreational facilities on being opened, only 46.7% reported to have actually been using them at least once a week, post their installation. Despite the non-active use, the respondents emphasized on the need of such facilities at their workplace. But at the same time, on posttest, 86% of the participants had reported that the new recreational facility had little influenced their approach to work. Additionally, their findings reported that the current facilities fail to address many aspects of health. As such, a lot of refinement has been suggested in the available recreational facilities to enhance participative health efforts among the faculty and staff. Their findings had further emphasized the importance of components recommended by Morrison and MacKinnon (2008) as essential to the success of workplace wellness programs. Cannady (2020) extended Williams and Burgess' (2007) work on finding a right combination of workplace and recreational noise exposure and stressed the importance of selection of proper recreational programs. He asserted that their design should emphasize inclusion of occupational health and safety standards.

In a study conducted on the managerial and non-managerial staff of The World Shopping Mall at the city of Bhubaneshwar (India), Samantaray (2014) has found that the work environment, recreational and refreshment facilities at the workplace, fun at the work initiatives, and health and safety facilities at the work place are essential to develop interpersonal relationships and overcome fatigue, boredom, and the associated stress resulting from the job. The characteristics of an effective work environment include trust, mutual respect, mindfulness, openness to diversity and cooperation, which are strengthened by recreational activities. Organizations should aim at generation of a work environment which ensures easing of the effort and stress, while eliminating the causes of frustration, anxiety, and worry. Creating healthy workplaces to foster a positive work environment requires detailed planning and good implementation. This may involve changes in the organizational structure, culture, systems, and practices, if required.

Morrison and MacKinnon (2008) have done extensive review of the literature and interviews regarding Workplace Wellness Programs (WWPs) at Canada and other places. The employers, who employ more than 50% of Canadian population, are in prime position to take initiatives to impact health of their employees. The new millennium WWPs focus on organizational stress, including work-life balance and morale issues by integrating a comprehensive approach to wellness. The success of Employee Assistance Programs (EAPs) shows that a WWP with personalized health counseling-based needs would improve the utility and consumption of the initiatives. The organizations must foster a culture, wherein wellness must be a core business process and should be integrated with the strategy to achieve optimal results. Findings support that workplace wellness programs have a substantial effect on the indirect costs of the organizations, with significant impact on absenteeism and productivity. Besides, properly structured wellness programs enhance the corporate image of the organizations and improve employee retention and engagement.

In her study, Caroline (2013) has tried to determine the effect of workplace recreation on the well-being and performance of employees at the Commission for University Education (CUE), Kenya. Trying to separately analyze the impacts of different aspects of the recreation, viz. the physical fitness programs, mental health programs, and workplace entertainment programs, the study was conducted on 66 employees of staff at varied organizational levels of CUE. The results show a strong positive correlation of employee well-being with physical fitness and mental health, while the correlation with entertainment programs has been found less significant. Lack of time, inadequate recreational facilities, and distrust in the employer have been found as major deterrents in the positive participation of the individuals in the activities. The researcher emphasizes on the need of organizations to evaluate their recreational schedules so that the employees may be allowed to participate in the activities on a part-employee, part-company time basis. Among major challenges faced by the organizations in implementation of the recreational activities, the problem is being unable to quantify benefits from the recreational programs and getting employees to participate in the same. Gupta (2019) analyzed the need for human resource departments in Indian IT sector to invest in workplace recreation.

3 Research Gap and Objectives

The discussion so far establishes the importance of recreational activities and wellness programs at the workplace. However, there is very little evidence from these studies about the real effectiveness in the scenario of Indian IT companies. Gupta (2019) attempted to understand the need for these activities in the Indian IT sector, but has not assessed their present nature and effectiveness. Hence, a need has been felt to address the proposed research question.

An attempt has been made to formulate well worked-out questionnaire for surveying employees working in IT organizations in India to know about the actual impact of recreational activities held at their respective workplaces. The survey provided insights into the actual effectiveness of recreational activities and the impact these activities have on employees' satisfaction level and whether these recreational activities are helpful in improving the employee productivity or not. To summarize, answers and insights have been sought for the following research question:

'Are the recreational activities really recreational at the workplace?'

After consolidating the data and concrete opinions of employees, the results have been presented with the help of representative and inferential statistics, followed by some insightful recommendations.

3.1 Rationale

- As organizations spend a fortune on recreational activities for its employees, it becomes essential to realize the actual benefits of implementing these recreational activities.
- As already mentioned, the employees' satisfaction level largely depends on the environment in which he/she works. An employee who might be going through all the recreational activities available in his/her office may claim to have a low satisfaction level and dull/boring workspace.
- The effectiveness of recreational activities has a great impact on an individual employee's stress level and overall health. The measure of the effectiveness of recreational activities might provide the actual intensity of stress and pressure that an employee handles in an organization.

- Most of the books and a plethora of widely available researches in the area claim positive impacts of recreational activities on organization's productivity but if employees do not participate in these activities willingly and intensively, the benefits of these activities for those employees might not be significant.
- To know the actual trend and how employees actually perceive these recreational activities.

4 Research Design and Methodology

The research undertaken is a descriptive research based on primary data backed by secondary data obtained from the literature review. An attempt has been made to evaluate the impact of recreational activities at the workplace on aspects such as employees' individual performance, team performance, motivation, and life quality.

For this purpose, the impact assessing questions were categorized into individual heads, viz., *individual performance index, team performance index, motivation index,* and the *life quality index*. The mean of responses for the respective questions (as per the categories mentioned in the Inferential Analysis Section) has been used to estimate and analyze the respective indices. These indices have been analyzed with respect to the frequency of usage, which is the determining variable of the effectiveness of the available facilities.

Figure 1 represents the conceptual model.

Quantitative tools have been used to analyze the relation between the recreational activities at the workplace and the above-mentioned aspects.

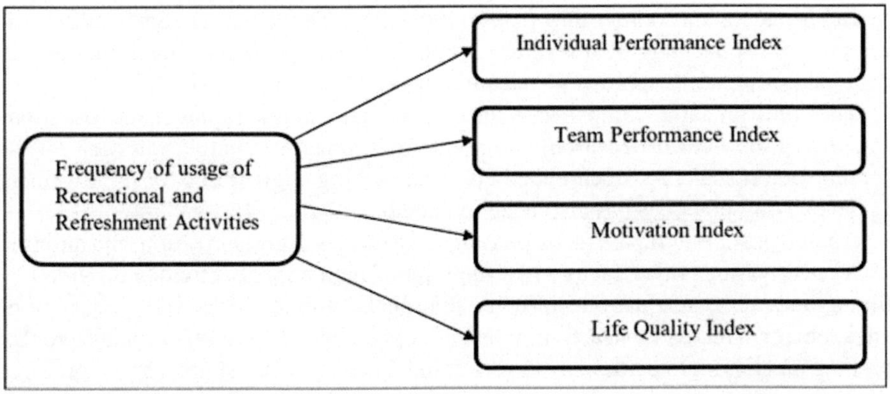

Fig. 1 Conceptual model

4.1 Sample Design and Size

The sample for the research constitutes the employees from different age groups, gender, and positions held in their organizations. The study has been limited to the Indian IT sector, which is one of the largest private sector employers. Further, the dynamic nature of IT sector may lead to increased workplace challenges and thereby higher stress levels implying the increasing need for the recreational activities at the workplace.

An approximate sample size between 100 and 150 was considered for the representative analysis. The objective was to ensure adequate representation of the target population. A total of 138 responses have been collected and analyzed.

4.2 Pilot Study

The pilot study done through the designed questionnaire was tested with responses from 20 employees. Cronbach's alpha value of 0.85 between the items assured the reliability of the questionnaire and set further stage for the full-fledged research.

4.3 Data Collection

Data has been collected from primary and secondary sources. The primary source of data has been the questionnaires, whereas the secondary sources of data include research papers and online information databases. The questionnaire method was used to collect data largely due to the simplicity and convenience in circulation and data management. Responses were sought using Google Forms.

The questionnaire comprised a mix of general demographic data, questions specific to the field of research, and a detailed impact-evaluating question on the 5-point Likert scale. An open-ended question seeking suggestions for improvement in the existing practices has also been included.

Apart from demographic factors like age, position in the organization, and duration of service, various other factors like the type of recreational activities provided by the organization, adequacy level of recreational activities, time and frequency of engagement in recreational activities by employees, employee motivational factors to participate and not to participate in recreational activities, most preferred workforce recreational activity by employees, company's priority toward recreational activities, and consideration of employee engagement in recreational activities for performance management system (PMS) have been considered as part of research.

The questionnaire has been normalized to clearly identify the impact of recreational activities at the workplace on employee morale, job satisfaction, motivation on the scale of 'highly negative impact, slightly negative impact, no significant impact, slightly positive impact, and highly positive impact.' A statement assuring them the confidentiality of the information provided was included.

4.4 Data Analysis

Quantitative analysis tools like MS Excel and IBM SPSS, and techniques like charting and correlation analysis have been used to analyze the data collected from the questionnaire. The analysis largely involved the use of descriptive statistics and inferential statistics. An attempt has been made to stratify the data in various strata depending on certain parameters, for instance, level of management. The objective of data analysis was to extract the information in the most meaningful and self-explanatory manner and to facilitate inferences and conclusions.

5 Results and Discussion

The primary data has been collected through questionnaire consisting of 17 questions, from 138 respondents and analyzed using appropriate tools, the salient findings of which have been summarized.

5.1 Descriptive Analysis

The descriptive analysis is based on the general and specific information collected from the survey. A total of 138 valid responses have been collected (where recreational facilities were available).

A significant 35% of the responses were from employees in significant decision-making positions of the respective organizations, whereas a good 44% of the responses were from employees who have been working in the organizations for more than three years. This gave good insights across all the categories and verticals of the organization (Fig. 2).

Fig. 2 Demographics of respondents

- Few intriguing facts have been unfolded about the perception of adequacy of recreational facilities as 45.7% responses report just adequate and only 8.6% responses report highly adequate.
- Indoor recreational activities have the lion's share in the type of recreational facilities provided by organizations with indoor games accounted to 79.4% responses followed by staff parties and gymnasium with 58.8% and 55.9%, respectively. Travel has least share with mere 5.9% responses.
- It is clearly evident from the survey that the motivational factor for employees to use the recreational activities is to reduce stress which accounted for 48.5% responses and the reason not to make use of recreational activities is lack of time which accounted for 60.3% responses. The top two preferred recreational activities among employees are found to be team building exercises and physical fitness activities which shared 60% and 55.4% of responses each.
- Around 50% responses stated that the organizations are giving moderate priority to the recreational activities at workplace, which shows a lack of systematic approach and significant weight attached to the activities.
- From the employees' perspective, it could be very well noted that the major reason for non-utilization of the facilities turned out to be *lack of time*. It is quite surprising to note that 72.5% responses reported that organizations are not taking employee participation in recreational activities into account in their performance evaluation system. The organizations care little about the use, nor do they let employees create some time for the same. Resultantly, the frequency of usage is very low among employees.
- Table 1 summarizes the various indicators used to develop further detailed insights on the sample data:

Table 1 Means and standard deviations of the responses

Indicators	Mean	Std. deviation
Frequency of usage	2.59	1.129
Impact on individual performance and productivity	3.28	0.998
Impact on individual work quality	3.33	1.080
Impact on individual job satisfaction	3.06	1.136
Impact on group participation and engagement	3.38	0.987
Impact on commitment and team performance	3.33	0.918
Impact on communication and confidence	3.71	0.842
Impact on absenteeism and motivation to work	3.10	1.214
Impact on morale	3.43	1.022
Impact on stress and anxiety	3.26	1.120
Impact on mental capability and alertness	3.39	0.958
Impact on work-life balance	3.10	1.059

The mean score of 2.59 for the frequency of usage with a standard deviation of 1.13 indicates that the employees do not use the available refreshment facilities in a very productive way. The reasons, from the results of other questions, is mainly because of the lack of time during the work time and lack of interest of the employers.

The mean scores of impacts of usage on different parameters are barely above 3, with a standard deviation of 1+ , which further indicates that there is no significant positive impact on the employees by making use of the existing recreational facilities.

5.2 *Inferential Analysis*

The impact on different indicators has been further analyzed with the help of *refreshment performance indices*, which have been obtained by clubbing and obtaining the means and standard deviations of the parameters, above. The indices have been classified as individual performance index, team performance index, motivation index, and life quality index. Each of these performance indices is discussed below.

5.2.1 Individual Performance Index (IPI)

This represents the impact of the recreational activities on the performance of the individual employees. It takes into account the following parameters:

- Impact on individual performance and productivity
- Impact on individual work quality
- Impact on individual job satisfaction

5.2.2 Team Performance Index (TPI)

This represents the impact of the recreational activities on the performance of the individual employees in their teams and workgroups. It takes into account the following parameters:

- Impact on group participation and engagement
- Impact on commitment and team performance
- Impact on interpersonal communication and confidence

5.2.3 Motivation Index (MI)

This represents the impact of the recreational activities on the motivation levels of the employees. It takes into account the following parameters:

- Impact on absenteeism and motivation to work
- Impact on morale

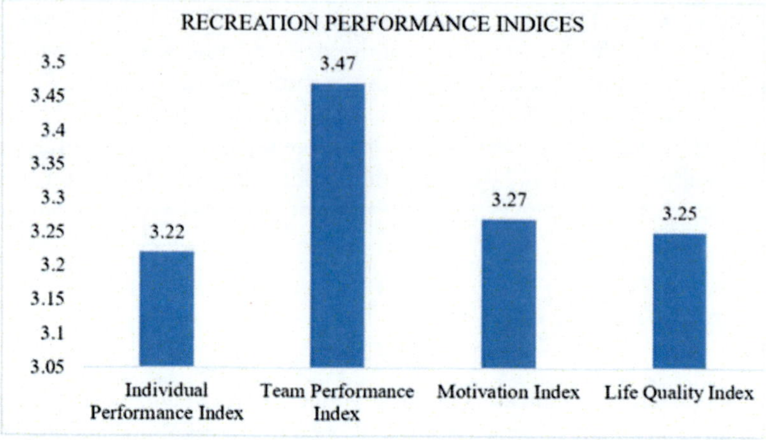

Fig. 3 Recreation performance indices

5.2.4 Life Quality Index (LQI)

This represents the impact of the recreational activities on the parameters determining the quality of life of the employees. It takes into account the following parameters:

- Impact on stress and anxiety
- Impact on mental capability and alertness
- Impact on work-life balance

Figure 3 summarizes the impact of refreshment activities as the respective indices.

The above results with means below 3.5 and standard deviation between 0.75 and 1 show that the impact of the recreational activities on improvement of the performance, motivation, or life quality has not been significant.

5.3 Correlation Analysis

The relation between the impacts of the recreational activities on different parameters has been analyzed with the help of Pearson's correlation obtained using statistical analysis tool—IBM SPSS Statistics 22. The correlation has been found between the frequency of usage of the recreational facilities and its impact on the individual performance index, team performance index, motivation index, and the life quality index. The detailed report of correlation analysis is available in Appendix. The results are as tabulated (Table 2).

Pearson's correlation coefficient of less than 0.3 in each of these indicates that there is little correlation between the usage of existing recreational facilities and performance of the employees. The correlation is least for the life quality index, which means that there has been no improvement in the quality of life of individual employees, which is the very purpose of the introduction of recreational facilities in the organizations.

Table 2 Correlations between frequency of usage and indices

Correlations

		Frequency of use	Individual Perf index	Team Perf index	Motivation index	Life Quality index
Frequency of use	Pearson correlation	1	0.207*	0.213*	0.291**	0.194*
	sig. (2-tailed)		0.015	0.012	0.001	0.023
	N	138	138	138	138	138

*Correlation is significant at the 0.05 level (2-tailed)
**Correlation is significant at the 0.01 level (2-tailed)

6 Conclusions and Recommendations

The findings suggest that that most of the workplaces do provide recreational activities at work and employees also find them as adequate or more than adequate. The corporate organizations are providing recreational activities at work in order to reduce the stress of work in them, help them in socializing with each other, developing skills like leadership, interaction and communication in them which in turn would boost the productivity of employees by improving their physical and mental strength, and thus will lead to improved organizational efficiency and profitability. But even after all such improvements in the organization, the employees are still not participating in those activities and the major reason which could be established from our study is the lack of time. Even though at the management level it is important that the employees should be motivated to improve their work performance, at the sub-level the culture which is followed is more toward achieving the targets at work rather than providing sufficient avenues/opportunities to let the employees participate in the recreational activities. Thus, it should be understood by the management that even though they could provide all the tools for recreational activities those will be of little use if they are not adequately utilized by the employees. Thus, the recreational activities should be well planned and managed in order to get the real outputs from them.

These recreational activities can be implemented in a more effective method by following some basic steps. Firstly, since each individual is different, it would be much better if an organization could know the hobbies of their employees and have those recreational activities which are more inclined to their hobbies. Secondly, the organization should encourage participation of employees in those activities. These can be done by giving them a day off from their work or by putting a hold on all the work at that time so that the employee will have only one choice and that to participate in those activities. The supervisors should make sure that the work of their subordinates is in line with those activities so that the work does not hinder the participation of employees in their recreation. The organizations should explore the opportunities for bottom-up approach while designing their recreational frameworks in order to use them as profit centers rather than the cost centers.

By following these basic steps, an organization can fully acquire all the benefits which the recreational activities can confer on them; otherwise instead of having a positive impact, these activities end up being just the cost centers, providing little benefit to the organization.

To summarize, the organizations in the Indian IT industry have invested in recreational and refreshment activities in order to improve their employees' productivity, motivation, and life quality. However, the present framework is not completely compatible with the design of their jobs, which is leading to underutilization of the facilities. Among those who use the facilities, there is no significant impact on their performance or life quality. Thus, the existing recreational framework may not be sufficient and the organizations need to review and redesign their frameworks to match to the requirements of the employees, so as to enhance the effectiveness of the facilities and positively impact the employee performance and work-life balance. As such, our very research question—'Are recreational activities really recreational at the workplace?' needs further exploration.

7 Scope for Future Research

This study challenges the effectiveness of the recreational framework in the Indian scenario and provides a framework for further research into this area. The research has been limited to the Indian IT industry only. Also, the sample size of 138 makes it difficult to generalize the study to the entire population. However, sufficient care has been taken to obtain the data and analyze it in the most objective manner possible.

For the aspiring researchers, this study may provide a platform to explore the scenario in other industries including manufacturing and service sectors. A cross-sectoral comparison of the approaches of managements toward recreation and employee well-being could reveal many more interesting facts. The difficulties in design, customization, and implementation of the recreational activities could be good area to delve into. If specific organizations could be accessed more formally, many more insights could be obtained. Further, some models could be designed and tested on pilot basis to help understand the behavior and aspirations of the Indian employees across sectors.

For the organizations, this study may serve as a mirror and provide food-for-thought for their betterment. Organizations may conduct much deeper internal analysis to find out specific reasons and factors and help resolve them and restructure their policies for the proper utilization of their resources. By trying to customize their organization-specific requirements, they might actually turn their human capital into their competitive advantage.

For the policymakers, regulatory authorities, and analysts, the study may help in understanding the differences across countries—why is the Indian scenario different from other countries, where the recreational activities have proven (as per the previous researches) to have a net significant positive impact. This may help in the making policy decisions.

Appendix

See Table 3.

Table 3 Correlations of performance indices

Correlations

		Frequency of use	Individual perf index	Team perf index
Frequency of use	Pearson correlation	1	0.207*	0.213*
	Sig. (2-tailed)		0.015	0.012
	N	138	138	138
Individual perf index	Pearson correlation	0.207*	1	0.715**
	Sig. (2-tailed)	0.015		0.000
	N	138	138	138
Team perf index	Pearson correlation	0.213*	0.715**	1
	Sig. (2-tailed)	0.012	0.000	
	N	138	138	138
Motivation index	Pearson correlation	0.291**	0.839**	0.762**
	Sig. (2-tailed)	0.001	0.000	0.000
	N	138	138	138
Refreshment index	Pearson correlation	0.194*	0.598**	0.673**
	Sig. (2-tailed)	0.023	0.000	0.000
	N	138	138	138

Correlations

		Motivation index	Refreshment index
Frequency of use	Pearson correlation	0.291**	0.194*
	Sig. (2-tailed)	0.001	0.023
	N	138	138
Individual perf index	Pearson correlation	0.839**	0.598**
	Sig. (2-tailed)	0.000	0.000
	N	138	138
Team perf index	Pearson correlation	0.762**	0.673**
	Sig. (2-tailed)	0.000	0.000
	N	138	138
Motivation index	Pearson correlation	1	0.609**
	Sig. (2-tailed)		0.000
	N	138	138
Refreshment index	Pearson correlation	0.609**	1
	Sig. (2-tailed)	0.000	

(continued)

Table 3 (continued)

Correlations

		Motivation index	Refreshment index
	N	138	138

*Correlation is significant at the 0.05 level (2-tailed)
**Correlation is significant at the 0.01 level (2-tailed)

References

Amber, V., & Mayer, K. A. (2016). Workplace related quality of life: Effect of available recreation facilities on physical activity and nutrition. *Virginia Henderson Global Nursing e-Repositry.*

Candice, M. B., Vurnakes, C., Martin, K., Perry, W., & Henderson, K. A. (2012). A case study of a workplace recreation-based physical activity program. *Leisure/loisir, 36*(1), 1–16. https://doi.org/10.1080/14927713.2012.701881

Cannady, R. (2020). Noise-not just in the workplace. *Professional Safety, 65*(03), 32–38.

Caroline, M. M. (2013). Effect of workplace recreation on employee wellbeing and performance: A case of the commission for university education (Cue). *Kenyatta University: Project Submitted to The School of Business In Partial Fulfillment of The Requirement For The Degree of Master of Business Administration.*

Gupta, B. (2019). The effect of participating in recreational activities on employee's productivity. *IME Journal, 13*(2), 113–120.

Gungaphul, M., Kassean, H., Ramnarain, T. (2012). Promoting recreation and leisure in the workplace. *African Journal for Physical Health Education, Recreation and Dance, 4*, 86–94. ISSN 1117-4315.

Harju, L., Hakanen, J. J., & Schaufeli, W. B. (2014). Job boredom and its correlates in 87 Finnish organizations. *Journal of Occupational and Environmental Medicine, 56*(9), 911–918.

Lacanienta, A., Duerden, M. D., & Widmer, M. A. (2018). Leisure at work and employee flourishing. *Journal of Leisure Research, 49*(3–5), 311–332.

Ledikwe, J. H., Semo, B. W., Sebego, M., Mpho, M., Mothibedi, H., Mawandia, S., & O'Malley, G. (2017). Implementation of a national workplace wellness program for health workers in Botswana. *Journal of Occupational and Environmental Medicine, 59*(9), 867.

Kerner, I., Rakovac, M., & Lazinica, B. (2017). Leisure-time physical activity and absenteeism. *Archives of Industrial Hygiene and Toxicology, 68*(3), 159–170.

Kohl, H. W., Craig, C. L., Lambert, E. V., Inoue, S., Alkandari, J. R., Leetongin, G., Kahlmeier, S., & Lancet Physical Activity Series Working Group. (2012). The pandemic of physical inactivity: global action for public health. *The lancet, 380*(9838), 294–305. https://doi.org/10.1016/S0140-6736(12)60898-8

Kukk, K., Tammaru, T., & van Ham, M. (2016). EthniCity of leisure: A domains approach to ethnic integration during free time activities.

Mokaya, S., & Gitari, J. W. (2012). Effects of workplace recreation on employee performance: The case of Kenya Utalii College. *International Journal of Humanities and Social Science, 2*(3), 176–183.

Morrison, E., & MacKinnon, N. J. (2008). Workplace wellness programs in Canada: an exploration of key issues. In *Healthcare Management Forum* (Vol. 21, No. 1, pp. 26–32). SAGE Publications. https://doi.org/10.1016/S0840-4704(10)60126-3

Okechukwu, C. S., Peace, N., & Ebele, O. (2019). Work stress and staff performance in selected banks in Anambra State. *International Journal of Management and Entrepreneurship, 1*(1), 143–162.

Samantaray, P. (2014). Strategy to develop an effective workplace environment. *International Journal of Language & Linguistics, 1*(1), 1–5.

Tuisku, K., & Houni, P. (2015). Experiences of cultural activities provided by the employer in Finland. *Old Site of Nordic Journal of Working Life Studies, 5*(1), 115–131.

Van den Brande, W., Baillien, E., De Witte, H., Vander Elst, T., & Godderis, L. (2016). The role of work stressors, coping strategies and coping resources in the process of workplace bullying: A systematic review and development of a comprehensive model. *Aggression and Violent Behavior, 29*, 61–71.

Williams, W., & Burgess, M. (2007). The combination of workplace and recreational noise exposure. *Acoustics Australia, 35*(3), 91.

Yang, X., Ge, C., Hu, B., Chi, T., & Wang, L. (2009). Relationship between quality of life and occupational stress among teachers. *Public Health, 123*(11), 750–755.

Green Employee Scorecard—A Conceptual Model to Align Individual Green Performance and Organizational Sustainability Goals

Arpita Ghosh and Shamima Haque

Abstract The globally growing concern for environmental sustainability has created obligation for every organization to adopt eco-responsive strategies in corporate sustainable agenda to achieve organizational excellence. An eco-protective organization culture with 'green' underpinning not only in thoughts and beliefs but also in practices and processes is possible only with transformation of employees into green employees. The present study attempts to construct a green employee assessment metric named Green Employee Scorecard to assess green contribution at individual level against four identified green perspectives, individual valuation indicators and relevant key result areas of Green HR. A research model was conceptualized which aimed to provide an understanding to Green HR practitioners, the strategic linkage of green result dimensions of the scorecard with environmental, financial and sustainability goals of the organization. The purpose was to assist Green HR managers to track and nurture green employees enabling strategic implementation of Green HRM.

Keywords Green employee scorecard · Green assessment tool · Green valuation indicators · Green HRM · Sustainability

1 Introduction

In recent times, the global business world is witnessing a paradigm shift from the traditional economic structure to a modern capacity-based economy where financial profit has to be accompanied with social and environmental well-being. The globally rising concern for environmental sustainability and the development of international

---

A. Ghosh (✉)
Department of Management, Maulana Abul Kalam Azad University of Technology, Kolkata, West Bengal, India

S. Haque
School of Management Studies, Techno Main Salt Lake, Sector V, Kolkata, West Bengal, India

© The Author(s), under exclusive license to Springer Nature Singapore Pte Ltd. 2022
A. Chandani et al. (eds.), *Achieving $5 Trillion Economy of India*, Springer Proceedings in Business and Economics, https://doi.org/10.1007/978-981-16-7818-9_7

benchmarks for environmental management have created obligation for every organization to accept corporate environmental strategies for being 'green' in their business practices with an aim to remain sustainably viable.

Sustainable development is conceptualized as utilization of human potential 'to improve their quality of life in ways which protect and enhance the earth's life support systems' (Parkin, 1999). Hence, no organization can implement its eco-focused business initiatives without its 'people' and their eco-sensitive approach towards performance. To reinstate, organizations can attempt a 'green' transformation only with its 'green' employees.

Green Human Resource Management (Green HRM) is referred to the concern of 'people' management measures and procedures towards the broader corporate environmental agenda.

Nowadays, Green HRM is significantly persuasive in enhancing employee consciousness and commitments on the issues of eco-sensitivity and to involve human resource initiatives to endorse sustainable business practices in the global context. Through its distinguished policies in recruitment, performance appraisal, training and development, discipline management, employee relations and reward systems, Green HRM aims to create, nurture and retain 'greening' within each employee of the organization so that the employee makes maximum individual contribution towards the achievement of 'green' business goals (Opatha, 2013).

A number of organizations across the globe have adopted Green HRM initiatives to successfully implement organizational and environmental strategies through different business functions. However, in India, Green HRM initiatives are still in a nascent stage. Here most of the initiatives in developing and nurturing 'green' employees seem to be confined only to few trainings, development and leadership efforts (Ghosh & Haque, 2019). From primary investigative discourses and informal talks with selected Green HR practitioners, the study has explored that the biggest challenge is to understand the dimensions of transforming a normal employee into green employee. There is no established tool depicting valuation criteria to evaluate individual green employee. Moreover, it is difficult to assess the contribution of individual green employee towards organizational profitability and sustainability.

Some organizations have established environmental management information systems and environmental audits (Carpenter et al., 1996) to monitor the level of pollution, resource usage, level of energy consumption and regulatory environmental requirements at the organizational level. The ISO 14001 provides the key performance indicators (like pollutant parts per million measures, weight to landfill, environmental audit scores, etc.) to help organizations in improving their environmental performance at the corporate level. Importantly, researchers argue that measuring employee green contribution in the organizational context is crucial to ensure realistic green performance at the institutional level in the long run (Milliman & Clair, 1996). Green HRM advocates integrating corporate environmental management objectives and targets with performance management system of the organization to specifically focus on 'green' valuation indicators at individual level. Firms need a green assessment tool to identify, track and measure each green employee at the operational level in order to nurture 'greening' within them. However, research works in this line are either inconclusive or sporadic. The present study attempts to propose a Green Employee Scorecard to evaluate the degree of employee eco-sensitivity and seeks to draw a plausible relevance of it to the strategic eco-protective vision.

HR Scorecard (Becker et al., 2001) aims to appraise employee behaviours resulting from the HR activities of an organization. Though it is in practice to estimate HR's contribution in generating organizational profitability and increasing shareholder value, HR Scorecard is not inclusive of the 'green' dimensions of HR. Extant literature indicates that successful implementation of corporate green initiatives demands strategic execution of Green HR that matches the organization's long-term objectives (Sudin, 2011). The present study attempts to construct a green employee assessment metric to identify the key result areas of Green HRM against four aspects of green employee purview (Opatha, 2013). This proposed tool is named as Green Employee Scorecard (Table 1), and it includes green valuation indicators against each key area to facilitate linkage of Green HRM with organizational profitability and sustainability goals through employee green results. The purpose is to assist Green HR managers to track and nurture green employees enabling strategic implementation of Green HRM.

2 Objective of the Study

The objective of the paper is manifold. Primarily, on the basis of the existing literature, the study aims to explore the concept of green employee and identify different dimensions and criteria to assess green employee.

Secondly, it proposes a conceptual measurement tool named Green Employee Scorecard to appraise green employees and assess green contribution at individual level.

Thirdly, a research model (Fig. 1) is conceptualized which aims to provide an understanding to Green HR practitioners of how the result dimension of Green Employee Scorecard can be linked with environmental, financial and sustainability goals of the organization.

Finally, the study aims to identify the key challenges in adopting and employing Green Employee Scorecard.

3 Literature Review

In recent years, the sustainable development concept is rapidly drawing attention to the corporate schedule. Business firms worldwide are adopting various environment management techniques to keep a balance between financial progress and conserving the environment for the future generation to flourish (Daily & Huang, 2001). Organizations need to channelize distinctive efforts of HRM for effective environmental management (Rothenberg, 2003). Green HRM aims to develop an environmentally

Table 1 Green employee scorecard: Dimensions of green employee scorecard indicating KRAs and indicators

Perspectives/dimensions	Key result area	Valuation indicators
Green competencies	Green recruitment/green selection/green training and development	Additional short-term courses/refresher programs/MDPs attended or completed regarding basic and contemporary environmental issues
		Green training hours (e.g. practical, seminars, conferences and lecture sessions) undertaken/attended per employee annually
		Total experience (e.g. green projects/efforts managed) in environmental management/sustainability
		Average time taken by the employee to transfer green training into operational efficiency
		Total number of ideas generated by the employee per year to develop new product/process/tool/solution regarding greening
Green attitude	Green culture/green job role analysis/green reward system	Belief: The extent to which the employee perceives greening as the most important virtue
		Affection: The extent to which employee can attach positive emotions such as happiness and satisfaction with greening
		Intention: The degree of seriousness and consistency attached with greening
		Motivation: The degree to which the employee is self-motivated regarding greening
Green behaviour	Green performance management/green reward system/green mentoring and leadership	Total number of voluntary green actions/activities the employee gets engaged with per year
		Total number of green official duties performed by the employee per year

(continued)

Table 1 (continued)

Perspectives/dimensions	Key result area	Valuation indicators
		Total number of green mentees per employee/leader/mentor per year
Green results	Green performance appraisal/green reward management	Percentage reduction in energy consumption per employee
		Percentage reduction in existing level of resource wastage achieved by the employee
		Percentage increase in revenue due to green initiatives per employee
		Number of green ideas generated/suggested by the employee that got implemented
		Number of green employees developed by the employee being assessed

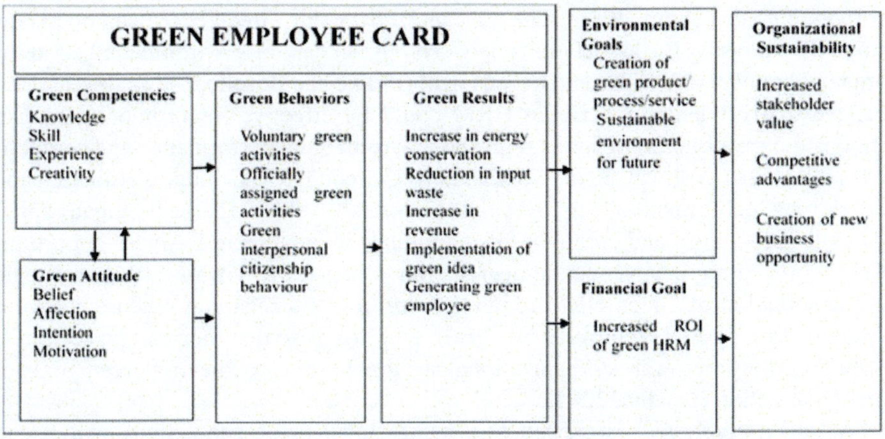

Fig. 1 Conceptual research model indicating linkages between individual performances with organizational sustainability goals

responsible and socially accountable workplace, and it helps to entwine corporate green management enthusiasm (Renwick et al., 2008) into all strategies, policies, processes and practices managing HR.

Green HRM attempts to amalgamate employee commitment and environmental compassion such that '… individual members embrace a concern for the natural environment in such a way that it becomes an integral component of the corporation's core values … it requires that the corporation seek, through attitudes and behaviours of its individual members, constantly and progressively to minimize the detrimental environmental impacts of all its activities …' (Keogh & Polonsky, 1998).

Environmental management experts argued that strategic eco-responsive efforts and initiatives of business firms should be incorporated into each individual job to mitigate the environmental degradation caused by the organizations (Arulrajah et al., 2015; Jabbour, 2011; Zoogah, 2011). Green management dimensions can be successfully entwined into individual job tasks and responsibilities and also as social, ecological and procedural stipulations making it imperative for job role (Jabbour, 2011), stating recruitment and selection criteria (Jackson et al., 2011; Renwick et al., 2013), developing consciousness, training and induction sessions (Daily et al., 2012; Renwick et al., 2013; Revill, 2000), assessing employee's job performance with regard to green-related criteria (Opatha, 2013; Renwick et al., 2013), framing environmental rewards and incentives (Jackson et al., 2011; Zoogah, 2011), organizing green discipline management (Arulrajah et al., 2015; Opatha, 2013) and employee relations and joint consultations (Renwick et al, 2008, 2013) for successful implementation of environmental procedures and policies. Ghosh & Haque (2018b) have attempted to design a gaming framework for the application of eco-responsive HR processes serving employees to enthusiastically appreciate and implement green initiatives adopted, through games that are playful and gainful at the same time.

Green HRM can be strategically used as a proactive tool that focuses on long-term corporate goals (Sudin, 2011). The concept of Strategic Green HRM can be understood by analysing the associations between human capital, environmental strategy, organizational performance and Green HRM (Paawe and Boselie, 2005). Researchers believe that implementing Green HRM could be effective for promoting human capital and resulting in organizational and environmental performance and competitive advantage (Deshwal, 2015; Opatha, 2013). Green HRM facilitates attracting and developing 'eco-sensitive' employees and provides a system to harness human capital (knowledge, energy and creativity of individual) in enhancing business opportunities by preventing environmental degradation (Bangwal & Tiwari, 2015). Strategic implementation of Green HRM requires recruiting and retaining green employees or converting normal employees into green employees so that they can make significant contribution towards organizational sustainability by achieving green goals of the organization (Opatha, 2013).

A 'green employee' is viewed as a nature lover or an eco-activist with green competencies and green attitude, who voluntarily or formally engages in green behaviour or stimulates others to become green and finally produces green results (Opatha, 2013). This view is supported by Daily and Huang (2001) who value green behaviour as a critical requirement of Green HRM and believe that without ample knowledge and skills in respect of 'greening', an employee cannot become green employee. Besides knowledge and skill, experience and creativity regarding 'greening' also add to green competencies. Green experience helps an individual to reduce the non-green behaviour (Muster & Schrader, 2011), and creativity drives an employee with innovative ideas about 'greening' (Chen, 2008).

Green attitude refers to appropriate 'cognition', 'affection' and 'intention' to believe and act 'green' (Opatha, 2013). A sense of joy, fulfilment and relatedness regarding 'greening' strengthens green attitude (Ashmos & Duchon, 2000). Green spiritual capital induces proactive inclination towards 'greening' through deeply driven intrinsic values, emotions and beliefs affirming environment-related capabilities (Ghosh & Haque, 2018a).

Green behaviour is a range of physical activities that contribute some positive impact on environmental sustainability as a whole. Green behaviour can be purely voluntary and deliberate or can be 'organizationally defined' and constitute a part of formal job requirements. When a green employee gets engaged in 'green interpersonal citizenship behaviour', he/she stimulates and persuades others to believe and behave 'green' (Opatha, 2013).

Producing green result is another critical dimension of green employee (Opatha, 2013). Such results essentially include those that are explicit and clearly oriented towards organizational performance. It might have two aspects, e.g. green innovations which refer to the implementation of innovative solutions to organization's environmental management and green outcomes that refer to the degree of accomplishment of precise environmental performance targets.

Numerous scholars feel that roles of green employee are of paramount significance in the success of organization's green initiatives (Arulrajah et al., 2015; Jackson et al., 2011; Opatha, 2013; Renwick et al., 2013). The correlation among green human resource initiatives, string of green competencies, competitive advantage and financial return is obvious in this context (Murad and Asaduzzaman, 2014). Though green result strategically contributes to organizational performance (both financial and environmental) and sustainability (Bangwal & Tiwari, 2015; Opatha, 2013), a majority of firms and managers failed to realize the connection as there is no assessment tool at practitioner's hand to trace the link. The research gap with regard to the valuation dimensions to track and collate green employee contribution and its discernible linkage to environmental, financial and sustainability objectives of the organization are proposed to be addressed by this study.

With its roots in Balanced Scorecard concept (Kaplan & Norton, 1992), HR Scorecard provides a comprehensive HR valuation model, which helps managers to pave the way to incorporate HR contribution to execute organizational all-level strategies (Murad and Asaduzzaman, 2014). It incorporates three perspectives—HR competency, HR engagement, and HR performance, for redefining the role of HR as a strategic partner (Murad and Asaduzzaman, 2014). However, HR Scorecard is relevant only to the practices of general HRM as it does not consider the 'green' aspects of managing human capital. Existing Green HRM literature suggests that assessment of green employee should be handled separately across different units of the firm and the indicators must be aligned with organizational strategic objectives (Arulrajah et al., 2015). In line with the literature survey, the study proposes a conceptual Green HR assessment tool to facilitate the strategic role of Green HR. Based on Green HR requirements, this tool includes four dimensions to tap the stock of green competencies, to track the level of employee engagement in green actions and activities and to explore the alignment between green result and strategic sustainable goals.

4 Methodology

The present study is qualitative in approach and attempts to define the concept of green employee and proposes to develop a conceptual assessment tool for Green HR. An extensive literature survey has been done to draw the logical inferences as the basis of this research work. Additionally, various investigative meetings with employees, HR managers and administrative staffs of different organizations have been conducted to support the research.

5 Findings

5.1 Concept of Green Employee

Based on the analysis of contemporary studies on Green HRM, the paper highlights the following key findings to define the concept of green employee:

(i) A green employee advocates preservation and conservation of nature and natural resources and prevents pollution by every possible means.
(ii) A green employee has sufficient amount of knowledge, skills, ability, experience and creativity regarding greening.
(iii) A green employee uses his green competencies and attitude as input to get engaged in green behaviour producing green results.
(iv) A green employee perceives 'greening' as one of the most important virtues and can associate positive emotions such as happiness and satisfaction with 'greening'.
(v) A green employee has the intention to seriously contribute towards 'greening'.
(vi) A green employee gets engaged in voluntary and assigned official green actions and activities in personal and professional life.
(vii) A green employee facilitates the organizational process of transforming a normal employee into green employee by motivating and assisting co-employees to think and act 'green'.
(viii) A green employee produces measurable green results which can directly be linked with organizational and environmental performance.

5.2 Green Employee Scorecard

A conceptual Green HR valuation tool named Green Employee Scorecard was developed to assess the degree of green component in an employee. The scorecard identified four perspectives of green employee that can be considered for evaluation—namely, green competencies, green attitude, green behaviour and green results. The scorecard essentially integrates the behavioural and results approach of individual performance management system for effective evaluation of both outcomes and outputs associated with greening. The study links these four dimensions to key result areas of Green HRM and identifies green valuation indicators against each perspective of green employee.

5.2.1 Green Competencies

Green competencies refer to sufficient amount of knowledge, skill, experiences and creativity regarding greening. Basic and contemporary knowledge regarding environmental sustainability helps employees to weigh various sides of an environmental problem and plays an important role in environmental decision-making. Awareness and experience regarding 'greening' enable employees to incorporate eco-accountability in business activities with an aim to minimize the impact of economic activity on the environment. Environmental education can be instrumental in contributing to behavioural changes within a normal employee and ultimately translating him or her into 'environmental citizen'. Employee ability to apply green knowledge in practice and to embrace environmentally friendly materials and technologies is crucial in generating significant green results. Creativity enables an employee to generate innovative ideas to create environment-friendly products, process or tools and apply competitive solutions to environmental problems. Employee Green Scorecard incorporated the following valuation indicators for green competencies:

(i) Additional short-term courses/refresher programs/MDPs attended or completed regarding basic and contemporary environmental issues.
(ii) Green training hours (e.g. practical, seminars, conferences and lecture sessions) undertaken/attended per employee annually.
(iii) Total experience (e.g. green projects/efforts managed) in environmental management/sustainability.
(iv) Average time taken by the employee to transfer green training into operational efficiency.
(v) Total number of ideas generated by the employee per year to develop new product/process/tool/solution regarding greening.

The key result areas in relation to green competencies may be green recruitment, green selection and green training and development.

5.2.2 Green Attitude

Green attitude that reflects the value and spirit of an employee towards eco-responsiveness is significantly shaped by green learning and perceptions. It is a psychological tendency that promotes positive inclination towards eco-focused activities. Green attitude combines appropriate belief, feelings and intention towards environmental activities. Belief may be conceived as the degree of importance an employee attaches to environmental protection. An employee's ability to associate positive emotions (such as joy, fulfilment and satisfaction). With 'greening' constitutes his or her feelings towards it. Intention to seriously contribute towards green agenda is imperative in producing impressive green results.

Green reward system has positive implication on green attitude as it motivates employees by linking financial and non-financial rewards with employee green initiatives. However, intrinsic motivation towards 'greening', which involves higher levels of personal involvement without an expectation, is vital in achieving incredible levels of performance and improvement in environmental management. Integrity is one of the most important ethical virtues employees need to inculcate in their green initiatives. Honest efforts in dealing with green issues in a consistent manner can ensure substantial progress towards environmental sustainability. Sincerity and truthfulness in 'greening' induce trust and help green employees play 'role models' setting noble examples for others. Green Employee Scorecard should include a composite green mindset index to assess the extent of employee cognition, affection, motivation and positive intention towards greening. This mindset index may incorporate the following indicators that can be measured using validated assessment tools:

(i) Belief: The extent to which the employee perceives greening as the most important virtue.
(ii) Affection: The extent to which employee can attach positive emotions such as happiness and satisfaction with greening.
(iii) Intention: The degree of seriousness and consistency attached with greening.
(iv) Motivation: The degree to which the employee is self-motivated regarding greening.

This dimension is related with green culture, green job role analysis and green reward system.

5.2.3 Green Behaviour

Green behaviour refers to employee engagement in green actions or activities that positively contribute to organizational green goals. Employee's eco-sensitive commitment depends on his perceptual experiences shaped from both personal life and professional life. Thus, green behaviour is facilitated in both life domains. Employees can get involved in discretionary green activity by setting personal agenda or they can accomplish it as official duties to fulfil formal job requirements. Employees can also be engaged in green behaviour by making other employees 'green'. Managers and leaders can act as green role models to stimulate and help normal employees to develop their green competencies and green attitude to be engaged in green behaviour. Green Employee Scorecard identified the following valuation indicators for green behaviour:

(i) Total number of voluntary green actions/activities the employee gets engaged with per year.

(ii) Total number of green official duties performed by the employee per year.
(iii) Total number of green mentees per employee per year (as a leader or mentor).

The key result areas against green behaviour include green performance management, green reward system and green mentoring and leadership.

5.2.4 Green Result

Finally, green result facilitates the link between employee green contribution and organization's financial, environmental and sustainability goals at strategic level. Green result refers to the ultimate green achievements accomplished by the employee. It refers to implementation and execution of green innovative ideas generated by the employee and specific green performance target achieved by the employee in the organizational context. The valuation indicators of green result include.

(i) Percentage reduction in energy consumption per employee
(ii) Percentage reduction in existing level of resource wastage achieved by the employee
(iii) Percentage increase in revenue due to green initiatives per employee
(iv) Number of green ideas generated/suggested by the employee that got implemented
(v) Number of green employees developed by the employee being assessed.

In Green Employee Scorecard, this perspective is linked with green performance appraisal and green reward management.

5.3 Linking Green Employee Scorecard and Organizational Goals and Strategies

The research model presents how Green Employee Scorecard dimensions can be connected with organization's financial, environmental and sustainability goals at the strategic level. Of the four dimensions, green competencies and green attitude are closely interrelated, and both of them significantly contribute in shaping green behaviour which in turn generates green results.

Green results such as reduction in input waste, increase in energy conservation, increase in revenue and decrease in costs, implementing innovative ideas to create eco-friendly products, processes and tools, directly contribute to strategic environmental objectives. An eco-protective organization culture with 'green' underpinning not only in thoughts and beliefs but also in practices and processes will promote and ensure sustainability in the long run benefitting the society and the planet and conserving for the future generations.

On the other hand, these green results enhance employee productivity by increasing operational efficiency and lowering cost, thereby contributing to the strategic financial objective by increasing ROI of Green HRM.

The achievement of the above financial and environmental objectives accentuates to ensure sustainability of the organization on a holistic perspective by creating new business opportunities, increasing competitive advantages and driving long-term shareholder value.

5.4 *Challenges in Implementation of Green Employee Scorecard*

Challenges for adopting and implementing Green Employee Scorecard would be in the establishment of structured green scoring framework with different valuation indicators across different units or specializations of the organization. Moreover, the process of collecting, recording, verifying and assessing correct employee data against each indicator would be cumbersome and time-consuming. Finally, Green Employee Scorecard may identify areas of an employee to be improved in order to transform him/her into green employee, but changing the employee behaviour can be demanding and lengthy.

6 Discussion

The finding of the study provides a comprehensive understanding of the concept of green employee to its readers. An approach towards environmental sensitivity can be self-stimulated or can be extrinsically generated through formalized structural framework of an organization. A conceptual assessment metric to gauge individual green contribution may not only serve an individual with gainful insights of his or her eco-responsive outcome vis-à-vis his comparable friends and peers but will also encourage the organization to implement a green 'auditable' framework for heightened environmental performance. Individual valuation indicators against each perspective should be further scaled down to quantifiable high, medium or low ratings and benchmarked against relevant point rating format. Scoring high or low points should motivate individual employees to 'act with responsibility' and participate in green initiatives and at the same time help organizational efforts channelize towards establishing a robust green culture to support and nurture 'every green thought, feeling, commitment and action' for sustainable viability.

7 Conclusion

Being 'green' in every practicable way is what the organizations should have in their strategic sustainable agenda to achieve organizational excellence. Green Employee Scorecard can be an effective individual assessment metric alongside an organizational interventional strategy to ensure green results and outcome in a structured manner. It can help HR practitioners' map the linkage of green employee contribution to verifiable green results that ultimately impact the 'triple bottom' deliverables.

After being empirically tested for reliability and validity, green individual scorecards can add substantial value in determining organizational 'green employee valuation index' as a measure of environmental performance.

8 Limitations and Scope of Future Research

The present study is conceptual and needs further empirical investigation for complete comprehension of its practical applicability. The indicators proposed against each dimension may undergo alteration, where new indicators may be added or proposed indicators may be dropped or modified for effective application in the organizations. Furthermore, the dimensions and indicators may be tailored to fit the requirements of the different organizations across sectors and job domains. The scorecard can be further extended, refined and represented as 'green employee maps' to appreciate the contribution of green employees in accordance with job roles or specializations or vertical and hierarchical differentiations.

References

Arulrajah, A. A., Opatha, H. H. D. N. P., & Nawaratne, N. N. J. (2015). Green human resource management practices: A review. *Sri Lankan Journal of Human Resource Management, 5*(1), 1–16.

Ashmos, D. P., & Duchon, D. (2000). Spirituality at work: A conceptualization and measure. *Journal of Management Inquiry, 9*(2), 134–145.

Bangwal, D., & Tiwari, P. (2015). Green HRM—A way to greening the environment. *IOSR Journal of Business and Management (IOSR-JBM), 17*(12), 45–53

Becker, B., Huselid, M., & Ulrich, D. (2001). *The HR scorecard: Linking people, strategy and performance.* Boston: Harvard Business School Press.

Carpenter, I., Milliman, J., & Clair, J. (1996). Best environmental HRM practices in the USA. In W. Wehrmeyer (Ed.), *Greening people—human resources and environmental management.* Sheffield, England: Greenleaf Publishing

Chen, Y. S. (2008). The driver of green innovation and green image—green core competence. *Journal of Business Ethics, 81*(3), 531–543.

Daily, B. F., Bishop, J. W., & Massoud, J. A. (2012). The role of training and empowerment in environmental performance: A study of the Mexican maquiladora industry. *International Journal of Operations and Production Management, 32*(5), 631–647.

Daily, B. F., & Huang, S. C. (2001). Achieving sustainability through attention to human resource factors in environmental management. *International Journal of Operations and Production Management, 21*, 1539–1552.

Deshwal, P. (2015). Green HRM: An organizational strategy of greening people. *International Journal of Applied Research, 1*(13), 176–181.

Ghosh, A., & Haque, S. (2018a). *Exploring green spiritual capital—a new dimension in green intellectual capital.* Paper presented at the 7th Annual International Conference on Sustainability (SUSCON), Shillong: IIM

Ghosh, A., & Haque, S. (2018b). *Gamification in Green HR: Utilizing employees' playful enthusiasm towards environmental sustainability.* Paper presented at the International Conference on Advances in Business Management (ICABM), Symbiosis Institute of Business Management, Pune

Ghosh, A., & Haque, S. (2019). *Exploring the role of green HRM towards the success of organizational green culture.* Paper presented at the International HR Conference on HR Trends 2030, West Bengal: IISW&BM

Jabbour, C. J. C. (2011). How green are HRM practices, organizational culture, learning and teamwork? A Brazilian study. *Industrial and Commercial Training, 43*(2), 98–105.

Jackson, S. E., Renwick, D. W. S., Jabbour, C. J. C., & Camen, M. M. (2011). State-of-the-art and future directions for green human resource management: Introduction to the special issue. *German Journal of Research in Human Resource Management, 25*(2), 99–116

Kaplan, R., & Norton, D. (1992). The Balanced scorecard—measures that drive performance. *Harvard Business Review*, 71–79

Keogh, P. D., & Polonsky, M. J. (1998). Corporate commitment to the natural environment: Issues in a team approach. In J. Moxon, & P. Strachan (Ed.), *Managing green teams: Environmental change in organizations and networks* (1st ed.). Sheffield, England: Greenleaf Publishing.

Milliman, J., & Clair, J. (1996). Best environmental HRM practices in the USA. In W. Wehrmeyer (Ed.), *Greening people—human resources and environmental management.* Sheffield, England: Greenleaf Publishing.

Murad, M. M. I., & Asaduzzaman, M. (2014). Human resource scorecard: A road map to balanced scorecard. *World Journal of Social Sciences, 4*(1), 70–79.

Muster, V., & Schrader, U. (2011). Green work-life balance: A new perspective for green HRM. *German Journal of Research in Human Resource Management, 25*(2), 140–156.

Opatha, H. H. D. N. P. (2013). Green human resource management: A simplified introduction. *Proceedings of the HR Dialogue, 1*(1), 11–21.

Paauwe, J., & Boselie, P. (2005). HRM and performance: What next? *Human Resource Management Journal, 15*(4), 68–83.

Parkin, S. (1999). Sustainable development—the human factor. In *Report of the Annual Conference: Environmental Management—using IT to Build More Sustainable Organisations*

Renwick, D. W. S., Redman, T., & Maguire, S. (2008). *Green HRM: A review, process model and research Agenda.* England: University of Sheffield.

Renwick, D. W. S., Redman, T., & Maguire, S. (2013). Green human resource management: A review and research Agenda. *International Journal of Management Review, 15*, 1–14.

Revill, C. (2000). The greening of personnel/human resource management an assessment. *International Journal of Applied HRM, 1*(3), 1–30.

Rothenberg, S. (2003). Knowledge content and worker participation in environmental management at NUMMI. *Journal of Management Studies, 40*, 1783–1802.

Sudin, S. (2011). *Strategic green HRM: A proposed model that supports corporate environmental citizenship.* Paper presented at the International Conference on Sociality and Economics Development, Singapore

Zoogah, D. B. (2011). The dynamics of green HRM behaviors: A cognitive social information processing approach. *German Journal of Research in Human Resource Management, 25*(2), 117–139.

A Study to Analyze Use of Social Media by Private and Public Sector Banks in India

Arti Chandani, Rajiv Divekar, B. Neeraja, Mita Mehta, and Rizwana Atiq

Abstract The banking system plays an important role in the modern Indian economy. Banking system had undergone a massive change or rather transformation post-1991 when banks have started seeing the face of competition from private and international players all around the world. Social media boon has also impacted banking sector, and use of social media for banking sector is increasing since past few years'. Present research focuses on how Indian Banks are using and can use social media as part of their strategy. This research has four major social media services as scope of the study for Indian Banks. These social media platforms are Facebook, Twitter, LinkedIn, and YouTube. Data for this research was collected through the official Web site of the banks. Kietzmann honeycomb model was used to analyze the collected data in terms of social media platform used by these private and public sector banks. This study focuses on Indian Banks which includes private and public sector banks together. Findings show that private sector banks are comparatively more active as compared to public sector banks. Researchers have shown interesting analysis in the paper which will be useful to Indian Banks.

Keywords Indian banks · Communication · Social media · Strategy · Public sector banks · Private sector banks

---

A. Chandani (✉) · R. Divekar · M. Mehta
Symbiosis Institute of Management Studies, Symbiosis International (Deemed University), Range Hills Road, Khadki, Pune, India
e-mail: arti.chandani@sims.edu

R. Divekar
e-mail: director@sims.edu

M. Mehta
e-mail: mita.mehta@sims.edu

B. Neeraja
Dr. MGR Educational and Research Institute University, Maduravoyal, Chennai, India
e-mail: neeraja.mba@drmgrdu.ac.in

R. Atiq
Integral University, Kursi Road, Lucknow, India

© The Author(s), under exclusive license to Springer Nature Singapore Pte Ltd. 2022

A. Chandani et al. (eds.), *Achieving $5 Trillion Economy of India*, Springer Proceedings in Business and Economics, https://doi.org/10.1007/978-981-16-7818-9_8

1 Introduction

Print and outdoor media has given boon to advertising and promotion to marketers. All these media's had one or the other limitations. For instance, you cannot get instant feedback of viewers on newspaper or print media which you can get nowadays on social media platform. Social media is a platform where user and marketer can get instant feedback and communication about subject matter. User on social media has benefit of feature of uniformity which means treating equal all irrespective of background. When we think of bank, we would think of formal and very professional bankers who would rather believe on more checklists or compliances rather than pleasing customers. The world is shifting now, and even banks are trying to raise community rather than appear rigid and imposing. Focusing on customer service and adopting the personality and create a brand through social media platform is one of the objective which bank seek to achieve through social media. Indian banking system has come a long way. From the notion of banks for few users to banks for all, it has been transforming tremendously over the last decade. Banks are not only improving in terms of its reach but also in terms of its presence on social media. Main objective of this research paper is to verify usage of the social media as strategy by Indian banks including public and private sector banks. This research aims at studying the social media platform usage by Indian Banks and how it can be differentiated. Social media is multidirectional and user-generated communication that is the main feature which differentiates social media from the traditional forms of advertising. Web sites mostly offer content from an entity or posted information about some products (Ashley & Tuten, 2015). It sounds difficult to measure the impact of message on social media. Whereas before implementing social media, organizations need to clarify the goal, objective, and measurement tools required to achieve the desired result of the adoption (Castelo Branco & Lima Rodrigues, 2006). Reasons for banks using or refraining itself for using social media could be lower demand from the side of customers for such interaction, probability of involvement of risks and hence more and more young banks are using it for marketing strategies rather than using social media for other purposes (Chandani et al., 2018). Marketing on social media is the use of a method which permits markets to engross with each other to pool resources and interact with the aptitude of those who share in it for the purpose of marketing products and services (Hanna et al., 2011). There are many ways through which social media marketing can be done but which are most popular and cost effective that organization has to decide based on the resources it has and goal it sets. Facebook and Twitter are the mail tools used by banks (Hanna et al., 2011). Most of the social media tools are used standalone, but if they are integrated based on strategic marketing tools and objectives, then it would turn social media into a firm's marketing communications strategy (https://about.linkedin.com/). Organizations have to make an attempt and integrated efforts for successful social media marketing. Incentivizing the participants, frequent updates, is creative, and experiential strategies should be used customer engagement which makes it more personal and effective (https://about.twitter.com/). There are different models through which social media platform usage can be analysed and one of those model is social organization model consisting of five different ways in which the marketer can establish social media message. These ways are centralized, coordinated, organic, and so on. This learning curve of social media strategy is intended to assist marketer in designing effective message which suits budget and content, beliefs, and values of particular organization. Social Engagement Journey model was coined by Sean O'Driscall from the Ant's Eye View firm in the year 2010 (https://en.wikipedia.org/wiki/Facebook). This model emphasizes some steps which would help organization in developing successful strategies for social engagement, viz. traditional stage, silo stage, operationalizing stage, and so on. These various stages and model can help organization to understand how to connect with audience with greater impact and effectiveness. Another model developed by authors Charlene Li & Josh Bernoff in the book Groundswell (HBR Press), known as POST model. Here, in the acronym, *P* refers to people, *O* refers to objectives, *S* refers to strategy, and *T* refers to technology. It is a proven framework for development of social media strategies (https://www.rbi.org.in/commonman/english/scripts/banksinindia.aspx#NB). Another model on social media strategy which researchers have followed is ACCESS model where *A* is for audience, *C* stands for concept, *C* stands for competition, and *E* for execution. Here, very important part which has been mentioned is about audience who is in reality going to deal with the content. Each business organization has some peculiar content especially designed as value propositions which intended to reach to its target audience. Social media visibility can be optimized by looking into its value proposition as well as the level of competition organization is facing (Kaplan & Haenlein, 2010). OASIS model has also been discussed in the area of social media research which helps a marketer in getting clarity in designing the campaign. Banks have more reasons to justify its existence among their clients through the use of social media (Kietzmann et al., 2011). Banks with higher visibility on social media show better performance and these banks have concern for better image through systematic disclosure as reported in the context of Portuguese banks (Kietzmann et al., 2011).

2 Materials and Methods

This research aims at understanding how Indian Banks are utilizing social media as their marketing tool. For this research, researchers have taken most famous four social media platforms which are Facebook, Twitter, YouTube, and LinkedIn. Researchers have used sample banks' Web sites to arrive at the social media usage of these banks, and data was collected. Kietzmann honeycomb model has been used to analyze and categorize how Indian banks are emphasizing on social media to market their products as well as their brands. To what extent social media platform is being capitalized is the aim of this research. For this study, researchers have taken entire census for the study including public and private sector banks. Kietzmann mentioned a root as to how social media tool may be used purposefully. This model is identified as a honeycomb model (Li & Bernoff, 2008). As a part of this research, researchers have used honeycomb model of social media to evaluate social media strategy among banks. This model gives insights about how user/customer engrosses into social media. This honeycomb model has seven blocks that permit specific aspect of social media and its consequences for organizations. Organizations can relate to this honeycomb model by analyzing which facet is more relevant to their social media strategy, and accordingly, they can comprehend and improve social media utilities and strategy for the messages.

Above figure shows the seven dimensions of honeycomb model used in this research for study of social media presence of Indian Banks. Dimension **Identity** of the model talks about identity of user and to what extent user reveals the information. The identity dimension has its analytical importance in social media marketing, mainly as it is central to how one targets leads with advertising as well as outreach. **Presence** dimension highlights the presence of other users on particular social media platform. Users do get influence by the existence of other users on the particular stage. Another dimension in the honeycomb model is **relationship** which highlights the level to which users can share to other users. The next part is **reputations** which means the range within which users may have faith on involvement in online social communications. Social platform features a large range of tools for quantification of repute of others, which includes likes, blue ticks, connections, and follower count. Another dimension is **conversation** which is the extent to which users interact and communicate with others. **Groups** dimension highlights how social media platforms enable users to form communities and groups. Some companies have some policy for being in group or guidelines that member has to follow. Marketers can focus on particular community and make focal point accordingly. For example, in the case of banks, those who are credit card users can make form of users' community to address their specific requirements. Another dimension is **sharing** which means how do users share content on social medial? Sharing of personal information like photos, videos and other information makes social media social. People will be encouraged to share on social media based on positive reinforcement they get on the channel or medium.

Based on extensive literature study, researchers have analyzed that there have been very less studies which have been conducted in the subject of social media usage by Indian Banks especially considering entire census in center. Based on best of knowledge, this study is exclusive and can be considered as one of the first such study of presence of Indian banks on social media by comparing major four social media Web sites. This study will be great useful to not only marketers but also to Indian Banks for further building on strategies. This research mainly focuses on following objectives:

1. To categories selected social media platforms as per honeycomb model
2. To evaluate the usage of social media by Indian Banks (public and private)
3. To classify banks based on their usage of social media tools.

As emphasized earlier, this research emphasizes over four trending social media tools, namely YouTube, Facebook, LinkedIn, and Twitter. Online social media presence of these banks was collected from their official Web site, and the time period for the study was the month of January, 2018. Data was gathered from all four social

Fig. 1 Honeycomb framework of social media

media and analyzed through Kietzmann's honeycomb framework (Fig. 1) which is very important in identifying the presence on social media.

This study has limited scope up to Indian banks. Official information of these banks has been gathered from Reserve Banks of India (RBI) Web site. Main objective of this research was to understand the social media as a tool used by these Indian banks to engage the customers. Wherever official media information was not sufficient for data, researchers have used social media search engine to get detail information.

3 Results

The components of social media have been categorized in the honeycomb framework's functionalities, and these components represent dependent variable of the study (Table 1).

Facebook

Facebook is widely known social networking site nowadays. Not only end users but companies are nowadays endorsing most of their products and carrying their social media pages on Facebook. Facebook is to be considered as most evolving marketing platform (Mitic & Kapoulas, 2012). Facebook-related data of Indian public sector

Table 1 Analysis of social media features as per honeycomb model

Function	Facebook	Twitter	YouTube	LinkedIn
Identity	Name of account, design, color, and logo	Name of account, design, color, and logo	Name of account, design, color, and logo	Name of account, design, color, and logo
Group	Page	Lists	Channel	Page
Relationships	Fans	Followers	Subscribers	Connections
Presence	Yes	Yes	Yes	Yes
Sharing	Photos, links, and posts	Tweets, retweets, and media	Upload video and views	Connections, videos, events, and News
Conversations	Discussion and comments	Tweets	Subscriber's and viewer's comments	Comments
Reputations	Verified information and content	Verified tweets	Channel design and views	Job posting, notification, and verified pages

banks has been mentioned in Table 2. For this analysis, gray color scheme has been used that shows the usage. Dark gray color means more usage and so on and so forth.

Most of the banks have clear identity, and it was visible through their logos and presence on social media. During research, it was observed that some places logos were not clear which would impact the presence and recognition of the particular bank. The number of active users on Facebook has increased more than 30% in the previous year that shows the importance of having corporate page on this social media site.

Presence of many Indian banks on social media is good sign. It was also found during this research that Facebook page was not found of Central Bank of India, Canara Bank, and Syndicate Bank. In this research, it has been seen that most of the banks are active on Facebook that shows and reflects the trust factor of banks on social media. Highest number of followers were of SBI representing the number of 15,139,880 while least followers were from UCO Bank with a number of just 1441.

Presence SBI is showing lead followed by other bank as far as the use of Facebook is concerned. Allahabad Bank has its Facebook page though not verified but is supposed to be managed by Allahabad Bank (as per online displayed credentials) from its headquarter—Kolkata. It did have one more page with about 6200 likes but is un-operational since December 23, 2012, and from its HQ at Kolkata only. Andhra Bank, apart from normal festive wishing posts, also wishes on board exam seasons (e.g., wishes for 10th board exam) catering to extreme insight to empathize with its customers via social media platform. Dena Bank does not hold any FB page, but surprisingly, its Facebook page is a fan made page by a person named Vijay Tondon and is regular in replies having 2962 followers which is way better than some banks having their FB page. United Bank of India's FB wall post, dated February 26, 2018, this bank won "Social Banking Excellence Awards 2017" under ASSOCHAM. This

Table 2 Indian public sector banks and Facebook usage

Banks	Identity	Group	Relationships	Presence	Sharing	Conversation	Reputations
State Bank of India							
Punjab National Bank							
Bank of Baroda							
Bank of India							
Canara Bank							
Union Bank of India							
IDBI Bank							
Syndicate Bank							
Central Bank of India							
Oriental Bank of commerce							
Allahabad Bank							
Andhra Bank							
Bank of Maharashtra							
Corporation Bank							
Dena Bank							
Indian Bank							
Indian Overseas Bank							
United Bank of India							
Punjab and Sind Bank							
UCO Bank							
Vijaya Bank							

bank is also the one which makes posts in National Language Hindi. Only six banks have verified account, viz. SBI; PNB; Bank of India; Bank of Baroda; Union Bank of India, and IDBI Bank. Syndicate Bank, Corporation Bank, Central Bank of India, Canara Bank, and Dena Bank do not have Facebook page at all.

Indian Private Sector Banks and Usage of Facebook

On Face book while doing survey about private banks, it was noticed that most of the banks had their logos and presence on social media, but some of banks such as Axis Bank, IndusInd Bank, Federal Bank, and City Union Bank were not very good (Table 3).

Presence of private banks on Facebook is quite more visible as compared to public sector banks. This shows that banks are taking these social media platforms quite seriously and actively. On Facebook, it was seen that number of followers can help these banks to connect with their customers. Yes Bank has the more numbers of the users or followers as the number was 7,186,889, while the least followers were 80 for Nainital Bank. It was also found that the City Union Bank page was not confirmed, by Facebook that is to be perceived as poor strategy. In this situation, users are

Table 3 Indian private sector banks and Facebook usage

Banks	Identity	Group	Relationships	Presence	Sharing	Conversation	Reputations
Axis Bank Limited							
Bandhan Bank Limited							
Catholic Syrian Bank Limited							
City Union Bank Limited							
DCB Bank Limited							
Dhanlaxmi Bank Limited							
Federal Bank Limited							
HDFC Bank Limited							
ICICI Bank Limited							
IndusInd Bank Limited							
IDFC Bank Limited							
Jammu and Kashmir Bank Limited							
Karnataka Bank Limited							
Karur Vyasa Bank Limited							
Kotak Mahindra Bank Limited							
Laxmi Vilas Bank Limited							
Nainital Bank Limited							
RBL Bank Limited							
South Indian Bank Limited							
Tamilnadu Mercantile Bank Limited							
Yes Bank Limited							

sometimes confused about the authenticity of page. HDFC Bank is using Facebook by providing news and tips on the union budget 2018. The usage of Facebook is not perceived much by other banks, including HDFC bank, in covering the important details of the Indian economy. Many of the above banks do not have verified pages, e.g., Bandhan, Catholic, City Union, Nainital Bank, etc. There are banks who have last updated anything on FB around 6 months back, E.g., Dhanlaxmi Bank and J&K Bank.

Twitter

Twitter is another most commonly used social media platform after Facebook. It is microblogging and news feeding site in year 2017, and the character limit was increased to 280. When it comes to banks, most of the times customers and users believe to go on Twitter page and read about the announcement of quarterly results and profit news feeds (Murdough, 2009). Twitter is considered as most official channel as compared to others based on the perception it has built so far among the users.

Indian Public Sector Banks and Twitter Usage

After collecting data about Twitter used as social media instrument by the public sector banks, researchers have analyzed the data. SBI has largest followers on the Twitter count at 3,049,530, shadowed by IDBI Bank which has 160,241 as followers. UCO Bank has least followers where the number stood as 46. It has also been observed that conversation is very important for Twitter page. Banks like SBI are dynamic when it is matter of optimum usage of Twitter, and they enthusiastically engage with their followers. This is seen by tweets and replied by SBI, tailed by Punjab National Bank and IDBI Bank those who have about 40 tweets/week. Union Bank and SBI are seen to be most active on Twitter and immediately respond to their customers. It was seen that PNB Banks reply in a minute and few banks reply in some hours that show the efficiency of banks on social media.

SBI tweeted 600 tweets/week or more, whereas Union Bank of India and Canara Banks are having 8–10 tweets per week. Central Banks of India and Syndicate Bank are not substantiated pages during the course of research. SBI and Bank of Baroda banks have been on Twitter for one or more news feeds relating to budgets and monetary policy as well as reviews. Same strategies can be used by other banks to be in news and heading the lead (Table 4).

Syndicate Banks and Central Bank of India had fake pages, and during the course of this research, it was found that SBI, Bank of Baroda, and Canara Banks, etc., did have verified page on Twitter. Bank of Baroda, Canara bank, and Punjab National Bank are using it soberly, while there is Bank of India and Oriental Bank of Commerce were not found on Twitter. Allahabad Bank joined Twitter in January 2018 only (though previously they had Twitter handles but are currently inactive) and has tweeted replica of their FB posts. UCO Bank has tried to open Twitter handle many times before but have been inconsistent to operate it. The recent one was opened in December 2017, may be to update about their platinum jubilee. Vijaya Bank is being very active on Twitter replies to customer's tweets in 2–3 days which should not be the case. This shows that they may have less number of people for social media, i.e., social media managers. This can also be verified by the fact that Twitter posts are almost similar to FB posts. Only five banks have verified Twitter handles, viz. SBI; BOB; Canara Bank; Union Bank of India; and IDBI Bank.

Use of Twitter by Indian Private Sector Banks

Yes Bank happens to be the largest bank follower of other Twitter users having a total of 3,611,649 followers, tailed by ICICI Bank with 394,358 supporters. Nainital Bank has least followers with 13 shadowed by Dhanlaxmi Bank. Marketing communication through Twitter is very important nowadays. The first one to have its presence on Twitter among the selected bank is Yes Bank which joined Twitter in May 2009, while most of other banks have joined in during 2010–2012. The latest to join Twitter is IDFC which joined in August 2015 (Table 5).

Banks like Yes Bank and ICICI Bank were found to be very live and active on Twitter. This was observed with the "Tweets and replies" by Yes Bank and ICICI Bank. Yes Bank has 9–10 tweets per week roughly, shadowed by ICICI Bank 8–9 tweets per week approximately. ICICI Bank is having on average 4–5 answers per

Table 4 Indian public sector banks and use of Twitter in accordance with honeycomb model

Banks	Identity	Group	Relationships	Presence	Sharing	Conversation	Reputations
State Bank of India							
Punjab National Bank							
Bank of Baroda							
Bank of India							
Canara Bank							
Union Bank of India							
IDBI Bank							
Syndicate Bank							
Central Bank of India							
Oriental Bank of commerce							
Allahabad Bank							
Andhra Bank							
Bank of Maharashtra							
Corporation Bank							
Dena Bank							
Indian Bank							
Indian Overseas Bank							
United Bank of India							
Punjab and Sind Bank							
UCO Bank							
Vijaya Bank							

day and is replying on daily basis. Yes Bank is extremely dynamic on Twitter and is responsive to the tweets every 45–50 min. Axis Bank has also been active and replies on daily basis. RBL Bank replies within 25–30 min. As seen, these are a few instances that show that banks that are fairly active in response. Research also shows that Twitter can be utilized in much better way than this. City Union Bank is having 2–3 tweets per month though RBL Bank, Yes Bank, Kotak Mahindra Bank, among others, have tweets that are frequent like 15–25 tweets/month. Furthermore, IndusInd Bank has also been quite active on Twitter. City Union Bank is taking total 148 tweets that are lowest among sample, and City Union Bank page is also not verified. Federal Bank's Twitter page is also not verified. HDFC Bank, ICICI Bank, and Yes Bank are using Twitter to notify to the consumers about the highpoints of the budget. Axis Bank had organized pre-budget meet in Mumbai, and this was tweeted by them. HDFC bank also shared a news on pre-budget which was given by their Chief Economist, Mr. Abheek Barua. RBL Bank had stated the tweets associated to the tax saving opportunities in the stir of forthcoming fiscal year completing as of March 2018, while ICICI Bank tax filing service offers on their Twitter page. Yes Bank also made their tweets on the Goods and Services Tax (GST) which was

Table 5 Use of Twitter by Indian private sector banks by using honeycomb

Banks	Identity	Group	Relationships	Presence	Sharing	Conversation	Reputations
Axis Bank Limited							
Bandhan Bank Limited							
Catholic Syrian Bank Limited							
City Union Bank Limited							
DCB Bank Limited							
Dhanlaxmi Bank Limited							
Federal Bank Limited							
HDFC Bank Limited							
ICICI Bank Limited							
IndusInd Bank Limited							
IDFC Bank Limited							
Jammu and Kashmir Bank Limited							
Karnataka Bank Limited							
Karur Vyasa Bank Limited							
Kotak Mahindra Bank Limited							
Laxmi Vilas Bank Limited							
Nainital Bank Limited							
RBL Bank Limited							
South Indian Bank Limited							
Tamilnadu Mercantile Bank Limited							
Yes Bank Limited							

implemented from July 1, 2017, in India. Other banks such as IDFC, Federal Bank, and Kotak Mahindra Bank did not have any major update of the budget or tax saving schemes. The liveliness and timeliness of the tweets and response banks had given. If banks can hire some of their talent pool to manage these social media tweets/pages, it is predictable to have more active announcement. Kotak Mahindra Bank, IndusInd, RBL Bank, and Axis Bank found to have fake profile as well, while there were some banks that did not have fake pages on Twitter such as Federal Bank, ICICI Bank, and HDFC Bank. Many of the above banks do not have verified pages, e.g., Bandhan, Catholic, City Union, Nanital Bank, etc. Tamilnadu Mercantile Bank does not have any presence on Twitter. Only few banks are there who are commenting back to the queries or complaints of the users on Twitter on regular basis. These are IndusInd, Karnataka, South Indian, RBL, and Yes Bank. Many of the banks have their pages which have certain amount of likes and followers but not even a single post is there on the accounts. For example, Dhanlaxmi Bank and Nainital Bank on Twitter have no tweets.

YouTube

YouTube social media Web site located at America. YouTube was established in year 2005. From year 2006, YouTube gave freedom to the user to upload content with condition to meet age criteria. YouTube gets chief source of revenue from various endorsements YouTube is able to pull over 1.8 billion consumers every month—and that is just the users who are just logged in. All these makes YouTube most popular Web site. There are nine banks within the sample that have their respective YouTube channels, namely Canara Bank, Union Bank of India, SBI, BOB, IDBI, Corporation Bank, Indian Banks, Andhra Bank, and Vijaya Bank. Banks such as Bank of India, Syndicate Bank, Central Bank of India, PNB, Indian Overseas Bank, United Bank, and Oriental Bank of Commerce, etc., do not have YouTube channel. Having YouTube channel can benefit banks to create content which can reach to the millions of active and prospective users at the same time. Having YouTube channel may not give instant benefits, but it will surely give benefits of presence.

Use of YouTube by Indian Public Sector Banks

The subscribers to the YouTube channel may not be the actual users of these banks. Also, counting channel viewers as customers or prospective users is also not correct approach. The correct approach is to integrate these YouTube channels to Facebook and Twitter, thereby getting benefits out of these. Researchers observed during research that there were 19 comments on IDBI video whereas no comments seen on SBI and Canara Bank. State Bank had highest upload of videos on YouTube which is more than 450 which was then seen by IDBI. Vijaya Bank of India has the least views as 25,431 as on January 27, 2018 (Table 6).

During this research, we found that there were no fake profile that is to be measured as decent. Few banks like State Bank of India and Bank of Baroda are steady in positioning the videos although other banks are not so steady in doing so. Andhra Bank posted almost 48 videos (90%) out of 53 videos all at once in October–November

Table 6 Use of YouTube by Indian public sector banks as per honeycomb model

Banks	Identity	Group	Relationships	Presence	Sharing	Conversation	Reputations
State Bank of India							
Punjab National Bank							
Bank of Baroda							
Bank of India							
Canara Bank							
Union Bank of India							
IDBI Bank							
Syndicate Bank							
Central Bank of India							
Oriental Bank of commerce							
Allahabad Bank							
Andhra Bank							
Bank of Maharashtra							
Corporation Bank							
Dena Bank							
Indian Bank							
Indian Overseas Bank.							
United Bank of India							
Punjab and Sind Bank							
UCO Bank							
Vijaya Bank							

2017, post which there are no further updates. Also, the videos are very good in terms of different procedures explained from customer's perspective. Only five banks have official (declared) YouTube channel, viz. SBI, Canara Bank, Union Bank of India, IDBI Bank, and Indian Banks.

Use of YouTube by Indian Private Sector Banks

HDFC and Axis Banks had 27 comments, while IndusInd and RBL had nine comments. There were no comments for other banks. Axis Bank has highest numbers of video upload in comparison with any other private bank, wherein this number stands at 996 followed by HDFC Bank and ICICI Bank at 372 and 359, respectively. City Banks did not have its own channel. Total views are maximum for ICICI Bank standing at 44,103,866 followed by HDFC Bank where the number of views was 34,176,199. The smaller banks such as IDFC Bank and RBL Bank had viewers 3,140,572 and 5,130,211, while Yes Bank had very less views as 288,073 as on January 27, 2018. Laxmi Vilas Bank had only one video, while the views were 28,441 for this. The foremost usage of YouTube channel by banks is with respect to notifying the customers on various offers, tips and procedures, and initiatives (Table 7).

It was observed that there were no fake profiles. Few banks such as Axis Bank was been regular in stationing the video, while other banks were inconsistent in doing the same. Many of the above banks do not have verified pages, e.g., Bandhan, Catholic, City Union, Nainital Bank, and few others. City Union Bank, Dhanlaxmi Bank, Karur Vysya Bank, Nainital Bank, and Tamilnadu Mercantile Bank do not have presence on YouTube. Only three banks are sharing regularly. These are Axis Bank, Kotak Mahindra Bank, and Yes Bank. There are banks who have been there for more than 2 years, but the number of videos posted by them is less than 10, e.g., Lakshmi Vilas Bank and Catholic Syrian Bank.

LinkedIn

Most professional networking site is LinkedIn network which was started 2003 and has more than 546 million memberships through 200 countries at present (O'Driscall, 2018). LinkedIn emphasizes professional data, inspiring members to make professional profiles on LinkedIn. LinkedIn users have made profiles that are very much specialized, with low data about interests and affiliation and all (Papacharissi, 2009). The connection on LinkedIn is hired to preserve and can be referred to each other (Safko & Brake, 2009).

Use of LinkedIn by Indian Public Sector Banks

Identity on LinkedIn ought to be considered as genuine. When it comes to banks, they are supposed to publish very intellectual information related to business or customer targets messages on the LinkedIn pages (Table 8).

During the course of research, it was found that SBI and IDBI were very active in publishing information on LinkedIn. SBI had 599,154 followers shadowed by 34,580 belonging to the IDBI Bank. Number of supporters also highlights status of banks. Union Bank had 234 followers which is to be considered as less. SBI had more than

Table 7 Use of YouTube through Indian private sector banks as per honeycomb model

Banks	Identity	Group	Relationships	Presence	Sharing	Conversation	Reputations
Axis Bank Limited							
Bandhan Bank Limited							
Catholic Syrian Bank Limited							
City Union Bank Limited							
DCB Bank Limited							
Dhanlaxmi Bank Limited							
Federal Bank Limited							
HDFC Bank Limited							
ICICI Bank Limited							
IndusInd Bank Limited							
IDFC Bank Limited							
Jammu and Kashmir Bank Limited							
Karnataka Bank Limited							
Karur Vyasa Bank Limited							
Kotak Mahindra Bank Limited							
Laxmi Vilas Bank Limited							
Nainital Bank Limited							
RBL Bank Limited							
South Indian Bank Limited							
Tamilnadu Mercantile Bank Limited							
Yes Bank Limited							

480 updates 139 of IDBI. Researchers also seen the career posting by various banks and found that SBI had some posting whereas few banks did not have.

Use of LinkedIn by Indian Private Sector Banks

RBL Banks and ICICI Banks were found very active in notifying through this medium. The total followers from ICICI Bank were 332,863, followed by 306,503 of Axis Bank. The numbers of followers were minimum for Tamilnadu Mercantile Bank. The numbers of update were 301 for RBL Bank and talk about the presence, followed by Yes Bank counted at 264. The job posts were made by Kotak Mahindra Bank, while the HDFC Bank, ICICI Bank, RBL Bank, and City Union Bank did not make the career posts during course of research (Table 9).

Many of the above banks do not have verified pages, e.g., City Union, Nainital Bank, Bandhan, Catholic, etc. Karur Vysya Bank, Karnataka Bank, Lakshmi Vilas Bank, Nainital Bank, and Tamilnadu Mercantile Bank have zero post and job openings on LinkedIn. Many of the banks have their pages which have certain amount of likes and followers but not even a single post is there on the accounts; for example, Karnataka Bank, Karur Vysya Bank, Lakshmi Vilas Bank, and Nainital Bank on LinkedIn have no posts.

Table 8 Use of LinkedIn by Indian public sector banks as per honeycomb model

Banks	Identity	Group	Relationships	Presence	Sharing	Conversation	Reputations
State Bank of India							
Punjab National Bank							
Bank of Baroda							
Bank of India							
Canara Bank							
Union Bank of India							
IDBI Bank							
Syndicate Bank							
Central Bank of India							
Oriental Bank of commerce							
Allahabad Bank							
Andhra Bank							
Bank of Maharashtra							
Corporation Bank							
Dena Bank							
Indian Bank							
Indian Overseas Bank							
United Bank of India							
Punjab and Sind Bank							
UCO Bank							
Vijaya Bank							

Table 9 Use of LinkedIn by Indian private sector banks as per honeycomb model

Banks	Identity	Group	Relationships	Presence	Sharing	Conversation	Reputations
Axis Bank Limited							
Bandhan Bank Limited							
Catholic Syrian Bank Limited							
City Union Bank Limited							
DCB Bank Limited							
Dhanlaxmi Bank Limited							
Federal Bank Limited							
HDFC Bank Limited							
ICICI Bank Limited							
IndusInd Bank Limited							
IDFC Bank Limited							
Jammu and Kashmir Bank Limited							
Karnataka Bank Limited							
Karur Vyasa Bank Limited							
Kotak Mahindra Bank Limited							
Laxmi Vilas Bank Limited							
Nainital Bank Limited							
RBL Bank Limited							
South Indian Bank Limited							
Tamilnadu Mercantile Bank Limited							
Yes Bank Limited							

4 Discussion

Honeycomb framework has been kept in center for this research to comprehend usage of social media by Indian private and public sector banks. Indian banks are lacking social media strategy in terms of building its brand. It is appealed through this research that if this model is used as benchmark for use of social media by banks, then it will give brilliant results (Skeels & Grudin, 2009). This research has used only four medium of social media research which are were popular. This research time period of 2018 January is its limitation. From the basis of this research analytics, the ten banks may be put in three categories, as represented hereunder.

Table 10 shows banks and their social media usage. Researchers have taken only three banks for active, partly active and inactive though the total number of banks is more than that. State Bank of India is very dynamic on all the four social media tools followed by IDBI which is active on three platforms except Facebook. Punjab National Bank (PNB) and Bank of Baroda (BOB) are partly active meaning that they have their presence and keep on updating their content but not so actively as SBI does. There are banks like Oriental Bank of Commerce (OBC), Syndicate Bank, and Central Bank of India, etc. which are in active in one or more social media platforms. ICICI Bank and Yes Bank are considered to be active among private sector banks, while in some parameters, these are not so active. Federal Bank is very active on YouTube and does regular update there, and same is the case with Karnataka Bank which is very active on Twitter. Axis Bank is partly active across all social media platforms, while Dhanalaxmi Bank, City Union Bank, Nainital Bank, etc., are inactive on these social media. The honeycomb model has some limitations in terms of indispensable as well as classifying the asset of each functionality. A lack of technical method to estimate the effectiveness of strength of social media lets researchers to use the most appropriate method in evaluating social media usage. Most of the banks data have been taken from the official Web site to understand banks and its social media usage (Tsitsi Chikandiwa et al., 2013). It has also been seen that some banks have resolved customer online issues in offline mode which is also good but it should be endorsed by banks efficiently on social media.

5 Conclusions

Social media is like a gold mine. How do you use these data/gold mine is based on your expertise and skills? Indian Banks which is still in the beginning stage in using social media needs to gear up in terms of more proactive then less information posting. Merely putting tweet or budgetary review is not enough, efficiency of banks lies in resolving customer complaints and gaining confidence.

Honeycomb model used in this study has analyzed presence in its way, and this can be analyzed in other way also. This research has highlighted that major public

Table 10 Classification of banks based on social media presence

	Very active				Partly active				Inactive			
	FB	Twitter	YouTube	LinkedIn	FB	Twitter	YouTube	LinkedIn	FB	Twitter	YouTube	LinkedIn
Public sector	SBI BOB Union	SBI Union IDBI	SBI Canara IDBI	SBI IDBI Vijaya	PNB IDBI Indian	PNB Vijaya Union	BOB Union Indian	BOB PNB Union	Canara Syndicate CBI	BOI OBC BOM	PNB BOI Syndicate	Central OBC Andhra
Private sector	ICICI IndusInd RBL	Yes Karnataka South Indian	HDFC ICICI Federal	Yes Axis ICICI	Axis HDFC Yes	Axis HDFC ICICI	Axis Karnataka IDFC	Karnataka South Kotak	Dhanlaxmi J&K Nainital	Catholic Laxmi Vilas Nainital	City Union Dhanlaxmi Karur	IDFC RBL City

sector banks are doing quite well on social media like State Banks, Bank of Baroda, and IDBI Bank whereas other public sector banks are very in active.

These banks have to do a lot more than what they are doing at present to optimize their social media presence.

In terms of private sector banks, ICICI Bank, Yes Bank, RBL, Federal Bank, etc., are considered to be active banks in these social media platform, while banks such as Axis Bank, HDFC, IDFC, etc., are partly active on social media. Certain banks such as City Union Bank, Nainital Bank, and Dhanlaxmi Bank are inactive where these banks either do not have presence or these are present for the sake of being present, doing no activity in order to engage with their customer base.

References

Arti, C., Akhilesh, R., Rajiv, D., & Mita, M. (2018). a working paper on use of social media by selected Indian public sector banks. In *2018 IEEE Punecon Conference*, Pune

Ashley, C., & Tuten, T. (2015). Creative strategies in social media marketing: An exploratory study of branded social content and consumer engagement. *Psychology and Marketing, 32*(1), 15–27.

Castelo Branco, M., & Lima Rodrigues, L. (2006). Communication of corporate social responsibility by Portuguese banks: A legitimacy theory perspective. *Corporate Communications: An International Journal, 11*(3), 232–248

Hanna, R., Rohm, A., & Crittenden, V. L. (2011). We're all connected: The power of the social media ecosystem. *Business Horizons, 54*(3), 265–273.

https://www.rbi.org.in/commonman/english/scripts/banksinindia.aspx#NB. Accessed on 03.02.2018

https://about.linkedin.com/. Accessed on 05.02.18

https://about.twitter.com/. Accessed on 04.02.18

https://en.wikipedia.org/wiki/Facebook. Accessed on 02.02.18

Kaplan, A. M., & Haenlein, M. (2010). Users of the world, unite! The challenges and opportunities of social media. *Business Horizons, 53*(1), 59–68.

Kietzmann, J., Hermkens, K., & McCarthy, I. P. (2011). Social media? Get serious! Understanding the functional building blocks of social media. *Business Horizons, 54*(3), 241–251.

Li, C., & Bernoff, J. (2008*). Groundswell: Winning in a World Transformed by Social Technologies.* Harvard Business School Press

Mitic, M., & Kapoulas, A. (2012). Understanding the role of social media in bank marketing. *Marketing Intelligence and Planning, 30*(7), 668–686.

Murdough, C. (2009). Social media measurement: It's not impossible. *Journal of Interactive Advertising, 10*(1), 94–99.

O'Driscall, S. (2018). The social engagement journey, Ant's eye view. Available at: www.antseyeview.com/social-journey accessed on December 2018

Papacharissi, Z. (2009). The virtual geographies of social networks: A comparative analysis of Facebook, LinkedIn and ASmallWorld. *New Media and Society, 11*(1–2), 199–220

Safko, L. & Brake, D. K. (2009). T*he social media Bible: Tactics, tools, and strategies for business success* new jersey. John Wiley & Sons, Inc.

Skeels, M. and Grudin, J. (2009). When social networks cross boundaries: A case study of workplace use of Facebook and Linkedin. In *Proceedings of the ACM 2009 International Conference on Supporting Group Work* (pp. 95–104). Sanibel Island

Tsitsi Chikandiwa, S., Contogiannis, E. and Jembere, E. (2013). The adoption of social media marketing in South African banks. *European Business Review, 25*(4), 365–381

Return Dynamics and Volatility Spill Over Effects of Stock Markets in G20 Countries

Viswanathan Thangaraj and John Ben

Abstract G20, a group of developed countries and major emerging markets, was formed in 1990. G20 aims to bring economic cooperation and the promotion of international financial stability. Economic cooperation of G20 countries has led to the integration of stock markets. The integrated markets may cause volatility of one market getting spillover into other markets. As a result, every market receives spillover and also contributes to the volatility of other markets. Understanding the market interdependencies and estimating the volatility spillover effect is an inherent process in portfolio management. Our study examines the return dynamics and volatility spillover effect among the G20 countries. The interdependencies of G20 stock markets are tested using cointegration test. We apply vector autoregression (VAR) to decompose the variance and created a methodology to calculate the spillover index for stock market volatility. The research is based on the major stock indices of G20 countries for the years between 2002 and 2018. The results indicate the presence of asymmetric volatility spillover effect among the stock markets of G20 countries. We observe a significant increase in volatility spillover from 1 to 5 weeks forecast of error variance. The shocks in the developed market trigger volatility to other emerging markets. The outcome of the study would facilitate the investors and portfolio managers to make an informed decision by considering the nature of stock market volatility.

Keywords Return dynamics · Volatility spillover · Cointegration · Vector error correction · Variance decomposition

---

V. Thangaraj (✉) · J. Ben
Symbiosis Institute of Business Management, A Constituent of Symbiosis International (Deemed) University, Bengaluru, India
e-mail: viswanathan@sibm.edu.in

J. Ben
e-mail: John.ben@sibm.edu.in

© The Author(s), under exclusive license to Springer Nature Singapore Pte Ltd. 2022

A. Chandani et al. (eds.), *Achieving $5 Trillion Economy of India*, Springer Proceedings in Business and Economics, https://doi.org/10.1007/978-981-16-7818-9_9

1 Introduction

Economic integration and regional cooperation have become the major driver of global trade and economic output. The world economy has seen various forms of economic integration post the Second World War. Starting from GATT in 1948, G6 in 1975, WTO in 1995, G20 in 1999, reformatted G8 to G7 in 2014, etc. Every financial crisis has led to the creation of new forms of alliances, bilateral and multilateral agreements. The formation of economic integration arrangements has created business and investment opportunities for member countries.

The G7 group originated in 1975 as a group of 6-member nations—France, Germany, Italy, Japan, the UK and the USA—also known as the "Group of Six" or G6. Later Canada and Russia joined the group in the year 1976 and 1998, respectively. In 2014, Russia was suspended from the group following the annexation of Crimea. G20 is one of the global economic groups with a membership of 19 countries and the European Union. The G20 countries account for 90% of the world's product, 80% of world trade and 2/3 of the world population.

The economic interdependence has deepened the financial connection among major economies. As a result, the integrated markets exhibit the mechanism of price discovery and the spillover effect. Any innovation or shock happens in one market, and getting percolated into other markets is described as the spillover effect. A constructive approach to quantify the spillover effect of many markets would facilitate the decision-making process of stakeholders in that market. Spillover happens due to the occurrence of primary, secondary and tertiary trends. The credit crisis of 1772, Great depression of 1929, OPEC oil shock of 1973, the Asian crisis of 1997 and the financial crisis of 2007–08 had signalled volatility across the global markets.

We undertake the present study to examine the interdependencies of the stock market of G20 countries. The nature of the integration of G20 stock markets is examined by cointegration test. The impulse response signal among the stock markets is analysed by creating spillover index for market returns and volatility. We construct the cointegration model and spillover effects based on the previous research contributions. We follow Diebold and Yilmax (2009) methodology to estimate the spillover index. They use vector autoregression (VAR) model to decompose the error variance of 19 different countries. Our objective is to examine the short-term transmission of volatility spillover effect of G20 stock markets.

The study examines the interdependencies of G20 stock markets using the stochastic process of vector autoregression. We apply restricted VAR to decompose the error variance of 5 weeks ahead volatility forecast of the stock markets of G20 countries. The vector error correction model reflects the partial adjustment of one stock market due to the shocks that happened in other markets. The variance decomposition of each country indicates how much of variance is coming from others and the variance contributed by the home country to others. For instance, if the decomposition result is 80% for India, that shows 80% of the stock market variance is due to happenings in India and 20% is due to shocks from other integrated stock markets. The overall adjustments are used as parameters to estimate spillover index at a time (t) for all G20 stock markets. The trends in spillover index over the forecasting horizon would indicate an increase or decrease in stock market volatility.

The rest of the paper is organised as follows. Section 2 shows the summary of the literature review. Section 4 deals with data description and return dynamics. In Sect. 5, we describe the methodology used to calculate the return volatility. Section 6 highlights the test of cointegration. The spillover index and the associated spillover table are explained in Sect. 7, followed by the conclusion in Sect. 8.

2 Review of Literature

A vast amount of research effort has been made in the past to gauge the volatility in the equity markets through the application of the family of ARCH models. Various studies directly or indirectly related to the objective of this study have been reviewed. There are various studies which appraise various aspects of Co-movement, i.e. return, risk, volatility, etc. Bollerslev (1986) introduced the GARCH (Generalised Autoregressive Conditional Hetroskedastic) models to consider the time-varying volatility.

A GARCH model is more robust and helps widely in modelling financial time series with varying volatility. Some previous works by Arshanapalli and Doukas (1993) and Hamao et al. (1990) displayed that international stock markets are sturdily integrated.

Shahzad et al. (2016) estimated the Co-movement among the stock markets applying ARDL and revealed the existence of co-movement among the markets. Majid and Aziz (2009) assessed the Co-movement among ASEAN-5 stock exchanges using Cointegration and found the existence of co-movement and Cointegration among the markets.

Jang and Saul (2002) studied the Co-movement and integration among the Asian markets using the Granger causality test and Johnsen cointegration test. Recently, many researchers have found the existence of Co-movement and integration of BSE with other markets, Mitra and Bhattacharjee (2015), Bhattacharjee and Swaminathan (2016) and Vohra (2016). Chen and Lian found the existence of disproportionateness in the equity markets of five ASEAN countries, viz. Malaysia, Singapore, Thailand, Indonesia and Philippines.

TARCH and EGARCH models achieved better results in forecasting the equity markets post-Asian financial countries. Most of the spillover studies for the emerging markets have been conducted for Central and Eastern Europe (Gilmore & McManus, 2003; Gündüz & Hatemi, 2005), Latin America and Asian countries. Lee et al. (2004) examined the linkages between the daily returns and volatility of the NASDAQ and Asian markets using EGRARCH and VAR-based methodology and found strong evidence of volatility spillovers from the US to Asia. Bennett and Kelleher (1988), Hamao et al. (1990) and Susmel and Engle (1994) displayed that US returns appear to cause the other countries and that lagged spillovers of price volatility are found between the major markets.

The extensive literature review highlights two broad areas. One is the scope of study concerning volatility spillover effect, and the other is the methodology used. We found the previous studies on spillover effect focus on stock markets, comparison of spillover effect between stock, commodities and foreign exchange markets. The studies have used VAR and GARCH models to forecast volatility. However, except Diebold and Yilmax (2009), other studies have not attempted to create an index that provides multiple benefits. An index can be used as an indicator to study the volatility before and after a major crisis and impulse response behaviour of integrated markets. Further, the world economy has been going through a major transformation post the financial crisis in 2008–09. The major transformation includes protectionism versus globalisation, preventive measures to global economic shocks and news forms of alliances among member countries. In this aspect, our study aims to examine the nature and direction of causality among G20 countries.

3 Objectives of the Study

The major objectives of the study are as follows.

1. To examine the nature of the association among G20 stock markets
2. To analyse the return dynamics and volatility of G20 stock markets
3. To forecast volatility and create a spillover index for the markets of G20 countries.

4 Data Description and Return Dynamics

We obtain the major stock market index data for G20 countries from Bloomberg. The benchmark composite indices for the respective countries are shown in Table 1.

The sample data for the study covers the period between 2010 and 2018. The frequency of data includes the weekly high, low, open and closing index. The weekly prices are observed from Monday to Friday for all the benchmark indices. The weekly returns are the log-returns calculated based upon the closing index value on every Friday.

$$\text{Return} = \ln(\text{CO}_t|\text{CO}_t - 1) \tag{1}$$

where CO_t is the closing price for the current period, and CO_{t-1} is the previous period closing price (Fig. 1).

Table 2 shows the descriptive statistics of weekly stock market returns of the benchmark stock indices of G20 countries. Among all G20 countries, Brazil has given a maximum weekly return of 16.56%, followed by Russia with 14.68%. Both the countries were rated as one of the best performing stock markets during 2016.

Table 1 Countries and indices

Countries	Index
Argentina	MERVAL
Australia	ASX
Brazil	IBOV
Canada	SPTSX
China	SHCOMP
EU	Euronext100
Germany	DAX
France	CAC
India	Nifty 50
Indonesia	JCI
Italy	FTSEMIB
Japan	Nikkei 225
Mexico	MEXBOL
Russia	RTS
Saudi Arabia	SASEIDX
South Africa	JALSH
South Korea	KOSPI
Turkey	XU100
UK	FTSE100
USA	S&P 500

Brazil has outperformed S&P 500, Russia, India, China, FTSE, Japan and other emerging markets. The stellar performance of the Russian stock market is due to the strong recovery of oil price, stabilisation of Rubble and investors optimum after the financial crisis in 2008. The negative skewness for all indices shows that the returns are skewed to the left that indicates more negative return during the period of observation. The standard deviation of weekly return varies between 1.61 and 4.46% (Fig. 2).

5 Return Volatility of G20 Countries

Volatility represents the variation in price movement. The methods to measure volatility include historical and implied volatility. While the historical volatility is based on the past data, implied volatility is a market estimate of future volatility. It can be inferred based on the option premium of a particular security. In this study, we attempt to estimate the spillover index for returns and volatility for all G20 countries. The forecasting horizon spans from short-run (one week) to long-run (5 weeks)

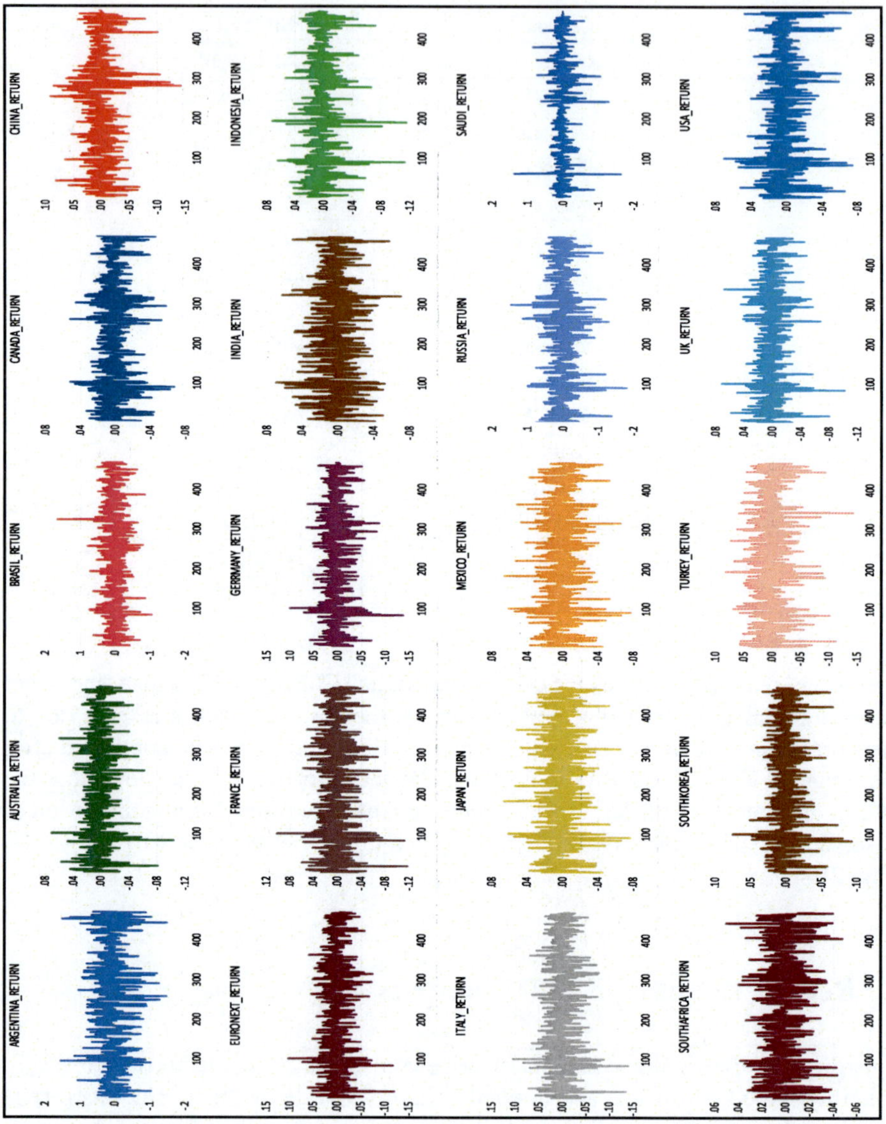

Fig. 1 Return summary of G20 Stock Market: 2002–2018. *Source* Compiled by the authors

Table 2 Descriptive statistics for the weekly return of G20 countries 2010–2018

Countries	Mean return	Median_return	Max_return	Min_return	Stdv_return	Skewness	Kurtosis
ARGENTINA	0.00544	0.008308	0.155418	−0.148674	0.044679	−0.272131	3.868642
AUSTRAILA	0.000657	0.002556	0.07081	−0.10398	0.019452	−0.601956	5.747515
BRASIL	0.000487	0.001736	0.165617	−0.105207	0.029697	0.178679	4.873358
CANADA	0.000411	0.001971	0.052298	−0.067531	0.017241	−0.594547	4.284238
CHINA	−0.000529	0.000179	0.090735	−0.142909	0.029251	−0.721776	6.200751
EURONEXT	7.81E−05	0.00311	0.103934	−0.11926	0.026736	−0.440723	4.557357
FRANCE	0.000429	0.002878	0.102376	−0.117869	0.02606	−0.480887	4.690036
GERRMANY	0.001562	0.00373	0.101666	−0.137974	0.026268	−0.567098	5.217417
INDIA	0.001592	0.002673	0.069719	−0.070264	0.02147	−0.035161	3.222213
INDONESIA	0.001872	0.00338	0.072763	−0.116139	0.021903	−0.925852	7.18552
ITALY	−0.000473	0.001333	0.10472	−0.140599	0.031521	−0.501951	4.165739
JAPAN	0.000519	0.001683	0.065797	−0.076561	0.020019	−0.200057	3.756244
MEXICO	0.000519	0.001683	0.065797	−0.076561	0.020019	−0.200057	3.756244
RUSSIA	−0.000627	−0.000302	0.146887	−0.179658	0.039029	−0.397198	4.969011
SAUDI	0.000473	0.001992	0.137621	−0.162698	0.02527	−0.860235	10.47131
SOUTHAFRICA	0.001485	0.002999	0.050909	−0.048132	0.016136	−0.278031	3.094319
SOUTHKOREA	0.000415	0.00253	0.075672	−0.093009	0.020049	−0.777278	5.492035
TURKEY	0.001103	0.00298	0.083366	−0.143708	0.031258	−0.663048	4.396444
UK	0.000511	0.002663	0.072373	−0.102819	0.020074	−0.515557	5.49398
SA	0.001725	0.002844	0.071284	−0.074603	0.019845	−0.595527	4.909666

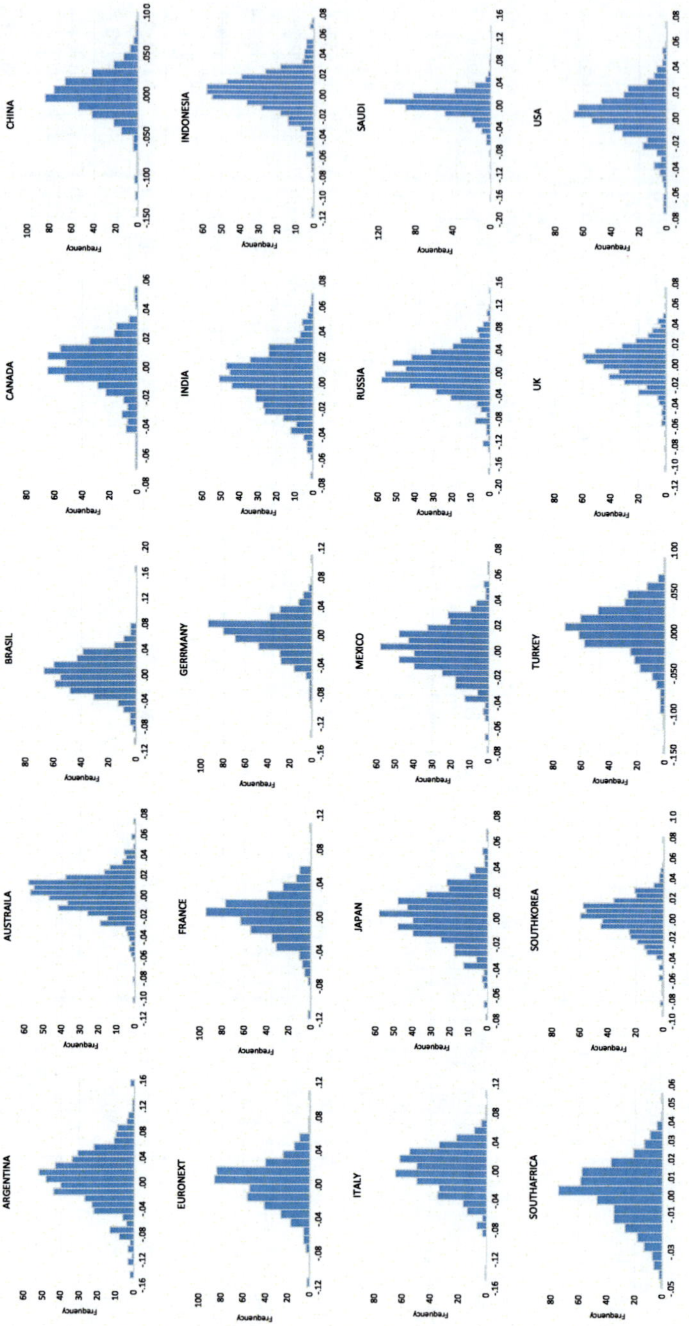

Fig. 2 Distribution plot of G20 Stock Market: 2002–2018

volatility for the sample period. So, the appropriate measure is to calculate the historical volatility and estimate the variance decomposition using a vector autoregression (VAR) model. The estimation of historical volatility will be highly influenced by the frequency of past data. The data gets smoothened when daily index movement is converted into a weekly or monthly average and so as the volatility. The choice of selecting data frequency depends on the intention of the trader/investor. Use of high-frequency data shows hourly or daily volatility. A day trader or scalper will be more institutive to know hourly volatility. An investor is concerned about how the volatility spans in the future. Short-run and long-run volatility are measured taking weekly or monthly data, respectively. We use the transformed price to calculate returns and volatility. The returns are calculated as log-returns, and volatility is calculated by converting the absolute weekly data into log transformation.

We examine various estimators to calculate volatility. The classical estimator of volatility is one of the simple methods to estimate volatility. The volatility is measured based on the squared difference between the closing price current period (C_t) and the previous closing price (C_{t-1}). Though the method is easy to use, it suffers from information bias. It is quite possible that the price of security opens at a price "X" on Monday and close at the same price "X" on Friday after going through some ups (high) and downs (Low). The difference between high and low price contains information that contributes to measuring volatility. Parkinson introduced an estimator, which calculates volatility based on the squared difference between high and low price. The main disadvantage is its failure to consider the joint effect of opening and closing price. Like Yilmaz, Diebold and Hwee Kwan Chow Tan, we follow Garman and Klass to measure weakly volatility of the benchmark indices. The estimator is comprehensive, and it addresses the limitations of classical and Pearson's volatility estimators. To calculate volatility, we obtain the highest (H_t), lowest (L_t), open (O_t) and closing price (C_t) for the week ending Friday.

$$\begin{aligned}\sigma^2 = 0.511(H_t - L_t)^2 - 0.019[(C_t - O_t)(H_t + L_t - 2O_t) \\ -2(H_t - O_t)(L_t - O_t) - 0.383(C_t - O_t)^2]\end{aligned} \tag{2}$$

In the equation, ($H_t - L_t$) measures the range, ($C_t - O_t$) shows the normalised close, ($H_t - O_t$) calculates the normalised high, and ($L_t - O_t$) scales the normalised low.

Table 3 and Fig. 3 show the summary statistics of return volatility (variance) of G20 countries. The skewness and kurtosis show the momentum of distribution. Stock returns often deviate from the normal distribution and show asymmetric distribution. The skewness and kurtosis value indicate the variance non-normal distribution of return volatility. The positive skewness shows that the variance is skewed to the right. There are more instance of higher market volatility of G20 countries as compared to low market volatility. The kurtosis value greater than 3 highlights occurrences of abnormal market volatility. Among the G20 countries, Argentina had seen the maximum stock volatility. The patterns of volatility clustering are observed in the series for all countries.

Table 3 Descriptive statistics of return volatility of G20 countries

	Mean_var	Median_var	Max_var	Min_var	Stdv	Skewness	Kurtosis
ARGENTINA	0.001416	0.000871	0.017894	4.82E−05	0.001851	4.059647	26.70109
AUSTRALIA	0.000355	0.000194	0.005279	1.18E−05	0.000557	5.023357	35.26567
BRASIL	0.000867	0.000583	0.007227	2.34E−05	0.000948	3.438032	18.31299
CANADA	0.000271	0.000154	0.003688	1.15E−05	0.000382	4.543069	30.95781
CHINA	0.000728	0.00039	0.01439	1.00E−05	0.001302	6.018514	51.82692
EURO	0.000664	0.000387	0.012095	2.85E−05	0.000946	5.65739	53.83193
FRANCE	0.000638	0.00037	0.01017	3.00E−05	0.000884	4.763426	37.90196
GERMANY	0.000613	0.00039	0.0087	1.00E−05	0.000846	4.737605	33.00272
INDIA	0.00043	0.00027	0.0153	2.00E−05	0.000807	13.84014	248.4756
INDONESIA	0.000443	0.00022	0.00798	2.00E−05	0.000741	4.816425	34.7838
ITALY	0.000954	0.0006	0.0142	6.00E−05	0.001205	4.841427	40.69838
JAPAN	0.000391	0.00024	0.00512	3.00E−05	0.000519	4.461684	29.96242
MEXICO	0.000392	0.0002	0.0051	0.00E+00	0.000519	4.430176	29.58909
RUSSIA	0.001364	0.0008	0.054	0.00E+00	0.002885	13.61381	239.9939
SOTHAFRICA	7.60E−05	6.00E−05	0.00046	1.00E−05	6.06E−05	2.229608	9.677821
SAUDI	0.000456	0.0002	0.0114	0.00E+00	0.00101	6.205177	53.4333
SOUTHKOREA	0.000334	0.0002	0.0083	0.00E+00	0.000543	8.183198	105.0258
TURKEY	0.000823	0.0005	0.0088	0.00E+00	0.00098	3.796378	22.03162
UK	0.000392	0.00022	0.0055	1.00E−05	0.000583	4.702511	31.43866
USA	0.000331	0.0002	0.0058	0.00E+00	0.000535	5.082484	38.878

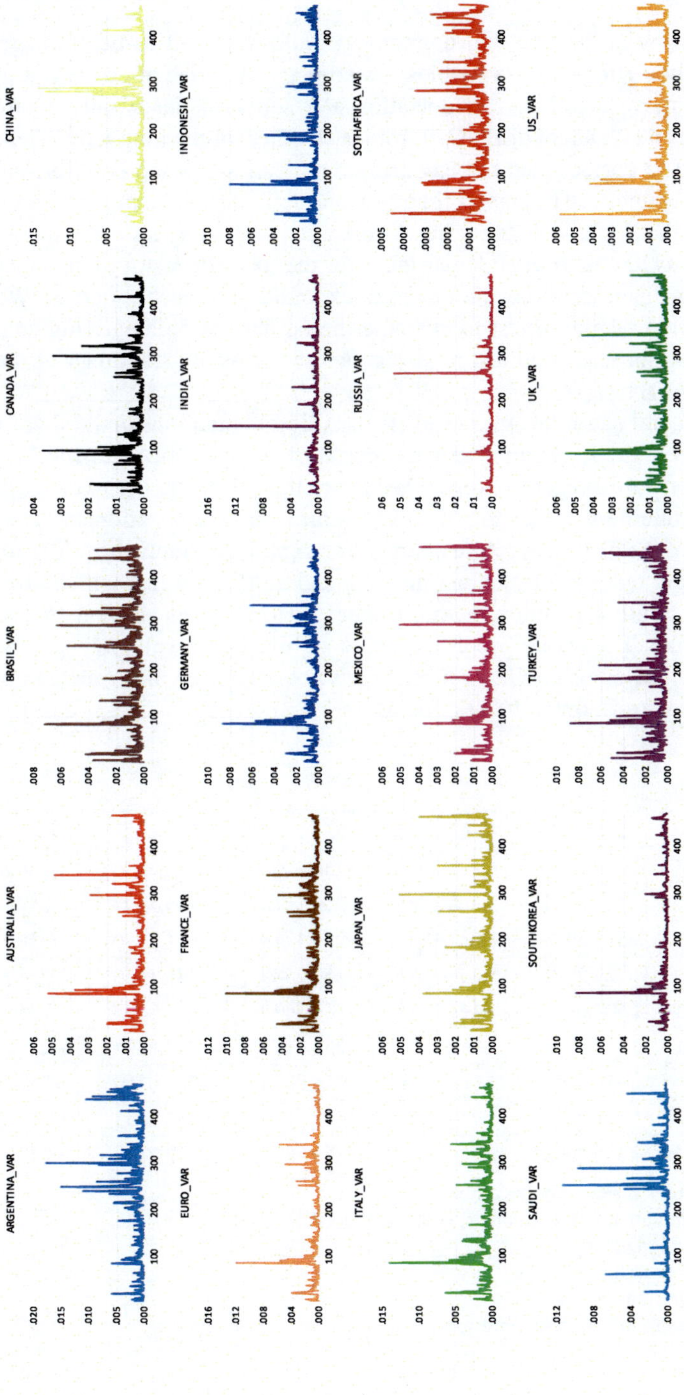

Fig. 3 Stock market volatility of G20 countries

6 The Test of Cointegration

Economic theory states that two or more variables are said to be cointegrated if the linear combination of the variables is stationary. A series of cointegrating variables tend to move together. Any deviation between variables is only a temporary phenomenon, and it cannot drift away from each other for the long term. Thus, these variables tend to correct themselves during deviation and bring equilibrium in the cointegrating equation. The lagged change in one variable has the power to predict the change in another variable in the series. Economic integration has led to the financial integration of G20 countries. It is pertinent for the trader/investor to understand the nature of long-run association among the stock markets of these countries. We apply the Johansen cointegration test to examine the number of cointegrating equations. Application of cointegration test requires that all series are stationary at the same order, either $I(\mathrm{O})$ or $I(\mathrm{I})$.

It is the general nature of stock markets to exhibit fluctuations in the short run and follow a trend in the long run. The trend could be flat (no slope), upward (positive slope) or downward (negative slope). We apply the augmented Dickey–Fuller unit root test to examine whether the historical return series are stationary. The visual examination of the historical return chart shows significant fluctuation. The unit root test is applied at three levels, i.e. no intercept and trend, intercept without trend and intercept and trend. The null hypothesis states that the series are non-stationary or there is unit root. The results are tested at 5% significance level. ADF test indicates that the return series of all G20 countries are non-stationary at levels and become stationary at first difference $I(1)$ (Table 4).

Table 4 Lag selection

Lag	LogL	LR	FPE	AIC	SC	HQ
0	58,077.59	NA	6.1e−137	−256.8920	−256.7100*	−256.8203
1	59,031.26	1818.711	5.3e−138*	−259.3418*	−255.5194	−257.8356*
2	59,392.83	657.5578	6.3e−138	−259.1718	−251.7090	−256.2310
3	59,814.77	729.9801	5.8e−138	−259.2689	−248.1656	−254.8935
4	60,181.90	602.6884	7.1e−138	−259.1235	−244.3797	−253.3135
5	60,512.08	512.8055	1.0e−137	−258.8145	−240.4304	−251.5700
6	60,931.53	614.3156	1.1e−137	−258.9006	−236.8760	−250.2214
7	61,267.79	462.7377	1.7e−137	−258.6186	−232.9535	−248.5049
8	61,647.54	488.9606*	2.3e−137	−258.5289	−229.2235	−246.9807

*Indicates lag order selected by the criterion
LR: sequential modified LR test statistic (each test at 5% level)
FPE: final prediction error
AIC: Akaike information criterion
SC: Schwarz information criterion
HQ: Hannan–Quinn information criterion

The historical weekly return series of G20 countries stock market have 469 weekly observations. It is the general nature of time series data to exhibit a lead–lag relationship. It is inferred that the current period return will be influenced by the previous period. An equation, whether it is OLS or GLS, should include the lag of the response variable. Inclusion of too many lags would lead to a loss in the degrees of freedom. If the lag length is too short, the equation becomes imprecise, and autocorrelation of the error term may lead to inefficient estimators. We run unrestricted vector autoregression to select the optimal lag length. The optimum lag is selected based on the minimum Akaike information criterion (AIC). The minimum AIC is observed at Lag 1.

6.1 Johansen Cointegration Test

We apply the Johansen cointegration test (1988, 1995) to examine whether stock markets of G20 countries are cointegrated. The cointegration test is appropriate to examine the long-run relationship between the stock market movements. The results of the unit root test indicate that the series of market returns of all G20 countries are integrated of the same order $I(1)$. We run unrestricted vector autoregression to estimate the number of cointegrating equations. The assumption made to run the model is no intercept and trend in cointegrating equation and vector autoregression.

Table 5 shows the results of cointegration test. The test results are interpreted based on two likelihood ratio (LR) statistics. First is the trace test, and the second is the maximum eigenvalue. To determine the number of the cointegrating equation, the null hypothesis is set as no cointegrating equation against the alternative of $k - 1$ number of equations, where k is the number of variables. The theoretical framework of Johansen test suggests that there may be zero or r number of cointegrating equations, where $0 > r < k$.

The following are the hypothesis of cointegration test.

H_0: $r = r_o$ (None—no cointegration).
H_1: $r_o < r < k$ (There exists r number of cointegrating equations).

The hypothesis has done sequentially starting from none and proceeding to (k) in steps until the null hypothesis cannot be rejected. The results are interpreted based on the obtained values of trace and Max-Eigen statistic value. The null hypothesis is rejected if the trace or eigenvalue is more than the critical value or the probability is less than 5%. Both trace test and maximum eigenvalues are statistically significant at 5% level for all null hypotheses. The trace test and maximum eigenvalue indicates seven cointegrating equations. It is inferred that the stock markets of G20 countries are cointegrated.

Table 5 Cointegration results

Unrestricted cointegration rank test (trace)				
Hypothesised no. of CE(s)	Eigenvalue	Trace statistic	0.05 critical value	Prob.**
None	0.467858	3008.965	NA	NA
At most 1	0.428267	2716.253	NA	NA
At most 2	0.388980	2456.839	NA	NA
At most 3	0.367946	2228.261	NA	NA
At most 4	0.361317	2015.387	NA	NA
At most 5	0.340372	1807.354	NA	NA
At most 6	0.335502	1614.293	NA	NA
At most 7	0.318327	1424.646	NA	NA
At most 8*	0.306327	1246.839	334.9837	0.0000
At most 9*	0.287963	1077.128	285.1425	0.0000
At most 10*	0.247057	919.5424	239.2354	0.0000
At most 11*	0.239512	787.8751	197.3709	0.0000
At most 12*	0.230205	660.8343	159.5297	0.0000
At most 13*	0.219051	539.4376	125.6154	0.0000
At most 14*	0.198779	424.7155	95.75366	0.0000
At most 15*	0.185164	321.8846	69.81889	0.0000
At most 16 *	0.153879	226.8724	47.85613	0.0000
At most 17 *	0.129218	149.3415	29.79707	0.0000
At most 18*	0.098927	85.14056	15.49471	0.0000
At most 19*	0.076259	36.80637	3.841465	0.0000
Unrestricted cointegration rank test (maximum eigenvalue)				
Hypothesised no. of CE(s)	Eigenvalue	Max-eigen statistic	0.05 critical value	Prob.**
None	0.467858	292.7121	NA	NA
At most 1	0.428267	259.4142	NA	NA
At most 2	0.388980	228.5779	NA	NA
At most 3	0.367946	212.8743	NA	NA
At most 4	0.361317	208.0327	NA	NA
At most 5	0.340372	193.0608	NA	NA
At most 6	0.335502	189.6474	NA	NA
At most 7	0.318327	177.8075	NA	NA
At most 8*	0.306327	169.7101	76.57843	0.0000
At most 9*	0.287963	157.5861	70.53513	0.0000
At most 10*	0.247057	131.6673	64.50472	0.0000
At most 11*	0.239512	127.0408	58.43354	0.0000

(continued)

Table 5 (continued)

Unrestricted cointegration rank test (trace)				
Hypothesised no. of CE(s)	Eigenvalue	Trace statistic	0.05 critical value	Prob.**
At most 12*	0.230205	121.3967	52.36261	0.0000
At most 13*	0.219051	114.7221	46.23142	0.0000
At most 14*	0.198779	102.8308	40.07757	0.0000
At most 15*	0.185164	95.01226	33.87687	0.0000
At most 16*	0.153879	77.53091	27.58434	0.0000
At most 17*	0.129218	64.20091	21.13162	0.0000
At most 18*	0.098927	48.33418	14.26460	0.0000
At most 19*	0.076259	36.80637	3.841465	0.0000

*Significant @ 5%
**MacKinnon–Haug–Michelis (1999) p-values

7 Spillover Index

Spillover is the transmission of volatility induced by one variable into other variables that are supposed to be cointegrated. The spillover effect occurs when one or more markets are interlinked. The spillover index measures the percentage of forecast error variance caused by own and other variables. We construct a spillover index for the return and volatility series of the stock indices of G20 countries.

We follow the stepwise conceptual process to model return and volatility spillover for the G20 countries. The procedural steps involved are as follows.

Step 1: Check whether the historical series of return are stationary using the augmented Dickey–Fuller test.
Step 2: Run unrestricted vector autoregression to estimate the optimum lag structure (p).
Step 3: Conduct Johansen cointegration test at (p) lags to check the number of cointegrating equations (r).
Step 4: Apply the decision rule to choose between vector autoregression (VAR) and vector error correction model (VECM). VAR model is used where there is no cointegration among the variables. VECM model is applied when there is at least one cointegrating equation among the variables.
Step 5: Estimate the parameters of the VAR model taking ($p - 1$) lag.
Step 6: Forecast 10 weeks ahead variance decomposition for return and volatility.
Step 7: Perform diagnostics test to check for model accuracy.
Step 8: Construct the spillover index separately for the series of return and volatility of G20 countries.

The sequential application of procedural steps shows that the historical series of return are stationary at first difference $I(1)$. The most commonly used approach to estimate volatility transmission across markets is to adopt VAR models. We follow Diebold and Yilmaz (2009) framework to model volatility and calculate spillover index. However, they used the VAR framework to measure the spillover of 19 countries. In our study, we attempt to calculate the spillover among G20 countries. Unlike the 19 countries, G20 countries are bound together with economic and financial integration. By running VAR model, we forecast the error variance for the next 5 weeks. We use Cholesky factor identification to orthogonalise the shocks among G20 countries and then estimate the spillover index (Fig. 4).

The spillover index is a simple measure to understand how the return and volatility spillover transmits across the G20 stock markets. The variance decomposition parameters of VAR are used to calculate the spillover index, and the results are shown in Tables 6 and 7. We have taken the full sample data of weekly returns and forecasted the error variance for the 5-week horizon to calculate the spillover index (SP). The spillover tables are to be read as $(i \times j)$ matrix. Every ijth value in the matrix shows the contribution of forecast error variance from country j to i for all $j \neq i$. For every country in a row (i), we estimate the contribution of error variance due to shocks or innovations from other countries by simply adding values of (j), for all $j \neq i$. The diagonal values in the matrix for every $i = j$ show the contribution from own to the forecast variance. The sum of values in every row (i) excluding $i = j$ or the diagonal element in the row shows a contribution from others. We then add all $i = 1 \ldots n$ to get the total contribution from others. The sum of columns (j) for all $j \neq i$ provides the contribution of every country to the forecast error variance of other countries. In simple terms, the sum of rows for all $j \neq i$ highlights the contribution from others. Similarly, the sum of columns for all $j \neq i$ shows the contribution to others.

$$\text{The spillover index (SP)} = \frac{\text{Contribution from others}}{\text{Contribution including own}}$$

For example, for one week ahead variance decomposition in Table 4, the total contribution from others is 902.28, and the total contribution including own is 1900. Thus, the spillover index = 902.28/1900 = 47.49%

We interpret the spillover index across the period by referring to the spillover table. The analogy of interpretation is the same for the return and volatility spillover index. The spillover table is flexible to decompose the spillover into input and output variance. For instance, in Table 6, the shocks from the S&P 500 (US) can cause 31.55% variance to FTSEMIB (Italy) for one week ahead forecast of Italy whereas shock in the US can cause only 20.66% variance to NIKKEI (Japan). Therefore, for one week forecast of return, the spillover from USA to Italy is larger as compared to Japan. The overall spillover index for one week ahead forecast in 47.49%. We forecasted the volatility from one to 5 weeks and calculated the spillover index. The spillover index for week 2 is shown in Table 7. The trend in spillover from one to 5 weeks is shown in Fig. 5.

The overall return and volatility spillover effect can be summarised by referring to the spillover index. An insight of spillover index for stock returns of G20 countries shows for one week forecast, and the spillover index is 47.49%. When the forecasting

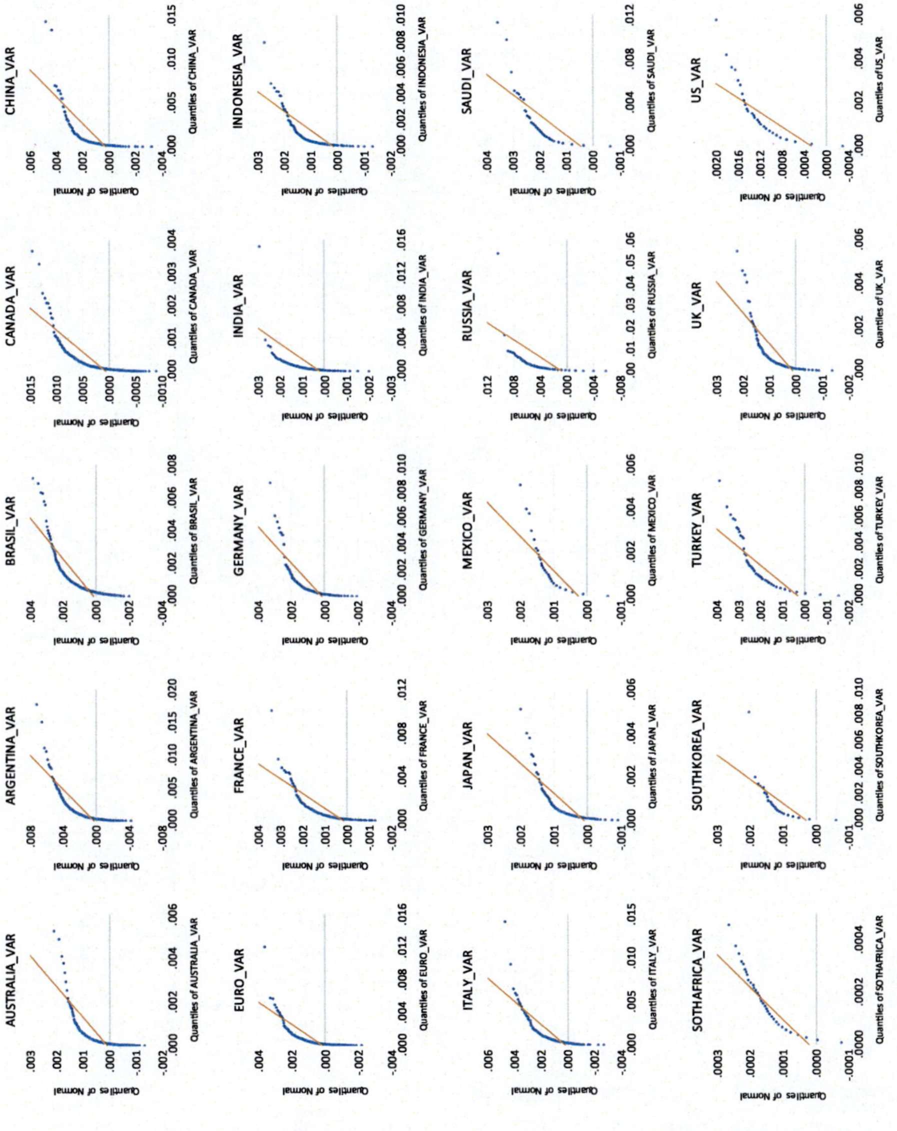

Fig. 4 Variance analysis of G20 countries

Table 6 One week ahead forecast of volatility spillover index of G20 countries

	USA	CHI	JAP	FRA	CAN	UK	GER	IND	AUS	SOK
USA	79.94	0.00	0.52	1.50	0.02	0.03	0.96	0.02	2.15	0.89
CHI	0.15	97.70	0.19	0.04	0.00	0.19	0.19	0.01	0.50	0.02
JAP	20.66	0.11	62.56	0.02	0.24	0.00	1.14	0.00	4.11	0.00
FRA	37.13	0.37	1.29	36.71	0.00	0.73	1.61	0.02	4.04	0.30
CAN	38.31	0.06	1.93	6.10	37.95	0.49	2.37	0.03	1.85	0.06
UK	32.78	0.08	2.34	24.41	1.19	18.43	2.22	0.03	4.65	0.40
GER	28.66	0.30	2.42	33.60	0.39	0.93	15.00	0.02	2.30	0.98
IND	0.86	0.04	0.77	0.21	0.04	0.26	0.15	94.96	0.04	0.39
AUS	31.21	0.06	2.15	24.96	0.56	19.45	2.06	0.04	6.91	0.27
SOK	16.98	0.05	2.90	4.66	0.39	1.55	8.41	0.24	4.83	42.10
SOA	7.99	2.02	0.52	0.75	0.38	0.03	0.72	0.21	0.50	0.26
BRA	18.58	0.23	10.36	0.95	0.77	0.01	0.22	0.29	2.74	0.91
RUS	0.85	0.98	0.13	0.07	0.38	0.10	0.03	0.03	0.48	0.11
ITA	31.55	0.05	0.52	19.50	0.05	0.52	1.33	0.12	5.09	0.27
SAU	0.18	0.71	0.12	0.52	0.81	0.88	0.73	0.01	0.33	0.66
INA	6.55	0.25	1.39	1.00	0.02	1.69	3.25	0.62	2.37	0.18
MEX	20.49	0.11	62.18	0.02	0.23	0.00	1.24	0.00	4.10	0.00
TUR	4.36	0.68	1.22	2.03	1.08	0.43	0.64	0.00	0.74	1.51
EUR	32.05	0.28	1.13	35.07	0.02	1.14	2.40	0.06	4.78	0.38
Contribution to other	329.35	6.38	92.07	155.41	6.57	28.43	29.66	1.76	45.60	7.58
Contribution including own	409.29	104.08	154.63	192.12	44.53	46.86	44.66	96.72	52.50	49.68

	SOA	BRA	RUS	ITA	SAU	INA	MEX	TUR	EUR	Contribution from others
USA	2.22	0.62	2.65	0.03	0.01	7.64	0.08	0.39	0.33	20.06
CHI	0.47	0.00	0.16	0.04	0.05	0.13	0.00	0.05	0.08	2.30
JAP	0.57	0.68	2.43	0.22	0.04	7.12	0.05	0.01	0.04	37.44
FRA	2.74	0.03	1.96	2.59	0.05	9.40	0.00	0.67	0.37	63.29
CAN	0.34	0.86	1.61	0.11	0.02	7.58	0.00	0.27	0.05	62.05
UK	2.32	0.25	1.97	0.52	0.09	7.46	0.02	0.70	0.15	81.57
GER	2.38	0.00	2.35	2.01	0.05	7.89	0.03	0.45	0.26	85.00
IND	0.01	0.06	0.04	0.01	0.02	1.93	0.08	0.05	0.09	5.04
AUS	2.13	0.28	2.03	0.55	0.07	6.39	0.05	0.67	0.17	93.09
SOK	1.65	0.03	0.89	2.73	0.02	9.46	0.00	0.35	2.74	57.90
SOA	85.83	0.00	0.00	0.49	0.10	0.04	0.08	0.06	0.01	14.17
BRA	2.34	55.58	2.99	0.64	0.09	2.98	0.00	0.07	0.26	44.42

(continued)

Table 6 (continued)

	SOA	BRA	RUS	ITA	SAU	INA	MEX	TUR	EUR	Contribution from others
RUS	0.38	0.60	94.74	0.37	0.15	0.14	0.01	0.33	0.12	5.26
ITA	1.95	0.27	2.24	26.99	0.01	6.86	0.05	1.10	1.52	73.01
SAU	2.89	2.05	0.09	0.04	89.13	0.31	0.02	0.19	0.35	10.87
INA	2.03	0.63	2.29	0.37	0.34	76.30	0.42	0.26	0.04	23.70
MEX	0.57	0.66	2.46	0.21	0.04	7.25	0.38	0.01	0.04	99.62
TUR	1.29	0.06	0.13	2.92	0.68	8.82	0.05	73.23	0.14	26.77
EUR	2.24	0.10	1.81	4.07	0.03	10.37	0.05	0.74	3.27	96.73
Contribution to other	28.51	7.19	28.10	17.92	1.83	101.78	0.99	6.38	6.77	902.28
Contribution including own	114.34	62.77	122.84	44.91	90.96	178.08	1.37	79.61	10.04	1900.00
Spillover index										47.49%

USA—America, CHI—China, JAP—Japan, FRA—France, CAN—Canada, UK—United Kingdom, GER—Germany, IND—India, AUS—Australia, SOK—South Korea, SOA – South Africa, BRA—Brazil, RUS—Russia, ITA—Italy, SAU—Saudi Arabia, INA—Indonesia, MEX—Mexico, TUR—Turkey, EUR—Euronext

horizon increases gradually from one to 5 weeks, the spillover index has increased from 47.49% in week 1 to 51.55% in week 5. It indicates in the short run, the spillover effect is less, and it becomes larger with an increase in time. Therefore, we conclude that the spillover effect is significant for return and volatility for G20 countries. Further, the volatility spillover is larger than the return spillover. In the long run, the shocks or innovations from other G20 countries make significant contributions to the volatility of the home country. Hence, it is inferred that the stock market of G20 countries is integrated (Table 8).

8 Conclusion

The interdependencies of the stock market in G20 countries have increased due to growing economic integration, the influence of technology and favourable economic policies. Like other groups of countries, the members of G20 countries make a significant contribution to the global trade and trade among the members. The economic cooperation, cross-broader investments, imports and exports bring financial integration to the market. Transmission of volatility is a common phenomenon in an integrated market. We apply the Diebold–Yilmax methodology to calculate spillover index for return and volatility. The spillover index is constructed through a variance decomposition process by running vector error correction model. We found out the presence of volatility transmission in return and volatility within the G20 countries.

Table 7 Two weeks ahead forecast of volatility spillover index of G20 countries

	USA	CHI	JAP	FRA	CAN	UK	GER	IND	AUS	SOK
USA	74.05	0.09	0.49	1.75	0.06	0.03	1.23	0.09	2.43	1.00
CHI	0.15	96.19	0.30	0.08	0.01	0.26	0.23	0.02	0.99	0.02
JAP	20.41	0.13	59.31	0.16	0.54	0.02	1.17	0.04	4.27	0.02
FRA	35.12	0.47	1.15	32.60	0.00	0.62	1.84	0.07	4.11	0.33
CAN	36.98	0.22	1.81	6.51	34.09	0.62	2.89	0.11	1.81	0.14
UK	31.50	0.20	2.08	22.58	1.05	15.94	2.63	0.08	4.98	0.45
GER	27.86	0.45	2.06	29.34	0.33	0.77	13.70	0.07	2.32	1.15
IND	1.05	0.04	0.77	0.21	0.05	0.27	0.18	93.99	0.05	0.41
AUS	30.22	0.16	1.92	23.16	0.53	16.90	2.40	0.09	7.17	0.31
SOK	16.82	0.05	2.74	5.01	0.37	1.38	8.99	0.28	4.60	37.46
SOA	9.23	2.63	0.48	0.80	0.41	0.16	0.72	0.20	0.46	0.32
BRA	18.47	0.28	9.92	1.36	0.76	0.06	0.22	0.28	2.93	1.00
RUS	1.02	1.37	0.13	0.08	0.41	0.10	0.03	0.04	0.48	0.14
ITA	30.47	0.05	0.47	18.69	0.07	0.50	1.41	0.13	4.98	0.24
SAU	0.18	0.96	0.23	0.50	0.77	0.83	0.71	0.02	0.38	0.79
INA	7.12	0.38	1.33	0.96	0.04	1.70	3.10	0.60	2.49	0.31
MEX	20.24	0.13	58.89	0.16	0.53	0.03	1.26	0.05	4.27	0.02
TUR	5.16	0.64	1.32	1.90	1.28	0.40	0.67	0.05	0.80	1.53
EUR	30.59	0.34	1.02	31.65	0.02	0.99	2.56	0.10	4.70	0.40
Contribution to other	322.59	8.61	87.07	144.90	7.21	25.67	32.23	2.33	47.07	8.57
Contribution including own	396.65	104.80	146.38	177.50	41.30	41.61	45.92	96.32	54.24	46.03

	SOA	BRA	RUS	ITA	SAU	INA	MEX	TUR	EUR	Contribution from others
USA	3.71	0.73	3.59	0.40	0.08	9.33	0.09	0.38	0.46	25.95
CHI	0.89	0.07	0.18	0.04	0.10	0.32	0.00	0.07	0.08	3.81
JAP	1.18	0.97	3.33	0.22	0.07	7.99	0.05	0.06	0.06	40.69
FRA	5.16	0.08	3.98	2.92	0.05	10.30	0.01	0.71	0.49	67.40
CAN	0.97	0.90	2.50	0.64	0.05	9.30	0.05	0.29	0.13	65.91
UK	4.24	0.36	3.44	0.88	0.08	8.48	0.02	0.69	0.32	84.06
GER	4.79	0.02	4.13	2.75	0.04	9.18	0.05	0.50	0.49	86.30
IND	0.03	0.08	0.11	0.03	0.04	2.41	0.08	0.05	0.14	6.01
AUS	3.96	0.39	3.48	0.91	0.06	7.28	0.05	0.68	0.32	92.83
SOK	3.31	0.25	2.61	2.77	0.03	10.38	0.00	0.33	2.62	62.54
SOA	82.69	0.05	0.03	1.22	0.21	0.15	0.08	0.07	0.09	17.31
BRA	3.05	53.22	4.03	0.88	0.08	3.11	0.01	0.07	0.27	46.78

(continued)

Table 7 (continued)

	SOA	BRA	RUS	ITA	SAU	INA	MEX	TUR	EUR	Contribution from others
RUS	0.57	0.76	93.36	0.55	0.18	0.16	0.02	0.44	0.15	6.64
ITA	3.67	0.26	4.30	24.89	0.03	7.14	0.05	1.19	1.47	75.11
SAU	4.07	2.28	0.08	0.14	86.60	0.77	0.02	0.27	0.38	13.40
INA	2.83	0.63	2.48	0.50	0.46	74.29	0.45	0.29	0.05	25.71
MEX	1.18	0.94	3.38	0.21	0.07	8.16	0.36	0.06	0.06	99.64
TUR	2.45	0.16	0.79	3.12	0.64	10.77	0.16	68.00	0.18	32.00
EUR	4.49	0.17	4.00	4.16	0.04	10.98	0.05	0.77	2.98	97.02
Contribution to other	50.56	9.10	46.45	22.31	2.31	116.23	1.24	6.92	7.74	949.10
Contribution including own	133.26	62.32	139.80	47.20	88.91	190.52	1.60	74.91	10.72	1900.00
Spillover index										49.95%

USA—America, CHI—China, JAP—Japan, FRA—France, CAN—Canada, UK—United Kingdom, GER—Germany, IND—India, AUS—Australia, SOK—South Korea, SOA—South Africa, BRA—Brazil, RUS—Russia, ITA—Italy, SAU—Saudi Arabia, INA—Indonesia, MEX—Mexico, TUR—Turkey, EUR—Euronext

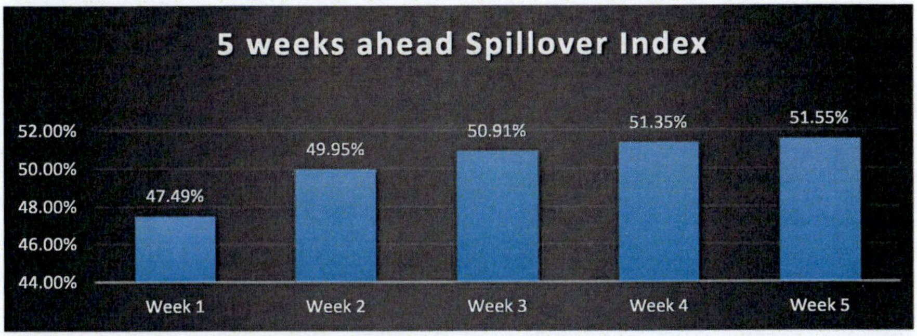

Fig. 5 Spillover index of return and volatility for 1 to 5 week forecast

The spillover index shows evidence of inward and outward transmission of volatility among the benchmark stock indices of G20 countries. The transmission of volatility increases significantly in the long run.

Table 8 Two weeks ahead forecast of volatility spillover index of G20 countries

	USA	CHI	JAP	FRA	CAN	UK	GER	IND	AUS	SOK
USA	71.95	0.21	0.47	1.92	0.07	0.03	1.24	0.09	2.35	1.04
CHI	0.18	95.51	0.32	0.08	0.02	0.27	0.25	0.03	1.12	0.04
JAP	20.54	0.20	58.17	0.17	0.66	0.02	1.14	0.05	4.22	0.04
FRA	34.66	0.69	1.07	30.96	0.01	0.58	1.80	0.07	3.91	0.34
CAN	36.50	0.37	1.74	6.52	32.50	0.65	2.93	0.12	1.72	0.22
UK	31.28	0.38	1.95	21.69	1.00	14.97	2.61	0.09	4.78	0.49
GER	27.73	0.67	1.90	27.61	0.30	0.72	12.91	0.07	2.18	1.18
IND	1.10	0.04	0.77	0.22	0.05	0.29	0.19	93.69	0.05	0.42
AUS	30.11	0.33	1.81	22.28	0.53	15.91	2.37	0.09	6.91	0.33
SOK	17.41	0.11	2.59	4.98	0.37	1.31	8.81	0.27	4.36	35.53
SOA	9.62	2.84	0.46	0.91	0.40	0.18	0.69	0.20	0.47	0.31
BRA	18.58	0.39	9.77	1.46	0.75	0.07	0.22	0.28	2.91	1.01
RUS	1.05	1.50	0.14	0.12	0.44	0.11	0.03	0.04	0.49	0.15
ITA	30.44	0.18	0.46	18.20	0.07	0.48	1.37	0.12	4.80	0.23
SAU	0.17	1.09	0.27	0.50	0.75	0.82	0.75	0.03	0.40	0.86
INA	7.36	0.46	1.31	0.95	0.04	1.69	3.05	0.59	2.52	0.37
MEX	20.38	0.19	57.73	0.18	0.64	0.03	1.24	0.05	4.22	0.05
TUR	5.43	0.65	1.31	1.86	1.32	0.40	0.65	0.06	0.79	1.53
EUR	30.47	0.53	0.96	30.16	0.02	0.93	2.49	0.10	4.47	0.41
Contribution to other	323.01	10.84	85.01	139.80	7.43	24.48	31.82	2.33	45.75	9.03
Contribution including own	394.97	106.35	143.18	170.76	39.93	39.45	44.73	96.02	52.66	44.56

	SOA	BRA	RUS	ITA	SAU	INA	MEX	TUR	EUR	Contribution from others
USA	4.69	0.73	3.95	0.63	0.12	9.57	0.09	0.38	0.48	28.05
CHI	1.15	0.14	0.18	0.06	0.13	0.35	0.00	0.08	0.09	4.49
JAP	1.60	0.97	3.47	0.27	0.10	8.19	0.05	0.06	0.06	41.83
FRA	6.55	0.08	4.51	3.24	0.06	10.24	0.01	0.71	0.52	69.04
CAN	1.65	0.86	2.88	1.03	0.08	9.67	0.07	0.31	0.17	67.50
UK	5.51	0.35	3.93	1.24	0.08	8.58	0.02	0.69	0.36	85.03
GER	6.35	0.02	4.70	3.20	0.05	9.28	0.06	0.52	0.56	87.09
IND	0.06	0.09	0.15	0.04	0.05	2.51	0.09	0.05	0.14	6.31
AUS	5.18	0.38	3.97	1.25	0.07	7.39	0.05	0.69	0.35	93.09
SOK	4.39	0.24	3.06	3.08	0.04	10.58	0.01	0.32	2.55	64.47
SOA	81.52	0.05	0.16	1.45	0.26	0.20	0.09	0.08	0.12	18.48
BRA	3.41	52.37	4.21	1.05	0.08	3.09	0.01	0.08	0.26	47.63

(continued)

Table 8 (continued)

	SOA	BRA	RUS	ITA	SAU	INA	MEX	TUR	EUR	Contribution from others
RUS	0.65	0.80	92.89	0.59	0.18	0.18	0.02	0.47	0.15	7.11
ITA	4.60	0.25	4.69	24.25	0.05	7.09	0.05	1.21	1.45	75.75
SAU	4.51	2.37	0.08	0.22	85.47	1.02	0.02	0.28	0.39	14.53
INA	3.29	0.62	2.54	0.59	0.49	73.35	0.46	0.28	0.06	26.65
MEX	1.61	0.95	3.53	0.26	0.11	8.37	0.36	0.06	0.06	99.64
TUR	3.12	0.18	1.02	3.14	0.64	10.99	0.16	66.57	0.18	33.43
EUR	5.77	0.16	4.49	4.42	0.06	10.87	0.05	0.77	2.87	97.13
Contribution to other	64.11	9.22	51.53	25.75	2.66	118.17	1.30	7.05	7.97	967.26
Contribution including own	145.63	61.58	144.42	50.01	88.12	191.52	1.66	73.62	10.84	1900.00
Spillover index										49.95%

USA—America, CHI—China, JAP—Japan, FRA—France, CAN—Canada, UK—United Kingdom, GER—Germany, IND—India, AUS—Australia, SOK—South Korea, SOA—South Africa, BRA—Brazil, RUS—Russia, ITA—Italy, SAU—Saudi Arabia, INA—Indonesia, MEX—Mexico, TUR—Turkey, EUR—Euronext

References

Arshanapalli, B., & Doukas, J. (1993). International stock market linkages: Evidence from the pre- and post-October 1987 period. *Journal of Banking & Finance, 17*(1), 193–208.

Bennett, P., & Kelleher, J. (1988). The international transmission of stock price disruption in October 1987. Quarterly Review, Federal Reserve Bank of New York, Summer, pp. 17–33.

Bhattacharjee, S., & Swaminathan, A. M. (2016). Stock market integration of India with rest of the world: An empirical study. *Indian Journal of Finance, 10*(5), 22–32. https://doi.org/10.17010/ijf/2016/v10i5/92934

Bollerslev, T. (1986). Generalized autoregressive conditional heteroskedasticity. *Journal of Econometrics, 31*(3), 307–327.

Diebold, F. X., & Yilmaz, K. (2009). Measuring financial asset return and volatility spillovers with application to global equity. *The Economic Journal*, 158–171

Gilmore, C. G., & McManus, G. M. (2003). Bilateral and multilateral cointegration properties between the German and central European equity markets. *Studies in Economics and Finance, 21*(1), 40–53.

Gündüz, L., & Hatemi, J. A. (2005). Is the tourism-led growth hypothesis valid for Turkey? *Applied Economics Letters, 12*(8), 499–504.

Hamao, Y., Masulis, R. W., & Ng, V. (1990). Correlations in price changes and volatility across international stock markets. *Review of Financial Studies, 3*(2), 281–307.

Jang, H., & Saul, W. (2002). The Asian financial crisis and the co-movement of Asian stock markets. *Journal of Asian Economics, 13*(1), 94–104.

Lee, B. S., Rui, O., & Wang, S. S. (2004). Information transmission between the NASDAQ and Asian second board markets. *Journal of Banking & Finance, 28*, 1637–1670.

Majid, M., & Aziz, H. A. (2009). Dynamic linkages among ASEAN 5 countries. *International Journal of Emerging Market, 4*(2), 160–184.

Mitra, A., & Bhattacharjee, K. (2015). Financial interdependence of international stock markets: A literature review. *Indian Journal of Finance, 9*(5), 20–33. https://doi.org/10.17010/ijf/2015/v9i5/71447

Shahzad, S., Kanwal, M., Ahmed, T., & Ur Rehman, M. (2016). Relationship between developed, European and South Asian stock markets: A multivariate analysis. *South Asian Journal of Global Business Research, 5*(3), 385–402.

Susmel, R., & Engle, R. F. (1994). Hourly volatility spillovers between international equity markets. *Journal of International Money and Finance, 13*, 3–25.

Vohra, P. S. (2016). A study of co-movement among indices of Bombay Stock Exchange. *Indian Journal of Finance, 10*(9), 11–29.

Can Effective E-Government Implementation Disrupt Corruption? An Exploratory Study

Punit Ahluwalia and Mohammad Merhi

Abstract The motivation of this study is to explore the relationship between e-government usage and corruption at a country level. This paper statistically assesses this relationship using data of 164 countries collected by credible organizations. Secondary data included in various reports published by international agencies were used for analyses. The sample of 164 countries makes the results more generalized than those published in previous studies. The empirical analysis shows that e-govt index is a significant antecedent of corruption index. The findings reported in this paper have important implications for policy makers and researchers.

Keywords e-government · Country-level analysis · Corruption · Government effectiveness · Percentage of individuals using the internet

1 Introduction

Many countries are plagued by high levels of corruption, and there is a widely held perception that this corruption can be decreased by e-government practices by limiting the human interaction between the citizens and the people in authority. For example, recently, the finance minister of India issued directions to the tax authorities that all notices for tax collection or inquiries must be processed through a central processing system (India Today, 2019). A 2016 UN Survey shows that governments of 148 countries provide some service using Internet channels (United Nations, 2016). The goal of e-government is to deliver government services to citizens in an effective and efficient manner to increase transparency and accountability, lessen corruption, grow revenue and/or reduce costs, while profiting from greater convenience (Merhi & Koong, 2016; World Bank, 2011). Although various studies report

P. Ahluwalia (✉)
The University of Texas, Rio Grande Valley, Edinburg, TX 78541, USA
e-mail: punit.ahluwalia@utrgv.edu

M. Merhi
Department of Decision Sciences, Judd Leighton School of Business, Indiana University South Bend, South Bend, IN, USA
e-mail: mmerhi@iusb.edu

© The Author(s), under exclusive license to Springer Nature Singapore Pte Ltd. 2022
A. Chandani et al. (eds.), *Achieving $5 Trillion Economy of India*, Springer Proceedings in Business and Economics, https://doi.org/10.1007/978-981-16-7818-9_10

that e-government is beneficial to both government and citizens, governments' initiative to simply provide these services to their citizens does not immediately translate to usage of these services. Adoption of e-government by citizens is hindered by a lack of trust and transparency in government, lack of awareness of technology, and low e-maturity levels (AlAwadhi & Morris, 2009; Belanger & Carter, 2008; Shareef et al., 2011). Many governments cite decreasing corruption as their primary motive of implementing e-government technology. This paper explores whether this belief of the negative relationship between e-government and corruption can be validated through rigorous statistical analysis. In other words, can it be established whether effective e-government policies, platform development, and implementation disrupt corrupt practices?

E-government has been defined as the use of information and communication technologies (ICTs) to improve the activities of public sector organizations (Ngafeeson & Merhi, 2013). Research shows that effective implementation and use of e-government-based systems enables many benefits such as increased technological innovation, greater self-efficacy of citizens, decreased cost of services, etc. (Hassan, 2017). Clearly, implementation of e-government systems requires a good IT infrastructure as well as high level of education among the citizens to be able to use these technologies.

Many governments are focusing on implementing e-government systems but research shows that a significant number of these systems are not successful because of low usage by citizens (Merhi, 2018). There may be several factors that determine citizens' usage but according to the technology diffusion model, technology factors are important drivers of technological innovation. Therefore, we use "percentage of people using internet (PII)" as an antecedent of e-government usage. The global data on PII are published by the United Nations for 164 countries and is used in this paper.

This study proposes a model that examines the relationship between e-government and corruption at country level. The model also includes two other factors, percentage of people using the Internet and government effectiveness index. This paper makes the following specific contributions:

1. Empirically investigates the relationship between e-government usage and corruption level at country level using data from one hundred and sixty four countries.
2. Analyzes and interprets the empirical relationships in the context of research and government policy opportunities.

This section presented the introduction. Next section (Sect. 2) describes the research model. The research design is presented in Sect. 3, followed by presentation of results in Sect. 4. The results are discussed in Sect. 5. Finally, conclusions and implications are presented in Sect. 6.

2 Research Model and Hypotheses

In this section, we provide details of each of the related factors included in the model. We also explain the relationships between these factors and corruption perceptions.

E-Government (EGOV)

The e-government development index measures the ability and willingness of a country's administration to adopt ICTs with the intention to provide information and services to its citizens. In this paper, we use this measure as e-government usage in a country.

Percentage of Individuals Using the Internet (PII)

According to the diffusion of innovation theory, adoption of technology is integral to diffusion of innovation in a social system (Rogers, 1962). Accordingly, the availability and adoption of Internet-based technologies that are fundamental to the use of e-government platforms reaching a critical mass. The International Telecommunication Union published the World Telecommunication/ICT Development Report which includes a measure of individuals using the Internet as a percentage of population (PII) (World Bank, 2016b). Thus, we hypothesize that percent of individuals using the Internet (PII) is a driver of e-government use.

Hypothesis 1 (H1): Greater the percent of individuals using the Internet (PII), greater is e-government usage (egov).

Government Effectiveness (GEI)

According to the World Bank, the government effectiveness index "measures the quality of public services, the quality and degree of independence from political pressures of the civil service, the quality of policy formulation and implementation, and the credibility of the government's commitment to such policies (World Bank, 2016a)." It can be argued that increased use of e-government improves the quality and delivery of public services because of increased speed, greater access, standardization of basic processes and insulating the citizen from government agents. Thus, we state the second hypothesis:

Hypothesis 2 (H2): Greater e-government (EGOV) use has a positive effect on government effectiveness (GEI).

Corruption

Corruption is defined as the "abuse of public power or authority for private benefit" (Anokhin & Schulze, 2009). Corruption manifests in forms of bribery, clientelism, embezzlement, lobbying, and patronage. Corruption creates distrust in citizens hindering effective delivery of public services (Damania et al., 2004). Many countries around the world face high levels of perceived corruption, and there is a widely held belief that corrupt practices are one of the biggest impediments to

Table 1 Countries with high and low corruption indexes

High CPI			Low CPI		
Country	CPI	GEI	Country	CPI	GEI
Denmark	90	1.89	Somalia	10	−2.18
New Zealand	90	1.86	South Sudan	11	−2.26
Finland	89	1.85	Syrian Arab Republic	13	−1.82
Sweden	88	1.79	Sudan	14	−1.41
Switzerland	86	2.03	Libya	14	−1.89

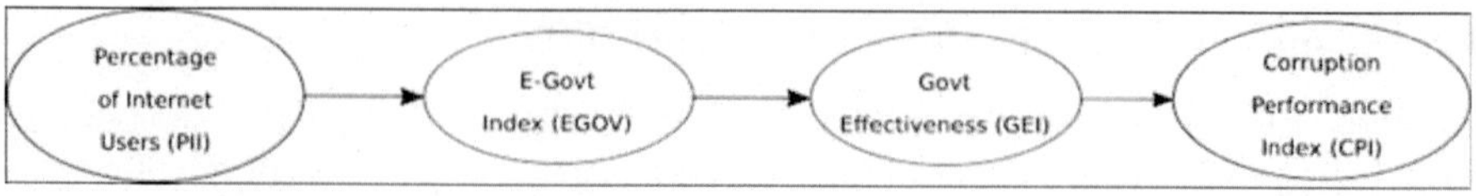

Fig. 1 Research model

the overall public good. Transparency International publishes a yearly Corruption Perception Index (CPI), which is a widely used indicator of corruption worldwide (ourworldindata.org). The countries with low CPI are plagued by untrustworthy and badly functioning public institutions (transparency.org) and negative government effectiveness index, whereas the countries with high CPI exhibit positive GEI. On the other hand, less corrupt countries tend to have higher degrees of information about the public expenditure and stronger standards when it comes to integrity for public officials (transparency.org). Table 1 shows CPI and GEI values from the data for select five countries ranked by high and low CPI measures.

Accordingly, we argue that more effective governments are better able to control corruption. Thus, we state the third hypothesis as:

Hypothesis 3 (H3): Greater the Government Effectiveness Index (GEI), Greater will be the Corruption Index (CPI).[1]

The three research hypotheses are shown in Fig. 1.

3 Research Design

Secondary data comprising of 164 countries were used for conducting the empirical analysis. The data are drawn from credible organizations that have the resources to collect data at a global level and are known for their integrity. The datasets used for analysis are drawn from the Transparency International "Corruption Index 2016,"

[1] Greater index values are associated with lesser corruption.

Table 2 Countries with high and low e-government indexes

High EGOV		Low EGOV	
Country	EGOV	Country	EGOV
United Kingdom	0.919	Somalia	0.027
Australia	0.914	Niger	0.059
Singapore	0.883	Central African Republic	0.079
Finland	0.882	Eritrea	0.090
Sweden	0.870	Guinea	0.123

and the "United Nations E-government Survey 2016." The variables of interest are now described.

E-government

The e-government development index presents the state of e-government development of a country. It assesses the Website development patterns in a country, as well as incorporates the access characteristics such as the infrastructure and educational levels to reflect how a country is using IT to promote access and inclusion of its country. The data for this factor were obtained from the United Nations data repository. See Table 2 for sample values in this index.

Government Effectiveness (GEI)

The GEI taps into the quality of public services, government policies, and their implementation. This measure also reflects insulation of civil service from political influences and government's credibility toward its policies. These data were collected in the United Nations E-Government Survey 2016. See Table 1 for representative sample values in this index.

Corruption (CPI)

Transparency International publishes index on perceptions about levels of corruption in a country. The CPI measures range between 0 and 100 which represents no corruption at all and 0 represents highest corruption. Table 1 shows CPI values from the data for select five countries ranked by high and low CPI measures.

4 Analysis and Results

Descriptive analysis is the first step in most statistical analyses as it helps in providing useful information about the data such as its distribution. For example, descriptive analysis may reveal that the data are not suitable for further analysis. The results of the descriptive statistics are presented in Table 3. Unlike structural equation modeling, the PLS method is not based on assumptions of normal distribution of data.

Table 3 Descriptive analysis

VARS	*N*	MEAN	SD	MIN	MAX	RANGE	SKEW	KURTOSIS	SE
PII	164	48.72	28.63	0.00	98.24	98.24	−0.02	−1.30	2.24
EGOV	164	0.50	0.22	0.03	0.92	0.89	−0.04	−0.99	0.02
GEI	164	−0.06	1.00	−2.26	2.21	4.47	0.24	−0.52	0.08
CPI	164	43.04	19.39	10.00	90.00	80.00	0.67	−0.34	1.51

Table 4 Inner model squared multiple correlations (R^2)

PII	EGOV	GEI	CPI
0.000	0.843	0.754	0.851

Table 5 Bootstrap SEs and two-tailed significance tests

Relation	Estimate	SE	*t*	*p* (regression)
PII EGOV	0.918	0.012	0.70	<0.5
EGOV GEI	0.868	0.019	0.45	<0.5
GEI CPI	0.922	0.012	0.81	<0.5

We used Matrixpls package offered by R statistical repository (Ronkko, 2017) to conduct multivariate PLS regression analysis. The R^2 values reflect the amount of variance in endogenous latent variables that is caused by their antecedent latents. Table 4 shows the R^2 values which show that significant variance in the dependent variables is explained by the independent variables included in the research model.

The standardized coefficients, *t* values and the regression coefficients are shown in Table 5. These results show data confirmed the three hypotheses as the *p*-values for all three relationships which are statistically significant, i.e., < 0.5.

5 Discussion

This paper explored empirical validation of widely reported assertion that effective e-government implementation and practices can reduce corruption. Although many factors may directly or indirectly influence corruption at a country level, we examined the stated hypotheses in the research model by drawing from secondary data published by the United Nations, World Bank, and Transparency International. The data confirmed all three hypothesis. This paper hypothesizes and confirms antecedent roles of PII, EGOV, GEI in influencing corruption. The results are mapped onto the research model and are shown in Fig. 2.

It is frequently argued that e-government systems help in reducing corruption. The results produced by the analysis presented in this paper suggest that effective e-government policies and implementation have a significant impact on corruption.

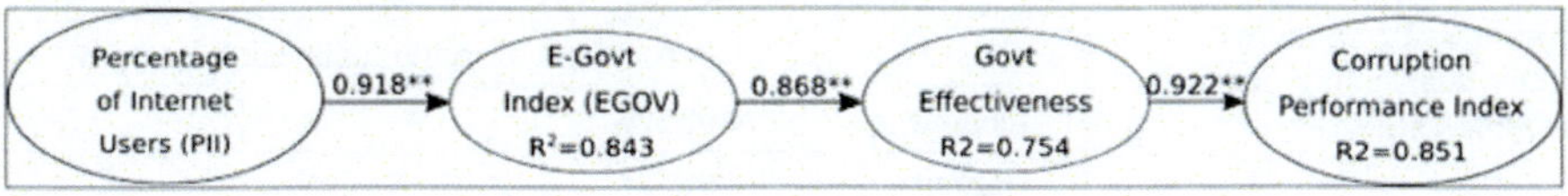

Fig. 2 PLS model: results

The coefficient of the relationship between corruption and government effectiveness is very high ($\beta = 0.922$).

The results also indicate that Internet usage by the citizens is a significant and strong ($\beta = 0.918$) antecedent to effective e-government practices. With the advances in social media and technologies, citizens are able to share news faster. Individuals can also access information in a very fast and convenient way. This confirms the assertions made by the innovation diffusion theory (Rogers, 1962).

In this paper, we also confirmed a positive relationship between e-government implementation and government effectiveness. Thus, it is important for the government to focus on effective implementation of e-government policies and platforms that would improve the quality of delivery of public services to its citizens.

6 Conclusions and Implications

The motivation of this study was to examine the empirical relationship between e-government usage and corruption. Using the secondary data published by very reputable international organizations, we explored these relationships. The data collected supported all the hypotheses postulated in this paper.

The ever-increasing adoption of e-government among varying governmental agencies has led to many studies that measure the adoption and usage of these systems by citizens of different nations. This research constructs a model that depicts the relationships between e-government usage and corruption index, and empirically test it. This study makes two important contributions to the literature. Even as most studies in e-government literature examine e-government use as the dependent construct, no study has yet investigated the research model postulated in this study. Thus, this research adds to the literature and the body of knowledge. Second, by empirically investigating the hypothesized relationships using a dataset with a greater sample size lends greater generalizability to the results. Previous studies that examined e-government usage and adoption have used smaller sample size.

A multitude of people is expected to find this paper useful and interesting. In addition to its contribution to the growing empirical base of literature on e-government and corruption, this study has significant implications for policy makers and people working with e-government technologies. During the last decade, it is witnessed that governments from all over the world are trying to develop efficient as well as effective government services and delivery systems by using technologies and especially e-government systems. Despite their attempt to achieve success, unfortunately some

Table 6 Percentage of individuals using internet: sample values

Country	Percentage of individuals using internet
Iceland	98.24
Bahrain	98.00
Luxembourg	97.49
Norway	97.30
Denmark	96.97
India	29.55

governments fail to accomplish their goals. The results obtained in this research suggests that effective government is a significant antecedent to corruption and that the effectiveness and quality of governments' delivery of public services can be significantly improved by effective e-government implementation and adoption.

The data also suggest that the Internet usage is a significant driver of e-government usage. This finding is supported by the diffusion of innovation theory. This finding may be especially important for Indian policy makers. Table 6 shows the top five rated countries as well as India's measure as reported in the United Nations ITU report (World Bank, 2016b). This shows that there is a huge opportunity for the practitioners to make improvement in this area of governance.[2] In this context, looking into the aspect of improving human capital and whether it can improve diffusion of e-government channels offers a worthwhile research opportunity.

It is important to know that effective implementation and adoption of e-government platforms can play an important role in disrupting established corrupt practices by lending themselves to ease of search and reporting. All these factors facilitate transparency which is considered to be the strongest anti-dote of corruption. Thus, when governments make greater use of digital technologies in their decision making, in providing information to its citizens, and to interact with various stakeholders, they help in strengthening the perceptions that their practices are free of corruption. Although this study looks at the Internet usage and effective government factors, other factors such as infrastructure, e-participation, and education may also be examined in how they impact corruption. Cultural dimensions are yet another set of factors that may shed more light into how to curb corruption through implementation of e-government platforms.

While this paper makes important contribution to theory and practice, it is necessary to acknowledge its limitations as well. The findings of the paper are a result of statistical analysis of secondary data. It is practically impossible to collect global level data by individuals or even group of researchers. Therefore, most studies that examine cross-country-level phenomena are dependent on secondary data. This also means that the studies can only assess the indexes that have been published by large organizations such as the United Nations and Transparency International. Second, this study examines the relationships of four macro-level factors and e-government adoption. Many other determinants have been found to also influence e-government

[2] Please note that this data was published in 2016. These measures may have changed over time.

adoption and corruption. However, the variables used in this study have been found to be both stable and useful in describing the phenomenon.

References

AlAwadhi, S., & Morris, A. (2009). Factors influencing the adoption of e-government services. *Journal of Software, 4*(6), 584–590.

Anokhin, S., & Schulze, W. S. (2009). Entrepreneurship, innovation and corruption. *Journal of Business Venturing, 24*(5), 465–476.

Bank, W. (2011). *Definition of e-government*. http://go.worldbank.org/M1JHE0Z280

Belanger, F., & Carter, L. (2008). Trust and risk in e-government adoption. *Journal of Strategic Information Systems, 17*, 165–176.

Damania, R., Fredriksson, P. G., & Mani, M. (2004). The persistence of corruption and regulatory compliance failures: Theory and evidence. *Public Choice, 121*, 363–390.

Hassan, S. A. (2017). Investigating the relationship of e-government, control of corruption, economic prosperity and environmental degradation: An analysis of Asian region. *International Journal of Innovation and Economic Development, 3*(2), 18–28.

India Today. (2019). *Finance minister Nirmala Sitharaman announces raft of measures to boost economy, more steps on anvil*. https://www.indiatoday.in/business/story/finance-minister-nirmala-sitharaman-announces-raft-of-measures-to-boost\\-economy-more-steps-on-anvil-1590974-2019-08-23

Merhi, M. I. (2018). Does national culture have any impact on e-government usage? *International Journal of Technology Diffusion, 9*, 29–45.

Merhi, M. I., & Koong, K. S. (2016). E-government effectiveness: A rocket model of contributing user-related factors. *International Journal of Business and Standards, 11*(1), 1–19.

Ngafeeson, M. N., & Merhi, M. I. (2013). E-government diffusion: Evidence from the last decade. *International Journal of Electronic Government Research, 9*(2), 1–18.

Rogers, M. (1962). *Diffusion of innovations*. The Free Press.

Ronkko, M. (2017). *matrixpls: Matrix-based partial least squares estimation*. R package version 1.0.5.

Shareef, M. A., Kumar, V., Kumar, U., & Dwivedi, Y. K. (2011). E-government adoption model (GAM): Differing service maturity levels. *Government Information Quarterly, 28*, 17–35.

United Nations E-Participation Index. https://publicadministration.un.org/egovkb/en-us/About/Overview/E-Participation-Index

World Bank. (2016a). *Government effectiveness (estimate)*. https://databank.worldbank.org/reports.aspx?source=1147&series=GV.GOVT.EF.ES

World Bank. (2016b). *Individuals using the internet (% of population): International telecommunication union, world telecommunication/ict development report and database*. https://data.worldbank.org/indicator/IT.NET.USER.ZS

Moderation of Income and Age on Customer Purchase Intention of Green Cosmetics in Bangalore

S. V. Krishna Kishore, Prabha Kiran, Jayanta Banerjee, and M. Vasudevan

Abstract Cracking the code of customer purchase behaviour is a challenge for market researchers as myriad factors interfere. Marketers are puzzled as competitors position a new product category in the market to create demand. Indian public perceived cosmetics composition as blend of "healthy" chemical extracts. Television commercials portrayed the presence of chemicals in cosmetics as a product performance booster. People attributed chemical presence to superior product performance. Saturated markets witnessed competitors aiming at increased sales with similar commercials. Under pressure to differentiate, the idea of organic cosmetics started. Companies invested heavily on product development, marketing and branding. Expected success was not achieved as buyers measured performance of cosmetics weighing the absence of chemicals. Scepticism on organic level of the products emerged as various brand commercials claimed their respective compositions a true organic product. Fewer studies explained purchase intention of green cosmetics without focus on health consciousness and consumer innovativeness. Product diffusions were strategized on the basis of consumer innovativeness. Health consciousness captured individual's weightage on health and well-being while purchasing a product. This paper explores relationship of health consciousness and consumer innovativeness with purchase intention development conducting exploratory factor analysis, regression analysis and interaction analysis on selected independent variables using dependent variables. The study found both consumer innovativeness and health consciousness leading to development of purchase intention of green cosmetics. Age and income moderated the relationship of consumer innovativeness and purchase intention.

Keywords Green · Cosmetics · Purchase · Intention · Age · Income · Health consciousness · Consumer innovativeness

---

P. Kiran (✉)
Westminster International University, Tashkent, Uzbekistan

S. V. Krishna Kishore · J. Banerjee · M. Vasudevan
School of Business and Management, Christ University, Bangalore 560074, India

© The Author(s), under exclusive license to Springer Nature Singapore Pte Ltd. 2022
A. Chandani et al. (eds.), *Achieving $5 Trillion Economy of India*, Springer Proceedings in Business and Economics, https://doi.org/10.1007/978-981-16-7818-9_11

1 Introduction

Green product category demand in recent times is on positive slope. But it is also evident that there is a sluggish customer acceptance of green philosophy. Green cosmetics manufacturer's attempts of customer's acquisition have not seen a convincing success (White et al., 2019a, b). In nineteenth century, cosmetics marketing techniques evolved. Marketing communications focused on benefits of beauty and health. Companies funded R&D activities embedding beauty and wellness ingredients in their products. Later, companies positioned products as treatable solution for oily skin-related problems. Cosmetics were associated with medicines.

UK cosmetic industry promoted wellness and organic lifestyle to target their customers (Dimitrova et al., 2009). Initial responses were impressive. Suppliers formed a robust distribution chain. Wellness promotion drove market growth at UK in the year 2010 (Mintel, 2010). Mintel (2010) had also reported spike investment in wellness ads and misleading information of companies entering into the category leading to decrease in customer confidence. In 2013, the industry registered 3.8% growth compared to 2012. In 2015, sales were estimated to cross 14 billion mark. Mintel (2018) found more than half of consumers in Britain favoured using cosmetics made from natural ingredients. In the present scenario, global consumers are confused to select green products due to confusion on definition of a green product.

Mason (2012) discovered health benefit elements driving the sales of organic cosmetics not features that used to be frequent part of market communications. Mason recommended organic cosmetic manufacturers to communicate benefits instead of ingredient details. In Hong Kong, knowledge dissemination about foods and their benefits amplified organic food product sales (Cheung et al., 2015). In Malaysia, Thambiah et al. supported the finding of food knowledge. Taiwanese believed cancer can be treated by adopting organic food habits (Tung et al., 2015).

According to Hill and Lynchehaun (2002), consumers already believed organic food products taste better as they do not consist of chemical ingredients. Previous studies found that consumer's health consciousness as a major driver of organic product sales (Huber et al., 2011; Patnaik et al., 2021; Sirieix et al., 2011; Van Loo et al., 2013).

Indian urbanites live in packed routines. They are vulnerable to illness than their ancestors. Health and wellness products are prioritized by urban dwellers. Products and services portraying well-being on their packages are being preferred. Market entrants skimmed pricing to make money. In the past, chemical cosmetics were sold in the market; cues of chemical cosmetic trend changes can be observed with managerial and marketing tweaks by companies. Modern urbanites demand green cosmetics and healthier lifestyle.

Cosmetics market was valued at USD 532 billion in 2017 and is forecasted to reach approximately USD 863 billion in 2024, growing at a CAGR of more than 7% between 2018 and 2024. India is one of the top ten countries in cultivable land availability for growing natural ingredients for green cosmetics (Laheri, 2015). The organic cosmetic industry in the world has gained momentum. Organic cosmetic sector's growth in India is at a snail pace. The reason for achieving fast growth momentum in world markets is not clear. As a first mover company in the market releases a green product, imitators flood the market causing distortion of customer's belief system and preferences. Customer purchase intention development needs a tranquil environment. This is absent due to aggressive competition –generating clutter. In 2010, Cosmetic Organic and Natural Standards (COSMOS) was formed to monitor the adherence of cosmetic brands to green theme.

A product is green when it preserves nature with less pollution backed with a concrete plan of recycling and disposal of wastes leading to sustained living of animal and plant species (McEachern & Mcclean, 2002). Shamdasani et al. (1993) had already made point of nature preservation and recycling in products. Csorba and Boglea (2011) argued that a cosmetic is considered green if the composition includes fruit- and botanical-based formulae (Csorba & Boglea, 2011). This argument was supported by Mintel report.

Super-premium, premium and mass green cosmetic brands have earned small revenues citing an important need to research and identify effective indicators of green cosmetics purchase intention (GVR, 2019). Factors influencing and interacting store visitors to buy the green brands have to be explored. The demographic variables like age, gender, income status reserve vital insights on customer purchasing behaviour (Roberts, 2021) – Research Gap.

Authors point at difference in consumer purchase behaviour of general cosmetics and organic cosmetics. Natural ingredients and organic ingredients are powerful purchase decision drivers followed by botanical ingredients, free from label claims, not tested on animals, fragrance- and gluten-free product properties. General products are weighed on the basis of cost and benefits. With enhanced green literacy rate in the market and exposure to health articles, consumers are aware of health implication by usage of chemical-based products (Blasi et al., 2020; Kotler, 2011). Overall review of all industry trends lead us to form research questions in Indian market scenario like.

- What influences the development of purchase intention of organic cosmetics?
- Do health consciousness and innovative consumers drive the purchase intention?
- Do age and income moderate the development of purchase intention?

The rising preference of organic elements in cosmetics is a challenge for (Dimitrova et al., 2009; Johri & Sahasakmontri, 1998; Kim & Seock, 2009). There are studies at various countries on increased production of green products relating to changing consumer tastes (Rybowska, 2014).

2 Review of Literature

Initial literatures indicated scholars acknowledging increase in the demand of organic cosmetics. Media promotions on wellness and fitness lifestyle amplified organic cosmetics sales. Li et al. (2019) observed modern cosmetic industry's reliance on innovation and technology. Companies are informed on customers preferences for younger appearances linked to organic products. Companies aimed at better understanding of consumer preferences and market conditions resulting in feeble rise in number of studies on organic products (Dimitrova et al., 2009; Johri & Sahasakmontri, 1998; Kim & Seock, 2009; Rybowska, 2014).

Laroche et al. (2002) observed that environmental concern among consumers solely need not necessarily lead to organic product purchases. On the contrary, Cervellon and Carey (2011) argued wider awareness of green products contributed to sales growth of green cosmetics category.

According to Organic Monitor (2012), in addition to efficiency at R&D organizational verticals creating green formulations, the summits organized on creating awareness about natural ingredients benefits connected with customers. Package Digest (2010) also reported similar findings. Cervellon and Carey (2011) observed gap in consumer's acceptance towards organic cosmetics. The solution for low adoption needs to be explored. Similar studies in past have been conducted in the area of China and Korea. Insight on Indian consumer cosmetic preferences is negligible in research world (Matić & Puh, 2016).

Lea and Worsley (2005) linked green products with demographic characteristics. Harper (2002) and Ahmed (2010) also found very small set of consumers consistently consume green product categories in India. The consumption depended on mostly demographic attributes. The gaps were identified from studies outside India, especially in Korea, Japan and Finland. Not many studies have been done in India with respect to cosmetics' market. Since most of the researches are based out of outside market, it is evident that Indian cosmetic market will be definitely different from others. According to Mintel, the male grooming product market grew almost 12% between 2006 and 2011. Still, more studies focussed only on female cosmetics and their perceptions. So far, studies conducted are mostly on consumer attitude and perception (Anjana, 2018; Baghel, 2020). → Research Gap.

2.1 Operational Definition

A definition of green cosmetics has been adopted in the study to clear define the scope of green cosmetics. According to Chin et al. (2018) Green cosmetics can also be called as organic cosmetics. They fit in the bracket of green theme if they adhere to environmental preservation and promotes ecological stability. Green, organic and natural cosmetics terms have been used to discuss and measure the consumer behaviour.

According to Gourville (2006) and Rogers (2003), there is complexity in purchase intention development of organic products compared to general products. They also argued that the set of general variables used to predict the purchase intention may not be sufficient. This makes clear that a specific set of variables that have consistently explained the purchase intention of organic cosmetics (Rybowska, 2014; Tsakiridou et al., 2008). A review of scholarly articles pointed us at variables like social influence, price sensitivity, general characteristics of the products, green cosmetics buying pattern and health consciousness were selected due to their relevance to the Indian market situation. According to Zelezny et al. (2000) and Tikka et al. (2000), from the year 2001, more females were worried on chemical effects and started preferring green cosmetics and products. According to Lea and Worsley (2005) and Ahmed (2010), psychological attributes acted as major influencers compared to other classifications in preferring green cosmetics. Mainieri et al. (1997) found that females would be loyal customers after trusting on green cosmetics. This was supported by Pillai (2013).

Also, most studies are done combing organic products and cosmetics. Specific studies on organic cosmetics are less. Besides users are still not familiar with all the categories and brand of green cosmetics; hence, overall research with respect to organic cosmetics is not valid for most of the occasion. There is a gap in studies on cosmetic preference across genders, as most of the studies are on female consumers. Indian customers are yet to adapt organic cosmetics. Until and unless proper study is conducted, the information gap will widen.

2.2 *Consumer Innovativeness*

Consumer innovativeness is a personality trait reflecting willingness to change. Consumer innovativeness is a tendency of an individual to adopt a new product earlier compared to others in the society (Rogers & Shoemaker, 1971). The propensity of consumer to purchase fresh releases in the market points at interesting dimensions of decision making (Hirschman, 1980).

Consumer innovativeness construct assumes that consumers would like to go for new experiences. Their mental and physical activities are in synch with motivations. Cote, Wood and Roehrich (2004) observed that innovativeness forms by change embracing behaviour of consumers. Researchers consider innovative consumers as prime segment in getting revenue inflow from the market (Cowart et al., 2008; Gil et al., 2000; Klink & Athaide, 2010). Bartels and Reinders (2010, 2011) observed that consumer innovativeness is different in its approach as it studies the behaviour with new product adoption perspective. Innovativeness could explain the consumer acceptance of new product based on cultural relativity. This gives key insight on connecting campaigns and the consumer's intention to study behaviour (Bartels & Reinders, 2011; Goldsmith & Flynn, 1992; Wood & Swait, 2002).

Bhate and Lawler (1997), Barrena-Figueroa and Garcia-Lopez-de-Meneses (2013) found that consumer innovators pay high prices to purchase new products earlier ignoring the conventional products in the market. This behavioural pattern of purchasing premium-priced novel products are found rapidly among innovators. Other classifications in diffusion of innovation model try lately. According to Leavitt and Walton and Chao et al. (2013), consumer innovativeness construct has consistently explained development of purchase intention on organic products. Hwang et al. (2020) also found that CI leading to purchase intention. Zhang et al. (2020) supported that CI explains the willingness to pay. There we hypothesized.

H1N: Consumers innovativeness of an individual does not lead to development of purchase intention of green cosmetics.

H1A: Consumers innovativeness of an individual leads to development of purchase intention of green cosmetics.

2.3 Health Consciousness

Health consciousness is the propensity of an individual to centre decisions on purchase and lifestyle on conscious of health (Gould, 1988; Jayanti & Burns, 1998). Kraft and Goodell (1993) identified that maintenance of nutritional choices and physical fitness led to health-based choices of the consumers. Health information for health conscious people is attractive as they believe life-threatening situation can be averted (Dutta-Bergman, 2004, 2006). Aldoory (2001), Iversen and Kraft (2006) found that health conscious consumers pay higher attention to health-based market communications (Dutta-Bergman, 2006; Moorman & Matulich, 1993). Dutta-Bergman, (2004) and Ahadzadeh et al. (2015) observed the same finding in the Internet. Health conscious consumers give prime importance to well-being and longevity. This was also later supported by Dutta-Bergman (2004), Kim and Chung (2011) and Newsom et al. (2005).

Michaelidou and Hassan (2008) observed health consciousness as prime motive behind the organic products purchases. Kim and Chung (2011) linked health consciousness to purchase intention of organic cosmetics. According to Kraft and Goodell (1993), Newsom et al. (2005), health consciousness is related to daily consumer purchase decisions. Consumers maintain elevated awareness of organic products that promote healthy lifestyle and wellness.

Johri and Sahasakmontri (1998) observed that health conscious people believe synthetic-free products give glowing skin and it lead to beautiful appearance. These individuals are more ingredients driven than the finished product. Tarkiainen and Sundqvist (2005) commented on keen interest in ingredients or being health consciousness does not affect the scale of the items purchased. Kim and Seock (2009) found that heath conscious people engaged themselves more in exercises and health clubs to promote wellness. This finding was further supported by Michaelidou and Hassan (2008) as well as Kim and Chung (2011). Female consumers were concerned on their lifestyles, health, self-image and economic considerations while purchasing of green cosmetic products (Pudaruth et al., 2015).

We found various studies linking animal well-being, environmental concern, health and safety as motive for female buyers to buy green cosmetics and healthcare products. However, it is interesting to observe women did not only buy cosmetics and beauty care products because of environmental concerns or personal beliefs but mainly due to health reasons (Vermeir & Verbeke, 2006). Leire and Thidell (2005) contended requirement for clear comprehension of female inspiration concerning eco-named beautifiers as female customers are more concerned on corrupt advertisers with "green" claims (Bhaskaran et al., 2006; Thogersen et al., 2010). As most of the consumers lack knowledge and awareness about green cosmetics, so they tend to opt for those products promote based on traditional methods. According to Tran et al. (2020) health consciousness mediated the marketing mix factors towards purchase intention. Nagaraj (2021) found health consciousness leading to purchase intention. So, we hypothesized.

H2N: Health consciousness of an individual does not lead to development of purchase intention of green cosmetics.
H2A: Health consciousness of an individual leads to development of purchase intention of green cosmetics.

Consistency in product quality leads to consumer loyalty (Chumpitaz & Paparoidamis, 2004). Thus, green customers see organic ingredients inclusion as the best quality point and judge green products as more secure because of the evaded danger of pesticide deposits in the makeup items (Cornelissen et al., 2008; D'Souza et al., 2006; Martenson, 2007; McWilliams & Siegel, 2001; Rios et al., 2006; Yiridoe et al., 2005).

2.4 Moderation of Age and Income

Demographic variables deepen the understanding of variables in the model.

Davies (1995) found age as vital determinant of purchase preferences compared to other variables among demographic variables. Lea concluded that moderately aged people have strong conviction and preferences towards natural products. Finisterra do Paco et al. (2009) found no critical relations among age and green attitudes. Mihic and Kuran focused on purchases rather than attitude and found age, income, marital status are important determinants of green cosmetic purchase.

As green product preferring segment is small resulting in purchases getting sluggish, the prices of these products are high. This brings income factor in demography as second important variable that explains offering (Davies, 1995; Chinnici, 2002; Lea, 2005). The literature provided on the product package played a vital role in forming of customer loyalty (Ahmed, 2010; Lockie et al., 2002).

Green cosmetics purchases were not studied on the basis of age and income role purchase intention development. Davies (1995) observed purchase decisions of organic cosmetics depend on age cycle of an individual. Im et al. tested demographic variables like age, education, income and concluded no moderating effect on consumer innovativeness. Lea and Worsley (2005) supported Im et al.'s findings but stated middle-aged persons are more likely to purchase organic items and with age, purchase preferences of organic cosmetics rises. Straughan and Roberts (1999) had already argued age and income explain eco-conscious buying behaviour of consumers. D'Souza et al. (2007) supported Straughan and Robert's findings and argued demographic factors as a lens for researchers with perspectives to look at consumer behaviour. No study area is there on income and gender moderation of organic cosmetics. Ali et al. (2019) supported the view of moderating demographic variables by testing age and financial costs. Therefore, we hypothesized.

H3 a (n): Age of an individual does not moderate the path of consumer innovativeness leading to purchase intention.
H3 a: Age moderates of an individual moderate the path of consumer innovativeness leading to purchase intention.
H3 b (n): Age of an individual does not moderate the path of health consciousness leading to purchase intention.
H3 b: Age of an individual moderates the path of health consciousness leading to purchase intention.
H4 a (n): Income of an individual does not moderate the path of consumer innovativeness leading to purchase intention.
H4 a: Income of an individual moderates the path of consumer innovativeness leading to purchase intention.
H4 b (n): Income of an individual does not moderate the path of health consciousness leading to purchase intention.
H4 b: Income of an individual moderates the path of health consciousness leading to purchase intention.

Davies (1995), Chinnici (2002), Lea and Worsley (2005) had already concluded that purchase of organic products can also be explained better with of income data of a region.

2.5 *Purchase Intention (Dependent Variable)*

Purchase intention is a will of an individual to purchase a particular product or a service. Purchase intention has a credible record as dependent variable in explaining the adoption phenomena in various cases (Chen & Chang, 2012) (Fig. 1).

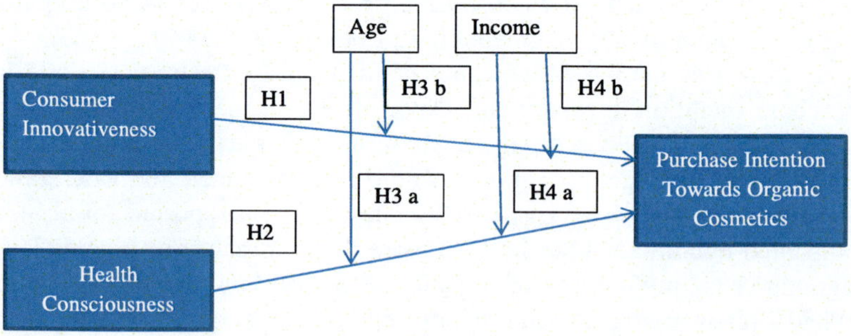

Fig. 1 Proposed conceptual framework of green cosmetics adoption. *Source* Literature review

Goldsmith and Hofacker (1991) observed consumer innovativeness as an immediate predictor of purchase intention. PI was widely used in new product purchase-based studies. Rashid (2009) concluded that purchase intention can explain new product adoption behaviour in all product categories. Rybowska (2014) identified consumers insensitiveness to price and perception of superior value on green products. There were enhancements in biotechnological extraction of natural ingredients. As consumers lacked knowledge and awareness about green cosmetics, consumers weighed old brands positioning methods than novel one (Lin et al., 2018).

3 Objectives of the Study

The main objective of the study is to observe factors resulting in development of purchase intention towards green cosmetics. The sub-objectives include identifying factors impacting purchase intention and to determine the strength of their relationship. Moderation effect of income and age on the path of independent variables (consumer innovativeness and health consciousness) leading to customer purchase intention development is also aimed.

4 Research Methodology

Descriptive approach was made to accomplish stated objectives. Data was collected through structured questionnaire. Non-probabilistic sampling was used to trace respondents. Sampling frame was not available. Under non-probabilistic sampling technique, convenience sampling was used to reach the respondents. Respondents were engaged outside the stores. It was hit or miss basis based on the consent of the respondent. Questionnaire was administered to collect data.

The questionnaire was tested prior to full-fledged data collection. Pilot study was conducted for a sample size of 36 to test reliability and internal consistency of data. The internal consistency check was done for the instrument. The Cronbach's alpha of reliability statistics need to reflect data reliability of more than 0.6. The results of reliability analysis is as follows (Table 1).

Each variable with their items was tested for reliability analysis. All variables had a satisfactory Cronbach's alpha value. Cronbach's alpha is a measure of internal consistency, that is, closely related set of items as a group. The value was more than 0.75 against the role of thumb 0.60. Overall model's value was at 0.82. The value was satisfactory for further analysis. Over 517 responses were collected. After scrutiny, 62 responses were removed for tabulation and coding as they were faulty. Four hundred nine responses were considered for further analysis. SPSS was used to analyse data.

Table 1 Summary of reliability analysis

S. No.	Variable items	Reliability (Cronbach's alpha)	Model's Cronbach's alpha)
1	Health consciousness	0.79	0.82
2	Consumer innovativeness	0.74	
3	Purchase intention	0.86	

Source Data analysis

5 Data Analysis and Interpretation

After tabulating and coding data, raw data was treated for outliers and missing data. After data cleaning process, the data set was subjected to reliability, factor analysis and multiple regression with interaction analysis. Factor analysis provides evidence about a scale in question being one-dimensional for further analysis. Exploratory factor analysis was conducted to checking dimensionality.

5.1 Demographic Variables

The demographic variables under investigation were gender age and income.

5.1.1 Gender

Out of 459 samples, 71.7% were females that are 329 and 28.3% of the total sample which was males that are 130. Apparently, in the store's cosmetic section, more females were seen than males.

5.1.2 Age

A frequency pie chart was generated on age. Age had four classifications in questionnaire apparently 20–24 yrs, 25–29 yrs, 30–35 yrs and more than 35 yrs. In the total sample, more number of samples was from 20 to 24 yrs age group classification with 44.2% followed by 25–29 yrs groups with 38/1% and 30–35 yrs group as well as above 35 yrs with 11.5 and 7% presence.

Table 2 Summary of reliability table

S. No.	Variable	Reliability–Cronbach alpha	Model reliability
1	Health consciousness (HC1, HC2, HC3)	0.899	0.842
2	Consumer innovativeness (Innov 1, Innov 2, Innov 3)	0.856	
3	Purchase intention (PI1, PI2, PI4)	0.861	

Source Primary data

5.1.3 Income (Per Month)

A frequency pie chart was generated on income. Income had three classifications apparently 0–20,000 per month, 20,000–50,000 per month and more than 50,000 per month. More samples were from 0 to 20,000 Rs per month income group classification with 47.8% followed by 20,000–50,000 Rs per month income group with 26.5% and more than 50,000 Rs per month income group with 25.7% presence.

5.2 Reliability Analysis

Exploratory Factor Analysis (EFA) was conducted to observe convergence of factors. Before running an EFA, reliability analysis was conducted to test internal consistency of data after complete data collection (Table 2).

All items of variables were loaded under their respective factors validating subject matter. This proved convergent and divergent validity of constructs. PI3 was removed during the pilot test as variance of the construct improved in its absence. Compared to 50% rule of thumb measure, all factors had reliability value of above 0.60 with health consciousness, consumer innovativeness and purchase intention recording Cronbach's alpha of 0.899, 0.856 and 0.861. The overall model reliability value of 0.842 signalled us to proceed for further analysis.

5.3 Sample Adequacy. Exploratory Factor Analysis and Multiple Regression

The Kaiser–Meyer–Olkin (KMO) measure of sampling adequacy examines the appropriateness of factor analysis. High value indicates factor analysis is appropriate, and low value implies that factor analysis may not be appropriate (Table 3).

Against the rule of thumb reading is 0.50. The KMO value was 0.778 signalling good sample adequacy and ample opportunity for factor analysis. The output was statistically significant with chi square value of 1809.940 (Fig. 2).

Table 3 KMO and Bartlett's test

Kaiser–Meyer–Olkin measure of sampling adequacy		0.778
Bartlett's test of sphericity	Approximately Chi-square	1809.940
	D*f*	36
	Sig.	0.000

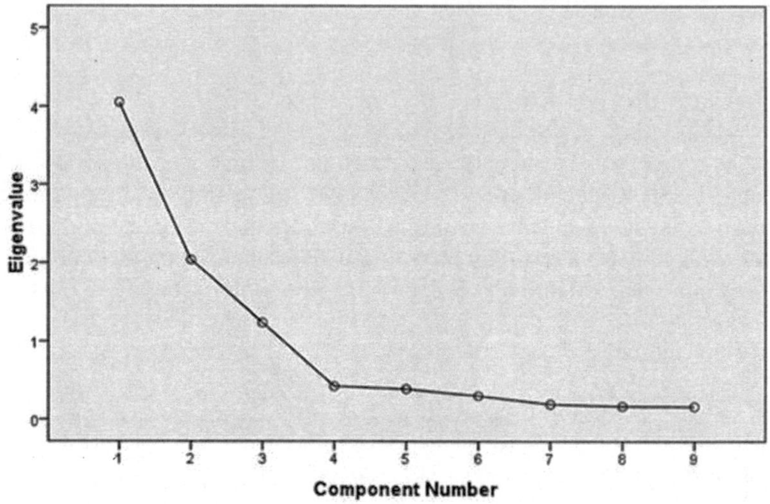

Fig. 2 Scree plot curve. *Source* Primary data

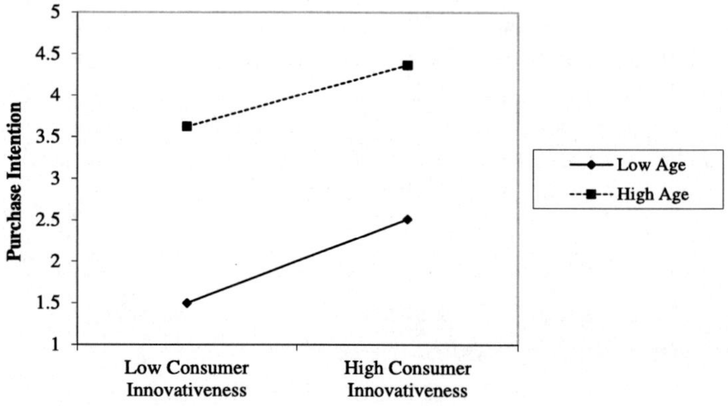

Fig. 3 Health consciousness and purchase intention. *Source* Primary data

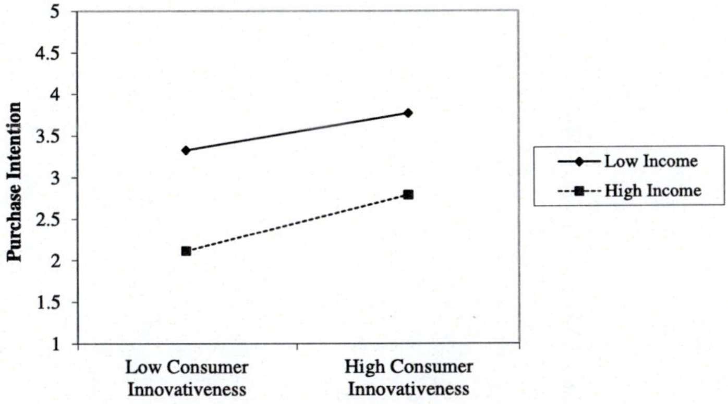

Fig. 4 Consumer innovativeness and purchase intention. *Source* Primary data

Scree plot curve deep dived lesser than 1 eigen value. Below the eigen value of 1 4th factor appeared. Factors with minimum eigen value of 1 were considered. Three factors with more or equal to 1 eigenvalue were selected. The total of three factors was extracted from EFA (Table 4).

As per the scree plot, table displayed a total variance of 13.734 with cumulative total percentage of 81.452. As per the rule of thumb, 60% should be cumulative value, and three factors were able to explain 81.452% of the data that is more than rule of thumb.

Selected three factors were rotated orthogonally using varimax method with Kaiser normalization. Table 5 consists of three factors and the item loadings. All items were loaded under their respective components. There were no cross-loadings proving convergent and divergent validity (Table 6).

Model summary table retained *r* value at 0.497 and *r* square at 0.247. Generally, these values are not considered excellent. In consumer behaviour the *R* squared values are expected low. While predicting consumer behaviour, behaviours linked to psychology, it is normal to have r squared values lower than 50%. Human behavioural patterns are difficult to conclude (Frost, 2016). Durbin Watson value with 1.758 was within the range. The value range of 1.5–2.5 was acceptable (Table 7).

R and *r* square values do not symbolize complete regression output. ANOVA output was also crucial output for observation to reach final interpretation of coefficient table. *F* value of 51.584 was statistically significant (Table 8).

Health consciousness and consumer innovativeness were related to development of purchase intention. The relationship was statistically significant with beta value of 0.429 and 0.177. Health consciousness was more strongly related to green cosmetics purchase intention development.

Table 4 Total variance explained

Component	Initial eigenvalues			Extraction sums of squared loadings			Rotation sums of squared loadings		
	Total	% of variance	Cumulative %	Total	% of variance	Cumulative %	Total	% of variance	Cumulative %
1	4.054	45.041	45.041	4.054	45.041	45.041	2.653	29.481	29.481
2	2.041	22.677	67.718	2.041	22.677	67.718	2.344	26.046	55.527
3	1.236	13.734	81.452	1.236	13.734	81.452	2.333	25.925	81.452
4	0.431	4.784	86.236						
5	0.396	4.398	90.635						
6	0.306	3.399	94.034						
7	0.198	2.195	96.228						
8	0.172	1.906	98.134						
9	0.168	1.866	100.000						

Source Primary data
Extraction method: principal component analysis

Table 5 Rotated component matrix

	Component		
	1	2	3
HC1	0.903		
HC2	0.849		
HC3	0.900		
PI1		0.868	
PI2		0.912	
PI4		0.696	
INNO1			0.913
INNO2			0.934
INNO3			0.750

Source Primary data
Extraction method: principal component analysis
Rotation method: varimax with Kaiser normalization

Table 6 Model summary[a]

Model	*R*	*R* square	Adjusted *R* square	Std. error of the estimate	Durbin–Watson
1	0.497[b]	0.247	0.243	1.86744	1.758

[a]Dependent variable: Purchase_Intention
[b]Predictors: (constant), Consumer_Innovativeness, Health_Consicious

Table 7 ANOVA[a]

Model		Sum of squares	*df*	Mean square	*F*	Sig.
1	Regression	359.778	2	179.889	51.584	0.000[b]
	Residual	1095.018	314	3.487		
	total	1454.796	316			

Source Primary data
[a]Dependent variable: Purchase_Intention
[b]Predictors: (constant), Consumer_Innovativeness, Health_Consicious

Table 8 Coefficients[a]

Model		Unstandardized coefficients		Standardized coefficients	*t*	Sig.
		B	Std. error	Beta		
1	(Constant)	1.785	0.370		4.820	0.000
	Health_Consicious	0.429	0.049	0.435	8.766	0.000
	Consumer_Innovativeness	0.177	0.049	0.179	3.605	0.000

Source Primary data
[a]Dependent variable: Purchase_Intention

5.4 Moderation Analysis of Path with Income and Age Variables

Moderation analysis was conducted using mean centring and Jeremy Dawson approach. Direct moderation could result in biased results leading to faulty conclusion. Initially, all variables health consciousness, consumer innovativeness and purchase intention were mean centred as per their respective grand means. Median split and mean centring are used as data cleaning methods in moderation analysis. Median split classifies the whole data set in to 1 and 2. This causes loss of data. Mean centring concentrates the power in variables resulting in accurate outputs.

5.4.1 Age Interaction on HC's Path to Purchase Intention

Age was subjected to moderation analysis in the path of health consciousness to purchase intention. Model summary table had *r* value at 0.524, *r* square at 0.275 and adjusted *r* square 0.268.

Model summary

Model	*R*	*R* square	Adjusted *R* square	Std. error of the estimate
1	0.524[a]	0.275	0.268	2.77579

[a]Predictors: (constant), age, health consciousness, Age_HC

ANOVA output is also crucial output for observation to reach final interpretation of coefficient table. *F* value of 39.543 was statistically significant with mean square values of 304.679.

ANOVA[a]

Model		Sum of squares	*df*	Mean square	*F*	Sig.
1	Regression	914.038	3	304.679	39.543	0.000[b]
	Residual	2411.672	313	7.705		
	Total	3325.710	316			

[a]Dependent variable: purchase intention
[b]Predictors: (constant), age, health consciousness, Age_HC

The mean centred variables health consciousness, age and hc combined and age loaded in coefficients table. Age and health consciousness were combined as an interaction effect.

Coefficients[a]

Model		Unstandardized coefficients		Standardized coefficients	t	Sig.
		B	Std. error	Beta		
1	(Constant)	4.305	0.661		6.516	0.000
	Healthconsciousness	0.495	0.078	0.423	6.309	0.000
	Age_HC	0.128	0.073	0.338	1.756	0.080
	Age	−0.818	0.647	−0.231	−1.264	0.207

Source Primary data
[a]Dependent variable: purchase intention

Health consciousness was related to development of purchase intention with the strength of 0.495. Age_HC, and age variables were not related as there was no statistically significance. This proved that age had no interaction effect in the path of health consciousness and purchase intention (Fig. 3).

5.4.2 Age Interaction on CI's Path to Purchase Intention

Age was subjected to moderation analysis in the path of health consciousness to purchase intention. Model summary table had *r* value at 0.436, *r* square at 0.190 and adjusted *r* square 0.182.

Model summary

Model	R	R square	Adjusted R square	Std. error of the estimate
1	0.436[a]	0.190	0.182	2.93333

[a]Predictors: (constant), innovativeness, age, Age_CI

ANOVA output is a crucial output for observation to reach final interpretation of coefficient table. F value of 24.504 was statistically significant with mean square values of 210.840.

ANOVA[a]

Model		Sum of squares	*df*	Mean square	F	Sig.
1	Regression	632.519	3	210.840	24.504	0.000[b]
	Residual	2693.191	313	8.604		
	Total	3325.710	316			

[a]Dependent variable: purchase intention
[b]Predictors: (constant), innovativeness, age, Age_CI

The mean centred variables consumer innovativeness, age and CI combined and age loaded in coefficients table. Age and consumer innovativeness were combined as an interaction effect.

Coefficients[a]

Model		Unstandardized coefficients		Standardized coefficients	t	Sig.
		B	Std. error	Beta		
1	(Constant)	4.375	0.587		7.450	0.000
	Age	0.995	0.477	0.281	2.085	0.038
	Age_CI	−0.067	0.052	−0.184	−1.286	0.019
	Innovativeness	0.440	0.065	0.475	6.787	0.000

[a]Dependent variable: purchase intention

Consumer innovativeness was related to development of purchase intention with the strength of 0.995. Age_CI and age variables were related with statistical significance. This proved age had an interaction effect in the path of health consciousness and purchase intention.

Jeremy Dawson's two-way unstandardized Excel Macro was used to plot the moderation effect. The moderation analysis portrayed age's interaction with in the path of consumer innovativeness and purchase intention. Age increased the relationship strength of consumer innovativeness and purchase intention increase.

5.4.3 Income Interaction in the Path of Consumer Innovativeness to Purchase Intention

Income was subjected to moderation analysis in the path of consumer innovativeness to purchase intention. Model summary table had *r* value at 0.424, *r* square at 0.184 and adjusted *r* square 0.176.

Model summary

Model	R	R square	Adjusted R square	Std. error of the estimate
1	0.428[a]	0.184	0.176	2.94530

[a]Predictors: (constant), Income_CI, innovativeness, income

ANOVA output is a crucial output for observation to reach final interpretation of coefficient table. *F* value of 23.458 was statistically significant with mean square values of 203.497.

ANOVA[a]

Model		Sum of squares	df	Mean square	F	Sig.
1	Regression	610.491	3	203.497	23.458	0.000[b]
	Residual	2715.218	313	8.675		
	Total	3325.710	316			

[a]Dependent variable: purchase intention
[b]Predictors: (constant), Income_CI, innovativeness, income

The mean centered variables consumer innovativeness, income and CI combined and age loaded in coefficients table. Income and consumer innovativeness were combined as an interaction effect.

Coefficients[a]

Model		Unstandardized coefficients		Standardized coefficients	t	Sig.
		B	Std. error	Beta		
1	(Constant)	5.775	0.570		10.132	0.000
	Innovativeness	0.280	0.070	0.302	3.974	0.000
	Income	−0.548	0.526	−0.140	−1.042	0.028
	Income_CI	0.099	0.058	0.267	1.703	0.010

[a]Dependent variable: PurchaseIntention

Consumer innovativeness was related to development of purchase intention with the strength of 0.280. Income_CI and income variables were related with statistical significance. This proved that income had an interaction effect in the path of consumer innovativeness and purchase intention (Fig. 4).

Jeremy Dawson's two-way unstandardized Excel Macro was used to plot the moderation effect. The moderation analysis portrayed income's interaction with in the path of consumer innovativeness and purchase intention. Income increased the relationship strength of consumer innovativeness and purchase intention increase.

5.4.4 Income Interaction in the Path of Health Consciousness to Purchase Intention

Income was subjected to moderation analysis in the path of health consciousness to purchase intention. Model summary table had r value at 0.538, r square at 0.289 and adjusted r square 0.282.

Model summary

Model	*R*	*R* Square	Adjusted *R* Square	Std. error of the estimate
1	0.538[a]	0.289	0.282	2.74807

[a]Predictors: (constant), Income_HC, health consciousness, income

ANOVA output is a crucial output for observation to reach final interpretation of coefficient table. F value of 42.460 was statistically significant with mean square values of 320.654.

ANOVA[a]

Model		Sum of Squares	*df*	Mean square	*F*	Sig.
1	Regression	961.963	3	320.654	42.460	0.000[b]
	Residual	2363.746	313	7.552		
	Total	3325.710	316			

[a]Dependent variable: purchase intention
[b]Predictors: (constant), Income_HC, health consciousness, income

The mean centered variables health consciousness, income and HC combined and income loaded in coefficients table. Income and health consciousness were combined as an interaction effect.

Coefficients[a]

Model		Unstandardized coefficients		Standardized coefficients	*t*	Sig.
		B	Std. error	Beta		
1	(Constant)	3.495	0.610		5.729	0.000
	Income	0.237	0.556	0.061	0.427	0.670
	Healthconsciousness	0.557	0.074	0.476	7.541	0.000
	Income_HC	0.051	0.068	0.113	0.758	0.449

[a]Dependent variable: purchase intention

Health consciousness was related to development of purchase intention with the strength of 0.557. Income_HC was not related as there was no statistical significance. This proved that income had no interaction effect in the path of health consciousness and purchase intention.

6 Findings

The study revealed that consumer Innovativeness and health consciousness leads to development of purchase intention. Health consciousness had strong influence on purchase intention compared to consumer innovativeness. Consumer innovativeness though had a less influential strength was able to explain the age and income moderation. Promotional strategies can be planned from health conscious perspective. The paths with beta values mentioned are shown in the below diagram.

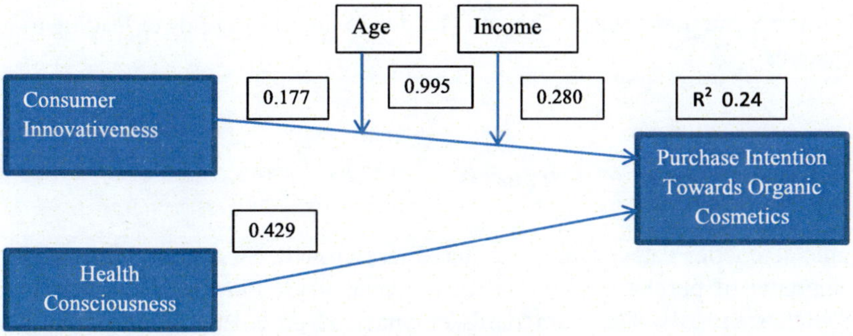

The satisfied hypothesis statements after the analysis as follows.

H1A: Consumers innovativeness of an individual leads to development of purchase intention of green cosmetics.
H2A: Health consciousness of an individual leads to development of purchase intention of green cosmetics.
H3 a: Age moderates of an individual moderate the path of consumer innovativeness leading to purchase intention.
H4 a: Income of an individual moderates the path of consumer innovativeness leading to purchase intention.

Age and Income moderated the path of consumer innovativeness and purchase intention. Age's moderation was far stronger than incomes moderation on health consciousness path to development of purchase intention.

7 Conclusion

Study was able to solve the puzzle of green cosmetics adoption with some insights. Health consciousness and consumer innovativeness and purchase intention variables were subjected to regression and moderation analysis. It is found that health consciousness and consumer innovativeness lead to development of green cosmetics purchase intention. Health consciousness of an individual compared to consumer innovativeness drives the development of green cosmetics purchase intention effectively.

It was also an interesting finding on how consumer innovativeness led to purchase intention development. If a consumer retains the tendency to be innovative in his/her preferences, then these individuals are likely to develop purchase intention of green cosmetics.

Interaction analysis revealed age moderation in the path consumer innovativeness to purchase intention. Study concludes that elder people have tendency of being innovative in their preferences. Income moderated the path of consumer innovativeness to purchase intention. Study concludes higher income individuals are more innovative in their purchase preferences. This may be due to purchasing power leading to more alternatives.

7.1 Future Scope of Research

Organic cosmetics category has registered less growth. Study provided insights on development of purchase intention. In the year 2013, European agencies created COSMOS standards. These standards emphasized on cosmetic manufacturer and country of origin. As these were shallow indicators to decide organic level of a product, buyers in retail stores were lost in making a purchase decision. Many products in FMCG sector have been widely banking on "organic" mantra to brand and sell their products. Despite these clutter in the market sector growth so far is positive. More studies in the line of recognizing the true nature of organize products taking statutory guidelines into account can shed more light leading clarity on organic nature of a product.

According to Cervellon et al., an environmentalist and health conscious consumer would buy organic product and believe that the purchase has contributed to environment. They spare no doubt in trusting about the performance of the product. The determinants and mind-set of health conscious consumers can be separately probed.

The variables were narrowed and selected based on the relevance of Bangalore demography. Moderation analysis also led to some key insights. More studies can research on relevant variables in a wider geography that would lead researcher's community to a theoretical framework explaining purchase intention development of green cosmetics.

References

Ali, Q., Salman, A., Yaacob, H., & Parveen, S. (2019). Financial cost and social influence: Factors affecting the adoption of Halal Cosmetics in Malaysia. *Academy of Entrepreneurship Journal, 25*(2), 1–17.

Ahadzadeh, A. S., Sharif, S. P., Ong, F. S., & Khong, K. W. (2015). Integrating health belief model and technology acceptance model: An investigation of health-related internet use. *Journal of Medical Internet Research, 17*(2), e45.

Ahmed, S. B. B. (2010). Organic cosmetic: A study on demographic characteristics and factors influencing purchase intentions among consumers in Klang Valley, Malaysia. *International Journal of Business Management, 5*(2), 105–118.

Aldoory, L. (2001). The standard white woman in public relations. In E. Toth & E. Aldoory (Eds.).

Anjana, S. S. (2018). A study on factors influencing cosmetic buying behavior of consumers. *International Journal of Pure and Applied Mathematics, 118*(9), 453–459.

Baghel, D. (2020). Interdependence of social and technical indicators of innovation: The case of cosmetic MSMEs in India. *Innovation and Development*, 1–19.

Barrena-Figueroa, R., & Garcia-Lopez-de-Meneses, T. (2013). The effect of consumer innovativeness in the acceptance of a new food product. An application for the coffee market in Spain. *Spanish Journal Agricultural Research, 11*(3), 578–592.

Bartels, J., & Reinders, M. J. (2010). Social identification, social representations, and consumer innovativeness in an organic food context: A cross-national comparison. *Food Quality and Preference, 21*(4), 347–352.

Bartels, J., & Reinders, M. J. (2011). Consumer innovativeness and its correlates: A propositional inventory for future research. *Journal of Business Research, 64*(6), 601–609.

Bhaskaran, S., Polonsky, M., Cary, J., & Fernandez, S. (2006). Environmentally sustainable food production and marketing: Opportunity or hype? *British Food Journal, 108*(8), 677–690.

Bhate, S., & Lawler, K. (1997). Environmentally friendly products: Factors that influence their adoption. *Technovation, 17*(8), 457–465.

Blasi, S., Brigato, L., & Sedita, S. R. (2020). Eco-friendliness and fashion perceptual attributes of fashion brands: An analysis of consumers' perceptions based on twitter data mining. *Journal of Cleaner Production, 244*, 117.

Cervellon, M. C., & Carey, L. (2011). Consumers' perceptions of 'green': Why and how consumers use eco-fashion and green beauty products. *Critical Studies in Fashion & Beauty, 2*(1–2), 117–138.

Chao, C. W., Reid, M., & Mavondo, F. (2013). Global consumer innovativeness and consumer electronic product adoption. *Asia Pacific Journal of Marketing and Logistics, 22*(2), 51–56.

Chen, S. Y., & Chang, S. C. (2012). Enhance green purchase intention: The roles of green perceived value, green perceived risk and green trust. *Management Decision, 50*(3), 502–520.

Chin, J., Jiang, B. C., Mufidah, I., Persada, S. F., & Noer, B. A. (2018). The investigation of consumers' behaviour intention in using green skincare products: A pro-environmental behaviour model approach. *Sustainability, 10*, 3922.

Chinnici, G. D. B. (2002). A multivariate statistical analysis on the consumers of organic products. *British Cosmetic Journal, 104*(3), 187–199.

Cheung, R., Lau, M. M., & Lam, A. Y. (2015). Factors affecting consumer attitude towards organic food: An empirical study in Hong Kong. *Journal of Global Scholars of Marketing Science, 25*(3), 216–231.

Chumpitaz, R., & Paparoidamis, N. G. (2004). Service quality and marketing performance in business-to-business markets: Exploring the mediating role of client satisfaction. *Managing Service Quality, 14*(2), 235–248.

Cornelissen, G., Pandelaere, M., Warlop, K., & Dewitte, S. (2008). Positive cueing: Promoting sustainable consumer behaviour by cueing common environmental behaviours as environmental. *International Journal of Research in Marketing, 25*(1), 46–55.

Cowart, K. O., Fox, G. L., & Wilson, A. E. (2008). A structural look at consumer innovativeness and self-congruence in new product purchases. *Psychology & Marketing, 25*(12), 1111–1130.

Csorba, L. M., & Boglea, V. A. (2011). Sustainable cosmetics: A major instrument in protecting the consumer's interest. *Regional and Business Studies, 3*, 167–176.

Davies, A. A. T. (1995). Who buys organic cosmetics? A profile of the purchasers of organic cosmetic in Northern Ireland. *British Cosmetic Journal, 97*(10), 17–23.

Digest, P. (2010). Cosmetics slow to embrace sustainable packaging. *Packaging Digest, 47*, 22.

Dimitrova, L. N., Kuroha, K., Tatematsu, T., & Inada, T. (2009). Nascent peptide-dependent translation arrest leads to Not4p-mediated protein degradation by the proteasome. *Journal of Biological Chemistry, 284*(16), 10343–10352.

D'Souza, C., Taghian, M., Lamb, P., & Peretiatkos, R. (2006). Green products and corporate strategy: An empirical investigation. *Society and Business Review, 1*(2), 144–157.

D'Souza, C., Taghian, M., Lamb, P., & Peretiatko, R. (2007). Green decisions: Demographics and consumers understanding of environmental labels. *International Journal of Consumer Studies, 31*(4), 371–376.

Dutta-Bergman, M. J. (2004). Primary sources of health information: Comparisons in the domain of health attitudes, health cognitions, and health behaviors. *Health Communication, 16*(3), 273–288.

Dutta-Bergman, M. J. (2006). Media use theory and internet use for health care. *The Internet and Health Care: Theory, Research, and Practice*, 83–103.

Finisterra do Paco, A., Barata Raposo, M. L., & Leal Filho, W. (2009). Identifying the green consumer: A segmentation study. *Journal of Targeting, Measurement and Analysis for Marketing, 17*(1), 17–25.

Frost, J. (2016). Understanding analysis of variance (ANOVA) and the F-test. *The Minitab Blog. Pridobljeno, 10*(01), 201.

Gil, J. M., Gracia, A., & Sanchez, M. (2000). Market segmentation and willingness to pay for organic products in Spain. *The International Food and Agribusiness Management Review, 3*(2), 207–226.

Goldsmith, R., & Flynn, L. R. (1992). Identifying innovators in consumer product markets. *European Journal of Marketing, 17*(6), 43.

Goldsmith, R. E., & Hofacker, C. F. (1991). Measuring consumer innovativeness. *Journal of the Academy of Marketing Science, 19*(3), 209–221.

Gould, J. L. (1988). Timing of landmark learning by honey bees. *Journal of Insect Behavior, 1*(4), 373–377.

Gourville, J. T. (2006). Eager sellers and stony buyers: Understanding the psychology of new product adoption. *Harvard Business Review, 84*(6), 98–106.

GVR. (2019). Grand view research report on skin care products market size, share & trends analysis report, by product (face cream, body lotion), by region (North America, Central & South America, Europe, APAC, MEA), and segment forecasts, 2019–2025. https://www.grandviewresearch.com/industry-analysis/skin-care-products-market

Harper, A. M. (2002). Consumer perception of organic cosmetic production and farm animal welfare. *British Cosmetic Journal, 104*(3), 287–299.

Hill, H., & Lynchehaun, F. (2002). Organic milk: Attitudes and consumption patterns. *British Food Journal, 23*(2), 12–22.

Hirschman, E. C. (1980). Innovativeness, novelty seeking, and consumer creativity. *Journal of Consumer Research, 7*(3), 283–295.

Huber, M., Rembialkowska, E., Srednicka, D., Bügel, S., & Van De Vijver, L. P. L. (2011). Organic food and impact on human health: Assessing the status quo and prospects of research. *NJAS-Wageningen Journal of Life Sciences, 58*(3–4), 103–109.

Hwang, J., Park, S., & Kim, I. (2020). Understanding motivated consumer innovativeness in the context of a robotic restaurant: The moderating role of product knowledge. *Journal of Hospitality and Tourism Management, 44*, 272–282.

Iversen, A. C., & Kraft, P. (2006). Does socio-economic status and health consciousness influence how women respond to health related messages in media? *Health Education Research, 21*(5), 601–610.

Jayanti, R. K., & Burns, A. C. (1998). The antecedents of preventive health care behavior: An empirical study. *Journal of the Academy of Marketing, Science, 26*(1), 6–15.

Johri, L. M., & Sahasakmontri, K. (1998). Green marketing of cosmetics and toiletries in Thailand. *Journal of Consumer Marketing, 15*(3), 265–281.

Kim, H. Y., & Chung, J. (2011). Consumer purchase intention for organic personal care products. *Journal of Consumer Marketing, 28*(1), 40–47.

Kim, S. K., & Seock, Y. (2009). Impacts of health and environmental consciousness on young female consumers' attitude towards and purchase of natural beauty products. *International Journal of Consumer Studies, 33*(6), 627–638.

Klink, R. R., & Athaide, G. A. (2010). Consumer innovativeness and the use of new versus extended brand names for new products. *Journal of Product Innovation Management, 27*(1), 23–32.

Kotler, P. (2011). Reinventing marketing to manage the environmental imperative. *Journal of Marketing, 75*(4), 132–135.

Kraft, F. B., & Goodell, P. W. (1993). Identifying the health conscious consumer. *Marketing Health Services, 13*(3), 18.

Laheri, V. K. (2015). Consumer behavior towards purchase of green products with specific product category. *Indian Journal of Management Science, 5*(1), 66.

Laroche, M., Bergeron, J., Tomiul, M., & Barbaro-Forleo, G. (2002). Cultural differences in environmental knowledge, attitudes and behaviours of Canadian consumers. *Canadian Journal of Administrative Sciences, 19*(3), 267–283.

Lea, E., & Worsley, T. (2005). Australians' organic food beliefs, demographics and values. *British Food Journal, 107*(11), 855–869.

Li, Y., Zhang, C., & Laroche, M. (2019). Is beauty a premium? A study of the physical attractiveness effect in service encounters. *Journal of Retailing and Consumer Services, 50*, 215–225.

Lin, Y., Yang, S., Hanifah, H., & Iqbal, Q. (2018). An exploratory study of consumer attitudes toward green cosmetics in the UK market. *Administrative Sciences, 8*(4), 71. https://doi.org/10.3390/admsci8040071

Leire, C., & Thidell, Å. (2005). Product-related environmental information to guide consumer purchases—A review and analysis of research on perceptions, understanding and use among Nordic consumers. *Journal of Cleaner Production, 13*(10–11), 1061–1070.

Lockie, S., Lyons, K., Lawrence, G., & Mummery, K. (2002). Eating green motivations behind organic food consumption in Australia. *European Society for Rural Sociology, 42*(1), 23–40.

Mainieri, T., Barnett, E., Valdero, T., Unipan, J., & Oskamp, S. (1997). Green buying: The influence of environmental concern on consumer behaviour. *Journal of Social Psychology, 137*(2), 189–204.

Martenson, R. (2007). Corporate brand image, satisfaction and store loyalty: A study of the store as a brand, store brands and manufacturer brands. *International Journal of Retail & Distribution Management, 35*(7), 544–555.

Mason, S. (2012). Ingredients innovation: Inspired by nature. *Global Cosmetic Industry, 180*, 44–47.

Matić, M., & Puh, B. (2016). Consumers' purchase intentions towards natural cosmetics. *Ekonomskivjesnik/Econviews-Review of Contemporary Business, Entrepreneurship and Economic Issues, 29*(1), 53–64.

McEachern, M. G., & Mcclean, P. (2002). Organic purchasing motivations and attitudes: Are they ethical? *International Journal of Consumer Studies, 26*(2), 85–92.

McWilliams, A., & Siegel, D. (2001). Profit maximizing corporate social responsibility. *Academy of Management Review, 26*(4), 504–505.

Michaelidou, N., & Hassan, L. M. (2008). The role of health consciousness, food safety concern and ethical identity on attitudes and intentions towards organic food. *International Journal of Consumer Studies, 32*(2), 163–170.

Mintel. (2010). Natural and organic beauty-UK-February 2010' Mintel Oxegen. http://academic.mintel.com/sinatra/oxygen_academic/search_results/show&/display/id=479857. Accessed 13 July 2018.

Mintel. (2018). Global beauty trends 2018. http://www.mintel.com/beauty-trends/. Accessed 12 November 2018.

Moorman, C., & Matulich, E. (1993). A model of consumers' preventive health behaviors: The role of health motivation and health ability. *Journal of Consumer Research, 20*(2), 208–228.

Nagaraj, S. (2021). Role of consumer health consciousness, food safety & attitude on organic food purchase in emerging market: A serial mediation model. *Journal of Retailing and Consumer Services, 59*, 102423.

Newsom, J. T., McFarland, B. H., Kaplan, M. S., Huguet, N., & Zani, B. (2005). The health consciousness myth: Implications of the near independence of major health behaviours in the North American population. *Social Science & Medicine, 60*(2), 433–437.

Organic Monitor. (2012). The greening of the cosmetic & personal care industry gathers pace' organicmonitor. http://www.organicmonitor.com/r1104.htm. Accessed on 1 June 2018.

Patnaik, A., Tripathy, S., & Dash, A. (2021). Identifying the features influencing sustainable products: A study on green cosmetics. In *Advances in mechanical processing and design* (pp. 631–640). Springer.

Pillai, S. (2013). Profiling green consumers based on their purchase behaviour. *International Journal of Information, Business and Management, 5*(3), 15–27.

Pudaruth, S., Juwaheer, T. D., & Seewoo, Y. D. (2015). Gender-based differences in understanding the purchasing patterns of eco-friendly cosmetics and beauty care products in Mauritius: A study of female customers. *Social Responsibility Journal, 11*(1), 179–198. https://doi.org/10.1108/srj-04-2013-0049

Rashid, N. R. N. A. (2009). Awareness of eco-label in Malaysia's green marketing initiative. *International Journal of Business and Management, 4*(8), 132–141.

Rios, F. J. M., Martinez, T. T. L., Moreno, F. F., & Soriano, P. C. (2006). Improving attitudes toward brands with environmental associations: An experimental approach. *Journal of Consumer Marketing, 2*(31), 26–33.

Roberts, R. (2021). 2021 beauty industry trends & cosmetics marketing: Statistics and strategies for your ecommerce growth. Commonthreads.com. https://commonthreadco.com/blogs/coachs-corner/beauty-industry-cosmetics-marketing-ecommerce

Roehrich, G. (2004). Consumer innovativeness: Concepts and measurements. *Journal of Business Research, 57*(6), 671–677.

Rogers, E. M. (2003). Diffusion of innovations (5th ed.). Free Press.

Rogers E. M., & Shoemaker, F. F. (1971). Communication of innovations: A cross-cultural approach. The Free Press.

Rybowska, A. (2014). Consumer's attitudes with respect to ecological cosmetic products. *Zeszyty Naukowe Akademi Morskiej w Gdyni, 84*, 158–164.

Shamdasani, P., Chon-Lin, G. O., & Richmond, D. (1993). Exploring green consumers in an oriental culture: Role of personal and marketing mix factors. *ACR North American Advances, 32*(2), 21–29.

Sirieix, L., Kledal, P. R., & Sulitang, T. (2011). Organic food consumers' trade-offs between local or imported, conventional or organic products: A qualitative study in Shanghai. *International Journal of Consumer, Studies, 35*(6), 670–678.

Straughan, R. D., & Robberts, J. A. (1999). Environmental segmentation alternatives: A look at green consumer behaviour in the new millennium. *Journal of Consumer Marketing, 16*(6), 558–575.

Tarkiainen, A., & Sundqvist, S. (2005). Subjective norms, attitudes and intentions of Finnish consumers in buying organic food. *British Food Journal, 107*(11), 808–822.

Thogersen, J., Haugaard, P., & Olesen, A. (2010). Consumer responses to ecolabels. *European Journal of Marketing, 44*(11/102), 1787–1810.

Tikka, P., Kuitunen, M., & Tynys, S. (2000). Effects of educational background on students' attitudes, activity levels and knowledge concerning the environment. *Journal of Environmental Education, 31*(3), 12–19.

Tran, T. A., Pham, N. T., Van Pham, K., & Nguyen, L. C. T. (2020). The roles of health consciousness and service quality toward customer purchase decision. *The Journal of Asian Finance, Economics and Business (JAFEB), 7*(8), 345–351.

Tsakiridou, E., Boutsouki, C., Zotos, Y., & Mattas, K. (2008). Attitudes and behaviour towards organic products: an exploratory study. *International Journal of Retail & Distribution Management*.

Tung, S. J., Tsay, J. C., & Lin, M. C. (2015). Life course, diet-related identity and consumer choice of organic food in Taiwan. *British Food Journal, 3*(4), 55–67.

Van Loo, E. J., Diem, M. N. H., Pieniak, Z., & Verbeke, W. (2013). Consumer attitudes, knowledge, and consumption of organic yogurt. *Journal of Dairy Science, 96*(4), 2118–2129.

Vermeir, I., & Verbeke, W. (2006). Sustainable food consumption: Exploring the consumer "attitude–behavioral intention" gap. *Journal of Agricultural and Environmental Ethics, 19*(2), 169–194.

White, K., Habib, R., & Hardisty, D. J. (2019). How to SHIFT consumer behaviors to be more sustainable: A literature review and guiding framework. *Journal of Marketing, 83*(3), 22–49.

White, K., Hardisty, D. J., & Habib, R. (2019). *The elusive green consumer*. Harvard Business Review (July–Aug 2019). https://hbr.org/2019/07/the-elusive-green-consumer

Wood, S. L., & Swait, J. (2002). Psychological indicators of innovation adoption: Cross-classification based on need for cognition and need for change. *Journal of Consumer Psychology, 12*(1), 1–13.

Yiridoe, E. K., Bonti-Ankomah, S., & Martin, R. C. (2005). Comparison of consumer perceptions and preference toward organic versus conventionally produced foods: A review and update of the literature. *Renewable Agriculture and Food Systems*, 193–205.

Zelezny, L. C., Chua, P., & Aldrich, C. (2000). New ways of thinking about environmentalism: Elaborating on gender differences in environmentalism. *Journal of Social Issues, 56*(3), 443–457.

Zhang, F., Sun, S., Liu, C., & Chang, V. (2020). Consumer innovativeness, product innovation and smart toys. *Electronic Commerce Research and Applications, 41*, 100974.

Study on Identifying the Opportunities for Defence Exports Initiative Towards Make in India Initiative

Aditya Kumar and Mita Mehta

Abstract India aims to make the country amongst the top 5 in the world in aerospace and military sectors, for which it has set a target of a turnover of USD 26 Bn and exports of USD 5 billion by 2025 which in FY15-16 was at USD 319 million. India's current defence import-to-export ratio stands at 194:1, making it one of the largest arms importers in the world. Larsen & Toubro (L&T) is a leading Indian private sector company in defence equipment and services, and it should aim to capitalise on the markets in Africa, Middle East and South Eastern countries to help the Indian government's target for 2025. This research examined the market opportunities for L&T in the MENA region, and a go-to-market strategy was formulated. For formulating the go-to-market strategy for L&T's defence product exports, parameters taken into consideration were GDP, military spending and arms imports. Data was collected using internal and external secondary resources. Analysis is done using standard frameworks, namely Political, Economic, Social, Technological, Environmental, Legal (PESTLE) and Segmentation, Targeting, Positioning (STP) analysis, and this research is restricted to the above-mentioned frameworks. Countries which were analysed were Oman, Saudi Arabia, UAE and Egypt.

Keywords Defence · Strategies · Export · New India · MENA · L&T

1 Introduction

L&T is a leading private sector company in defence equipment and services. Its offerings range from home grown air defence, land-based and naval weapon launch systems and their modernisation to communication, missile systems and avionics.

A. Kumar · M. Mehta (✉)
Symbiosis Institute of Management Studies, Symbiosis International (Deemed) University, Range Hill, Pune 411020, India
e-mail: mita.mehta@sims.edu

A. Kumar
e-mail: aditya.kumar2019@sims.edu

© The Author(s), under exclusive license to Springer Nature Singapore Pte Ltd. 2022
A. Chandani et al. (eds.), *Achieving $5 Trillion Economy of India*, Springer Proceedings in Business and Economics, https://doi.org/10.1007/978-981-16-7818-9_12

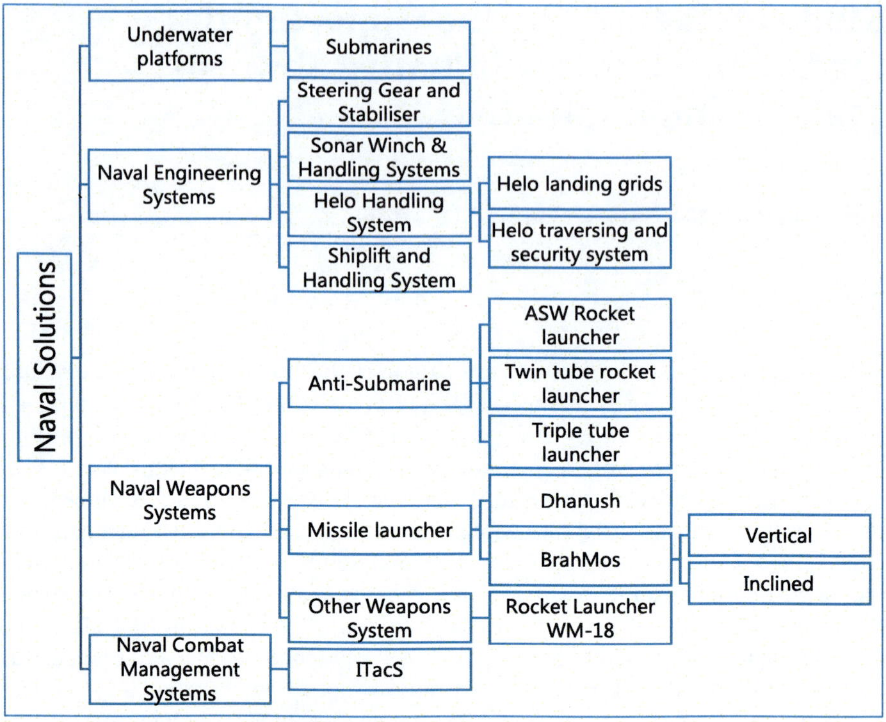

Fig. 1 Naval systems' capabilities (www.larsentoubro.com)

Apart from these, it also offers solutions such as military bases, storage facilities and modernisation of current facilities.

Its capabilities in the different fields are highlighted below (Figs. 1, 2, 3 and 4).

2 Objectives of the Study

2.1 Problem Statement

The government of India wants to make India among the top 5 countries in world in aerospace and military sectors.[1]

In this regard, it has set a target for the year 2025 to achieve a turnover of $26 billion and exports of $5bn. To achieve this, majority of the opportunities it can target lies in Africa, Middle East and South Eastern countries. L&T is one of the leading defence product and service providers in India and should aim to capitalise on this market.

[1] https://theprint.in/security/govt-spells-out-defence-industry-vision-5-billion-exports-by-2025-leader-in-ai-cyberspace/44005/.

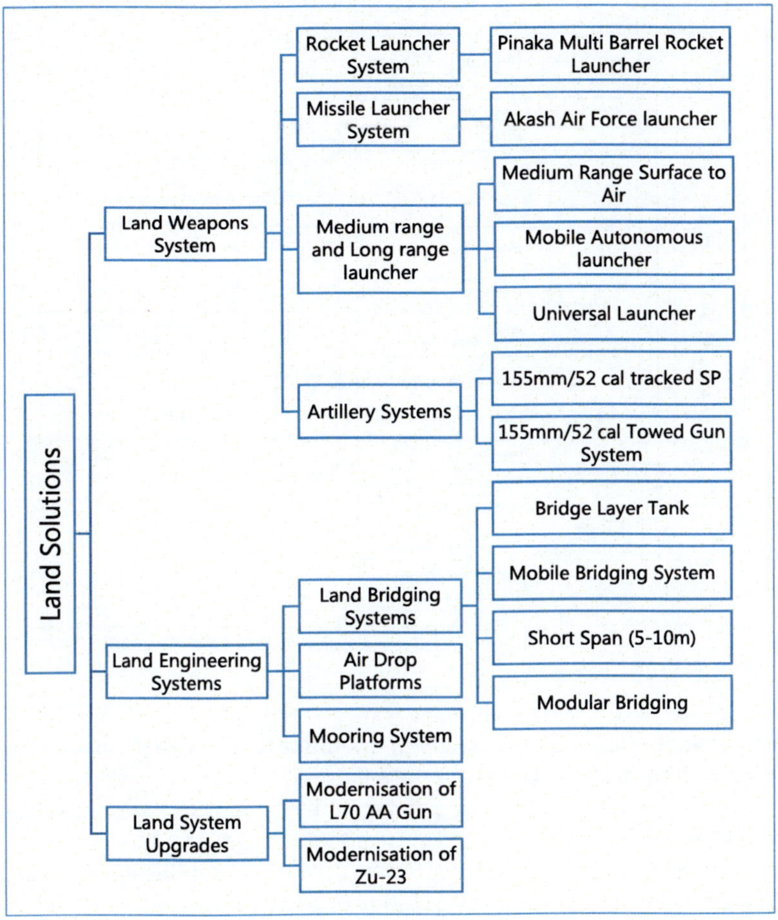

Fig. 2 Land system solutions

However, India's current defence import-to-export ratio stands at 194:1, making it one of the largest arms importers in the world. The Middle East is already dependent on the USA for majority of its arms supplies,[2] whereas Africa is dependent on China for its defence imports. As per published data for FYI 2016-17, the export value stood at \$166.13 mn compared to \$309.52 mn in 2015–16.[3]

Should the same situation continue the target of achieving \$5billion exports could be difficult to achieve. The Middle East is looking to increase its spending on defence imports. Therefore, L&T as well other private defence goods and services manufacturing companies should look to export here.

---

[2] http://bigthink.com/strange-maps/mapping-the-worlds-biggest-weapons-exporters-nil-and-their-best-customers.

[3] http://ddpmod.gov.in/sites/default/files/Annual%20Report%202016-17.pdf.

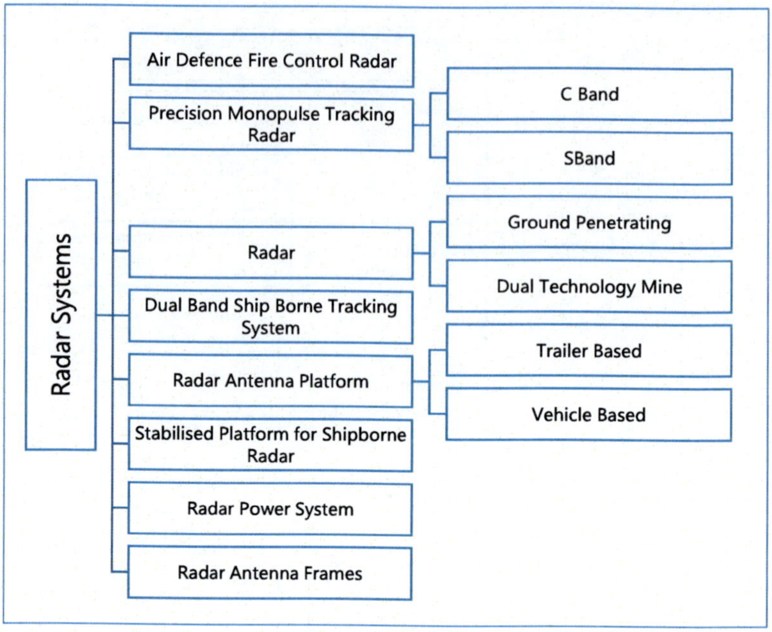

Fig. 3 Radar systems

This research examines the market opportunities for L&T in these regions and to formulate a go-to-market strategy.

For selecting the specific countries to target, key parameters taken into consideration are GDP, military spending and arms imports (Figs. 5 and 6).

As the graphic indicates, in comparison to Africa and Americas, the Middle East holds a significantly larger share of the arms imported.

Military spending as of last year also points to the fact that the Middle East spends a significant % of its GDP in comparison to most parts of Africa. However, we need to consider the size of the GDP as well (Table 1).

On comparison of the GDP of both regions, we can see that the Middle East has a higher GDP in comparison to most African nations (Fig. 7).[4]

On the basis of the parameters taken into consideration, the focus will be on the Middle East region, whereas in the North African region, only Egypt would be taken into consideration.

The countries examined in this research are:

- Saudi Arabia
- UAE
- Oman
- Egypt

[4] https://www.sipri.org/research/armament-and-disarmament/arms-transfers-and-military-spending/military-expenditure.

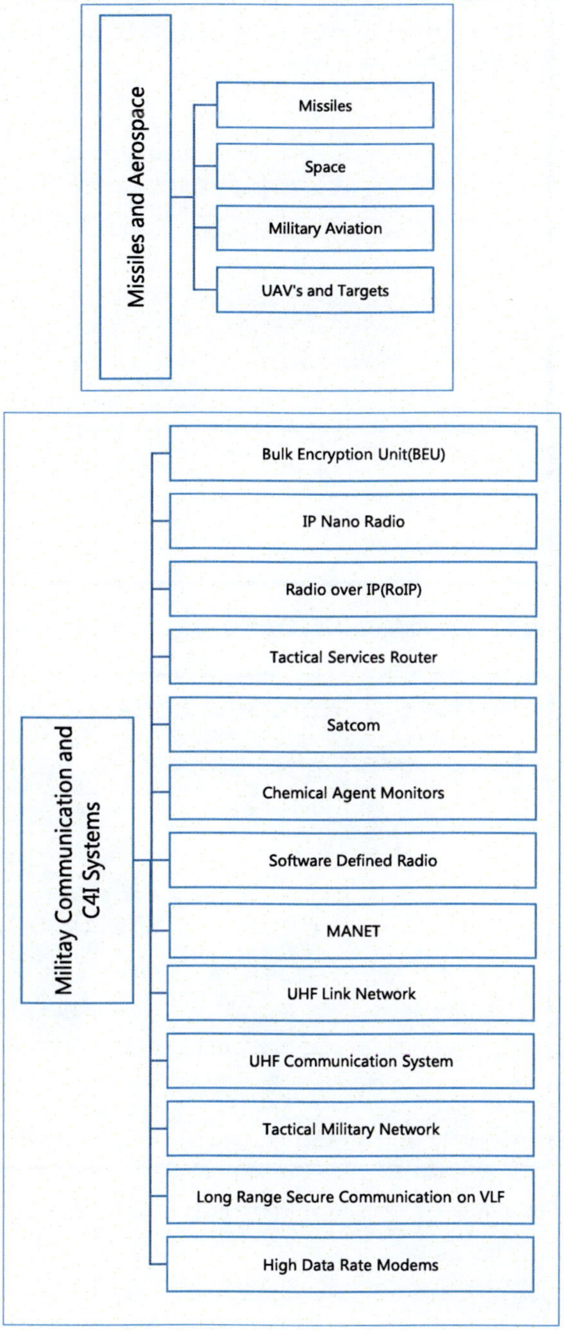

Fig. 4 Missiles and aerospace. Military Communications and C4I Systems (www.larsentoubro.com)

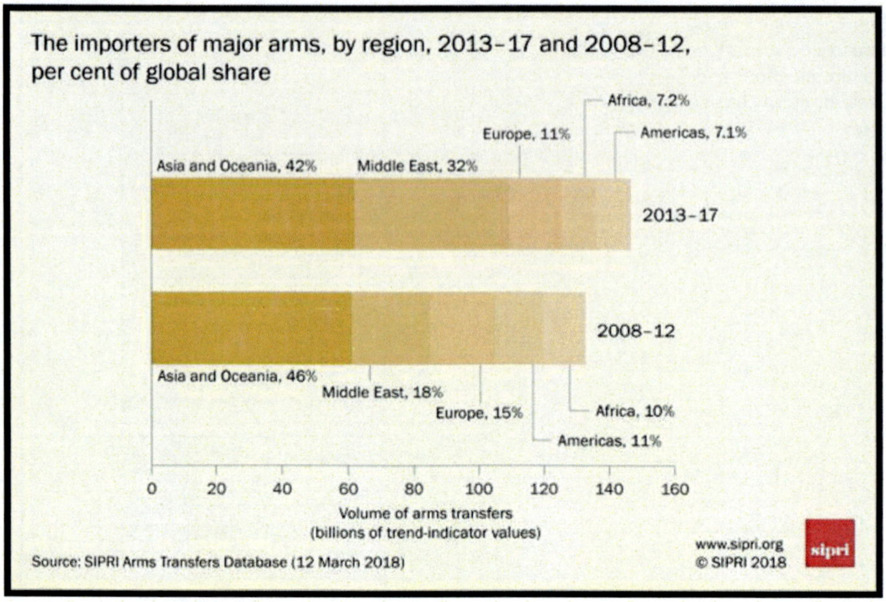

Fig. 5 Comparison to Africa and America (https://www.sipri.org/)

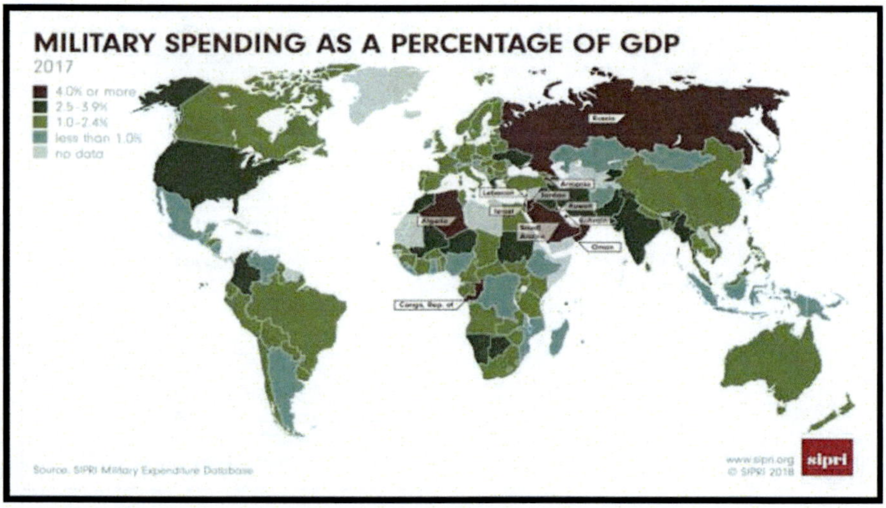

Fig. 6 Military spending as a percentage of GDP (https://www.sipri.org/)

Table 1 GDP of Middle East and African countries

Middle East			North Africa		
Rank	Country	GDP (in crores USD)	Rank	Country	GDP (in crores USD)
1	Saudi Arabia	64,643.84	1	Egypt	33,279.10
2	Iran	41,897.67	2	Algeria	15,905.00
3	UAE	34,874.43	3	Morocco	10,360.63
4	Israel	31,774.45	4	Tunisia	4,206.25
5	Iraq	17,489.00	5	Jordan	3,865.47
6	Qatar	15,245.19	6	Malta	1,099.04
7	Kuwait	11,087.56			
8	Oman	6,629.33			

https://data.worldbank.org/indicator/NY.GDP.MKTP.CD?locations=ZQ&year_high_desc=true

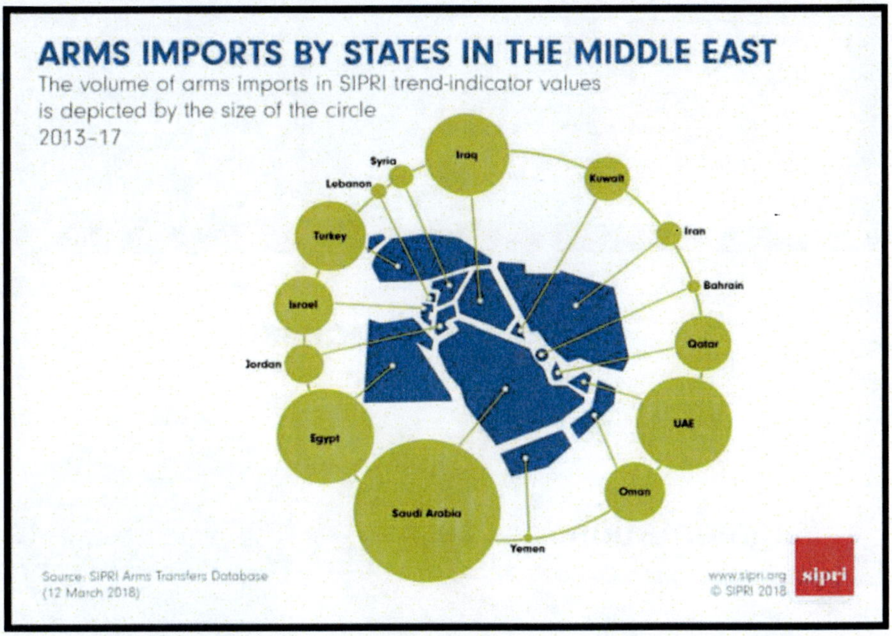

Fig. 7 Arms imports by states in the Middle East

3 Methodology

- The method of research for preparing the strategy in this report is quantitative
- The type of data used is secondary with data being collected from
  - Internal secondary resources

   - External secondary resources

- The data was analysed using standard frameworks, namely PESTLE and STP (Fig. 8)

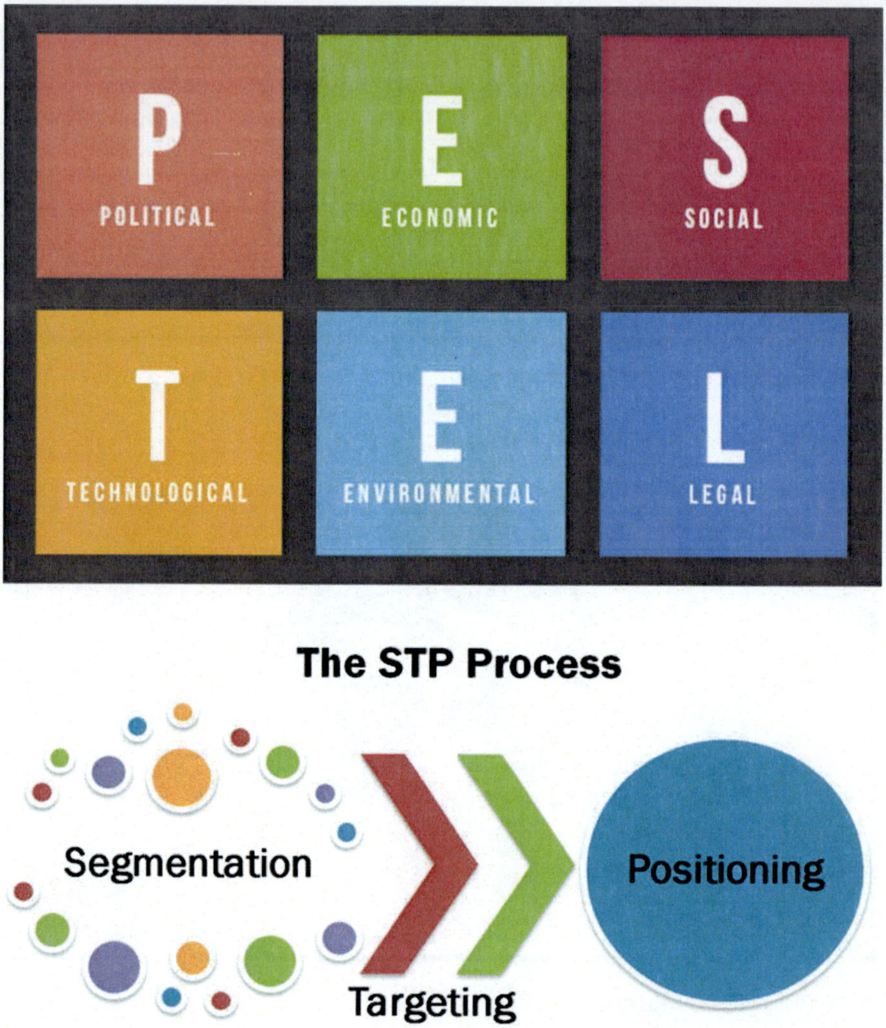

Fig. 8 PESTEL and STP process (http://www.covalconsultores.com/herramientas-sencillas-de-gestion-i-analisis-pestel/, http://stpsamsungmobiles.blogspot.com/)

3.1 Indian Competitors[5]

- **Tata Aerospace and Defence**

They design, produce and manufacture in the field of land mobility solutions, aerospace, weapons systems, sensors and command control and C4I. It has tied up with Lockheed Martin Corp. and is pitching for providing aircrafts to the Indian Air Force. It manufactures airframes for Pilatus Aircraft Ltd. It also manufactures fuselages for the Apache attack helicopters. They also manufacture armoured vehicles and troop-carrying vehicles.

- **Mahindra and Mahindra Ltd**

Mahindra and Mahindra Ltd has a group of subsidiaries which design and manufacture defence equipment and services. They cater to the fields of armoured vehicles, radar systems for fixed and rotary wing aircrafts, naval vessels and ground-based systems, communication systems and border security solutions.

- **Reliance Naval and Engineering Ltd**

Reliance Naval and Engineering Ltd is a group company of Reliance Ltd. It has the capability of designing and manufacturing OPVs, LPDs, frigates, destroyers, corvettes, submarines and aircraft carriers. It has won a contract from the Indian Govt. for five OPVs. It also manufactures CMS systems for naval vessels and land systems.

- **Adani Defence and Aerospace**

It is a subsidiary company of Adani Group. Adani Defence and Aerospace is a relatively new entrant in the defence sector. It has tied up with Israel's Elbit systems for providing UAVs. It has also tied up with Saab Ab to bid for the contract for providing aircrafts to the Indian Air Force.

- **Mazagon Dock Shipbuilders Ltd**

It is the prime shipyard of India. It designs and manufactures naval ships and submarines. Some of its products include Nilgiri class, Godavari class, Khukri class, Delhi class, Shivalik class, Kolkata class, Shishumar class and Scorpene class submarine.

- **Cochin Shipyard**

It is one of the largest shipbuilding and maintenance facilities in India. It has undertaken the repairs of INS Viraat and has been contracted by the Indian Govt. to locally build Vikrant class aircraft carriers.[6]

---

[5] https://www.livemint.com/Industry/FLQDiv0sdMc2Io61PEaCFL/Inside-Indian-industrys-big-defence-play.html.

[6] https://www.indiannavy.nic.in/content/iac-vikrant-undocks-cochin-shipyard-limited.

- **Hindustan Shipyard Limited**[7]

It undertakes the repair and maintenance of warships and submarines. It has been contracted by the Govt. in partnership with Hyundai to manufacture five support vehicles for the Indian Navy.[8] It also manufactures onshore and offshore patrol vessels for the Indian Navy and Indian Coast Guard.

- **Garden Reach and Shipbuilders Ltd**

It manufactures frigates, corvettes, landing crafts, OPVs and landing ship tanks. Some if its products include Brahmaputra class, Khukri class, Kora class, Seaward class, Trinkat class, Bangaram class, Car Nicobar class, Aditya class, Magar and Shardul class vessels. It has been contracted by the Govt. to build four Kamorta class corvettes and seven Project 17A class frigates. It has exported a patrol vessel MCGS Barracuda to Mauritius.[9]

- **Bharat Electronics Ltd**[10]

It manufactures defence communication systems, land-based radars, naval systems, electronic warfare systems, avionics, weapons systems and C4I systems.

4 Analysis and Interpretation of Data

4.1 Middle East

4.1.1 Saudi Arabia

Current Leader: King Abdullah bin Abdul Aziz Al-Saud.

Currency: Saudi riyal.

Political

Government Structure

- Saudi Arabia is an absolute monarchy. The King is the head of state as well as head of the government. The Quran is said to be the constitution and is governed based on Islamic Laws

[7] https://www.hslvizag.in/content/49_1_ProductsProfile.aspx.

[8] http://www.thehindu.com/news/national/andhra-pradesh/hyundai-hsl-to-build-first-of-five-fleet-support-ships/article19679125.ece.

[9] https://economictimes.indiatimes.com/news/economy/foreign-trade/garden-reach-shipbuilders-and-engineers-to-export-first-warship-to-mauritius/articleshow/45307196.cms.

[10] http://bel-india.in/Default.aspx.

- The King is appointed from amongst the sons of the first King. He is subject to the approval of the religious leaders. He is also the Prime Minister and presides over the Council of Ministers
- The complete Government budget is not fully disclosed to the public

Tax Policies

- Corporate income tax rates vary between 25 and 45% based on levels of profit
- Petroleum and other hydrocarbon-producing companies are charged a flat rate of 85% of net operating income
- Tax holiday of 5 years can be granted to foreign companies which enter into joint ventures with local companies. Agricultural product manufacturers can be granted 10 years

Entry and Trade Regulations

- Foreign companies which want to conduct business can enter the Saudi market in the following ways:
  - **Limited Liability Company**—Joint venture with Saudi partner.

    Minimum capital investment to be SAR 500,000
  - **Partnership**—Entering into a limited partnership.

    It is a separate business entity which could comprise of several companies or individuals.
    It has to comprise of at least on general partner and limited partner
  - **Joint Stock Corporation**—At least five shareholders holding transferrable shares.

    At least SAR 2 million for private JSC and SAR 10 million for public
  - **Branch Office**—Wholly foreign-owned branch office

    Can engage in any government or private sector work within scope of licence
  - **Sponsorship and Temporary Commercial Registration (TCR)** Sponsorship by a Saudi company for private sector or a temporary commercial registration for government sector

    If a contract is awarded with the Saudi govt., to a company which doesn't have a presence in the above-mentioned forms it has to obtain a TCR.
    It also has to appoint a Saudi Service Agent

Economics

GDP fell by ~1.2% in 2016, triggered by falling oil prices. As of 2016, 44% of the GDP was due to its hydrocarbon sector. Future plans with regard to Vison 2030 aim to

Table 2 GDP growth rates

	Last (2016)	Previous (2015)	Highest	Lowest	Unit
GDP growth rate	1.00	−0.20	8.50	−2.00	%
GDP annual growth rate	−1.20	−0.40	24.20	−20.70	%
GDP	646.44	654.27	756.35	4.19	USD billion

https://tradingeconomics.com/saudi-arabia/gdp

Table 3 Interest rates

	Last (2016)	Previous (2015)	Highest	Lowest	Unit
Interest rate	2.25	2.25	7.00	1.50	%
Interbank rate	1.99	1.90	5.24	0.60	%
Deposit interest rate	2.65	2.65	9.04	0.50	%
Reverse repo rate	1.75	1.75	6.75	0.25	%

reduce dependence on hydrocarbon sector and diversify the economy by developing retail, private and renewable energy sector and defence industries (Table 2).

Interest Rates[11]

Saudi Arabia hiked its Repo and reverse repo rates by 0.25% points. The reason is to maintain parity with the US federal rates. Repo and reverse rates indicate the borrowing and lending ability and the tendency to do the same (Table 3).

Inflation Rate

Saudi inflation rate in the year 2018 reached 3% vs 2017 where it was at about -0.5%. This is attributed to the VAT introduced in 2018 (Fig. 9).[12]

Saudi arm imports as indicated in the above graph have shown an uptick over a period of 17 years. In 2017, the value of arms imports stood at $4.11bn compared to $2.98bn in 2016.

Defence Offsets

- Saudi Arabia implements its military offset policy on an ad hoc basis. The offset is **at least 30%** of the value of the contract
- Foreign companies which are awarded Govt. contracts have to subcontract **at least 30%** to be wholly owned Saudi subcontractors subject to the subcontractor's ability

[11] https://tradingeconomics.com/oman/interest-rate.

[12] https://tradingeconomics.com/saudi-arabia/inflation-cpi.

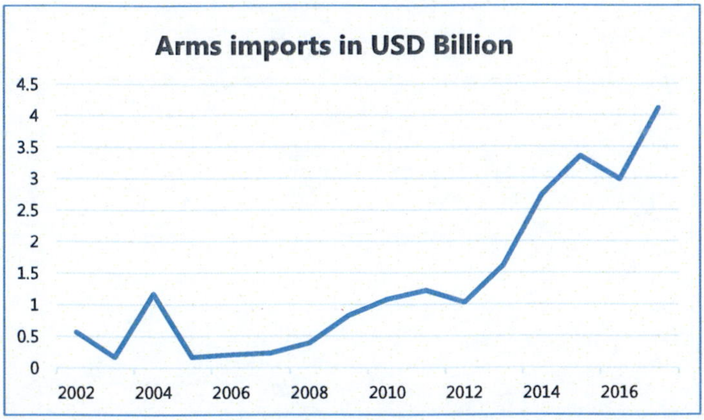

Fig. 9 Military expenditure (https://data.worldbank.org/indicator/MS.MIL.MPRT.KD)

- The primary goals of programme are technology acquisition, economic growth and diversification towards sectors such as petrochemicals, health care and education
- It follows an indirect offset approach[13,14]

Social

Literacy Rate

- As of 2013, Saudi literacy rate stood at ~95%.
- For females aged 15 and above, literacy rate stood at 91.36%
- For males aged 15 and above, literacy rate stood at 96.5%[15]
- Median age of males was 27.9 and females 26.2[16]
- As per Saudi Arabia General Authority for Statistics, total female population was 49.05% and male population at 50.95%
- Unemployment rate as of 2016 stood at 6% increasing by about 0.2% year on year (Figs. 10 and 11)

Technological

Saudi Government as a part of its Vision 2030 is investing heavily in indigenous technology development. To this effect, it has an independent scientific organisation

[13] https://idsa.in/jds/3_1_2009_ASurveyofSuccessfulOffsetExperiencesWorldwide_AMitra.

[14] http://www.mepc.org/journal/offsets-middle-east.

[15] data.worldbank.org.

[16] http://worldpopulationreview.com/countries/saudi-arabia-population/.

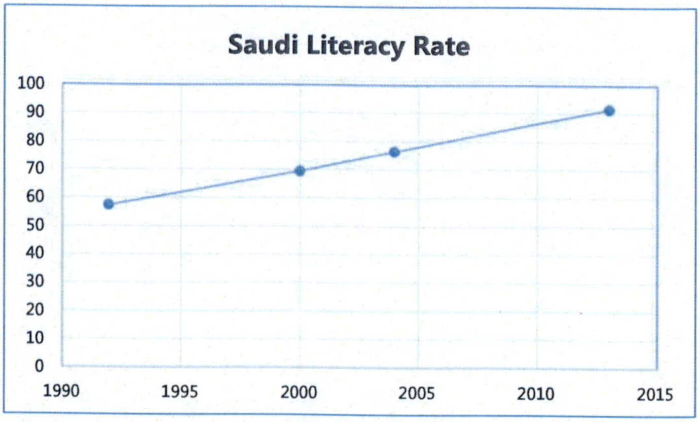

Fig. 10 Literacy rate of Saudi (https://www.indexmundi.com/facts/saudi-arabia/literacy-rate)

(KACST). It has also set up several universities with the curriculum dedicated to science and technology with curriculum ranging from biotechnology to geophysics.

As of 2016, Internet users stood at 64.7% of the population contributing to about 0.6% of the world's Internet users.

Online content restriction is regulated by the Saudi government with content such as pornography, gambling and anti-government opinions completely banned.

Environmental

Energy Consumption

- Saudi has the capacity to produce 318 bn kWh energy where its consumption accounts for 292.8 bn kWh
- Per capita consumption stands at 9072 kWh which is almost 68% more than per capita Europe consumption
- It is capable of 604.37 bn kWh using fossil fuels and 604.88 mn kWh using renewable energy

Environmental Protection Laws

- General Authority of Metrology and Environmental Protection is the body of Saudi govt. which handles all environmental policies
- Due to the abundance of oil, fossil fuel consumption for energy generation is high. Also due to the subsidies provided carbon emission has been increasing substantially[17]
- KAUST, an institute created by the Govt., is working on a model where energy usage is supported only by nuclear and renewable sources

[17] https://bit.ly/2K5AEw0.

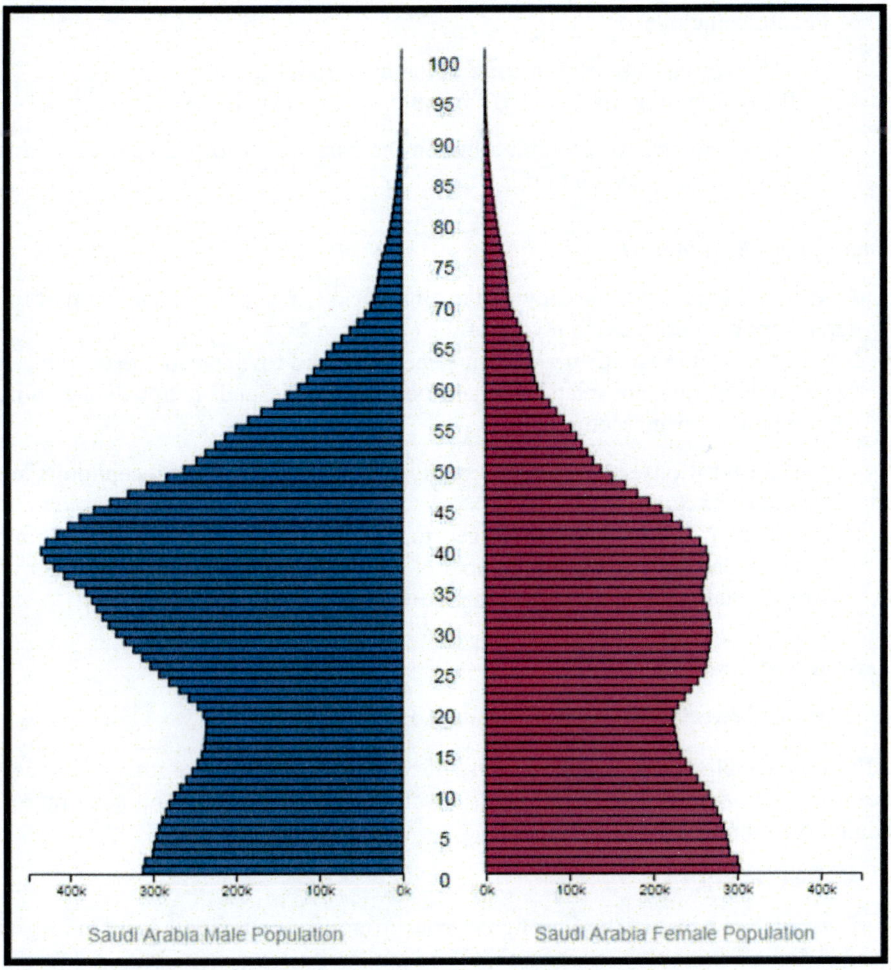

Fig. 11 Population demographics

Legal

Competitive Regulations

- The competition law came into effect in 2005. It is not applicable to Govt. corporations and fully owned state entities
- The law aims at avoiding monopolistic practices to provide fair competition
  - Regulating merger and acquisitions which results in a dominating position in the market
  - Illegalising the abuse of dominant position by a firm (40% of total sales for 12 months)

- Penalties include

  A fine of up to SAR 5 mn, multipliable on reoccurrence
  Daily fine of up to SAR 10,000 until violation is removed

- The government can prohibit a bid on the basis of its low price if the bid is 35% below the prevalent prices

Employment Regulations

- A written contract is to be provided to employees. In its absence any term of the agreement is interpreted in favour of the employee
- Number of working hours per week in general is 8 and 6 h in the month of Ramzan
- As per the Saudisation plan, a certain percentage of Saudi nationals are to be employed by private sector firms
  - Certain positions such as HR, security guards, treasurer and receptionist are restricted to Saudi nationals
  - As of 2016, policies have changed to include a point-based system. Points are awarded on the basis of number of Saudi staff, average salary, number of women staff amongst several other criteria[18]

Existing Players

- **Advanced Electronics Company (AEC)**

AEC was established in 1988 and has offices in Riyadh and Dammam. Its business areas are avionics and electronics, electronic warfare, command and control, communication.

- **Airbus Group**

Airbus which is a part of the Eurofighter consortium is developing a local industrial base in Saudi for maintenance, overhaul and modernisation programmes.

- **Al Salam Aerospace Industries**

Established in 1988, it undertakes maintenance, repair, overhaul and modernisation of civil and military aircrafts. It is located in Riyadh. Primarily involved in the F15S to F15S-A modernisation program

- **BAE Systems Plc.**

BAE are involved in training the Saudi nationals in high-skilled fields. It also provides military solutions in the area of IT, electronics and security systems.

---

[18] https://bit.ly/2rvFUBn.

- **Boeing**

Boeing has a joint venture with Saudi Arabian Military Industries. It is the sole provider of sustainment services of all planes and helicopters of the Saudi military fleet.

- **Lockheed Martin**

Saudi purchased its first C-130J Hercules in 1965. Since then Lockheed Martin as a result of several joint ventures and partnerships with various firms has established itself in Saudi.

Some of the significant ones are Lockheed Martin and TAQNIA for manufacturing two communication satellites. As well as facility in Saudi where the advanced sensor system of the F15's would be repaired.

- **Northrop Grumman Corporation**

Northrop Grumman provides services in the field of defence, security, cyber security and communications. Significant services/products being Longbow Fire Control Radar for AH-64 helicopter. They also work with Aramco for protection of sites. They have a joint venture with NG Mission systems Arabia and Vinnell Arabia.

As a part of its Vision 2030, Saudi aims to localise production of defence equipment from 2 to 50%. As a result, it is backing Saudi Arabian Military Industries (SAMI) (Fig. 12).

Opportunities

Self-propelled Artillery

With the M-109 (early 1960-present), M-60 Patton (1960–1987), AMX-GCT (1977-present) being manufactured about 30–40 years ago, it provides an opportunity for defence manufacturers to provide alternatives and upgrades to these.

The M-109 is of US origin and has multiple variants with the latest being the "Paladin" currently being used by the US army. As the Saudi Army currently employs about 150 M-109 s, it provides an opportunity for upgrades to the existing vehicles to bring them up-to-speed with the current technologies.[19]

Tanks

The M-60A3 was produced by the USA from 1960–1987. The Saudi army has currently 450 of them. Raytheon, the manufacturer, is providing an option to upgrade

[19] http://www.dsca.mil/major-arms-sales/kingdom-saudi-arabia-155mm-m109a6-paladin-medium-self-propelled-howitzer-system.

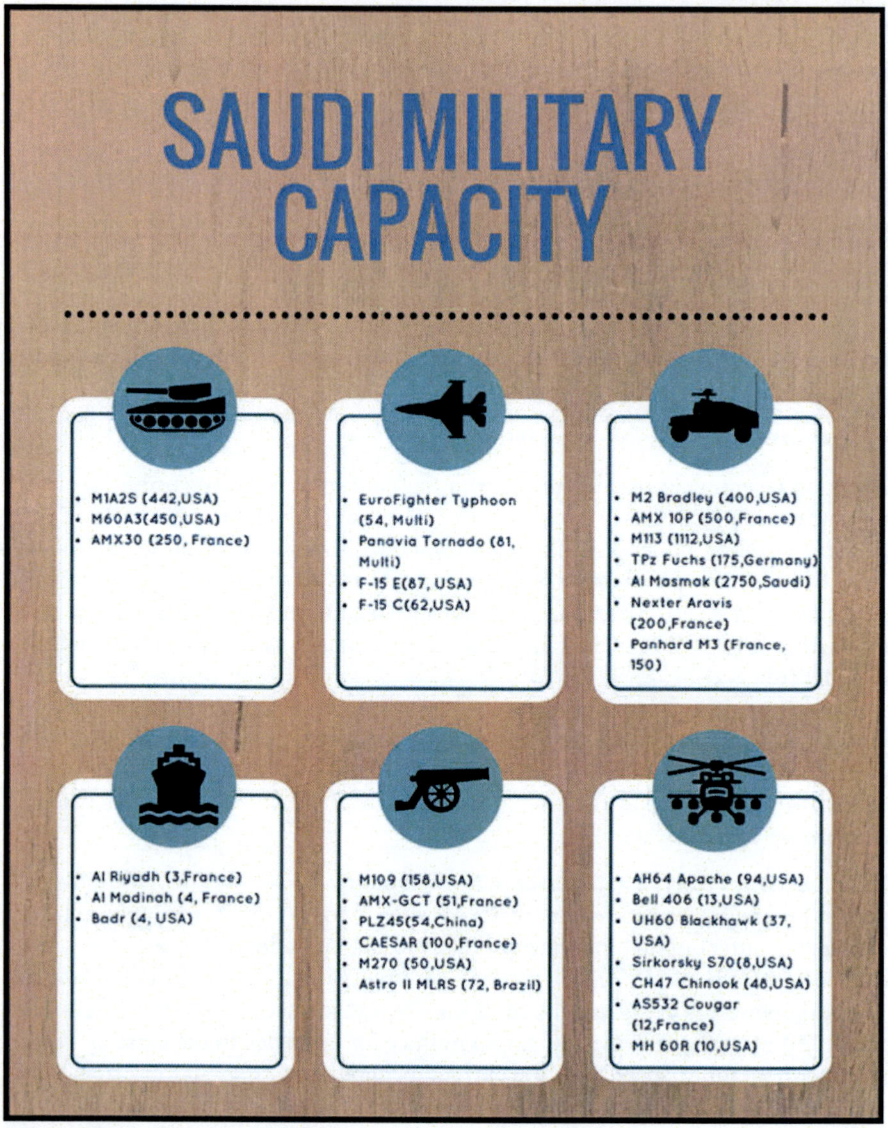

Fig. 12 Saudi military capacity. *Source* https://bit.ly/2kg2Rpi

these tanks to make them up-to-date and competitive with the modern tanks. This provides an opportunity to upgrade these.[20]

[20] https://www.popularmechanics.com/military/a21009/raytheon-wants-to-hot-rod-old-patton-tanks/.

Saudi Army owns about 450 M1A2 tanks. As they have requested for acquisition of M1A2S tanks and upgrade packages for the M1A1/A2 tanks. It provides an opportunity to upgrade.[21]

Reconnaissance Aircraft

US DOD announced the modernisation programme for Saudi E-3A AWAC planes. This provides an opportunity to upgrade these.[22]

Attack Aircraft

The Pentagon announced the modernisation of Saudi F15S to F15S-A configuration. This provides an opportunity to upgrade these (Fig. 13).[23]

Foreign Relations

Iran

- Iran and Saudi Arabia have a very strained relationship, despite being Muslim dominated countries. Iran consists primarily of Shia Muslims, whereas Saudi consists of Sunnis. Both the nations want to have Islamic leadership over the Gulf region
- The relations have further strained over Syrian and Iraq war. Iran is also said to support extremist groups such as Hezbollah, Hamas and the Houthis which have anti-Saudi and anti-Sunni motives
- Iran also opposes the monarchy system, saying that it goes against the teachings of Islam

Israel

- Saudi is a supporter of the creation of Palestine as a separate state and wants Israel to move out of the areas it occupied post the Yom-Kippur war. They are of the opinion that Palestinian Arabs should be allowed to back to Israel and reclaim the lands they held before. Israel which believes in democracy opposes this as this would lead to the majority population being Arabs and ceasing of Israel's identity as a Jew state

---

[21] http://www.dsca.mil/major-arms-sales/kingdom-saudi-arabia-m1a2s-saudi-abrams-main-battle-tanks-and-m88ala2-heavy.

[22] http://www.arabianaerospace.aero/boeing-s-240-million-saudi-awacs-contract.html.

[23] http://www.arabianaerospace.aero/saudi-air-force-to-get-upgraded-f-15s-as-part-of-modernisation-deal.html.

Fig. 13 Brief history

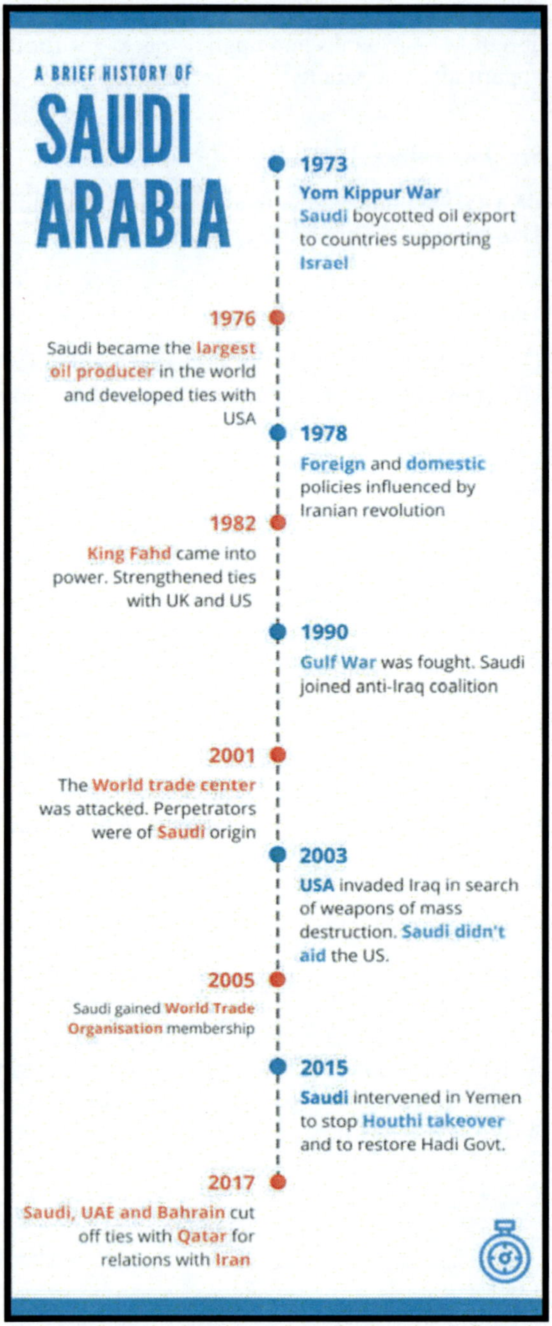

China

- Diplomatic relations between China and Saudi Arabia was established in 1990. The relations between the two countries grew stronger in 2000
- Saudi was the largest contributor when the Sichuan earthquake occurred in 2008.
- By 2010, China became the largest trading partner of Saudi

India

- Saudi is one of the largest oil suppliers to India. Saudi employs a majority of its labour force from India to work in the construction and oil business
- It also contributed to India in the 2001 earthquake

Pakistan

- The relations between Pakistan and Saudi have been mostly friendly. Saudi supported Pakistan when Bangladesh wanted to separate from it
- It is known as the closest non-Arab ally of Saudi Arabia. Pakistan plays an important role in the development of Saudi Arabia. It provides assistance in the field of technology, science and infrastructure development
- Saudi also provided asylum to Nawaz Sharif while he was exiled from Pakistan for 8 years

United States

- Saudi and the USA have had relations since 1930s when the USA recognised the government of King Saud. The USA has helped train the Saudi military and has had full diplomatic relations since 1930
- Relations between USA and Saudi started to strain in 2001 after the World Trade attacks. The major reason being that majority of the terrorists had Saudi roots.
- The relations were further strained when Saudi refused to support USA in the Iraq war. Under the Obama administration, USA relations with Iran and the nuclear deal was a major reason of worry for Saudi

Segmentation

Based on its proximity to countries with which it has conflicts in the region with which it shares its borders such as Yemen, Iraq, Iran and Israel, Saudi Arabia invests heavily on its defence and offensive capabilities. It has a large coastline which is close to strategic entities such as the Gulf of Aden and the Persian Gulf. It is amongst the largest Gulf countries and enjoys a major decision-making role in the GCC (Fig. 14).

Behaviour

Saudi Arabia in terms of arm imports has become the largest in the world as of 2016 (Source: sipri.org). Ninety-eight percent of the arms imported were from USA and

Fig. 14 Geography. *Source* https://sites.google.com/site/kjkmlt/saudi-arabian-flag

Europe. This is further supported by the fact that most of the major arms of Saudi are either of US or Europe origin. With regard to military expenditure in a span of 10 years, Saudi arms imports have increased by about 200%.

Demographics

Saudi is dominated by Sunni Muslims who comprise of about 90% of the population. It follows the ideology that the government should only comprise of Sunni. Thus, it is involved in the ongoing conflicts in Syria and Yemen which it believes are being influenced by Iran which is a Shia governed country.

- A point for concern for India in terms of trade is Saudi's relationship with Pakistan and its opinion of the state of Kashmir. However, several visits by the current Government has caused the opinion to shift

Targeting

Criteria Size

With several factors contributing to the hike in military spending such as the instability in Yemen and Iraq, extremist tendencies of ISIS and Al Qaeda and the growing influence of Iran, military spending has shown an upward trend (Figs. 15 and 16).

Based on the above graph which shows the military imports of Saudi, it shows that it has a huge market. As of 2017, its arms imports stood at $4.111 billion. As per SIPRI reports, Saudi is ranked as the second highest arms importer after India.

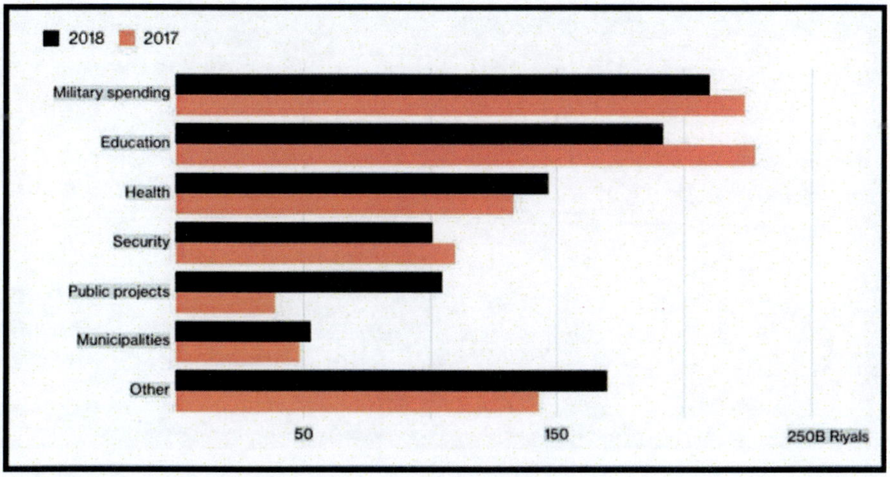

Fig. 15 Saudi Ministry finance. Sourcehttps://bloom.bg/2wAq524

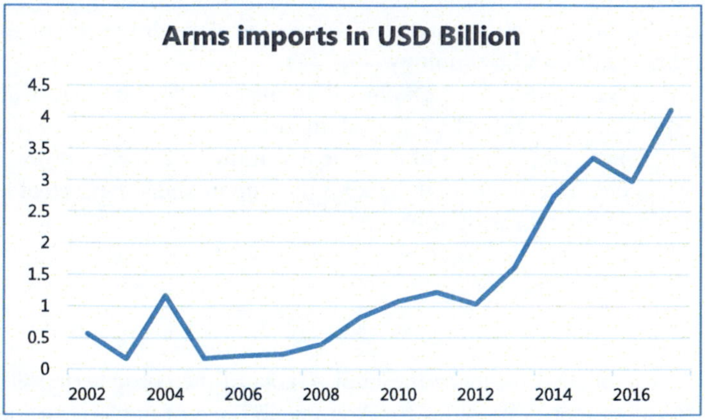

Fig. 16 Arms imports. *Source* data.worldbank.org

Market

Majority of Saudi's aviation requirements including civil and military fixed wing and rotary aircraft are met by Boeing, Airbus, BAE and Northrop Grumman as shown in the analysis. Opportunities for entering the arms market are in the naval and land forces.

The Government has set a military budget of SAR 210 bn for the year 2018. Additionally, SAR 26.5 bn is allocated for improving military readiness and capabilities by the local defence industrial sector.

It has appointed the government body general authority for military industries as the major source for military procurement. The focus as per Vision 2030 is also

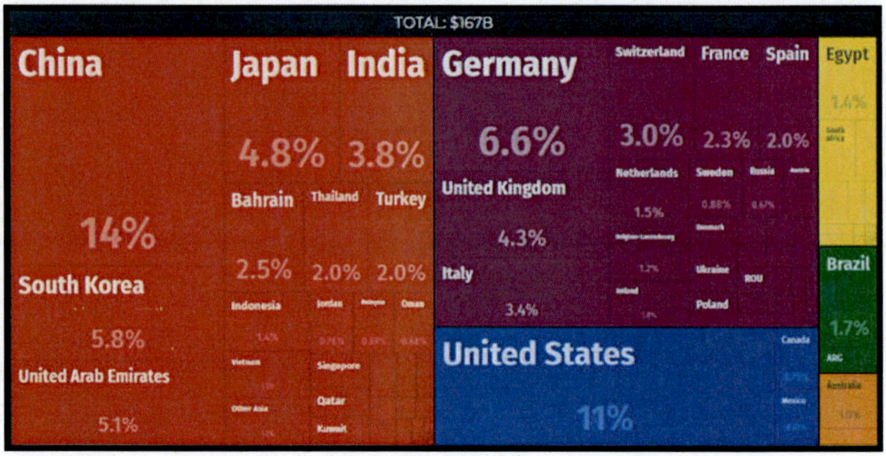

Fig. 17 Trade imports (https://atlas.media.mit.edu/en/profile/country/sau/)

shifting towards local production rather than imports. This also provides an opportunity to establish a long-term market in the region. One drawback of the move is transfer of knowledge and technology (Fig. 17).

As we can see from the above graphic, in terms of trade (imports), USA, Europe and China dominate in terms of % of total imports.

As of now, the manufacturing of defence and military equipment doesn't permit foreign investment. The Saudi govt. handles the import and clearance of customs as part of the sale and purchase of arms.

Positioning

L&T has an established presence in Saudi Arabia in the construction field, having built gas production deck modules for Aramco and one of the longest transmission lines for the government.

However, in terms of defence equipment none of the Indian companies have achieved any significant success.[24] Catering to the products manufactured by L&T, naval and land forces could be the focus points. Offering in-house solutions should be the way forward. With in-house built interceptor boats and patrol vessels already in service with the Indian Navy and Coast Guard and the K9 Vajra-T howitzers with the Indian Army, solutions like these could be offered.

[24] https://www.defenseindustrydaily.com/cat/geographical-focus/asia/asia-india/.

Go-to-Market Strategy

- The analyses suggest that for an entry into the Saudi market, a partnership with a local firm will have to be formed
- In the case of winning a contract on tender allocation, a Temporary Commercial registration can be applied for
- As a part of the defence offset, at least 30% has to be subcontracted to local companies, having a local company as a partner is a feasible approach
- In order to tackle the offset policy, a team should be set up to look into the possible initiatives which can be taken such as upskilling the Saudi nationals and training them
- In this case, partnering with an e-learning institution is a feasible idea
- This would help with the Saudisation programme as well which demands a certain % of the employees to be locals
- L&T should focus on the naval and land forces based on its product portfolio
- Positioning has to be as a solutions provider
- From L&T's perspective, Interceptor Boats and OPVs should be the products on offer as Saudi doesn't have a strong naval presence[25]
- Another offering could be the modernisation of self-propelled artillery; M-109 and AMX-GCT and M1A2, M-60A3 tanks for which Saudi is planning upgrades[26]

4.1.2 United Arab Emirates

Current Leaders: Sheikh Khalifa bin Zayed.

Currency: United Arab Emirates dirham.

Political

Government Structure

- The UAE is an absolute monarchy. The ruler of Abu Dhabi is the President of the Federation. The ruler of Dubai serves as the Prime Minister of the federation
- The Legal system is derived from the Civil Law System as well as Islamic (Sharia) laws
- Each Emirate has its own ruler who runs his own local government. For the Seven Emirates, appointed amongst them are the President, Vice President, Prime Minister, Cabinet Ministers and a 40-member assembly known as the Federation National Council. The Supreme Court operates as an Independent Judiciary

---

25 https://bit.ly/2ICNLIK.

26 https://oxfordbusinessgroup.com/overview/forward-facing-defence-increased-spending-and-modernisation-under-way-sector-continues-expand-and.

Table 4 Rates of GDP

	Last (2016)	Previous (2015)	Highest	Lowest	Unit
GDP annual growth rate	3.00	3.40	9.80	−5.20	%
GDP	348.74	357.95	403.20	2.85	USD billion
GDP per capita	40,864.20	40,159.60	113,682.00	35,049.10	USD

Tax Policies

- As per Index of Economic Freedom UAE ranks 10th in the world with a score of 77.6. The index takes into account Govt. integrity, Govt. spending, Business, Trade and Investment freedom amongst several factors
- UAE doesn't charge corporate tax except for oil companies, production companies and foreign banks
- Oil and gas exploration companies are taxed on the basis of their working incomes. Varying from 10 to 55%
- As of 2018, UAE has implemented VAT at rate of 5% which is overseen by the Federal tax authority

Trade and Entry Mode Regulations

- For doing business in UAE if not a part of the free zone, a foreign business should have either:
  - UAE national sponsor
  - Agent
  - Distributor
- For a government contract, a company should be pre-qualified and registered
- To bid for federal projects, the individual should be a UAE national or a company with at least 51% shares held by UAE nationals
- The above won't be applicable for defence contracts which local companies cannot fulfil
- There is no formal requirement to subcontract from local companies

Economics

As of 2016, GDP annual growth rate fell by about 0.4% as a result of falling oil prices.[27] As per UAE Central Bank's forecast estimated growth was predicted at about 1.6% due to the decrease in production of oil. As a result of a robust non-oil-based sector and rising oil prices, the GDP growth is said to be at about 3.6% for 2018. This helps us get an idea about their spending capability (Table 4).

[27] https://tradingeconomics.com/united-arab-emirates/gdp.

Table 5 Interest rates

	Last (2018)	Previous (2017)
Interest rate (%)	2.00	2.00
Interbank rate (%)	2.46	2.46
Foreign exchange reserves (AED billion)	326	348

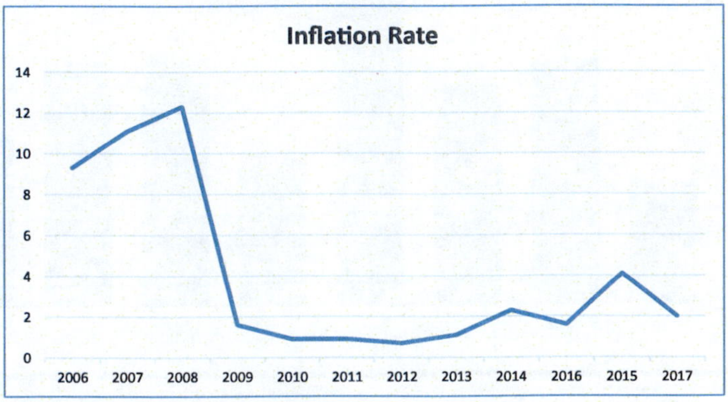

Fig. 18 Inflation rates (https://bit.ly/2ILaIsx)

Interest Rates

UAE Central Bank hiked the interest rates by ~25 basis points to 2%. The highest since 2010. This is said to be in accordance with the hike by US federal reserves (Table 5).[28]

Inflation Rate

The inflation rate doubled to 4.8% in 2018 from 2.7% in 2017 as a direct result of the VAT introduced by the UAE govt. Transport costs increased by about 12.8% as gasoline prices increased (Fig. 18).[29]

Military Expenditure

With its involvement in various conflicts such as Syria, Yemen and Iraq as well as its proximity to Iran, UAE has shown an uptick with regards to arms imports. With plans to acquire F35's from the USA and other latest defence equipment, the rate of arms imports as well as military expenditure is predicted to rise (Fig. 19).[30]

[28] data.worldbank.org.

[29] https://www.khaleejtimes.com/uae-inflation-rises-with-new-tax-in-jan.

[30] https://wapo.st/2IMkBGm.

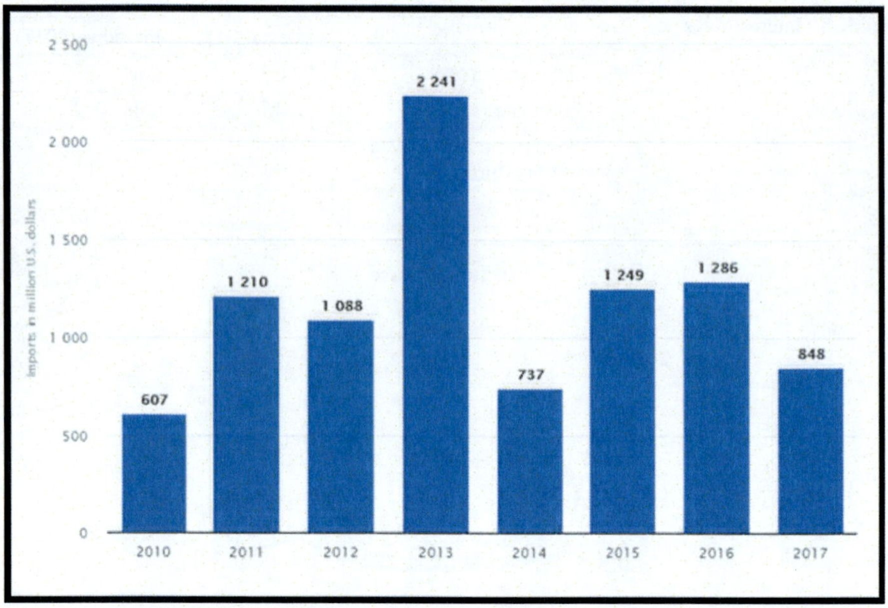

Fig. 19 Military expenditure (https://www.statista.com/statistics/677220/uae-arms-imports/)

Defence Offsets[31]

- A foreign defence contractor who is awarded a contract worth more than $10 mn has to participate in the Tawazun Economic Programme.
- Any defence contract when awarded is linked to the signing of TEP agreement. The defence contractor would have an obligation of **60% of the supply contract** value towards sectors such as aerospace, defence, cyber security or autonomous systems with capabilities including designing, engineering, manufacturing, etc.
- The project could focus on final or subassembly, key technical services or major components
- The obligations should be fulfilled over a period of seven years
- The said obligations are fulfilled by earning input (30% of total obligations) and output credits (70% of total obligations)
- Credits can be earned through
  - Joint ventures—51–49% partnership (local–foreign). Input credits are cash, capabilities or assets transferred to UAE economy. Output credits are profits, and jobs for locals
  - Work package—Providing capabilities or supply contracts to established UAE company. Input credits are same as above, and output credit is the value of contract to the UAE company

[31] https://tec.tawazun.ae/the-program/.

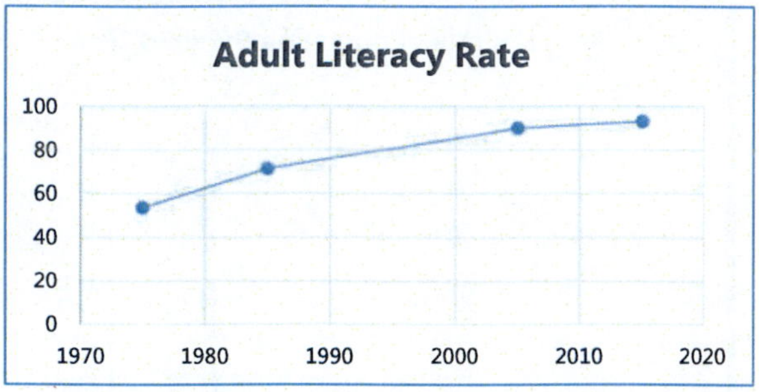

Fig. 20 Literacy expenditure (https://bit.ly/2Gexdkm)

Social

Literacy Rates

- As of 2015, adult literacy rate stood at 93%
- Male literacy rate as per UNESCO report 2015 stood at 93.1%
- Female literacy rate stood at 95.8% (Fig. 20)

Population Demographics

UAE as a popular destination for work and its tax laws attracts nationals from all countries. To an extent that majority of the population of the UAE is comprised of Indians, Pakistanis and Bangladeshis. The Emirati population stands at about 11% of the entire population of UAE (Figs. 21 and 22).

- Of the entire population females comprise ~28% and males ~72%
- Median age of males stood at 32.1 years as of 2017
- Female median age stood at 25 years[32]

Technological

- Amongst the Emirates, Dubai is considered the most developed. It aims to be the smartest city by 2020
- One advantage UAE has over other developed and developing nations is its spending power. UAE has launched four satellites between 2009 and 2013
- UAE has a nuclear power plant in the city of Abu Dhabi
- It ranks 31st on the Global Innovation Index

[32] https://www.cia.gov/library/publications/the-world-factbook/fields/2177.html.

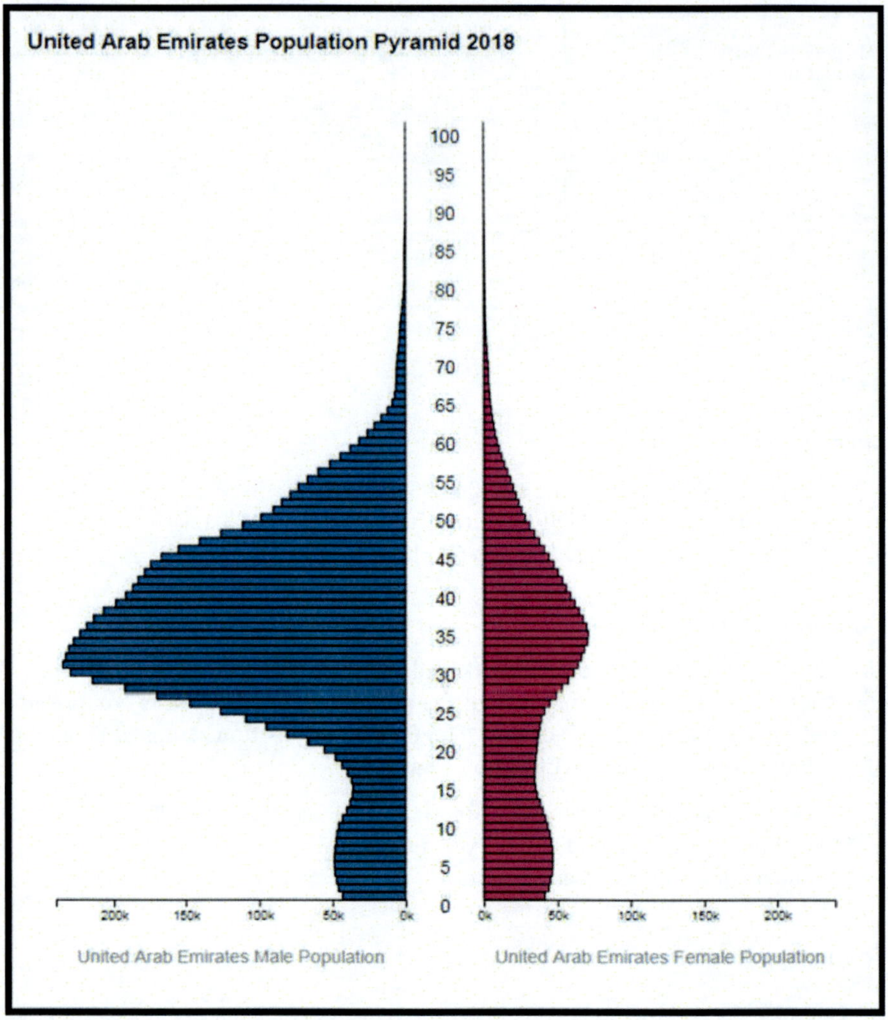

Fig. 21 Population demographics (http://worldpopulationreview.com/countries/united-arab-emirates-population/)

Environmental

Energy Consumption

- UAE has an annual consumption of 119.70 bn kWh with its own consumption amounting to 110.6 bn kWh
- Per capita consumption stands at 11,931.5 kWh in comparison to Europe's 5412.25 kWh

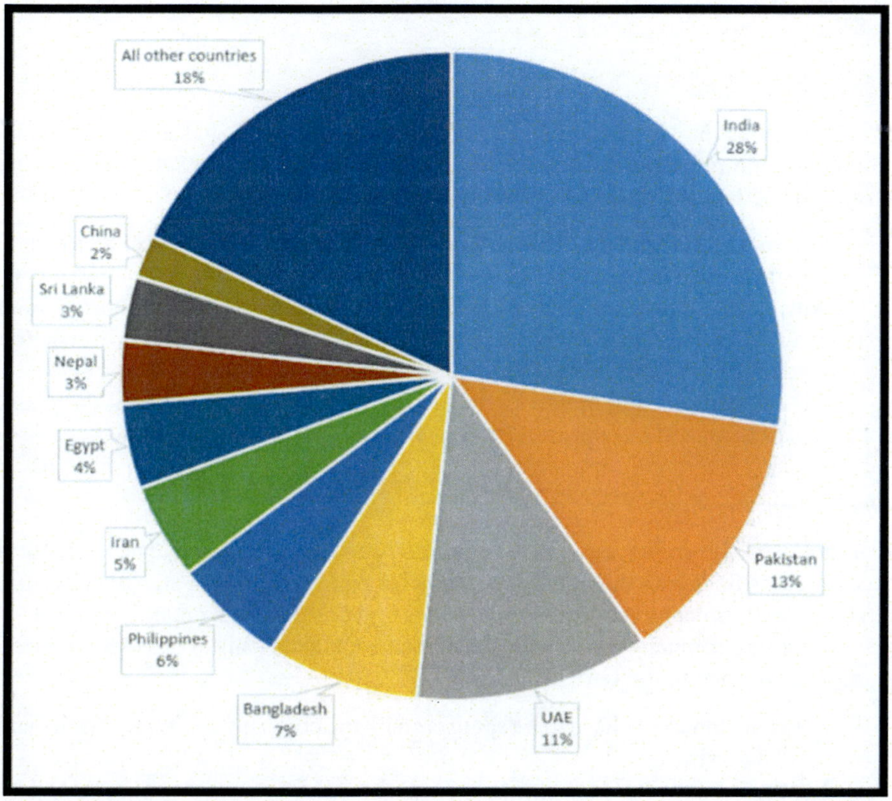

Fig. 22 Comparing population with other nations. http://worldpopulationreview.com/countries/united-arab-emirates-population/

- Of this the potential energy production value due to fossil fuels stands at 251.9 bn kWh and renewable energy at 1.21 bn kWh

Environmental Protection Laws

- Each Emirate has its own policy on electricity and are enacted independently
- There aren't any federal laws in place for governing renewable energy
- With energy demands growing by about 9% every year, Dubai's Integrated Energy Strategy Plans to reduce CO_2 emissions by about 30% by 2030
- ADWEA and DWEA are the regulatory bodies for power supply, transmission and distribution of electricity and water in Abu Dhabi and Dubai, respectively
- FEWA is the regulatory body for the northern emirates

Legal

Competitive Regulation

- The competition law doesn't apply to SME's, specific regulated sectors with own competition rules and Federal or Emirate establishments.
- As per the law, the businesses shouldn't engage in the following:
  - Restrictive agreements such as price fixing, collusion in tenders and offers, hoarding, excluding new market entrants, etc.
  - Any establishment occupying a dominant position (40% of total transactions) shouldn't misuse its position such as influencing selling conditions, restriction on dealing with others, falsifying price information, etc.
  - All acquisitions and mergers which result in a business holding a dominant position have to be approved by the Ministry of Economy

Employment Regulations

- Employers and employee need to enter into two written contracts. The short-form contract is filed with the Labour Ministry for employment visa and work permit. The long-form contract provides the terms and conditions in detail
- Any foreign company which wants to hire and conduct business has to be licenced and established in the UAE
  - Foreign employees have to be sponsored by the company for work permits and residence visa
  - Foreign companies not registered in the UAE can hire an independent contractor for undertaking work

Existing Players

- **Emirates Defence Industries Company**

EDIC MRO Land: It was established in 2006 and is involved in the maintenance, repair and overhauling of the equipment and components.

EDIC Geospatial services: Mapping, surveying and geospatial services.

EDIC Tech Services: It is a merger of three companies Naval Advanced Solutions, Secure Communications and C4 Advanced Solutions. It deals with importing equipment, services and technology.

- **Textron**

Textron and its sister company Bell have set up offices in Abu Dhabi for maintenance and providing in country training for its equipment, primarily the Bell Helicopters and C17 Globemaster.

- **Lockheed**

Lockheed Martin was established in 1995 in the UAE. It takes care of the maintenance, repair and overhaul of Block 60 F16, THAAD Air Defence System and Black Hawk helicopters.

- **Boeing**

Boeing established its defence, space and security office in 1999. UAE operates the AH-64 Apache and CH-47 Chinook helicopters. Boeing looks after the maintenance, repair and overhauling as well as marketing and sale of its products in Abu Dhabi (Fig. 23).

Opportunities

Self-Propelled Artillery

UAE purchased M-109 in the year 1999 after which it hasn't undergone modernisation. This provides an opportunity for offering upgrades for these.

K9 Vajra-T guns could also be offered as a solution (Fig. 24).

Foreign Relations

Egypt

UAE since its creation has had strong ties with Egypt. It ranks first amongst the Gulf countries who invest in Egypt. They have close political, cultural and economic ties.

USA

USA and UAE have strong diplomatic relations. This relationship was further strengthened when UAE-aided USA during the Persian Gulf War. To an extent where USA has the maximum number of ships after its own. They signed a nuclear co-operation deal under the Bush Administration which was further endorsed by the Obama administration. As a part of the Saudi Navy Expansion programme, a contract has been signed with Lockheed Martin for four Freedom class frigates.

Iran

Iran and UAE share very close economic relations. There is a matter of dispute over islands which Iran claims to be theirs.

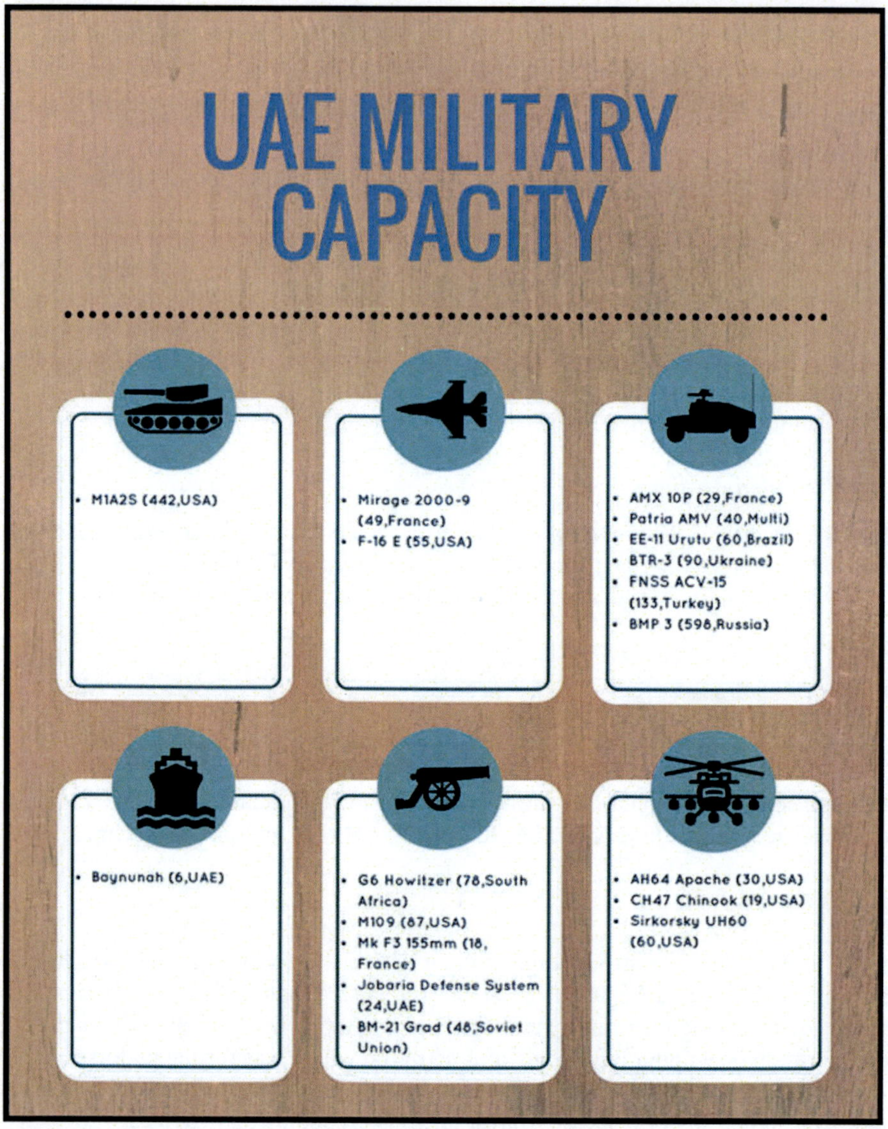

Fig. 23 UAE military capacity (https://bit.ly/2IpfOHr)

India

UAE and India share close trade ties, which date back centuries. Both are each other's main trading partners.

With its open trade policies and growth opportunities, Indians make up the second largest ethnic group in UAE which contributes to roughly 30% of its population.

Fig. 24 UAE history

Pakistan

Pakistan and UAE share very close relations based on the shared faith and religion. UAE is a major source of economic assistance in Pakistan.

Pakistan was the first country to officially recognised UAE as an independent nation. Pakistan has a majority of its expatriates living in the UAE.

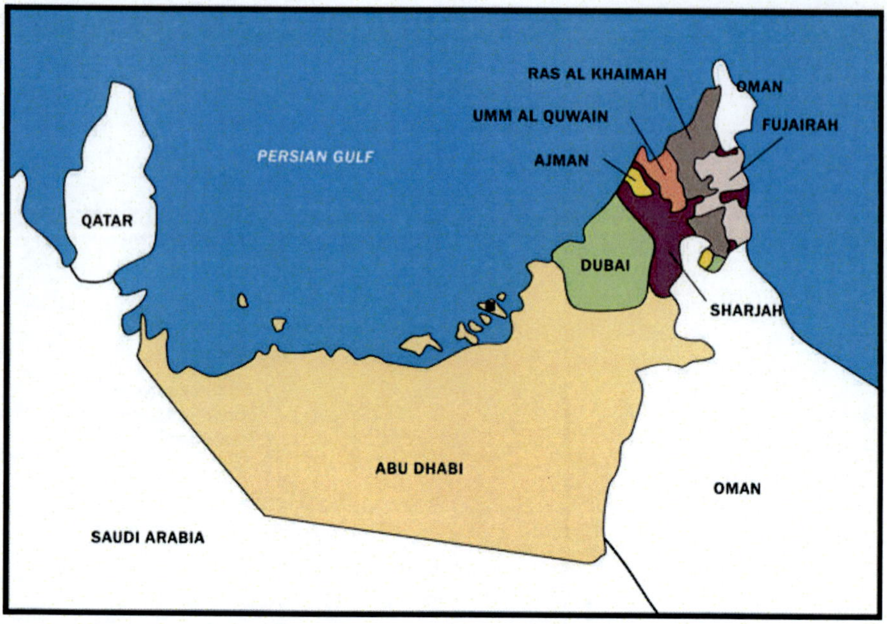

Fig. 25 Geography of Saudi Arabia

France

France and UAE have a defence co-operation agreement. It is one of the largest exporters of defence goods and services to UAE.

This agreement was primarily signed to reduce its dependence on the USA. France has a permanent military base in the UAE.

Segmentation

Geography

UAE is a part of the Saudi-led coalition to resolve the conflicts in Syria, Yemen and Iraq. It is also located close to Iran which is considered to be an enemy country by the GCC. It is located close to strategic trading routes such as the Gulf of Oman and the Persian[33] Gulf (Fig. 25).

[33] https://www.vecteezy.com/vector-art/126944-uae-map-vector-boundary.

Behaviour

According to SIPRI data, UAE increased their major arms imports by 63% in 2012–16 from 2007 to 11. Majority of the arms owned by UAE are of US or European origin. About 62% of the major arms owned by UAE are of US origin.

Demographics

UAE's population is dominated by Indians, Pakistanis and Bangladeshis. The Emirati population constituted about 11% of the entire population. Arab is the official language of UAE. Majority of the population is concentrated in Abu Dhabi, Dubai and Sharjah.

Targeting

Criteria Size

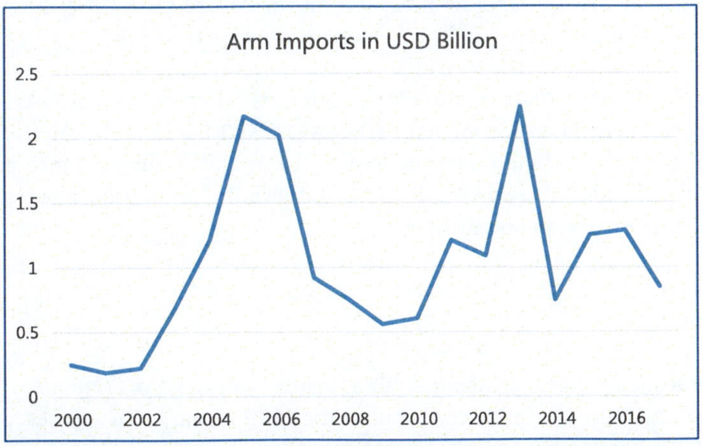

As the graph indicates in a span of about 20 years, on average UAE has spent about $1.014bn a year on major arm imports.[34] As of 2016, UAE contributed to about 1.3% of the world's military expenditure compared to 36% by USA and 3.8% by Saudi Arabia. With its participation in ongoing conflicts in Yemen and Syria, an upward trend in spending can be expected.

Market

A majority of the major arms in possession of the UAE is either of US or European origin. In terms of fixed and rotary wing aircrafts, land-based vehicles, US and Europe

[34] https://data.worldbank.org.

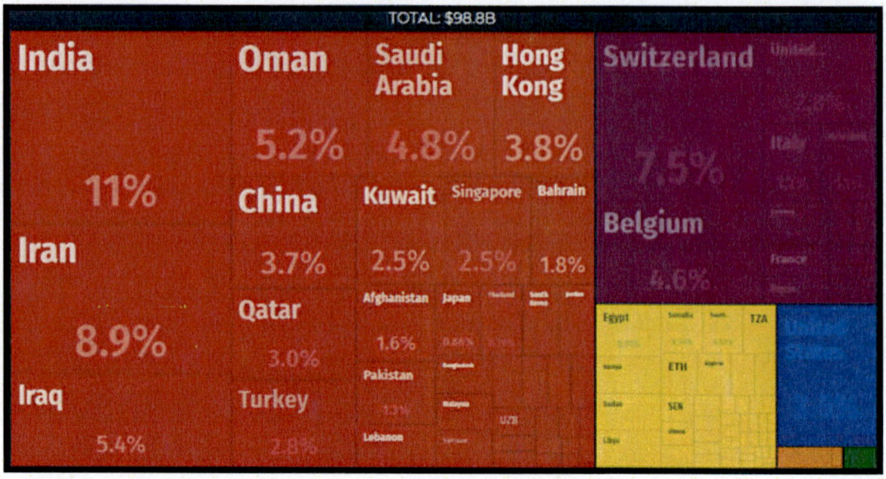

Fig. 26 Other nations exports (https://atlas.media.mit.edu/en/profile/country/are/)

are the leaders. USA accounts for 62% of arms imports of UAE for 2012–16. Russia has also started to gain a share of the market accounting for about 2.5% of UAE arms imports for the same period (Fig. 26).

As per the above graphic, India is the major export destination for UAE. Whereas in terms of imports, India accounts for 10% of UAE's total imports, ranking 3rd after China and USA. With both countries looking to establish local defence production capabilities, UAE could become a destination for India for long-term presence in the Middle East and African countries.

Positioning

Following a similar trend as Saudi Arabia, majority of the arms imports of UAE are from USA and Europe. In order to gain a foothold in the UAE market, partnering with a US- or Europe-based defence firm would be essential.

As 60% of the supply contract has to be invested in UAE (for order >$10 mn), a training establishment for the nationals or for making the subcontractors able could be created.

In terms of offerings, L&T should approach with a naval vessel-based mind-set and to be cost competitive. Fast-attack crafts and offshore patrol vessels along with maintenance, repair and modernisation is a likely approach.

Go to Market Strategy

- UAE is relatively the most liberal amongst the Gulf states when it comes to ease of doing business. With its relaxed entry regulations as well as tax policies, it has resulted in the setting up of branches or offices by several businesses
- As per the PESTEL analysis, a foreign firm looking to enter the UAE market needs to have either an UAE sponsor, agent or distributor. Partnering with local firm could be a good approach
- The defence offset accounts for 60% of the value of the contract, partnering with a local company could be an approach
- A team should be set up to for examining the possibilities for offset opportunities
- Modernisation for M-109 howitzers could be an approach which have been in service since 1999 and haven't undergone any upgrades
- Another approach could be offering the K9 Vajra-T

4.1.3 Oman

Current Leader: Qaboos Bin Said Al Said.

Currency: Rial.

Political

- Oman is an absolute monarchy. The Sultan of Oman is the head of the state as well as the Govt.
- The Sultan also serves as the Prime Minister, Minister of Defence, Foreign Minister, Supreme Commander of the forces and Chair of Central Bank
- It has no legislature or political parties
- There are three court levels: Elementary, Court of Appeal and Supreme Court

Tax Policies

- Corporate tax rate is set at 15%, increased from 12% in 2017
- A VAT of 5% to be implemented by all the members of the GCC is to be implemented in 2018
- Tax exemption of OMR 30,000 has been eliminated in the latest budget (2018)
- Companies in the field of oil exploration are charged 55% from the revenue generated from the sale

Entry and Trade Regulations

- Foreign companies can establish operations in Oman in the following ways
  - **Limited Liability Company**—Omani partner with 30% shares

Table 6 Oman interest rates

	Last (2016)	Previous (2015)	Highest	Lowest	Unit
GDP annual growth rate	−5.10	−14.10	13.10	−14.10	%
GDP	66.29	69.83	81.03	0.04	USD billion
GDP per capita	17,071.00	17,132.10	19,408.60	713.67	USD

Minimum share capital of OMR 150,000 is required to register an LLC. At least two shareholders are required

- **Joint Stock Company**—Omani partner with 30% shares

  Companies whose shares are not offered for public subscription are called privately held JSC. Min share capital required is OMR 500,000
  Companies whose shares are offered for public are called publicly held JSC. Min share capital required is OMR 2,000,000

- **Branch**—Only to execute a contract with the govt. or related bodies.

  Registration is limited for the period of contract
  A company could be allowed to register without a contract if the Council of ministers deem it to be of national importance

- **Commercial Agency**—Foreign companies without commercial licence can do business through commercial agents
- **Commercial Representative Office**—Purpose of marketing and promotion of products or services

  Not permitted to sell products or services or engage in other forms of commercial activities
  To aid importing products and services

Economical

Oman in the years 2015 and 2016 went through a recession owing to the fall in prices of crude oil. This was after a 5-year growth period where crude oil prices followed an upward trend (Table 6).[35]

Interest Rates

Oman Central Bank hiked rates on capital deposits from 0.5 to 1.5% in 2018 as a result of rise in market interest rates which in turn were in response to hikes in US rates (Table 7).[36]

35 https://tradingeconomics.com/oman/gdp.

36 https://tradingeconomics.com/oman/interest-rate.

Table 7 Oman interest rates' comparison

	Last (2018)	Previous (2017)	Highest	Lowest	Unit
Interest rate	2.41	2.38	5.00	1.00	%
Deposit interest rate	3.19	1.90	9.04	1.90	%

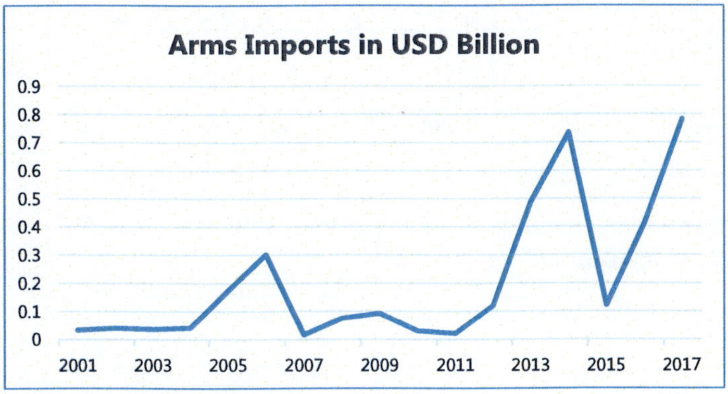

Fig. 27 Military expenditure of Oman

Inflation Rates

As of April 2018, the inflation rate has risen by about 0.58% over the same period in 2017. This is due to the increase in cost of segments such as education, transport and furnishing and household equipment. Others reasons were higher interest rates and removal of subsidies amongst several.[37]

Military Expenditure

Oman is amongst the few members of the GCC which has remained largely free from internal and external conflicts. It hasn't participated in the Saudi-led coalition in Yemen. It shares strong diplomatic and military relations with Iran as well. It hasn't joined the Arab states either in severing relations with Qatar (Fig. 27).[38]

Defence Offsets

- The offset obligations are applied through the partnership for development program. The obligations are applicable when a military or security equipment contract exceeds OMR 5,000,000. The obligations are 50% of the value of contracts towards direct or indirect offsets

---

[37] https://knoema.com/atlas/Oman/Inflation-rate.

[38] https://bit.ly/2IPlEFx.

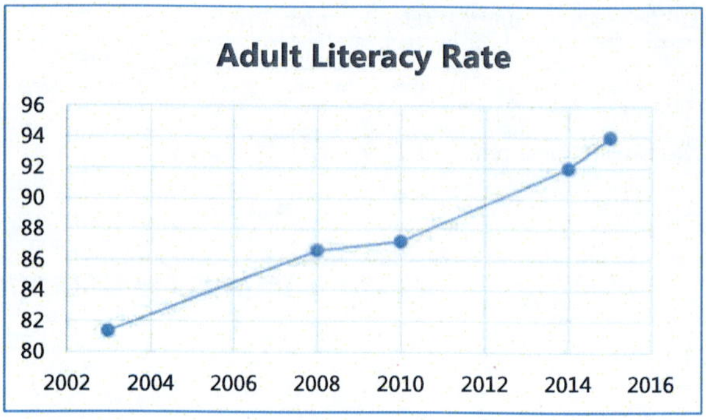

Fig. 28 Adult literacy rate in Oman (http://worldpopulationreview.com/countries/oman-population/)

- The Omanisation programme requires at least 35% of the workforce to be Omani nationals compulsorily.[39]

Social

Literacy Rates

- As of 2016, female youth literacy rate stood at 98.98%
- Male youth literacy rate stood at 98.51%
- For adults, female literacy rate was at 86.04% and male at 96.63%[40]

Population Demographics

The official language spoken in Oman is Arabic. About 33% of the entire population lives in Muscat. The currency in use is the Oman Rial (Figs. 28 and 29).

- The median age of Oman is 25.4 years
- Male median age is 26.5 years
- Female median age is 24 years

Technological

- Oman in 2016, launched a $200 mn Oman technology fund to invest in start-ups locally and abroad
- Oman is ranked 80th in the Global Innovation Index with a score of 31.8. In comparison, UAE is ranked 31st, Qatar 49th and Saudi 55th
- Internet content is monitored by the Govt., thus video chat services are not available

[39] https://oapfd.om/en/PFD/Pages/PFDRegulation.aspx.

[40] https://knoema.com/atlas/Oman/.

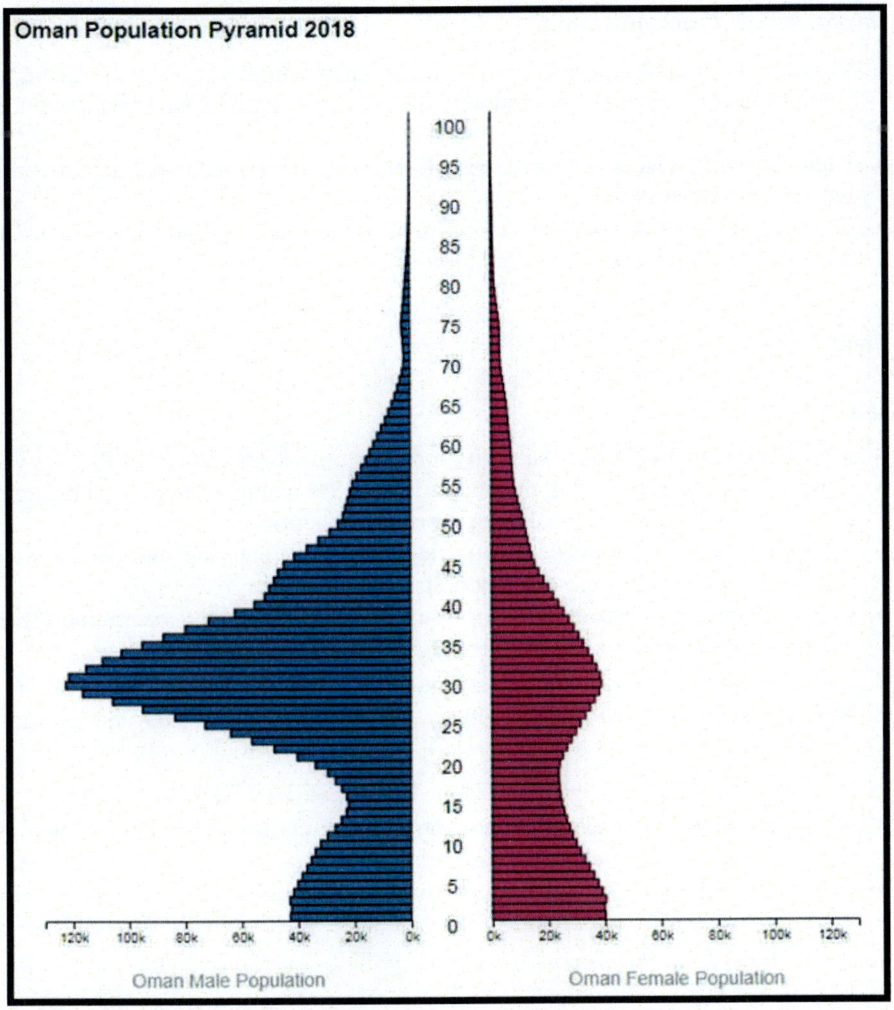

Fig. 29 Population demographics of Oman

Environmental

- Total energy production capacity of Oman is 30.79 bn kWh
- Own consumption is at 27 bn kWh with a per capita consumption of 6242.14 kWh
- It is capable of producing 68.93 bn kWh of energy using fossil fuels

Environmental Protection Laws

- The UN environment programme credited Oman with having a good record in environmental conservation, maintenance of ecological balance and pollution control in 2009
- It has declared 18 natural reserves with the reserves diversified into desert, marine, mountainous reserves
- The laws are governed by Ministry of Environment and Climate Affairs set up in 2007. It has also ratified the Kyoto protocol

Legal

Competition Law

- It is enforced by the Public Authority for Consumer Protection (PACP)
- It prohibits a company in a dominant position (35% market share) from engaging in activities which would weaken or prevent competition
- It prohibits businesses inside or outside Oman from entering into contracts or agreements for the purpose of monopolising the market
- It also requires a company looking to create an economic concentration (35% market share) to take a clearance from PACP. Above 50% is prohibited
- Consequences for violating the law could result in sanctions ranging from administrative fines to imprisonment

Employment Regulations

- For a private sector employee, the contract must contain basic details such as names of parties, place of residence, nationality, etc.
- The contract could be for a definite or an indefinite period
- Working hours of a maximum of 45 h a week is permitted. For Ramzan, a maximum of 6 h a day

Existing Players

- **Thales**

It has a presence of over 30 years in Oman. In 2012, it was contracted for supplying sensors and combat management systems for the Royal Navy.

- **Esnaad**

It has been certified by the Govt. of Oman to supply military and defence equipment. It represents US-based companies and has been accredited by the US dept. of state.

- **MSA Global LLC**

It is an Omani company. Its products include airborne surveillance platforms, military vehicles, mobile surveillance platforms and security systems.

- **Electroman**

It is a wholly Omani-owned company with products in the field of security systems and telecommunications (Fig. 30).

Opportunities

Tanks

Oman purchased the M-60A1 tanks in 1980 and M-60A3 tanks in 1990 after which they haven't undergone modernisation. This provides an opportunity for providing upgrades for these tanks.[41]

Self-propelled Artillery

Based on the age of inventory, Oman purchased the 155 mm G6 in 1995 after which they haven't undergone any modernisation. This provides an opportunity for upgrading them.

It also provides an opportunity for offering the K9 Vajra-T howitzers.

Foreign Relations

Saudi Arabia

Oman was one of the founding members of the GCC along with Saudi Arabia. It was a part of the coalition during the Iraq war in 1990.

Yemen

Oman and Yemen were involved in the Dhofar rebellion with the Yemen army helping the separatists. As of now, both countries share diplomatic relations with Oman providing refuge to Yemeni nationals affected by the Yemen war.

[41] http://www.inss.org.il/he/wp-content/uploads/sites/2/systemfiles/(FILE)1275907930.pdf.

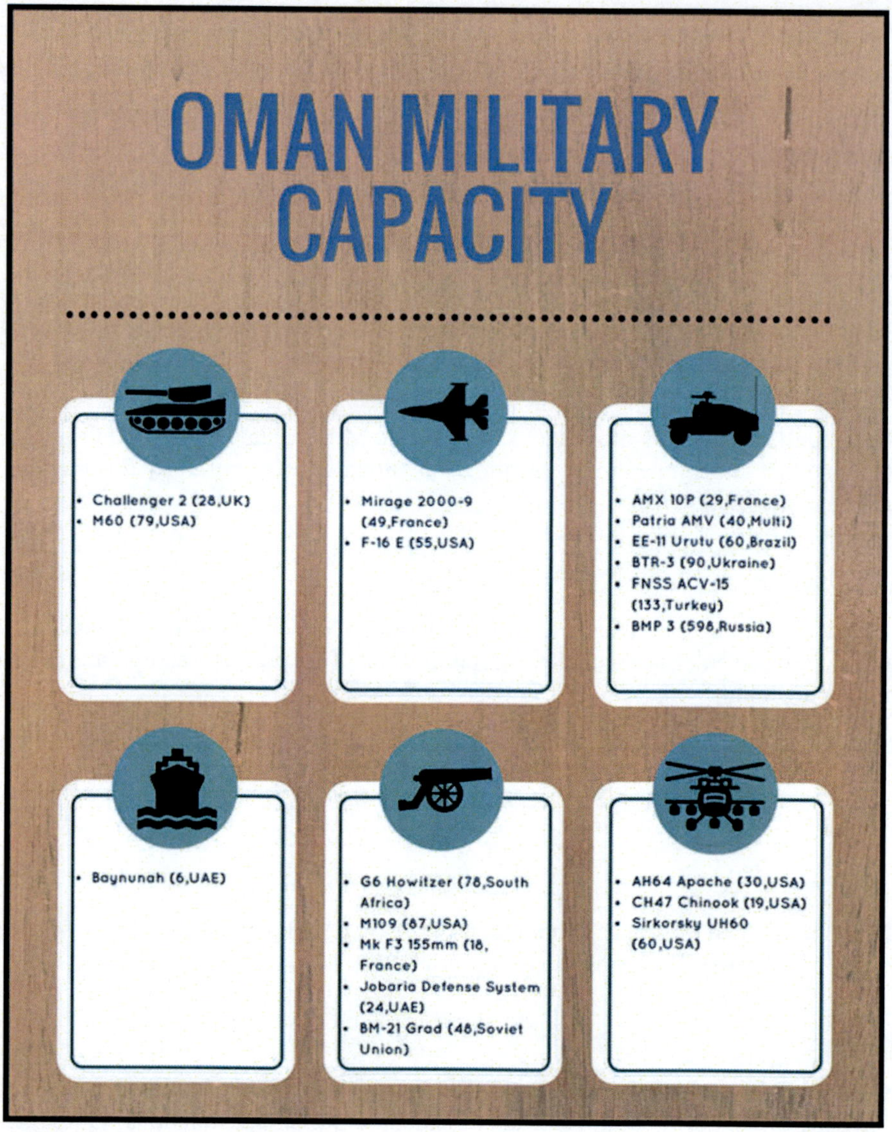

Fig. 30 Oman military capacity ([42])

India

Oman and India share diplomatic relations. It was the first Gulf nation to establish defence ties with India. In 2016, various deals including defence were signed (Fig. 31).

[42] https://bit.ly/2IFGFDk

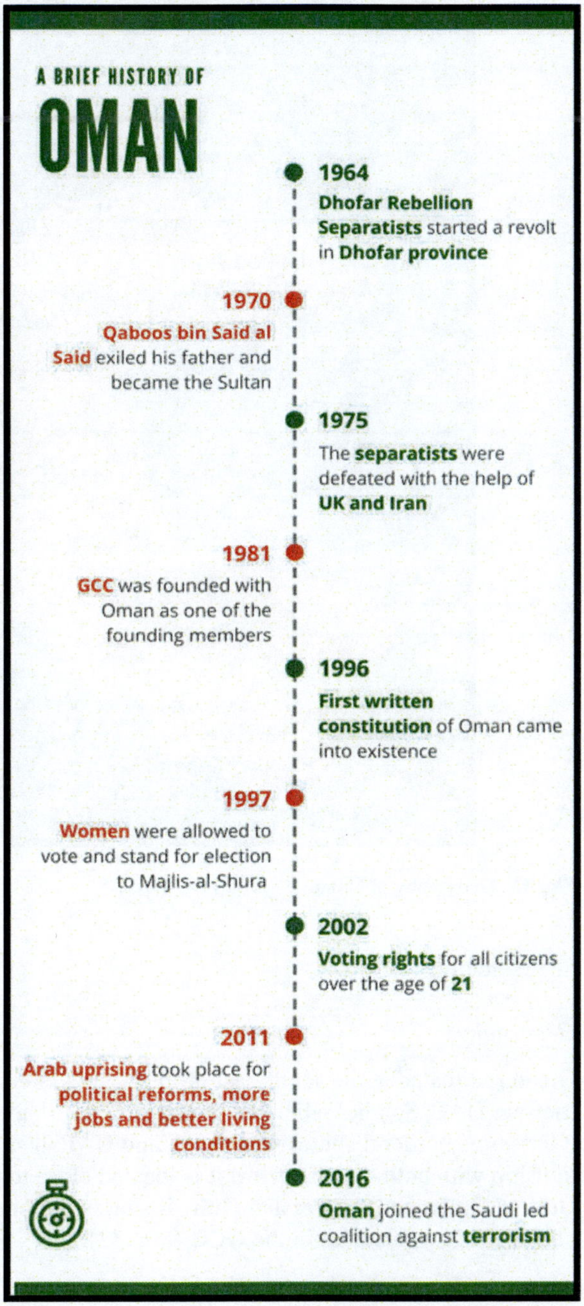

Fig. 31 Oman history

Fig. 32 Geography of Oman

Segmentation

Geography

Oman is situated at the south-east of the Arabian Peninsula. Its neighbouring countries are UAE, Saudi Arabia and Oman which it shares its borders with.[43] Although it has some border disputes with Saudi and UAE, it shares a relatively peaceful relationship with both the countries. It is located close to strategic locations such as the Gulf of Oman and the Persian Gulf. It shares diplomatic relations with Iran being one of the few countries in the GCC (Fig. 32).

---

43 https://www.infoplease.com/country/oman.

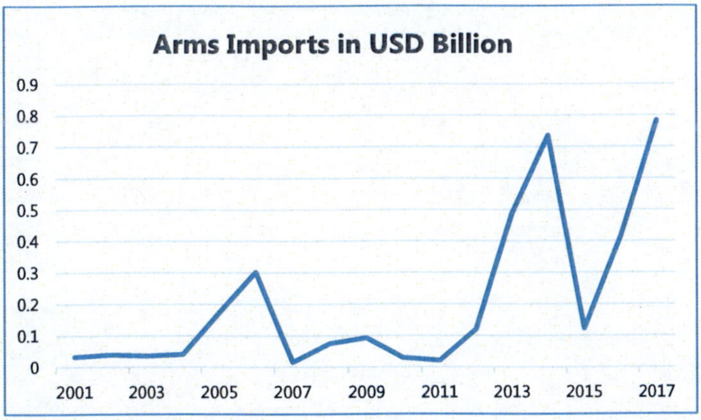

Fig. 33 Arms imports in Oman (https://bit.ly/2IplEFx)

Behaviour

As per SIPRI data, Oman has a military budget of $8.7bn with majority of the arms imported from USA and Europe.

Demographics

Primarily, the ethnic groups living in Oman are Arabs, Baluchi and South Asian. The languages spoken are Arab, Baluchi, English, Hindi and Urdu. Immigrants constitute about 45% of the entire population. Majority of its population is located in Muscat.

Targeting

Criteria Size

As per SIPRI data in 2016, Oman spent about 16.7% of its GDP on military expenditure. Arms imports accounted for $0.78 bn in 2017. Its arms imports ranked amongst the highest in the world for % of GDP spent. Majority of the arms imported from Oman have either US or UK origin. For UK, military exports to Oman account for 14% of its overall sales with Saudi accounting for 49% (Fig. 33).

Market

In terms of explosive ammunition US accounts for 79% of the imports and 100% for the military weapons. USA accounted for 35% of all major arms imports, whereas UK accounted for 23% (Fig. 34).

In terms of imports, India accounts for 5.4% of the total imports whereas 4.4% of its exports. India can capitalise on its trade relations with Oman to extend it to

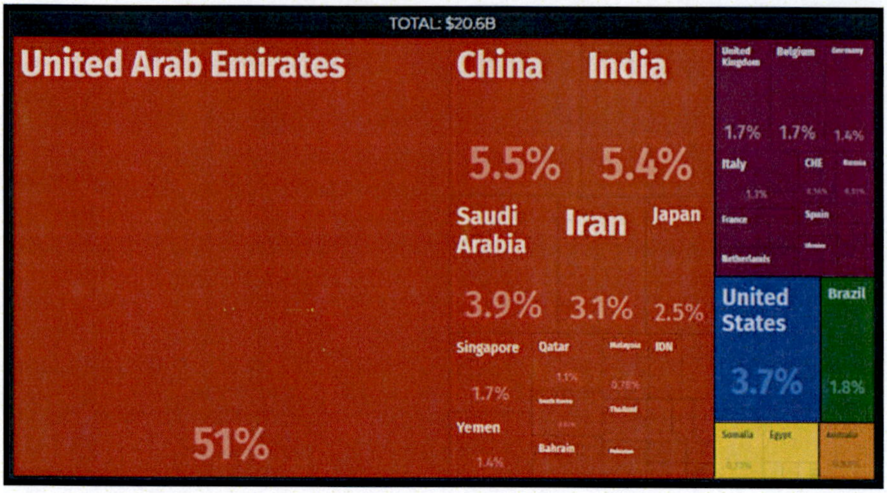

Fig. 34 International market. *Source* https://atlas.media.mit.edu/en/profile/country/omn/

defence equipment as well. With the worsening situation in Yemen and the presence of extremist forces such as Al-Qaida and ISIS, military expenditure is expected to show an upward trend.

Positioning

L&T already has a presence in Oman in the form of L&T Oman LLC. It can capitalise on its reputation and the work already undertaken to gain a market share in the defence sector as well.

Like most of the GCC countries, Oman too imports its major arms from USA and Europe. In order to do gain a market share, cost competition would be a good method to follow. As it is located close to strategic locations such as the Gulf of Oman and the Persian Gulf, a naval vessel-based approach should be followed. L&T could offer fast-attack crafts as well as OPVs.

Go-to-Market Strategy

- Possible modes of entry could be partnering with a local firm or to market products independently by setting up a commercial representative office
- A team should be set up to handle the offset requirement planning
- An approach to tackling the offsets could be upskilling the nationals in order to cater to the Omanisation requirements

- As L&T already has a presence in Oman (L&T Oman LLC), it could look to expand its business scope from construction, power transmission and distribution to defence contracts as well.
- An approach could be offering OPVs as the naval strength of Oman in this area is weak
- Marketing campaign could be aimed at securing its shores and the safety of its offshore extraction and exploration vessels
- Another approach could be offering modernisation solutions for 155 mm G6 Howitzers which were purchased in 1995 and haven't undergone any modernisation[44]

4.2 *North Africa*

4.2.1 Egypt

Current President: Abdel Fattah el-Sisi.

Current Prime Minister: Sherif Ismail.

Currency: Egyptian Pound.

Political

Government Structure

- Egypt follows a semi-presidential system which was implemented after the Arab Springs in 2011. The President is elected for a 4-year term which can be renewed once
- The principle legislative body is the House of Representatives. It sits for a 5-year term
- A new constitution was adopted in 2014 after the removal of Mohamed Morsi after a coup

Tax Policies

- Corporate tax is levied at a rate of 22.5%. However, different tax rates are applicable for the petroleum authority, Suez canal authority, Central Bank and Oil and Gas exploration and production companies
- Capital gains tax is applicable for the sale of unlisted shares at the rate of 22.5% for corporate shareholders
- A VAT of 14% is applicable for all goods and services. An exception is for machinery and equipment used for production. They are charged at 5%

[44] http://www.inss.org.il/he/wp-content/uploads/sites/2/systemfiles/(FILE)1275907930.pdf.

Entry and Trade Regulations

- For a foreign company to enter the market, the possible forms are:
  - **Joint Stock Company**—At least three shareholders and at least three Board of Directors. Capital requirement of 250,000 EGP.

    Can be 100% foreign owned but doesn't have the right to import. For importing company needs to be wholly owned by Egyptian shareholders. No restriction on activities that can be undertaken
  - **Limited Liability Company**—At least two partners and at least one manager for administrative work. At least one Egyptian manager

    Allowed to engage in all business activities and can be 100% foreign owned. Not allowed to import unless wholly owned by Egyptian shareholders
  - **Representative Office**—Only for market analysis, no commercial activity. A manager should be appointed for administrative work

    Not liable for corporate tax. Minimum of $1000 to be deposited in the office's account by the Head office
  - **Branch**—For the purpose of implementing a contract in Egypt. A manager has to be appointed for administrative work

    No capital requirement but a deposit of 5000EGP in the branch account
- At least 250 Egyptian employees should be employed

Economics

Interest Rates

The Central Bank cut the deposit rates by 100 basis points to 16.75% and 17.75%, respectively (Fig. 35; Table 8).

This was done because the inflation fell to 14.4% and borrowing costs were increased. This helps us know the investment and borrowing capability and tendency.[45]

Inflation Rate

Inflation rates reached a high of 33% in 2017. This was a result of Egypt devaluing the pound as well as cuts in energy subsidy. The Consumer Price Index has reached 13.3%, the lowest in two years.[46]

---

[45] https://tradingeconomics.com/egypt/interest-rate.

[46] https://knoema.com/atlas/Egypt/Inflation-rate.
https://knoema.com/atlas/Egypt/Arms-imports.

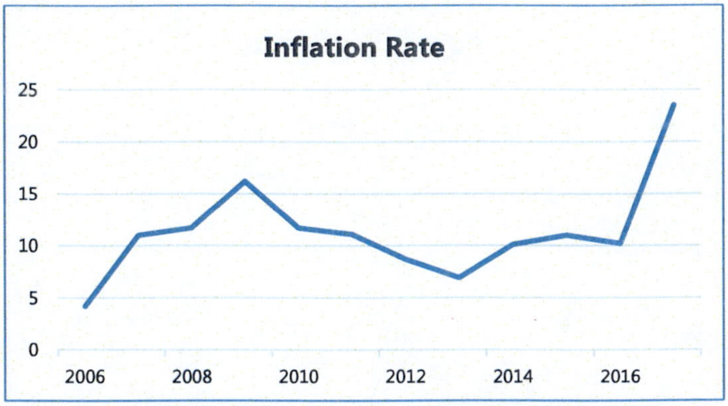

Fig. 35 Inflation rates of Egypt

Table 8 Interest rates in Egypt

	Last (2018)	Previous (2017)	Highest	Lowest	Unit
Interest rate	16.75	16.75	21.40	8.25	%
Deposit interest rate	12.09	7.86	12.09	6.02	%
Lending rate	17.75	17.75	19.75	9.25	%

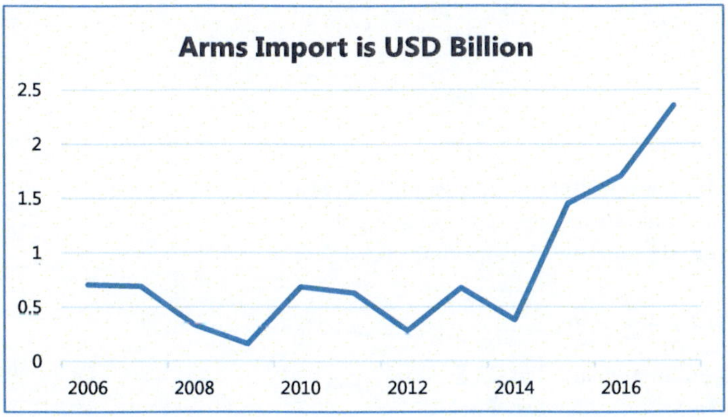

Fig. 36 Arms imports in Egypt

Military Expenditure

As per SIPRI data, Egypt was the third largest arms importer in 2013–17. Imports grew by 215% compared to 2008–2012. Of the total arms imports, France accounted for 37%, USA for 26% and Russia 21% (Fig. 36).

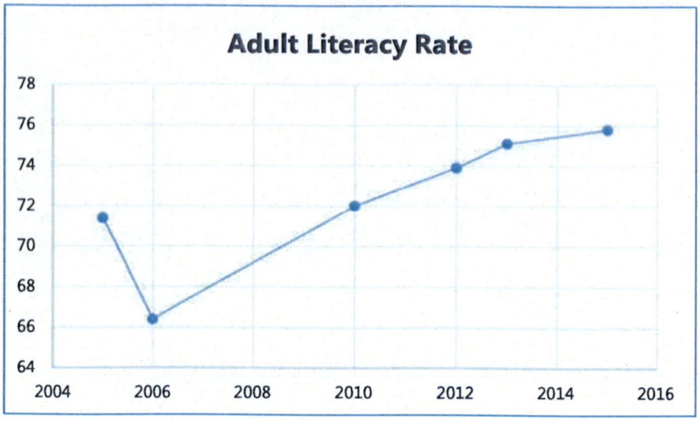

Fig. 37 Literacy rates in Egypt

Defence Offsets

- No mentions of an offset policy followed by Egypt was found
- The local defence industry develops defence equipment and systems through technology transfers and licencemanufacturing
- The procurement programme is largely funded by the USA in the form of foreign military financing program.[47]

Social

Literacy Rate

- As of 2015, adult literacy rate stood a 75.8%
- The adult male literacy rate stood at 82.2%
- Adult female literacy rate stood at ~65.4% (Fig. 37)[48]

Population Demographics

- Total median age stood at 23.8
- Median age for males was 23.4
- Median age for females was 24.1 (Fig. 38)[49]

[47] https://bit.ly/2kmW2Cn.
[48] https://bit.ly/2J4AJTT.
[49] https://bit.ly/2HpX4XV.

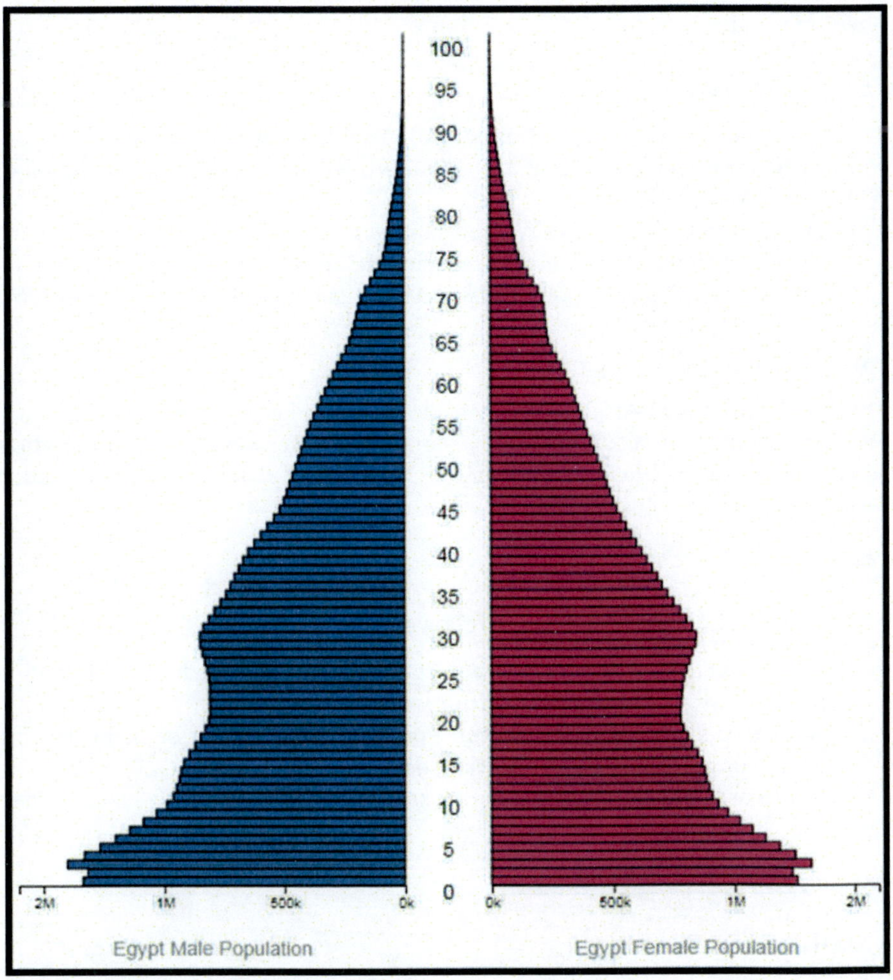

Fig. 38 Pollution demographic of Egypt

Technological

- Egypt ranks 105th on the Global Innovation Index with a score of 26
- As of 2016, 33% of the Egyptian population were Internet users[50]
- Egypt has set up the HCST and STDF for boosting innovation and development

[50] https://bit.ly/2fSdXBg.

Environmental

Energy Consumption

- Total production capacity of all production facilities is 171.9 bn kWh
- Its own consumption stands at 150.4 bn kWh with a per capita consumption of 1571.76 kWh
- Its energy imports are 43 m kWh and exports 1.16 bn kWh
- Of the total theoretical production capacity of 340.6bn kWh, fossil fuels account for 308.23 bn kWh, water power 24.86 bn kWh and renewable energy 7.5 bn kWh

Environmental Protection Laws

- Egypt Environment Affairs Agency is the main regulatory body
- Water resources are taken care of by Ministry of Water Resources and Irrigation
- Law 4/1994 is the Environmental law and its most important piece of legislation

Legal

- The competition law prohibits the following
  - Agreements and contracts between competing persons leading to fluctuation of prices for profit, hoarding, territory marking, etc.
  - Agreements and contracts between a person and contractors or clients leading to affecting freedom of competition, decline in quality, etc.
  - Abuse of dominant position (market share >25%)

Existing Players

- **AOI Aircraft Factory**
  - It manufactures and assembles aircraft for the Egypt Air Force such as the Alpha Jet, ordnance and knockdown kits for M-60 and M1A1 tanks
- **Sakr Factory for Developed Industries**
  - It is the primary facility for ballistic missiles and long-range artillery development. It also produces surface-to-air, air-to-air and anti-tank missiles
- **Kader Factory for Developed Industries**
  - It specialised in the development and production of armoured vehicles, aircraft guidance systems and aircraft bombs (Fig. 39)

Fig. 39 Egypt military capacity

Opportunities

Self-propelled Artillery

As the M110A2 which were purchased in 1996 haven't undergone any modernisation plans yet, it provides an opportunity.

Foreign Relations

USA

Diplomatic relations were re-established after the Yom Kippur war in order to reach a peace treaty with Israel in 1974. Post the strengthening of relations, USA has provided Egypt with military and economic aid. The relations seem to be weakening after Egypt started to purchase weapons from Russia.

India

Egypt and India together are the founders of the Non-Aligned movement. India supported Egypt and the Arabs during the Arab–Israeli war. Both nations have strong diplomatic and trade relations.

Iran

Egypt initially had diplomatic relations with Iran, but they weakened after Egypt supported Iraq in the Iraq–Iran war. Other reasons were Egypt's close relations with USA and other Western countries, Gaza war where both the sides blamed each other for escalating and Iran's alleged part in supporting terrorist organisations such as Hamas and Houthis.

Israel

Egypt and Israel have had a strained relationship over a history of wars and Egypt's stance on the Gaza strip (Fig. 40).

Segmentation

Geography

Egypt is bordered on the west by Libya, on the south by Sudan and on the East by Israel.[51] Other countries in the proximity are Saudi Arabia and Syria. It has diplomatic relations with Libya. Egypt was against the separation of Sudan and relations have weakened over land disputes. Egypt and Israel have a strained relationship over the wars fought between the two and Egypt's stance on Gaza and Palestine. Relations with Saudi Arabia have weakened after (Fig. 41) Egypt's limited participation in the Yemen war. Egypt is situated close to strategic locations such as Port Said and Suez Canal.

---

[51] https://bit.ly/2LCxdyI.

Fig. 40 Brief history of Egypt

Fig. 41 Geography of Egypt

Behaviour

Egypt ranks third in the world in terms of arm imports globally.[52] It accounted for 4% of the arms import globally. Compared to 2008–12 period, in 2013–17 arms imports increased by 215%. France was the largest contributor during this period, accounting for about 37% of total arms. Other exporters of arms to Egypt include USA, Russia and UK.

Demographics

Egypt's population is predominantly Sunni Muslims, who account for about 99.6% of the country's population. Muslims constitute for about 90% of the country's ethnic structure. Christianity is the other major religion.

[52] https://bit.ly/2sp9UQ8.

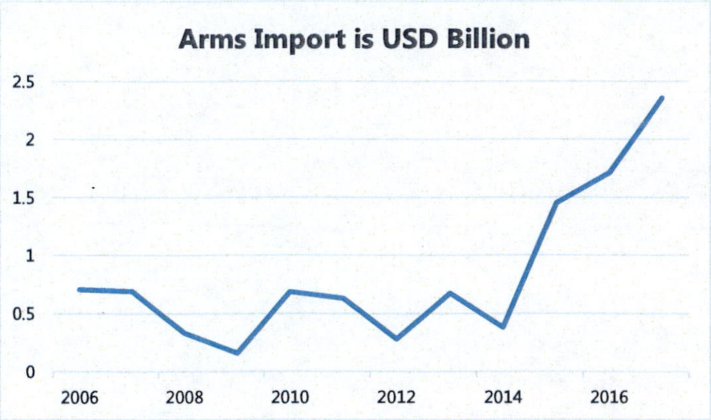

Fig. 42 Arms imports in Egypt

Targeting

Criteria Size

In terms of military expenditure, Egypt spent about 1.67% of its GDP as of 2016. In 2017, the arms imports amounted to $2.355 bn. As per SIPRI data, Egypt ranks 3rd in the world in terms of arms imports with the major contributors being France, USA and Russia (Fig. 42).[53]

Market

As of 2016, USA accounted for 79% of the explosive ammunition imported by Egypt (Fig. 43).[54]

Of the total imports, India accounts for 3.2%. Chemicals, animal products and transportation account for the majority of the imports. In terms of exports, India accounts for 2.8% of the total exports with mineral products and textiles accounting for the majority of the imports.

Positioning

Egypt's military ranks 12th in the world. Higher than most Arab states and Israel except Turkey.

---

[53] https://bit.ly/2xnXFcj.

[54] https://atlas.media.mit.edu/en/profile/country/egy/.

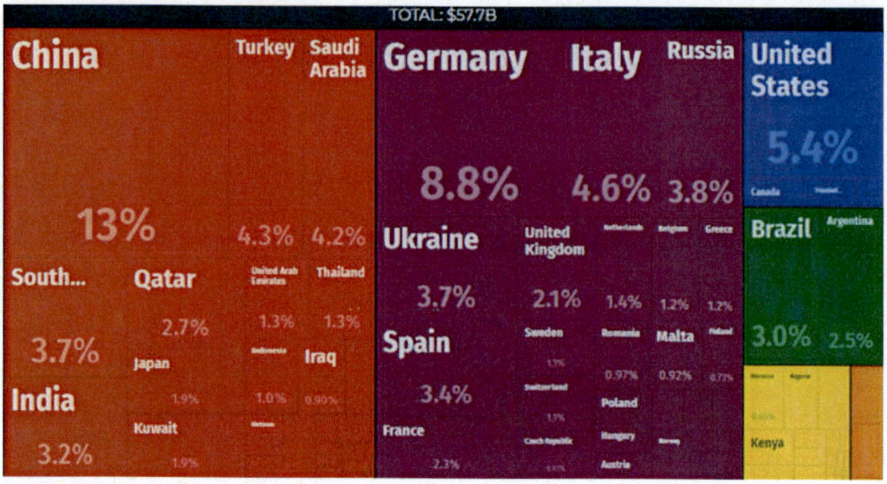

Fig. 43 International market of Egypt

Majority of the major arms imported by it are of US, Russian or European origin. In order to gain a market share in Egypt, partnering with a firm from the above-mentioned countries could be an approach. As most of the defence industries in Egypt are Govt. owned partnering with them wouldn't be a feasible option.

The arms imports when it comes to naval vessels, fixed and rotary wing aircrafts as well as land vehicles are imported from USA, Europe or Russia. L&T could approach the market by providing maintenance and repair solutions. Another product L&T could offer is OPVs.

Go-to-Market Strategy

- From the analysis, the possible mode of entry for a foreign firm looking to capture market share in Egypt would be to partner with the local defence firms
- Although Egypt allows to establish joint stock companies or LLCs, importing would be allowed only if the company is wholly owned by Egyptian shareholders.
- Based on its arms import history, the imports are likely to show an upward trend which would make it a feasible market
- A large proportion of the defence procurement is funded by the foreign military aid given by the USA, also a reason for the large % of the US origin arms.
- An approach for entering the market could be offering modernisation solutions for the M110A2 SP howitzer which haven't undergone modernisation plans[55]

[55] http://armorama.com/modules.php?op=modload&name=features&file=view&artid=6395.

Recommendations

Countries are arranged in the order of priority:

Oman

L&T has an LLC in Oman which would save costs on marketing. A team should be set up for handling the defence offsets policy.

Marketing strategy can be focused on the security of offshore oil extraction and exploration vessels as well as proximity to strategic locations such as the Gulf of Oman and the Persian Gulf.

Naval vessels should be the focus. Products that can be offered are OPVs, fast-attack crafts, modernisation solutions for M-60A1 and M-60A3 tanks and G6 SP howitzer.

Saudi Arabia

For entry into the market, partnering with a firm of US, Russian or European firm could be an approach.

Partnering with local firms to fulfil the 30% subcontracting from local companies is a feasible solution.

A team should be set up for handling the defence offset policy.

Partnering with an e-learning platform for upskilling Saudi Nationals could be a possible option. Modernisation solutions for M-109 and M-60 SP howitzers as well as M1A2 and M-60A3 tanks can be offered which haven't undergone modernisation programs. As an alternative K9 Vajra-T SP's could also be offered as a solution.

Another approach could be offering OPVs and fast-attack crafts with the marketing campaign focused on protection of its shores and offshore oil extraction and exploration vessels.

UAE

Amongst the countries which are a part of this research, UAE has the highest defence offset of 60% of contract value in direct offsets.

Another aspect is that they have a shipbuilding company place (Abu Dhabi Ship Building) who have already manufactured ships for UAE Navy.

An aspect which could bc focused on is the modernisation of M-109 SP howitzers which haven't undergone any modernisation programs since their purchase in 1999. As an alternative, K9 Vajra-T guns could be offered.

Egypt

Egypt has a strong navy in place. It is ranked highest in military ranking amongst all Middle East nations with the exception of Israel.

Also, technology transfer is an aspect that the Govt. focuses on in the case of purchase of foreign arms.

An approach which could be followed is the modernisation of M110A2 howitzers which haven't undergone any modernisation programs since their purchase in 1996.

References

Saudi Arabia

(n.d.). Retrieved from http://www.iaforum.org/Content/ViewInternalDocument.cfm?ContentID=8289

Africa's economies ranked by GDP, which is really the largest? (2017, October 21). Retrieved from https://www.cnbcafrica.com/zdnl-mc/2017/10/21/africas-economies-ranked-gdp-really-largest/

Al Jazeera. (2018, May 02). *US, China and Saudi Arabia top list of military spending*. Retrieved from https://www.aljazeera.com/news/2018/05/china-saudi-arabia-top-list-military-spending-180502060524362.html

Beauchamp, Z. (2014, March 31). *What is Zionism?* Retrieved from https://www.vox.com/cards/israel-palestine/zionism

Beauchamp, Z. (2017, November 06). *The purge in Saudi Arabia, explained*. Retrieved from https://www.vox.com/world/2017/11/6/16613088/saudi-arabia-princes-arrested-mohammed-bin-salman

Dudley, D. (2018, February 14). *Middle East Governments are cutting their military budgets even as wars rage around the region*. Retrieved from https://www.forbes.com/sites/dominicdudley/2018/02/14/middle-east-military-budgets/#66cc3c591de3

Caffrey, C., & IHS Jane's Defence Weekly. (n.d.). *Saudi Arabia increases defence budget*. Retrieved from http://www.janes.com/article/76607/saudi-arabia-increases-defence-budget

Energy consumption in Saudi Arabia. (n.d.). Retrieved from https://www.worlddata.info/asia/saudi-arabia/energy-consumption.php

Fioramonti, L. (2017, November 27). The 'Africa rising' bubble tells us why GDP growth is not a real indicator of prosperity. Retrieved from https://scroll.in/article/856161/the-africa-rising-bubble-tells-us-why-gdp-growth-is-not-a-real-indicator-of-prosperity

Focus, E. (n.d.). *Expat focus*. Retrieved from http://www.expatfocus.com/expatriate-saudi-arabia-taxation

History. (n.d.). Retrieved from https://www.uae-embassy.org/about-uae/history

Husein, A. T., Akel, A. A., & Balouziyeh, J. (2017, May 11). *Defense contracting in Saudi Arabia*. Retrieved from https://www.lexology.com/library/detail.aspx?g=39818115-a77c-4a7a-8f55-c2442bd382d9

INDIAN DEFENCE EXPORTS. (n.d.). Retrieved from http://www.defproac.com/?p=1427

Manfreda, P. (n.d.). 8 countries that had arab spring uprisings. Retrieved from https://www.thoughtco.com/arab-spring-uprisings-2353039

Middle Eastern Laws. (n.d.). Retrieved from http://www.mideastlaw.com/middle_eastern_laws_saudi_arabia.html

Military Budgets in the Middle East. (n.d.). Retrieved from http://militarybudget.org/middle-east/

Military expenditure (% of GDP). (n.d.). Retrieved from https://data.worldbank.org/indicator/MS.MIL.XPND.GD.ZS?view=map

Rahman, S. (2017, June 23). India's Middle East Balancing Act. Retrieved from https://thediplomat.com/2017/06/indias-middle-east-balancing-act/

Rashad, M. (2018, March 15). *Saudi central bank raises key interest rates ahead of U.S.* Retrieved from https://www.reuters.com/article/us-saudi-rates/saudi-central-bank-raises-key-interest-rates-ahead-of-u-s-idUSKCN1GR2H2

Saudi Arabia: The Competition law regime. (n.d.). Retrieved from https://www.tamimi.com/law-update-articles/saudi-arabia-the-competition-law-regime/

Sawhney, P. (2018, February 05). *In defence budget 2018, political goals masquerade as military objectives*. Retrieved from https://thewire.in/economy/defence-budget-2018-procurement-make-in-india

Subscribe to the FT to Read: Financial Times Britain Changes Strategy on Selling Arms to India. (n.d.). Retrieved from https://www.ft.com/content/35b0f918-1eab-11e7-a454-ab04428977f9

Tristam, P. (2017, November 6). *When the United Arab Emirates Won Independence From Britain.* Retrieved from https://www.thoughtco.com/united-arab-emirates-won-independence-2353661
Viswanathan, R. (2017, July 21). *Why It's important for India to trade with Latin America.* Retrieved from https://thewire.in/diplomacy/trade-india-latin-america
Writer, S. (2017, December 01). *Raytheon to help develop Saudi's defence industry.* Retrieved from http://gulfbusiness.com/raytheon-help-develop-saudis-defence-industry/

UAE

McAuley, A. (2014, September 21). *New UAE law in the works to curb misuse of energy.* Retrieved from https://www.thenational.ae/business/new-uae-law-in-the-works-to-curb-misuse-of-energy-1.240136
Taxation—The Official Portal of the UAE Government. (n.d.). Retrieved from https://government.ae/en/information-and-services/finance-and-investment/taxation
United Arab Emirates—Trade Barriers UAE—Trade Barriers. (n.d.). Retrieved from https://www.export.gov/article?id=United-Arab-Emirates-trade-barriers

Oman

Anti-Monopoly and Competition Law in Oman. (2017, September 18). Retrieved from https://omanlawblog.curtis.com/2017/09/anti-monopoly-and-competition-law-in.html
Employment & Labour Law|Oman|Laws and Regulations—Global Legal Insights. (n.d.). Retrieved from https://www.globallegalinsights.com/practice-areas/employment-and-labour-laws-and-regulations/oman
Market Forces in Oman: The New Competition Law—Al Tamimi & Company. (n.d.). Retrieved from https://www.tamimi.com/law-update-articles/market-forces-in-oman-the-new-competition-law/
Ministry of Environment and Climate Affairs—Oman. (n.d.). Retrieved from https://meca.gov.om/en/index.php
Oman—Country Information—Resources—Campaign Against Arms Trade. (n.d.). Retrieved from https://www.caat.org.uk/resources/countries/oman
Oman country profile. (2018, April 25). Retrieved from http://www.bbc.com/news/world-middle-east-14654150
Oman central bank raises rate on capital deposits to 1.5 pct from ... (2018, March 15). Retrieved from https://www.reuters.com/article/oman-cenbank-rates/oman-central-bank-raises-rate-on-capital-deposits-to-1-5-pct-from-1-0-pct-idUSL1N1QX0EC
Oman's Foreign Policy in the Twenty-First Century|Middle East Policy Council. (n.d.). Retrieved from http://www.mepc.org/omans-foreign-policy-twenty-first-century
P. (n.d.). Oman: Major changes to corporate income tax and withholding taxes. Retrieved from https://www.pwc.com/m1/en/services/tax/me-tax-legal-news/2017/oman-major-changes-to-corporate-income-tax-withholding-taxes.html
The World Factbook—Central Intelligence Agency. (n.d.). Retrieved from https://www.cia.gov/library/publications/the-world-factbook/geos/mu.html

Egypt

Defence About Us|Tata Motors Limited. (n.d.). Retrieved from https://www.tatamotors.com/about-us/

Mahindra Defence Systems & Military Vehicles—Mahindra Rise. (n.d.). Retrieved from http://www.mahindra.com/business/defence

Make In India. (2018). Mazagon Dock Shipbuilders Limited. https://mazagondock.in/Make-In-India.aspx

Navigation. (n.d.). Retrieved from http://www.rnaval.co.in/web/rnaval/defence-programs

P. (n.d.). *Doing business in the Middle East*. Retrieved from https://www.pwc.com/m1/en/services/tax/doing-business-guides-middle-east.html

Shukla, T. (2017, September 25). *Inside Indian industry's big defence play*

UPDATE 2-Egyptian inflation rates fall to lowest levels in almost 2 ... (2018, April 10). Retrieved from https://www.reuters.com/article/egypt-economy-inflation/update-2-egyptian-inflation-rates-fall-to-lowest-levels-in-almost-2-yrs-idUSL8N1RN12P

Effect of Age on Employees' Attitudes at Workplace—A Study

N. Srividya and Rita Basu

Abstract The age of a person denotes that how long he has been alive on this earth. Out of that number of years, except the early years of his birth that is around five years, all the rest of his life he is learning and moulding himself towards all the situations and events he comes across. This paper studies the effect of age of a person on his attitude in workplace. Data is collected through an instrument called questionnaire with a random sample size of 468 across the country. Few parameters such as attitude towards efficiency, risk-taking nature and self-image portrait are considered under employees' attitude and are analysed against the age of the respondents. The data is analysed with suitable statistical tools and techniques. The results are interpreted aptly making some meaning sense out of them. It is observed that with the age of the person, the attitude of the person towards workplace changes a lot. This research can further be extended towards career planning and succession planning in corporate world.

Keywords Attitude · Age · Self-image portrait · Risk taking nature and workplace

1 Introduction

It is quite understood and observed that for higher positions and for certain positions of jobs in corporate world, the age is mentioned mandatorily, that the criterion should be met without fail. With the progression of age, the attitude of the person changes gradually. His learning process is enhanced by his socialisation and observation of things. That is why we can easily observe a difference between students who are in hostels, abroad or out of their native places and those who are at home or hometown.

N. Srividya (✉)
Techno India School of Management Studies, Techno Main Salt Lake, Kolkata, India

R. Basu
University of Calcutta, Kolkata, India

© The Author(s), under exclusive license to Springer Nature Singapore Pte Ltd. 2022

A. Chandani et al. (eds.), *Achieving $5 Trillion Economy of India*, Springer Proceedings in Business and Economics, https://doi.org/10.1007/978-981-16-7818-9_13

1.1 Background of the Study

Keeping all these in mind, it is desired to do a research to decide how the age and attitude of a person vary and emerge gradually. While most of the research available in this field is highly concentrated on the medical terms, this study concentrates the managerial personnel and their development of attitudes in relation with their growing age.

1.2 Research Problem

The research problem considered here how the age and their attitudes are connected with each other. As the attitude is the vast subject involving several aspects of the personality, few personality traits are considered for the study. Concentrating on few aspects of personality, an attempt to make an extensive research is made. Moreover, the sampling population is also considered keeping managerial needs in mind. This research is mainly helpful to the managers and prospective managers.

1.3 Objectives of Study

Considering the applicability and importance of the managerial traits in a workplace, the following objectives are considered. Out of many personality traits, attitude towards achieving efficiency, risk-taking nature while doing their jobs and the way they portray their self-image are considered for in-depth study.

1. To study the effect of age on attitude towards efficiency
2. To study the effect of age on risk-taking nature
3. To study the effect of age on self-image portrait.

2 Review of Literature

Review of literature is done to check the previous literature that exists in the field. It also provides a broad framework and an idea about the existing literature and its depth and extent of the topic as well.

2.1 Introduction

As mentioned earlier, there is a huge literature on the said topic in medical field. There is very less literature in the management field.

Rezaei and Zamani-Miandashti (2013) studied the relationship between the self-efficacy, anxiety and the attitude towards research. They conducted this study on agricultural graduate students.

This paper studies the association among self-efficacy, the personal and professional characteristics. Respondents are the agricultural students at Shiraz University in Iran. A stratified sample of size 210 was selected, and through questionnaire, the data is collected. A *t*-test is conducted, and it is proved that reasonable amount of fretfulness, great self-efficacy and an optimistic approach is maintained towards the study.

Saleh and SweKhine (2013) study the research about the attitudes in the field of science. They also considered the measurements that are contemporary and classic.

This manuscript is about examining the classical views on science attitudes in addition to exploring contemporary attempts in measuring attitudes. This is a book of edited research papers by various researchers. The chapters of this book consist of the research papers edited.

Sorce et al. (2005) conducted a research on the relationship between attitude and the differences in age while buying online.

This research studies the spending behaviour of virtual buyers based on their age and attitude. A sample of 300 students from a US university is taken for buying 17 products. It is found that younger generations purchase more products online. This research is helpful to retail managers in understanding the consumer behaviour on online purchasing.

Klimova et al. (2016) studied the relationship between the attitudes of the senior citizens while using the information and communication technologies. This is done in Czech Republic.

This study is on the job of ICT on the living of senior citizens in Czech. Comparison of various research studies is done along with the review of literature on the topic.

Yim and Kim (2021) conducted a research on the effects of fit and novelty in collaboration with product attitude with a moderating effect on age.

They conducted in separate ways for novelty and fit each in the impact of brand collaboration with product attitude and moderating effect of age in association with novelty and attitude. They used four instruments to match all the scenarios and real brands. This recommends two paths, namely similar and non-similar to test the product attitude with each novelty and perceived fit. They also tested the moderating effect of the age. They tested the effect of perceived novelty fit on product attitude. They took a sample size of 250, and the study found that the degree of perceived novelty and fit with the type of brand had a positive influence on product attitude. They also confirmed that the age has a moderate relationship with novelty and attitude.

2.2 *Gap Analysis*

A lot of literature is available on the attitudes of the people in workplace. But no literature is found on the effect of age on the employees' attitude in the workplace.

Mostly in medical field, this research is done to correct the attitudes or in treating cancer, etc.

3 Methods

3.1 Background of the Study

Age plays a very important role in the attitude of the employees in the workplace. This paper tries to study this effect. This is done by considering the following parameters under the attitude of the employees.

1. Attitude towards efficiency
2. Risk-taking nature
3. Self-image portrait.

3.2 Aim

While doing the career planning or succession planning in the corporate world, the age is most important factor to be considered. With age, maturity arrives. This paper tries to explore the effect of age on the attitude.

3.3 Objectives of the Study

1. To study the effect of age on attitude towards efficiency
2. To study the effect of age on risk-taking nature
3. To study the effect of age on self-image portrait.

3.4 Importance of Study

This study is helpful to understand the importance of age in recruitment, promotions and as a whole career planning.

3.5 Scope of the Research

This research can be helpful in corporate world while planning and devising the recruitment and career planning. As there is a relationship between the age and his working attitude of a person, it is easily understandable that this can be used in appraisal system to draw his career planning and goal.

3.6 Sampling Technique

Random sampling.

3.7 Sample Size

468.

3.8 Population

All types of people from all parts of India, covering all ages and educational backgrounds.

3.9 Data Collection Method

Questionnaire.

3.10 Hypotheses

To analyse the data collected, few hypotheses are framed and are tested with suitable tests. The following hypotheses are formed based on the objectives and aim of the study.

Ho 1: **Age** and **attitude towards efficiency** of respondents are related each other.
Ho 2: **Age and risk-taking nature** are related each other.
Ho 3: **Age** and **self-image portrait** of respondents related each other.

3.11 Tools Adopted

Descriptive analysis, charts, group statistics, *t*-test and correlation.

3.12 Analysis of Data

First mean, mode and median, skewness and kurtosis are found using the descriptive analysis for the scale. All these values are calculated for all the item scores individually and the parameter as whole. Even for the overall total scores are also calculated.

For *t*-tests, the age and the educational qualification are grouped further into two ways, age as above thirty and below thirty. *t*-tests are conducted at the level of 0.05 significant level for all the parameters as shown in the hypotheses. All those hypotheses are tested individually.

3.13 Limitations

1. The results hold good only for this research and the study. It cannot be generalised to all.
2. The research is purely based on the data collected through the questionnaire.
3. The topic of the paper itself is highly subjective dealing with the dispositions about one's self, the respondents too might have felt uncomfortable in giving their true opinions. Even while filling the questionnaire also, they might felt highly hesitant or scared to reveal their actual dispositions or thoughts about themselves, how much ever it is ensured that the responses are kept highly confidential and are meant only the research purpose and nothing else.
4. The research holds good only for the dispositions of the respondents given. Neither can it be generalised to all the self-dispositions of the respondents nor to all the people in general.

3.14 Scope for Further Research

This research can be extended to career planning and succession planning.

3.15 Applied Value of the Research

This can be very well applied in workplace while considering the attitudes of the employees.

4 Data Analysis

Before proceeding further to analyse the data, first the validity and reliability test is done.

For both the scales, item validity and estimation of reliability are considered and checked.

4.1 Reliability and Validity Test

(a) **Item Validity**

For item analysis, appropriate constituents and their allied parts are chosen that highly correlate with the aggregate value. This is done by internal criterion method. Accordingly, for testing the consistency of the items of the selected domains, as well as, for total scale, correlations were computed for the following three different sets of scores for each of the tests.

(i) 'Individual item score—Individual enquiry area score'.
(ii) 'Individual enquiry area's score—Total score of all test items'.
(iii) 'Individual item score—Total score of all items'.

Suitable and selected components were retained for each of the final scales based on the correlation results that are more than 0.40. The results of the correlation analysis of respective scale have been presented in Table 1.

1. Attitude towards efficiency
2. Risk-taking nature
3. Self-image portrait.

The individual item scores which have the value less than 0.4 are removed. Those are as follows.

The item "Achieve OK", under the parameter 'Image' is deleted due to its low value.

Table 1 Consolidated picture of item validity measures of core beliefs scale on the basis of data collected from respondents ($N = 468$)

S. No.	Name of enquiry areas	Correlational values (r)		
		Individual enquiry area—individual item score	Individual item score—item total score	Enquiry area—total score
1	Attitude towards efficiency	0.65–0.793	0.303–0.533	0.593
2	Risk-taking nature	0.396–0.736	0.031–0.411	0.400
3	Image	0.234–0.642	0.009–0.256	0.342

Table 2 Revised values of item validity measures of core beliefs scale on the basis of data collected from respondents ($N = 468$)

S. No.	Name of enquiry areas	Correlational values (r)		
		Individual enquiry area—individual item score	Individual item score—item total score	Enquiry area—total score
1	Attitude towards efficiency	0.65–0.793	0.303–0.393	0.604
2	Risk-taking	0.496–0.746	0.031–0.463	0.400
3	Image	0.584–0.772	0.329–0.516	0.432

Again, the values for individual item scores are calculated, and the correlation tests for individual item score and item total score are calculated.

Again here, the enquiry areas with low values have been removed, and the values are recalculated. Further, the correlation test for enquiry area and total score is calculated.

The revised values are as Table 2.

Results of the correlation analysis for item validity results showed that all components of all the scales and subscales for each enquiry areas are content-wise valid (Table 3).

Again, the results of inter enquiry area correlation matrix showed that any modification in the values of the components will influence the respective scales. Only one dimension of the set of domains in each of the scale is also observed. Further, positive and noteworthy inter-enquiry areas correlation, individual item score—total score of all test item score correlation, as well as individual item score—individual component enquiry area score correlation confirmed that the scales are factor-wise valid.

Table 3 Inter-components correlation matrix for core beliefs scale on the basis of data collected from respondents ($N = 468$)

	Average attitude towards efficiency	Average risk-taking nature	Average self-image
Average attitude towards efficiency	1	0.162	0.213
Average risk-taking nature	0.162	1	0.352
Average self-image	0.213	0.352	1

Table 4 Group statistics between age and the average of attitude of the respondents

Result of the set

	Age	N	Mean	Standard deviation	Standard error mean
Average of attitude	≥ 30	336	3.911	0.610	0.033
	< 30	132	3.796	0.828	0.072

$\text{Var}_1 = \text{SD}_1^2 = (0.828)^2 = 0.686$ and $\text{Var}_2 = \text{SD}_2^2 = (0.610)^2 = 0.372$
$n_1 = 132$ and $n_2 = 336$ and the degree of freedom $= n_1 + n_2 - 2 = 466$

4.2 *Descriptive Statistics*

None of the parameters has skewness less than – 1.00 or greater than 0.5 which means that all of them are approximately symmetrical.

The kurtosis for **all the parameters** is negative, which means that the peak is flatter and the tails are thinner. This means that most of the respondents responded identically.

4.3 *Testing the Hypotheses*

t-tests are conducted to find whether there is any significant difference between the said groups. For this, total sample is divided into groups based on education. They are

i. The people who have their education level less than PG
ii. The people who have their education level more than PG

Hypothesis

Ho 1: Age and attitude of respondents are related (Table 4).

Interpretation

The mean value for the respondents with age more than 30 is greater than that of the respondents with age below 30. It can be said that the respondents with age more than 30 are to be more competent, perfect, efficient and generous (Table 4).

Interpretation

Result of *t*-test (1.654) is significant at 0.01 level. Hence, null hypothesis is rejected. This means that there is a significant difference for the attitude towards efficiency or perfection due to variation of age group (less 30 and greater than 30). Hence, we can infer that attitude towards efficiency or perfection increases with the increases of the age.

Hypothesis

Ho 2: Age and risk-taking nature of respondents are related (Table 6).

Table 5 *t*-test for independent samples (age below 30 and above 30) for the average of attitude of the respondents

		t	Sig. (two-tailed)	Difference in mean	Difference in standard error	Confidence interval of the difference at 95%	
						Lower	Upper
Average of attitude	Assumption of equal variances	1.654	0.099	0.115	0.069	– 0.022	0.252

Table 6 Group statistics between age and the average of risk taking of the respondents

Results of the set					
	Age	*N*	Mean	Standard deviation	Standard error mean
Average of risk taking	≥ 30	336	3.536	0.504	0.027
	< 30	132	3.250	0.441	0.038

$\text{Var}_1 = \text{SD}_1^2 = (0.441)^2 = 0.194$ and $\text{Var}_2 = \text{SD}_2^2 = (0.504)^2 = 0.254$
$n_1 = 132$ and $n_2 = 336$ and the degree of freedom $= n_1 + n_2 - 2 = 466$

Interpretation

The mean value for the item "Willing to take risks in life" is high for the parameter 'Risk Taking Nature'. This means that most of the respondents are willing to take risk in life (Table 6).

Interpretation

Result of *t*-test (5.710) is considerable at 0.01 level. Hence, null hypothesis is not accepted. This shows that there is a considerable difference in trust of people due to variation of age group (less 30 and greater than 30). Hence, we can infer that risk-taking nature increases with the increases of the age.

Hypothesis

Ho 3: Age and image of respondents are related (Table 8)

Table 7 *t*-test for independent samples (age below 30 and above 30) for the average of risk taking of the respondents

		t	Sig. (two-tailed)	Difference in mean	Difference in standard error	Confidence interval of the difference at 95%	
						Lower	Upper
Average of risk taking	Equal variances assumed	5.710	0.000	0.286	0.050	0.187	0.384

Table 8 Group statistics between age and the average of image of the respondents

Result of the set					
	Age	*N*	Mean	Standard deviation	Standard error mean
Average of image	≥ 30	336	3.655	0.595	0.033
	< 30	132	3.000	0.285	0.025

$\text{Var}_1 = \text{SD}_1^2 = (0.285)^2 = 0.081$ and $\text{Var}_2 = \text{SD}_2^2 = (0.595)^2 = 0.354$
$n_1 = 132$ and $n_2 = 336$ and the degree of freedom $= n_1 + n_2 - 2 = 466$

Table 9 *t*-test for independent samples (age below 30 and above 30) for the average of image of the respondents

		t	Sig. (two-tailed)	Difference in mean	Difference in standard error	Confidence interval of the difference at 95%	
						Lower	Upper
Average of image	Assumption of equal variances	12.101	0.000	0.655	0.054	0.548	0.761

Interpretation

The respondents with age more than 30 feel that they can face the outside world as they are and feel that if they do so, people would accept them (Table 8).

Interpretation

Result of *t*-test (12.101) is considerable at 0.01 level. Hence, the hypothesis is not accepted. This shows that there is a considerable difference in the image of people due to variation of age group (less 30 and greater than 30). Hence, we can infer that image towards people increases with the increases of the age.

5 Findings, Suggestions and Conclusions

Before going further towards the findings and suggestions, we glance at the hypotheses along with interpretations (Table 10).

It is found that age has a major role in moulding the attitude of a person. The employees with age more than thirty are more competent towards efficiency. They also take higher risks in their work life. With the age, the employees also gain maturity, and thereby, their attitude may develop or enhance. With the age, their experience would increase, and with the help of good amount of experience, they can handle better their jobs. Their efficiency would also increase with their learning. Experience is the best teacher.

Table 10 Overview of the hypotheses with respect to age of the respondents

S. No.	Hypothesis	Accepted/rejected	Interpretation
1	Age and attitude of respondents towards efficiency are related	Rejected	The respondents with age more than 30 are to be more competent, perfect, efficient and generous
2	Age and risk-taking nature of respondents are related	Rejected	The respondents with age more than 30 are willing to take risks in work life
3	Age and image of respondents are related	Rejected	The respondents with age more than 30 feel that they can face the outside world as they are and feel that if they do so, people would accept them

With the advance of their age, their exposure to the world or socialisation would develop them into good and efficient employees. They would probably know where to take risks and where to not. With the good amount of exposure or socialisation, they can take good decisions, and they can portray themselves with right attitude.

References

Klimova, B., Simonova, I., Poulova, P., Truhlarova, Z., & Kuca, K. (2016). Older people and their attitude to the use of information and communication technologies—A review study with special focus on the Czech Republic (older people and their attitude to ICT). *Educational Gerontology, 42*(5), 361–369. https://doi.org/10.1080/03601277.2015.1122447

Rezaei, M., & Zamani-Miandashti, N. (2013). The relationship between research self-efficacy, research anxiety and attitude toward research: A study of agricultural graduate students. *Journal of Educational & Instructional Studies in the World, 3*(4), 69–78, 10 p.

Saleh, I. M., & SweKhine, M. (Eds.) (2011). *Attitude research in science education: Classic and contemporary measurements* (p. 305). IAP. ISBN: 1617353264, 9781617353260

Sorce, P., Perotti, V., & Widrick, S. (2005). Attitude and age differences in online buying. *International Journal of Retail & Distribution Management, 33*(2), 122–132. https://doi.org/10.1108/09590550510581458. Download as RIS Publisher: Emerald Group Publishing Limited Copyright © 2005, Emerald Group Publishing Limited, pp. 361–369. Accepted author version posted online: 24 Nov 2015, Published online: 03 Mar 2016

Yim, Y.-K., & Kim, G.-G. (2021). The effects of fit and novelty according to brand collaboration on product attitude: the moderating effect of age. *Ilkogretim Online-Elementary Education Online, 2021, 20*(3), 1212–1221. http://ilkogretim-online.org, https://doi.org/10.17051/ilkonline.2021.03135

An Econometric Approach Towards Exploring the Impact of Workers Remittances on Inflation: Empirical Evidence from India

Vaishali Jain and Monika Mathur

Abstract This paper attempts to study short and long run impact of increased worker's remittances on general price level. It uses the real GDP growth, real effective exchange rate (REER), M3 (broad money), fiscal deficit to gauge the impact of foreign remittances on inflation. The study makes use of VAR/VECM framework to gauge the impact of worker's remittances on inflation. Inflation is measured in terms of CPI and WPI, real income or GDP at constant prices is taken as a measure of GDP growth, REER is used for exchange rates and M3 is taken as a proxy for money supply. Monthly data of all these variables has been taken from Bloomberg and World Bank data base. The findings provide important insights into the nature of association between remittances and inflation suggesting causality between inflation, remittances, real GDP, real effective exchange rates and money supply due to increased worker's remittances. The findings have policy implications for decisions to channelize worker's remittances in a way to increase real GDP growth and money supply while at the same time not causing the general price levels to soar. The present study focuses on how increased (decreased) worker's remittances is leading to increase (decrease) in general price levels in India.

Keywords Worker's remittances · Consumer price index · Wholesale price index · Inflation · Exchange rate · Money supply · GDP · Vector autoregression · Granger causality

1 Introduction

Workers remittances have been one of the major sources of foreign exchange earnings for developing countries including India. Due to COVID-19 pandemic, economists

V. Jain (✉)
Christ (Deemed University), Lavasa, Pune, India
e-mail: vaishali.jain@christuniversity.in

M. Mathur
Manipal University Jaipur, Jaipur, India
e-mail: monika.mathur@jaipur.manipal.edu

© The Author(s), under exclusive license to Springer Nature Singapore Pte Ltd. 2022

A. Chandani et al. (eds.), *Achieving $5 Trillion Economy of India*, Springer Proceedings in Business and Economics, https://doi.org/10.1007/978-981-16-7818-9_14

are of the view that the country requires a huge amount of FDI in order to be able to compensate for lower remittances in many years that have passed (Singh, 2020). As per a few estimates, India has earned more than two times in terms of remittances as compared to FDI in last few years. The remittances which these workers send home have been increasing every year, and as per World Bank report, high skilled migration has picked up in last few years. India has led the position in terms of recipient of worker's remittances from 2008 to 09 onwards and received 83.132 billion US $ in year 2019. Thus, workers' remittances, their importance and their impact on growth including financial development cannot be ignored and have been studied in detail by researchers.

On the other hand, inflation is one major issue for all developing economies of the world including India. Controlling inflation rate and stabilizing price level has been one of the top agendas of all macroeconomic policies in India. Therefore, study of its determinants and their relative impact would be crucial for policy making. As per the World Bank remittance data for April 2020, India received US $ 83,131 million in 2019 which was 2.8% of its GDP (Bank, 2020). India being one of the economies with highest growth rate, huge size in terms of GDP (PPP) and scale (number of consumers) also has been facing the issue of inflation from time to time in its growth trajectory. But the impact of the same must be analysed, and this paper attempts the same. Conceptually, if remittances rise in an economy, an increase in consumer spending and therefore price levels would have an effect. It also impacts the country's monetary base, resulting in an increased supply of money that is more inflationary in nature and has a negative effect on the real exchange rate. Moreover, in developing countries, the fiscal deficit plays an important role in growing price levels. Thus, there are three approaches to explain determinants of inflation in any economy, i.e. monetary approach, public fiancé approach and structural explanations. In context of India, although the amount of remittances has been high and increasing always, its ratio with GDP has been constant. Thus, whether inflation in India has been due to increased remittances is a subject matter of study.

2 Literature Review

Growth impact of remittances has been analysed by various economists in detail (Fayissa & Nsiah, 2010; Feeny et al., 2014; Javid et al., 2012; Meyer & Shera, 2017; Dahal, 2014; Dastidar, 2017) and many more. Most of the economist suggest a positive relationship between economic growth and worker's remittances. But the workers' remittances are utilized by people in different forms of expenditures made and that may lead to increased purchasing power and money supply in the economy which further results in inflation. There are not very conclusive studies available on relationship between inflation and worker's remittances, specifically in India. Studies by (Iqbal et al., 2013; Streimikiene et al., 2019; Mumuni & Quaidoo, 2016; Narayan et al., 2011) have tried to assess the impact of remittances on inflation, and findings suggest a positive relationship in long run. Muktadir-Al-Mukit (2018) studies GDP (real), interest rate, imports, money supply and exchange rate as the determining factors of inflation in Bangladesh. An assessment on investment by Mallick (2008) reveals that remittances are positively related with private consumption but has a negative influence on private investment. Using a money demand and supply function, (Adhikari & Kumar, 2013) try to evaluate impact of remittances on the domestic price level in India but find an insignificant effect. As per a study, remittances and real GDP growth had an insignificant effect on inflation rate in South Asia when analysed through the model adopted for time series data (Upadhyay & Upadhyaya, 2011).

Lim and Papi (1997) study the factors determining inflation in Turkey and find that exchange rate and public sector deficits plays an important role. A similar study by Moser (1994) concludes that expansionary fiscal policy and depreciation in Nigerian currency have been responsible for increasing inflationary pressure on its economy. A panel data study of 47 countries explains fiscal deficit, flexible exchange rate regime, wage indexation and central bank's independence as four major determinants of inflation (Cottarelli, 1998). Studying the impact of nominal exchange rate on inflation, Ghosh et al., (1997) conclude that inflation is slow and low under pegged exchange rate regimes. An evaluation of inflation by Kandil and Morsy (2009) studied the domestic and external factors leading to inflation in oil-producing gulf countries and found that among foreign factors, inflation in trading partner countries has maximum influence while credit expansion is one major domestic reason for rising price level in GCC. On the other hand, government spending to ease out capacity constraints has a moderating effect on inflation.

Bashir et al. (2011) use the Johansen's cointegration and vector error correction approach to conclude that long run consumer price index is positively influenced by money supply, gross domestic product, imports and government expenditures in Pakistan. Another study on inflation dynamics in Pakistan by Raza et al. (2013) analysed data from 1971 to 2012 with the same approach and findings suggested that GDP, M2, energy crises, import and current government expenditure, output gap and adaptive expectation generate inflationary pressure while development expenditure negatively corrected with inflation.

Several papers on determinants of inflation in India have studied gross domestic product and concluded that broad money supply leads to rise in price level while interest rate and the exchange rate have a negative influence on inflation (Sahadudheen, 2012). Researchers have also found a long-run relationship between inflation, interest rate, and GDP while no influence of import prices and money supply (Ajmair, 2019). Mohanty & John (2015) concluded a steady influence of monetary policy on inflation and changed dynamics of various factors were found to affect inflation over a period of time. Money supply, depreciation of the currency, and supply bottlenecks are predominating determinants of inflation in the short run while supply bottlenecks have an insignificant impact in long run (Alam & Alam, 2016). Using Engel Granger and Johansen—Julius cointegration analysis, Nair (2014) envisages that industrial production has a negative relationship with inflation while money supply has a positive impact. Kaur (2019) tries to study the macroeconomic determinants of inflation in India and effect of fiscal deficit on inflation. Author suggested the presence of long-term association among inflation, gross fiscal deficit, money supply, exchange rate, prices of crude oil and output gap. Behera et al., (2018) analyse the determining factor of inflation in India using a Phillips curve framework and conclude that exchange rate movements and excess demand have impact on inflation and confirm existence of a traditional Phillips curve. While studying global inflation trends and their driving forces, Kamber and Wong (2020) find relatively more impact of global factors on inflation in emerging economies than developed ones. While discussing properties of core inflation in India, Durai and Ramachandran (2007) concluded that inflation is highly correlated with growth of broad money (M3). Perera et al., (2013) studied the link between the financial strength of central bank and inflation and found an inverse relationship which was robust for deeper factors of inflation.

3 Research Gap and Objectives

There are indeterminate conclusions related to causal factors of inflation in India in short and long run. Therefore, objectives of this study are:

(a) To study the short- and long-term causal relationship between worker's remittances, GDP growth rate, fiscal deficit, real effective exchange rate and money supply (independent factors) and consumer price index.
(b) To study the short- and long-term causal relationship between worker's remittances, GDP growth rate, fiscal deficit, real effective exchange rate and money supply (independent factors) and wholesale price index.

4 Data and Methodology

The present study aims at exploring the impact of workers' remittances over inflation, with specific reference to India. Inflation is measured in terms of CPI and WPI, real income or GDP at constant prices is taken as a measure of GDP growth, REER is used for exchange rates and broad money or M3 is taken as a proxy for money supply. Monthly data from 2012 to 2019 for all these variables has been taken from Bloomberg and World Bank data base.

A unit root test has to be performed as a pre-essential, to study the stationarity properties of the data, for which, ADF (Dickey & Fuller, 1979) test has been employed. A time series is considered stationary when the statistical properties are constant over the time and tends to return to same path aftershock. ADF unit root test holds the H0 that unit root is present in time series. If the value calculated is lesser than the value critical, the Ha is accepted, and H0 is rejected. The bigger the negative value, the stronger is the support for the rejection of the hypothesis.

4.1 Johansen's Cointegration Test

Johansen (1988) is used to analyse the indices for the long-run integration. The test is used to study cointegration among three or more time series. The max eigen value test confirms the trace test. The H0 of trace test is the rank $(\pi) = r0$. On the other hand, the Ha of test is $r0 <$ rank $(\pi) < n$, where n is the maximal potential cointegration. If the H0 is rejected, the test proceeds with new H0, i.e. rank $(\pi) = r0 + 1$ and Ha, $r0 + 1 <$ rank $(\pi) < n$. The H0 of max eigen value test examines the that rank (π) $= 0$ and the Ha is rank $(\pi) = 1$. There is no cointegration and the H0 is accepted if the rank is 0. If the rank is non zero, then-largest eigen value, $\lambda 1$ is at least 1 and there could be more cointegrating vectors. Similarly, a series of tests are conducted for the null hypothesis, $(\pi) = 1, 2, 3\ldots.$ and alternative hypothesis, $(\pi) = 2, 3, 4\ldots$

4.2 VECM and VECM Granger Causality

Granger (1969) is employed to study the short-term causative association among all the time series. The Granger causality employed to examine if a time series may be used to use for forecasting another. The test has been performed to test if X carries any statistical information about variable Y if it does then "X Granger-cause Y" otherwise "X does not Granger-cause Y". Granger causality is performed using VECM model to check the causality relationship and direction determining the direction of causation between time series.

5 Empirical Results

To begin with the analysis, firstly, descriptive statistics were calculated for all the variables, and the same are presented in Table 1. After calculating the descriptive statistics, ADF test was used to check if the data is stationary and at what level. Results of ADF test, as presented in Table 2, indicate that all the variables are stationary at first difference at both 5 and 10%.

Since all the variables were found to be $I(0)$, cointegration test was performed to study the long-term association among the variables. Table 3 presents the outcomes for assessing the long-term relation between CPI, GDP, fiscal deficit, REER, money supply and workers' remittances. Since it is a multivariate model, Johansen's cointegration test is used. Both trace test and maximum eigen value test indicate four cointegration equations implying that there is a possibility that at least four out of the six variables seem to converge in the long term, even if they are found to diverge in the short run.

Table 4 presents the results for the long run relation between WPI, GDP, fiscal deficit, REER, money supply and workers' remittances. Both trace and maximum

Table 1 Descriptive statistics

	CPI	FD	GDP	M3	REER	RMT	WPI
Mean	5.928404	50,588.33	1.557235	0.868395	96.61596	2.363508	3.137340
Median	5.090000	52,761.00	1.699740	0.731330	97.65000	1.176997	3.560000
Maximum	11.24000	209,109.0	6.869909	4.442335	104.5900	38.19708	7.810000
Minimum	1.540000	– 206,132.0	– 4.195208	– 1.888510	84.11000	– 23.97571	– 4.950000
Std. Dev.	2.720888	64,147.13	1.942717	1.057426	5.101199	11.61781	3.162133
Skewness	0.486020	– 0.648092	0.059328	0.691526	– 0.517898	0.455000	– 0.629091
Kurtosis	1.884398	5.721660	3.845625	4.160956	2.524831	3.713380	2.682572
Jarque–Bera	8.575274	35.59280	2.855883	12.77087	5.086413	5.236634	6.594808
Probability	0.013737	0.000000	0.239802	0.001686	0.078614	0.072925	0.036979
Observations	94	94	94	94	94	94	94

Source Own Calculations by Authors

Table 2 Results of stationarity test

Variables	At level			At first difference		
	Without constant	With constant	With constant and trend	Without constant	With constant	With constant and trend
CPI	– 1.128773 (0.2340)	– 1.971965 (0.2986)	– 1.177290 (0.9089)	– 6.761333 (0.0000)	– 6.736553 (0.0000)	– 6.907833 (0.0000)
WPI	– 1.828173 (0.0645)	– 2.327320 (0.1657)	– 2.198221 (0.4846)	– 5.929172 (0.0000)	– 5.900718 (0.0000)	– 5.901532 (0.0000)
GDP	– 0.673463 (0.4224)	– 2.345687 (0.1604)	– 2.985478 (0.1426)	– 5.483727 (0.0000)	– 5.455496 (0.0000)	– 5.556921 (0.0001)
M3	– 0.551271 (0.4754)	– 1.00819 (0.2354)	– 1.643287 (0.4721)	– 8.648077 (0.0000)	– 8.592797 (0.0000)	– 8.530705 (0.0000)
REER	0.460294 (0.8121)	– 1.168127 (0.6855)	– 2.458824 (0.3476)	– 9.079048 (0.0000)	– 9.082901 (0.0000)	– 9.016955 (0.0000)
Fiscal Deficit	0.736778 (0.8718)	– 1.045825 (0.7333)	– 2.532003 (0.3124)	– 13.68724 (0.0000)	– 13.69154 (0.0001)	– 13.70976 (0.0000)
Workers' Remittances	– 1.202234 (0.2083)	– 1.837536 (0.3601)	– 1.846024 (0.6730)	– 3.264750 (0.0014)	– 3.241945 (0.0211)	– 3.980162 (0.0133)

Source Own Calculations by Authors

Table 3 Cointegration results for CPI model

Hypothesized No. of CE(s)	Eigen value	Trace statistic	Max eigen statistic
None*	0.926719	521.6105 (0.000)	214.3030 (0.0000)
At most 1*	0.845521	307.3075 (0.000)	153.1511 (0.0000)
At most 2*	0.571886	154.1564 (0.000)	69.56608 (0.0000)
At most 3*	0.551198	84.5903 (0.000)	65.69628 (0.0000)
At most 4	0.146308	12.89402 (0.065)	12.97113 (0.0000)
At most 5*	0.069683	5.922893 (0.000)	5.922893 (0.0000)

*Rejection of null hypothesis at 0.05 level

Table 4 Cointegration results for WPI model

Hypothesized No. of CE(s)	Eigen value	Trace statistic	Max eigen statistic
None*	0.952035	499.3719 (0.0000)	246.0192 (0.0000)
At most 1*	0.868474	253.3527 (0.0000)	164.3123 (0.0000)
At most 2*	0.533032	89.0404 (0.0000)	61.68112 (0.0000)
At most 3	0.168215	27.3593 (0.093)	14.91864 (0.295)
At most 4	0.112275	12.4406 (0.137)	9.646584 (0.236)
At most 5	0.033906	2.7941 (0.095)	2.7941 (0.095)

eigen value test indicate 3 cointegration equations implying a possibility that at least three out of the six variables seem to converge in the long term, even if they are found to diverge in the short run.

Tables 5 and 6 present the error correction terms for the two models. Error correction terms or ECTs are the speed of adjustment in the dependent variable when the series deviates from the equilibrium in the previous period. Since it is a correction term, it has to be in the opposite direction of the disequilibrium, ECT should be negative and to be significant, absolute value of observed t-statistic should be greater than 1.64 and 1.96 at 1% and 5%, respectively. The results show that while the ECT is significant for CPI and the disequilibrium of previous periods are corrected at a speed of 4.797% in the following period, the ECT is not significant for WPI.

Tables 7 and 8 present the results for Granger causality for CPI and WPI. The

Table 5 Error correction terms for CPI

Cointegrating Eq.	ΔCPI	Standard error	*t*-statistic
ECT(-1)	− 0.04797	(0.03362)	[− 1.92676]
D(DCPI(-2))	− 0.329714	(0.10917)	[− 3.02014]
D(DFD(-2))	4.55E−07	(7.7E−07)	[0.59057]
D(DGDP(-2))	− 0.00831	(0.06850)	[− 0.12131]
D(DM3(-2))	− 0.02039	(0.05425)	[− 0.37583]
D(DREER(-2))	0.038263	(0.04214)	[0.90805]
D(DRMT(-2))	0.003339	(0.00955)	[0.34970]
C	0.022153	(0.07274)	[0.30456]

Source Own calculations by Author(s)

Table 6 Error correction terms for WPI

Cointegrating Eq.	ΔWPI	Standard error	*t*-statistic
ECT(-1)	1.78E−07	(6.0E−07)	[0.29719]
D(DFD(-2))	8.09E−07	(1.0E−06)	[0.78170]
D(DGDP(-2))	0.045148	(0.08823)	[0.51169]
D(DM3(-2))	0.116444	(0.07048)	[1.65226]
D(DREER(-2))	− 0.025275	(0.05473)	[− 0.46182]
D(DRMT(-2))	0.014389	(0.01255)	[1.14612]
D(DWPI(-2))	− 0.289331	(0.10982)	[− 2.63465]
C	0.022134	(0.09393)	[0.23565]

Source Own calculations by Author(s)

Table 7 Granger causality results for CPI

Dependent variable: D(DCPI)		
Excluded	Chi-sq.	Prob.
D(DFD)	0.646065	0.7240
D(DGDP)	0.914351	0.6331
D(DM3)	1.190459	0.5514
D(DREER)	1.252220	0.5347
D(DRMT)	0.598938	0.7412
All	4.077367	0.9438

Source Own calculations by Author(s)

results envisage that though there is a long-term integration between the variables, there is no causative association between CPI and the independent variable, i.e. none of the variables are found to granger cause CPI in short term. Contrary to this, workers' remittances are found to granger cause WPI in short run.

Table 8 Granger causality results for WPI

Dependent variable: D(DWPI)		
Excluded	Chi-sq.	Prob.
D(DFD)	2.159207	0.3397
D(DGDP)	0.627705	0.7306
D(DM3)	2.809024	0.2455
D(DREER)	0.343135	0.8423
D(DRMT)	10.14994	0.0063
All	16.99551	0.0745

6 Conclusion

The aim of this paper is to study the association between workers' remittances, money supply, fiscal deficit, GDP growth rate and real effective exchange rate with inflation index WPI and CPI in India. The study concludes that while worker's remittances does have a causal relationship with WPI in short term, no such relation holds for CPI. In fact, the analysis shows that CPI does not have causal relationship with any of the explanatory variables in long run. The Johansen's cointegration test shows association between these variables and CPI and WPI in short run. The vector correction term is insignificant and does not show any convergence in long run. Individually, all the five variables, i. e. workers' remittances, GDP growth rate, fiscal deficit, real effective exchange rate and money supply are granger causing inflation but that is also not very strong and significant relationship. The other explanatory variables also fail to show any impact on inflation in long run. Thus, this paper also confirms the previous conclusions of insignificant positive impact of workers' remittances in India and a positive long run relationship. But it also highlights that some of the major factors like growth rate of GDP, fiscal deficit (which is one of the major problems of developing economies due to rising developmental expenditure), money supply and real effective exchange rate were not responsible for the CPI numbers in Indian during the period of study.

Future study of additional variables may be made to understand the causes of inflation in India over the period. This study takes into consideration time frame of 2012–2019 due to data availability, a study with extensive period may be made to deeply study these determinants.

References

Adhikari, D. R., & Kumar, K. (2013). An econometric study of the effect of remittances on inflation in India. In *Proceedings of academy of studies in international business* (pp. 1–7). Jordan Whitney Enterprises.

Ajmair, M. (2019). Determinants of inflation in India. *The Indian Economic Journal*, 248–254.

Alam, M. Q., & Alam, M. S. (2016). The determinants of inflation in India: The bounds test analysis. *International Journal of Economics and Financial Issues*, 544–550.

Bank, W. (2020, August 8). *Annual Remittances Data (Inflows)*. Retrieved from https://www.worldbank.org/, https://www.worldbank.org/en/topic/labormarkets/brief/migration-and-remittances

Bashir, F., Nawaz, S., Yasin, K., Khursheed, U., Khan, J., & Qureshi, M. J. (2011). Determinants of inflation in Pakistan: An econometric analysis using johansen cointegration approach. *Australian Journal of Business and Management Research*, 71–82.

Behera, H., Wahi, G., & Kapur, M. (2018). Phillips curve relationship in an emerging economy: Evidence from India. *Economic Analysis and Policy*, 116–126.

Cottarelli, C. (1998). *The nonmonetary determinants of inflation: A panel data study*. International Monetary Fund.

Dahal, P. (2014). The impact of remittances on economic growth. *Asia Pacific Journal of Public Administration*, 261–282.

Dastidar, S. G. (2017). Impact of remittances on economic growth in developing countries: The role of openness. *Global Economy Journal*, 33–44.

Dickey, D. A., & Fuller, W. A. (1979). Distribution of the estimates for autoregressive time series with a unit root. *Journal of American Statistical Association, 74*, 427–431.

Durai, S. S., & M. Ramachandran. (2007). Core inflation for India. *Journal of Asian Economics*, 365–383.

Fayissa, B., & Nsiah, C. (2010). The impact of remittances on economic growth and development in Africa. *The American Economist*, 92–103.

Feeny, S., Iamsiraroj, S., & McGillivray, M. (2014). Remittances and economic growth: Larger. *The Journal of Development Studies*, 1055–1066.

Granger, C. W. (1969, August). Investigating causal relations by econometric models and cross-spectral methods. *Econometric, 37*(2), 423–438.

Ghosh, A. R., Gulde, A. M., Ostry, J. D., & Wolf, H. C. (1997). *Does the nominal exchange rate regime matter?* National Bureau of Economic Research.

Iqbal, J., Nosheen, M., & Javed, A. (2013). The nexus between foreign remittances and inflation: Evidence from Pakistan. *Pakistan Journal of Social Sciences*, 331–342.

Javid, M., Arif, U., & Qayyum, A. (2012). Impact of remittances on economic growth and poverty. *Academic Research International*, 433–447.

Johansen, S. (1988, June–September). Statistical analysis of cointegration vectors. *Journal of economic dynamics and control, 12*(2–3), 231–254.

Kamber, G., & Wong, B. (2020). Global factors and trend inflation. *Journal of International Economics*, 1–14.

Kandil, M., & Morsy, H. (2009). *Determinants of inflation in GCC*. International Monetary Fund.

Kaur, G. (2019). Inflation and fiscal deficit in India: An ARDL approach. *Global Business Review*.

Lim, C. H., & Papi, L. (1997). *An econometric analysis of the determinants of inflation in Turkey*. International Monetary Fund.

Mallick, H. (2008). *Do remittances impact the economy? Some empirical evidences from a developing economy*. Trivendrum, India: Centre for Development Studies, Trivendrum Working Papers 407.

Meyer, D., & Shera, A. (2017). The impact of remittances on economic growth: An econometric model. *EconomiA*, 147–155.

Mohanty, D., & John, J. (2015). Determinants of inflation in India. *Journal of Asian Economics*, 86–96.

Moser, G. (1994). *The main determinants of inflation in Nigeria*. International Monetary Fund.

Muktadir-Al-Mukit, D. (2018). Determinants of inflation in Bangladesh: An econometric approach. *International Journal of Business and Economics*, 277–293.

Mumuni, A. A., & Quaidoo, C. (2016). Effect of international remittances on inflation in Ghana using the bounds testing approach. *Business and Economic Research*, 192–208.

Nair, M. S. (2014). *Inflation dynamics in India: An analysis*. Munich University.

Narayan, P. K., Narayan, S., & Mishra, S. (2011). Do remittances induce inflation? Fresh evidence from developing countries. *Southern Economic Journal*, 914–933.

Perera, A., Ralston, D., & Wickramanayake, J. (2013). Central bank financial strength and inflation: Is there a robust link? *Journal of Financial Stability*, 399–414.

Raza, H., Ahmed, F., Hussain, A., & Lal, I. (2013). Determinant of inflation in Pakistan: An econometric analysis, using johansen co integration approach. *European Journal of Business and Management*, 115–122.

Sahadudheen, I. (2012). A cointegration and error correction approach to the determinants of inflation in India. *International Journal of Economic Research*, 105–112.

Singh, A. (2020, May 3). https://www.deccanherald.com/. Retrieved from https://www.deccanherald.com/, https://www.deccanherald.com/business/india-needs-strong-fdi-flows-to-compensate-for-remittances-833161.html

Streimikiene, D., Ahmmed, R. R., Vveinhardt, J., Qureshi, K. S., & Ghauri, S. P. (2019). The effects of remittances on inflation (CPI and WPI) and exchange rate: A case of Pakistan. *Romanian Journal of Economic Forecasting*, 146–165.

Upadhyay, M. P., & Upadhyaya, K. (2011). Effects of remittances on inflation and real exchange rate in South Asia. *Himalayan Journal of Development and Democracy*, 88–96.

A Robot Maker for Health Sector

Om Prakash

Abstract Coronavirus infections have once again highlighted the need to accelerate the companies, especially in health care to adopt automation. *Countless robots have been made since last more than 50 years, but still we do not find their ubiquitous presence.* Consequently, countless doctors, nurses and healthcare workers have risked, are currently risking and may continue to risk their precious lives, while tending the dependents. Countless families have suffered as their lone breadwinner succumbed to a risky act while tending coronavirus-affected patients. The paper suggests that it is high time now that companies delegate only the *risky* tasks to robots. The industry is currently in version 4.0, which is digitalization, and a universal need is felt to accelerate the companies toward adopting intelligent automation. While automation is the next version in industrialization of the world, the question still arises as to whether the state-of-the-art technologies are available to usher the companies toward the new era of automation or not. There are innumerable researches on robotics, and even the kids are being prepared to construct a robot at some places. However, it seems to be an aimless proliferation of robotics undertaking the ordinary or cliché jobs so much so that the whole activity appears clichéd. It is high time that a focused research is undertaken to construct a universal robot that can help to make robots that are secure and harmless to humans and replace preferably risky tasks. This not only will prepare the world in moving in right direction, but would also ensure safety and security of human race as the automation could be directed to replace only the risky tasks. This work is therefore aimed at constructing a universal "automaton" to understand any requirement and assist in creating safe and secure robots with the help of 3D printers. A prototype to this effect was developed and is available for further research and development in this area.

Keywords Corona virus · Robotics · Humanoid · Robotic assisted surgery · Universal automaton

O. Prakash (✉)
Real Apps, New Delhi, India
e-mail: director@db-migration.co.in

© The Author(s), under exclusive license to Springer Nature Singapore Pte Ltd. 2022

A. Chandani et al. (eds.), *Achieving $5 Trillion Economy of India*, Springer Proceedings in Business and Economics, https://doi.org/10.1007/978-981-16-7818-9_15

1 Introduction

As the second wave began, no less than 174 doctors, 116 nurses, 199 health workers died due to COVID-19 as of February 2021. The list is growing as we have entered the next wave of infections and some speculate that the 3rd wave, mostly infecting kids, may be imminent (PTI, 2021). Astonishingly, *Amnesty International states that over 17,000 health workers* have died due to coronavirus (Amnesty International, 2021). As the states are again reeling with upsurge in cases and curfew-like situations are being considered or imposed, the situations in hospitals continue to be grim. While patients tend to be admitted and discharged and there is an end to their ordeal, but there is no respite for hospital staff and healthcare workers and experts. Day in and day out, they have to continuously work with these patients and every single second they are in real danger of contracting the deadly disease. In some hospitals, they are working beyond their regular times and they cannot even take a day off as the situation continues to be very serious. And what do some get as a bargain—nothing but a deadly disease as a reward to their exemplary social service to mankind (PTI, 2021).

Apparently, there is no alternative for them as they are the best bet for everyone, as who else can replace them? So, is it not fair that the technologists come forward to their rescue? If these healthcare workers are risking out their lives for the mankind, is it not the duty of the society, technology companies, taxpayers, angel investors and even the government agencies to do a little bit to take them out from such a terribly sticky situation? *So far, a zillion of robots have been constructed and deployed, but still one does not find them at common healthcare centers or hospitals assisting for common jobs.* This paper considers that certainly one can and a possible answer is to develop a robot to assist these workers and even the healthcare experts in their daily chores. Certainly, the robots cannot replace the human nurse or doctors, but can surely assist them in the tasks like undertaking preliminary diagnosis of a patient like initial registration, Aadhar Card verification, providing those tokens, recording the temperature and even tending them for plausible treatment. The object is to simulate the job of human nurse so that instead of the humans, these robots may come into the contact with the patient as there is no way that a robot can be affected or contract the deadly disease (Kaiser et al., 2021).

2 Hypothetical Situation

Shyama (fictitious name) is the only breadwinner for her family. She had been completely dedicated to the hospital, would leave every day on time and would also return on time after the completion of her shift. Her old mother would be waiting for her every single day. Her mother was about 80 years old, would wait for her and was completely dependent on Shyama. Shyama never married as her father had died while she was still young, and she sacrificed for the sake of her mother. But, this was not the only sacrifice, as after the spread of COVID-19, one day she left her house, never to return back again (Masceranhas, 2021).

Dr. Ravi recently married and had been happily living with her wife and a little daughter. His wife and daughter used to take dinner with him, and till date, they never dined without him, especially his daughter who was absolutely fond of him and her biggest fan. That day, Dr Ravi promised to come on time for special occasion for a special dinner, but never returned back. The reason was that he was in charge of COVID-19 facility and was not feeling well throughout the afternoon. By evening, he had to be admitted to the ICU of the same hospital. He was responsible to discharge countless patients, but that day he could not be discharged. Henceforth, his daughter and wife will have to take the dinners all alone as he will never return (AHA, 2021). Should we allow this to happen? Perhaps, the real stories could be similar or even grimmer as so many did sacrifice their lives for us! What if a healthcare worker just has small kids only, waiting for him or her to come back to them? (AHA, 2021).

3 State-of-the-Art Robotics Helping Healthcare Workers and Units

There are currently very expensive state-of-the-art robots that have been deployed so far in various countries. Earlier, USA had identified their first infection by the coronavirus in its territory. He was admitted to Everett Regional Medical Center in Washington. There, to prevent the spread of the virus, every detail counts and technology had become a great ally. From the first minute, doctors had communicated with the patient through a robot called Vici that has a screen, speakers and a microphone. The device, which looks like a tablet on wheels and was developed by the company InTouch Health, also has a stethoscope and allows basic tests such as temperature measurement. Like Vici, there are other machines that can contain the escalation of the coronavirus and help reduce the workload of doctors. For example, the Guangdong Provincial People's Hospital in southern China has started using robots capable of opening and closing doors and taking the elevator autonomously to deliver medicines to patients, according to Chinese public television CGTN (Kaiser et al., 2021).

In the pandemic situations, it is essential to avoid contagion and spread. Robots can be used to test citizens, detect possible diseases and prevent other people or medical personnel from being infected. Everything indicates that the coronavirus is spread between people who are close through contact, for instance, through the small drops of saliva that the virus carrier excretes when coughing. Therefore, minimizing human contact is critical. Among those killed is Liang Wudong, who was one of the doctors treating patients in Wuhan, the epicenter of the corona virus. He was one of the first health workers killed due to the deadly infection. The death of the 62-year-old doctor has highlighted the risks to which medical personnel are exposed. Already in 2003, with the severe acute respiratory syndrome (SARS) epidemic, a large part of the health personnel was affected while caring for infected people. Therefore, it is rather a pity that robots could not find its place in terms of common and easily affordable equipment, like other rather ubiquitous machines, for instance, X-ray machines or ultrasound machines. Currently, the robots are very expensive to the tune of over 100,000–400,000 Euros which are mostly out of reach for a popular healthcare center in the 3rd world countries like India (Katevas, 2001).

4 Waitress Robots in COVID Era

But hospitals are not the only places where technology can help. A Chinese urbanization uses a drone with thermal cameras to take the temperature of the neighbors without having them to leave their houses. In addition, at a hotel in Hangzhou, a city of nine million people in eastern China, an autonomous robot named Peanut is in charge of bringing food to about 200 quarantined people, according to China Xinhua News. These guests, as reported by the same media, will remain in isolation for at least two weeks as a preventive measure because they traveled on the same plane as passengers from Wuhan. Incidentally, cost of waitress robots is about INR 300,000–400,000 in India (Kaiser et al., 2021).

5 The Peanut Robot

"Hello! Peanut is serving the food," the machine greets as it moves slowly down the hall, door-to-door with the aim of having guests grab the menu. In a video uploaded to Twitter, a man with a mask, wearing a robe and slippers comes out of his room and takes his food. "Take advantage. Please contact the hotel staff via WeChat if you need anything else," adds the robot, after serving the food to the man. By using WeChat, the most widely used instant messaging application in China, it is intended to avoid any direct contact with hotel workers. This robot, developed by the Keenon Company, is designed to serve in restaurants, hotels, hospitals, offices, banks or airports. In fact, they are already present in a restaurant chain in Madrid. The company explains on its Web site that Peanut has a voice recognition system and is equipped with artificial intelligence. To make the communication "more interesting," you can change the shape of your eyes to show the emotions of happiness, anger or sadness (Korn, 2019).

6 Robots that Clean and Disinfect

In addition to the robots that interact with patients and those that bring them food, there are also those that can clean and disinfect different spaces. Xenex is a Texas-based company that sells robots to kill pathogens. These machines, as the company explains on its own Web site, are used to quickly disinfect any room in just five minutes. "LightStrike disinfection technology has been proven to effectively reduce coronavirus contamination in clinical settings," he adds. Another company called Dimer has offered some airlines a robot to prevent the spread of the virus. The company states on its Web site that commercial airlines play a direct role in how diseases spread around the world. "Airplanes have the unique ability to transport germs across continents and oceans," he says. The system, which has been developed specifically for airplanes, uses ultraviolet light to eliminate "99.99% of the germs" present in these means of transport (Korn, 2019).

7 Other Useful Robots from Pre-COVID Era

Machines that are already used in China on a regular basis could also be useful to the rest of the world. However, their cost is still somewhat USD 50,000–USD 100,000. For instance, it is a robot implanted in some preschools in China to detect diseases in children early, according to the Daily Mail. Every morning, before entering the school, it performs a medical checkup on the minors in just three seconds. Thanks to a temperature measurement system and cameras that scan children's faces, it is able to detect possible diseases. These robots of less than one meter, would serve to avoid contagion and keep a temperature control. It would be quite interesting to use them to diagnose those people who experience the first symptoms. The problem, however, is that sometimes they can have a risky operation as these are of very hard material and non-collapsible. In contrast, the robots made through soft material, like the ones created through 3D printers, are not only soft, but can potentially be constructed with much lower cost. Such low-cost robots can be useful in common schools and even healthcare centers in India. Even in China, there is lack of popular use of robots in common schools and hospitals, as they mostly rely on manual works as carried out by human workers (Balasubramanian & Santos, 2014).

In the same way, it underlines that Xiaoyi could be used. This robot, developed by the artificial intelligence company iFlytek, passed with flying colors the examination that medical students must take to practice as doctors in the Asian country, according to China Daily. "It is capable of reviewing patient records and giving recommendations to the specialist," he says. At a time when hospitals are overwhelmed, it could be used to "analyze the results of an analytical or temperature check."

8 Technological Innovations to Face COVID-19

The research and development work carried out by engineers and scientists in universities, industrial companies and other organizations is reflected in numerous innovations that have a strong positive impact on people's work, health and social activities. Hence, there is an importance of promoting the study of Science, Technology, Engineering, and Math (STEM) careers among young people. Robotics is being regarded as an ally to promote social distancing. Although the use of robots for productive, educational, health or social purposes was experiencing an expansionary phase before the pandemic, the arrival of Covid-19 stressed their assessment in terms of the contribution they can make to protect the exposure of humans beings to corona virus or interact with infected people without unnecessarily exposing health professionals (Kaiser et al., 2021).

RoomieBot, created by the Mexican company Roomie IT Services, identifies suspected cases of coronavirus infection in hospitals, taking body temperature and detecting breathing difficulties. It is a converted prototype, since before the pandemic it operated in banks and companies, as a customer service device, payment for services and product guidance.

Pepper, the SoftBank Robotics robot, recognized worldwide for being the world's first social humanoid robot capable of recognizing faces and basic human emotions, is supporting the battle against the coronavirus by fulfilling tasks of detecting the use of masks in offices, businesses, airports and other closed places. Optimized for human interaction, it is able to interact with people through conversation and its touch screen (Korn, 2019).

More than 2000 companies around the world have adopted Pepper as an assistant to receive, inform and guide visitors in an innovative way. It is also used in educational institutions.

Tommy, nurse robot, helps save lives of people affected by the COVID-19. As the newspaper El Comercio points out, it collaborates with doctors and nurses to treat infected patients at the Circolo Hospital in Varese (Italy).

Moxi is a nursing assistant robot developed by Texas Health Resources. It works with the clinical staff in the neurology unit at Texas Health Presbyterian Hospital Dallas, helping to search, collect and deliver intake kits, laboratory samples and linen bags. It was designed to give clinical staff more time to focus on patient care.

Cruzr: Antwerp University Hospital (Antwerp) uses a robot supplied by the Belgian company Zorabots, which automatically detects the temperature of patients and whether or not they are wearing masks when entering the hospital. These types of robots have been assisting people for years, but the pandemic has made them a checkpoint in hospitals.

Luchi, humanoid or gynoid robot, treats patients with COVID-19 at the National Medical Center November 20 in Mexico City. It measures 1.40 m in height, can receive instructions via Wi-Fi from anywhere in the hospital or outside of it and has an assisted movement with proximity sensors, an attachment to avoid obstacles in its transit and a system of recognition of people through vision by computer.

Spot is the quadruped robot of the Boston Dynamics Company, in Singapore, and monitors that humans respect social distancing to avoid coronavirus infections.

However, the problem is that such robots are effective, but are highly expensive. These robots need extensive care in operations, and some of them are built with material that may potentially cause risk to patients, if such robot happens to malfunction. The need of today is to build inexpensive robot, made of soft material, and must operate in a risk-free manner, with an option to auto-switch off on malfunction.

Apart from providing direct help to patients and healthcare workers, robotics can also be involved in creating accessories that help in pandemic age. For example, face shields, masks and equipment like air purifiers can be prepared with accuracy using robots. Before the pandemic, the market for face masks was limited to a few models, while full face shields were reserved for use in laboratories, industries and other work environments. However, the urgency to equip the entire world population with effective protection elements against the coronavirus in a few weeks led to the creation of numerous prototypes: from automated versions to those that incorporated a research process by professors and university students. This involved in development of gadgets to offer higher levels of security. Even large industrial corporations joined in their efforts.

In this research, the object was to collect the details of such developments and innovations in manufacturing of such accessories. Many devices were created in recent months, including those devised by three academic members of ISTEC: University of South Florida (USA), University of the Republic (Uruguay) and National University of La Plata (Argentina).

PuriCare: LG created a portable air purifying mask with a respiratory sensor and a double fan that features different speeds, allowing you to take in clean filtered air and achieve normal breathing. Additionally, it has a case with UV rays to sanitize the device.

LEAF is a transparent mask that offers health security, while others see the identity of the wearer and read their lips or facial expressions. It is the first FDA-registered mask to have standard N99 air filtration capabilities, as well as a self-purification feature, thanks to a built-in UV-C light.

Micrashell Body Suit is the suit created for safe interaction with large groups of people, including a drink delivery system, smartphone integration, speakers, voice communicator and security camera. The helmet uses a filtration system based on the N95 standard to clean the breathing air of any viruses.

HelloMasks is a set of mask that combines transparency, protection and porosity, developed with a specially designed polymer.

Face shield for health personnel (UNLP) is an initiative of students and teachers of the National University of La Plata, an academic member of ISTEC that allows the manufacture of transparent plastic masks for those who are on the front line of battle against COVID-19. The La Plata Aero-modeling School and the 3D Printing Community also participate in the project. The mask consists of only 5 pieces (visor, elastic, fixative to give rigidity to the transparent screen, a wedge to secure the visor and an A4 size acetate sheet) and is made using 3D printing.

LUCIA Project is a team of technicians from the Faculties of Engineering, School of Design and Sciences of the University of the Republic (Uruguay), an academic member of ISTEC, which designed and built a system to disinfect N95 masks using ultraviolet light. All plans, code, etc., can be accessed of the LUCIA project that is released under Creative Commons license type 4 (it can be copied, modified and used, indicating the original reference).

University of South Florida Senior Research Engineer Michael Celestin, PhD (USF College of Engineering's Mini-Circuits Design for X Laboratory), developed an assembly line to produce face shields for Tampa General Hospital medical staff. Celestin's team is using materials like Mylar, elastics and foam to produce one face shield per minute. In addition, the USF Advanced Visualization Center (AVC) also works to help address the shortage of personal protective equipment and collaborates on several projects with the institution's medical and engineering schools, including the development of nasal swabs printed on 3D. USF is an academic member of ISTEC (Korn, 2019).

ASICS, a mask for runners developed by the ASICS Institute of Sports Science, allows them to breathe normally and give their maximum potential.

Tyler Glaiel: The renowned video game creator built a very particular homemade electronic mask, using an Arduino Nano Development Board and an LED matrix to produce a light pattern that mimics the movement of the mouth when speaking. It is not suitable for use by children, but provides a new relationship experience for young people and adults.

C-Face: Donut Robotics developed a smart mask with technology that translates Japanese into eight other languages and connects to the Internet. You can record and transcribe conversations into text messages via Bluetooth. It also amplifies the user's voice and makes calls, connected to a smartphone. The goal is to break down the communication barriers imposed by the pandemic.

BioVYZR 360° face shield and personal air purifier that filters out pathogens, allergens and pollutants, was created in Canada. It consists of a bubble-shaped case that fits over the head and wraps around the torso.

ISPHERE is a protective sphere covering the entire head created from the mandatory mask use regulations in Berlin (Germany). Inspired by science fiction comics, it has a built-in microphone and speaker.

Maskalike: Designer Danielle Baskin devised a mask that has the part that is covering each person's face printed on it. It allows who is using it to be recognized.

Vue Shield: Joe Doucet designed a face shield with integrated sunglasses.

VitalMask: The device generated by Vita Innovations (a start-up created by a group of students from Cornell University) consists of a mask for use in hospitals. Printed in 3D, it has a HEPA filter on the front and sensors around the earlobes, nose and mouth, which monitor body temperature, heart rate, blood oxygen levels and respiration.

These are extraordinary creations. But, the mass creations need the intervention from robotics so that they are produced in a low-cost method and make them available for the 3rd world countries.

9 Inventions to Guarantee Social Distancing

M-Rad Test Units: Mobile and transportable test sites detect COVID-19 and the presence of antibodies in the body, which could help relieve pressure in hospitals.

AIR LOCK is created by Plastique Fantastique so that doctors can treat patients safely; it is a portable personal space, which has a positive air pressure so that air flows continuously without leaking contaminated air.

CURA is a container that creates negative pressure and biocontainment levels similar to normal room insulation. Designed by Carlo Ratti Associati, its first installation in a temporary hospital took place in Turin, Italy.

Shield is a project that proposes to integrate plexiglass dividers to public seats to keep people safe and distant, with limited visual impact on the surrounding environment.

The Vital House is a structure to contain infectious diseases, which can be quickly built inside a house and allows visual contact with the rest of the family members during the isolation period. These units would have health parameters monitored.

Plex'Eat is a hanging clear plexiglass protective shield that hang above each diner, so they can dine or have lunch with others without the need to wear chinstraps. They can be quickly dismantled and disinfected. It is a solution for restaurants and bars and even can be extended for their use in hospitals.

Washi: Designers Ana María González Londoño and Farhad Saffari Ghandehari imagined a small device to save water and better promote hand hygiene, which works with proximity sensors.

Butterfly seating is a flexible seating solution for economy and premium classes on airplanes.

Qworktine is an airtight office system in the shape of a hexagon for those who cannot work from home. The doors are hands-free and controlled by facial recognition.

Mediamatic is a restaurant in Amsterdam, created through fully glazed private greenhouses for each table to ensure social distancing.

Soffio is inflatable face shield that creates a wide protective barrier and blocks air droplets, allowing you to meet friends in restaurants and bars.

10 Technology to Predict Disease Outbreaks

> "If something is to kill more than 10 million people in the next few decades, it will probably be a highly infectious virus, rather than a war," warned the Microsoft founder in 2015 during a TED talk. "There will be no missiles, but microbes," I assure you. Ten years later, the pandemic that we are suffering today arrived. It is possible to anticipate epidemics the same way as the climate. Its creators argue that Microsoft Premonition can help in the global fight against disease outbreaks by predicting the distribution and evolution of disease-carrying microbes, viruses and animals in the earth's biome or in life around us. In an article published in the Microsoft News Center, Suzanne Choney argues that if the biome could be monitored

> like the weather, environmental pathogens could be detected earlier and outbreaks could be predicted before causing major epidemics. "Microsoft Premonition shifts the paradigm from reacting to known pathogens to continuously looking for them as they evolve," said Ethan Jackson, senior director, Microsoft Premonition. "These signals could help us detect potential threats earlier, respond faster, and develop new interventions before outbreaks occur."

Microsoft Premonition is an advanced early warning system that combines robotic detection, artificial intelligence, predictive analytics and cloud-scale meta-genomics platforms to autonomously monitor disease-carrying animals such as mosquitoes, robotically collect environmental samples and then scan them at the genomic level in search of biological threats. Like weather forecasting, your analytics pipelines use cloud-scale computing to take advantage of the latest advancements in Azure IoT and Azure Data Lake on Microsoft Azure. Today, Premonition pipelines have scanned more than 80 trillion base pairs of genomic material from environmental samples for biological threats (Yogesh et al., 2020).

10.1 Robotic-Assisted Surgery

Today, robotic-assisted surgery and, in general, the use of robots in medicine mark a qualitatively new stage in the development of minimally invasive technologies and endovideosurgery due to the high level of accuracy, functionality and ergonomics of modern robotic systems. With the help of robotic technologies, the quality of diagnostic manipulations increases, and the results of therapeutic procedures and surgical interventions are improved, which ultimately leads to an improvement in the prognosis and quality of life for patients. However, this also significantly expands the possibilities of clinicians being diminished. Earlier diagnosis, increased efficiency and the effectiveness of the therapeutic measures in combination with improved surgical treatment methods led to an improved prognosis and functional results for patients, increasing in life expectancy and constantly the expansion of the boundaries of survival. As a result, the role of clinicians undoubtedly became associated with the processing of a large number of multimodal noisy, multidimensional, multi-scale intervention on metabolic and systemic information, in addition to the anatomical details. Early diagnostic provides less lesion in volume of organs in the pathological process, requiring not only minimally invasive access, but also maximum precision of intervention, often superhuman agility, vision, analysis and decision making. In this respect, medical robotics plays an important role in the development of the surgery of the future (Broadbent et al., 2010).

10.2 History of Robotic Developments to Assist Surgery

Today, robot-assisted surgery and the use of robots in medicine mark a qualitatively new stage in the development of minimally invasive technologies called endovideo-surgery. But, the philosophy of automation was first laid out by the ancient Greek thinker Aristotle in the fourth century BC. There is evidence that automatic machines were created on the territory of ancient Greece, ancient China, ancient India and ancient Rome. In 322 BC, ancient Greek inventor Archytas of Tarentum created a wooden Blue Bay, flying with jets of steam. Large contribution to the development of mechanics, hydraulics and pneumatics was contributed by the Alexandrian mathematicians Andsofas, Heron and Ctesibius, who lived at the end of the third century BC, many of whose inventions turned ideas about human capabilities. At the end of the fifteenth century, the great artist and inventor Leonardo da Vinci for the entertainment of queen's family designed a mechanical knight, clad in armor, which can be called the first anthropomorphic robot. Inside the armor, there was a mechanism that sets in motion the artificial person with the help of the rollers, that allowed him to imitate human movements. Detailed drawings of this mechanisms were found in the 1950s. Pierre Jaquet-Droz created the surviving to this day "Automatons" (anthropomorphic mechanisms—artist, musician, calligraphers). An important milestone in robotics is at the end of the nineteenth century. In 1898, the ingenious inventor Nikola Tesla demonstrated for the first time the possibility of remote control devices by creating a boat with radio control future (Broadbent et al., 2010).

The term "robot" itself appeared only in 1920, thanks to the Czech science fiction writer Karel Czapek and his brother and co-author Josef. Into action one of his plays, "RUR," the author introduced a human similar mechanisms and called them "robots" (from Czech "robota"—hard physical labor). In the literature, the theme of robots was developed by the writer Isaac Azimov, and the collection of stories "I, Robot" brought him worldwide fame. In 1951, Raymond Goertz, who worked in the nuclear power missions in the USA, designed a mechanical remote-controlled manipulator for working with radioactive substances, excluding direct contact with the person. Several years later, the first industrial robot "Unimate" came into existence, used for welding and casting at the company's factories at General Motors. "Unimate" served as the first prototype robot used in medicine. In 1977, V. Shainman designed a robot system PUMA 560 (Programmable Universal Machine for Assembly), which was improved and used in 1985 in neurosurgery for the precise direction of movement of needles during a brain biopsy of a person. This moment is considered the starting point in the history of medical robots. In 1988 urologist John Wickham, who owns the term "minimally invasive surgery", along with Brain Davis of the Imperial College of London presented a robotic system PROBOT, created specifically for transurethral resection of the prostate. The first operation using this system was successfully performed in London in 1991. A year later, Integrated Surgical Systems presented a surgical system ROBODOC for use in orthopedics for hip arthroplasty. Subsequently, similar devices were developed for use when replacing a knee replacement and in temporal bone surgery, which are used to this day (Katevas, 2001).

In 1993 at Computer Motion Inc., a robotic device was presented to fix and change the position of the video camera during laparoscopic operations, which received the name Aesop ("Aesop"). Highly complex surgical robot was attached to the operating table or cart and moving the endoscope was achieved using voice control or was allowed to install the endoscope manually. In 1995, Computer Motion Inc. combined two robot manipulators with tools and Aesop, to create the ZEUS system ("Zeus") to manipulate the arms of the robotic complex. These could be guided by the surgeon who performed the movement using management tools (joysticks) on the surgeon's console. Technically, ZEUS was not a robot because it did not follow the programmed movements, but rather was a computer tele-manipulator with interactive robotic arms. To improve the accuracy of the movement of the instrument, ZEUS filtered out hand tremors and could massage the stack sweeping movements of the surgeon's hand in short and precise tool movements. ZEUS surgical system has been used for the first ever trans-Atlantic surgical operation (Lindbergh's operation).

French professor, Marescaux from New York (USA), performed cholecystectomy to a patient at a distance of several thousand kilometers, in Strasbourg (France). In 1999, Intuitive Surgical Inc. (USA) put into operation a robotic surgical da Vinci system. Like ZEUS, da Vinci is a tele-controlled system, which consists of three components:

- the surgeon's console on which the manipulator controls;
- patient trolley equipped with four manipulator arms, one of which serves to fix the endoscope, another is used to transmit image to the monitor built into the console and the rest are intended for fixing tools;
- endovideosurgical stand (Katevas, 2001).

Precision of movement of mechanical manipulators surpasses the capabilities of human hands, since they have seven degrees of freedom and bending capacity by 90°. The screen displays a 3D image of the operated area. Surgeon controls manipulators using touch joysticks, and this lets movements of the surgeon with an absolute precision reproduced by robotic tools, providing improved articulation that increases the ease of overlays and allows you to perform the most complex manipulation with maximum accuracy. In the end, this ensures high quality of the operation and increases the safety of its implementation.

11 Modern Robots in Various Fields of Medicine

In 2001, the first clinical trials began on CyberKnife apparatus. It represented a minimally invasive radio-surgical robotic system used for the treatment of tumors of the skull and spine, as well as cancer of the prostate gland, lungs, liver and pancreas, using linear accelerators. The system uses control according to the image and a robotic arm with a computer control, allowing continuous tracking to live the movement of the tumor and the patient for at the procedure and carry out the appropriate corrective actions. Thanks to its exclusive precision, the system does not require invasive frames for fixing the head or other parts of the patient's body, which significantly increases flexibility of robotic systems. The radio-surgical system has the possibility of online target tracking and irradiation with breath synchronization. This system is known for the standard technology of radiation therapy for carcinogenic diseases. More than 100,000 patients are being treated all over the world. CyberKnife is an example of a commercially available and widely used frameless radio-surgical robot. In 2007 by Endocontrol (France), the first robotic system was developed for Laparoscopic Surgery with Voice management, called VIKY, which is used in gynecology, general surgery and urologic, thoracic surgery and includes a number of 150 devices around the world. In the same year, robotic bathroom magnetic navigation system Niobe (Stereotaxis, USA) was developed for endovascular operations on the heart, as well as endoscopic manipulations in gastroenterology (capsule endoscopy). The stem consists of two magnets with a robotic control next to the operating table. During the procedure, the doctor uses 3D navigation, an intuitive computer interface for setting the magnetic field around the patient, so that it allows precise guidance of catheter movement or capsules with a built-in magnet. Hansen Medical in 2007 released a specialized robotic system for Sensei for endovascular transcatheter interventions on the heart, in particular correction of supraventricular tachycardia, tremoratria, as well as complex ablation procedures for the treatment of atrial fibrillation. Also, like the Niobe system, there is a remote control version providing stability, precise positioning and insertion of the catheter, tagged navigation system at Senseiis 3D mapping, fluoroscopy and ultrasound (Katevas, 2001).

Another example of this is a group of medical robots is a systemCorPath GRX, created over the years by Corindus Vascular. It was marked by further development of guided flexible catheters for endoluminal access and work in restricted areas, inaccessible for rigid laparoscopy. In 2011, American company Mazor Robotics developed a specialized robotized complex Renaissance for neurosurgery. The system allows doctors to advance plan all stages of surgical intervention and think over the size of the required implant goods and fixing materials. After installation, the robotic platform could be directly placed on the patient's spinal column and synchronize with the current position. The platform runs the planned volume of surgical intervention with a maximum high precision up to 1.5 mm. At this moment, most of the world's execution experience robotic interventions on the spine. Over time, the priority in medical robotics is creating more compact, lighter and safer robotic systems with improved artificial intelligence that can easily be integrated into the clinical workers (Karwowsk & Rahimi, 1992).

Due to developments in the field of highly specialized surgical robots, orthopedic robotic systems Mako (Stryker, USA) and Navio (Smith & Nephew, UK) produce devices that are semi-active. Robotic systems are used to replace knee joint. Mako uses a 3D model of the knee of the patient's joint for preoperative planning and ratio of surgical intervention. System provides both auditory and tactile feedback, limiting the workspace borax. Navio does not use preoperative CT scan as the system constantly monitors both the patient's anatomy and the robotic device using infrared cameras and optical instruments. Mako is a parallel manipulator (surgeon and robot work together to move the tool). Navio is a sequential robot (the surgeon holds and moves the robot, which moves the tool). Flex Robotic technology has been an approved platform (Medrobotics, USA), which is the first specialized surgical platform based on the manageable and customizable volume of robotics. Flexible-tiered single-point controlled endoscope access can be carried out on nonlinear twisted anatomical paths.

Another promising development in the field of robotic endoscopy is a company represented in 2018 by Auris Health Inc. Monarch System. This robotic system was created to carry out diagnostic medical and therapeutic bronchoscopy, and it provides access to the bronchi of a sub-segmental order. Thanks to 3D-MSCT navigation in combination with high-definition video transmitted with an endoscope, as well as ergonomic control, it allows you to perform targeted biopsy of the peripherical formations of the lungs. Its advantages provide access to anatomical calls within 360 degrees from one port to minimize the invasiveness of the procedure and significantly increase the efficiency of transoral surgical interventions (Pickover, 2012).

12 Medical Robot Classification

With the advent of medical robotic technologies, new terms have appeared. In particular, telesurgery has appeared that uses surgery interfering with master-master devices, in which the master and slave components are physically separated. The surgeon who is located at a remote distance from the operating room table carries out active control of the toolcops. Data exchange between the surgeon's console and tools is carried out by telecommunication lines. Although the master–slave devices are usually located in the same room during surgery, the procedure can be performed using a surgical console, located in another room or even in another region. Today, all existing surgical robots can be divided as follows:

Passive robots do not have autonomous mode and so are manually operated and independent movement is not performed (for example, Neuronavigator).

Tele-controlled robots do not possess autonomy. Retain surgical instruments controlled by a person remotely (e.g., da Vinci).

Semi-active (interacting) robots are "true robot assistants." Operator constantly monitors the system. The robot provides some control. Examples include robots with virtual functions (semi-active—Renaissance, Navio; interacting—Mako).

Active robots have autonomous framework of a specific task. Here, an operator performs discrete control, and the robot performs a certain task in autonomous mode, but with the initiative of the operator.

Active robots are autonomously complete with the planned movement, conditionally auto-nominal robots. Operator builds and confirms surgical/treatment plan. The robot performs the procedure in autonomous under operator control (e.g., CyberKnife) (Pickover, 2012).

13 The Future of Robotic Surgery

Robots are with a high level of autonomy—robots capable of making medical decisions under human control (at the moment does not exist). Fully autonomous robots that may be capable of performing a complete surgery without human intervention are at the moment a Science fiction. Also, medical robots can be divided by their scope:

1. Surgical robots:
   - Neurosurgical—during surgical interventions on the spinal column and brain (Neuromate, Renaissance).
   - Endoscopic—used for bronchoscopy (Auris Monarch), ENT surgery (μRALP), manipulation lesions on the digestive tract and upper respiratory paths (Flex Robotic System, i-Snake).
   - Endovascular—controlled flexible catheters for endovascular intervention sessions on the heart and blood vessels (Magellan, Niobe, Sensei, CorPath).
   - Radiosurgery robots—CyberKnife.
   - Universal laparoscopic robots—tele-controlled manipulators (Aesop /ZEUS, VIKY, Da Vinci).
2. Auxiliary medical robots.
   - Rehabilitation—nursing robots (RIBA), companion robots (PARO), robotic exoskeletons (ALEX, LOPES, RUPERT).
   - Pharmacological – robots-pharmacological delivery systems (RPDS), targeted drugs delivery robots through the bloodstream (micro-bots / micro-robots / nanobots).
   - Service (hospital) robotic for disinfection (Xenex Robot), robots for observation, training and telepresence (InTouch tele-robotic system), autonomous mobile manipulators for transporting, equipment, consumables (TUG), social robot administrators/c-secretaries capable of recognizing dozens of languages (Pepper, Nao).
3. Other medical robots
   - Robotic hair transplant system (ARTAS).
   - Venipuncture robot (Veebot).
   - Robotic systems for resuscitation branches (The AutoPulse Plus, LS-1). Da Vinci surgery

In recent years, competition has begun to appear in the market of medical robots. The most tough of potential opponents of Intuitive Surgery are from the companies like TransEnterix, TitanMedical, Accuray, MAKO Surgical, Mazor Robotics, Hansen Medical et al. Despite this, it is Intuitive Surgical that has for a long time monopolist in the global robotics market. Thanks to the huge number of patented technologies used in da Vinci, the company possesses over 1700 national and international technology patents. da Vinci is the only one in the universal world robotic system with remote control and is widely used on all continents. According to Intuitive Surgical Inc., today in the world, almost 5500 robotic da Vinci surgical systems are operative, out of which about 3000 are in the USA and about 900 in European countries (Pickover, 2012).

13.1 The Universal Automaton

Robotic mechanism intention is to replace manual work with machines, essentially in intensive operations and tasks that are risky and repetitive, for instance, in hospital industry. The intent of this research is the development of universal robot as this sector is characterized by being a great hand absorber in risky chores and dangerous as well as risky tasks in patient tending. Robots can act as manipulators having the characteristics with a degree of technical development that proves to be sufficient to meet the needs in various tasks. Harnessing the potential and virtuosities of the progress of robotics can lead to changes in the robot construction process from the conception and project phase up to the execution technologies at the healthcare sites and at hospitals. Thus, it is investigated for the performance of robots in the current production sites of the robotic construction as well as hospital sites and the applicability potential of the robotics in upstream industries with manufacturing tasks performed in an environment controlled, in the form of constructive processes liable to be executed in the traditional factory.

In this work, an application of universal robots is developed to help in the execution of risky chores like human nurse tending a patient affected from significantly contagious diseases like COVID-19. In recent years, there has been a great technological development in the mastery of programmable automata (robots) and their use in various industries, with clear advantages over manual production processes. In fact, we live in a global and very competitive market, where demands are very diverse, often defined by the customer himself, looking for a low price and with higher quality. The industry also experiences continuous pressure to increase productivity and realize the final product with uniform quality. This pressure from the market means that the industry has to bet more and more in flexible production systems (FPSs) that can be easily adapted to changes one want. These FPSs are preferably computerized systems where the installation of manipulator robots is essential due to its flexibility (since they are reprogrammable systems), being adaptable to several functions in which its high precision and repeatability are not affected.

On the other hand, the transition from fully manual processes to automated processes or quasi-automatons assists to increase productivity, and this is also the key to the success of robotic systems. Thus, the industrial robot has in many cases become the ideal solution for automation of production systems, allowing for very flexible systems and the introduction of frequent product modifications, at a minimum cost. Besides, the industry is obliged to put aside the rigid production systems, needed in mass production, and provide for an intermediate stage of storage. Depending, of course, on our software and the suitability of the tool for the function to be performed, there are several industrial sectors that have already invested in making their lines of automated and robotic production systems, the automotive industry being one of pioneering examples in several countries. In short, robotics have proliferated and infiltrated too many different domains.

14 Research Model

A prototype of universal automaton was prepared by taking into account the movement of robots as well as the manipulation of objects that imply the knowledge of position and orientation, especially at the end of the robot. Particularly important aspect is the study of the robot control and the analysis of the interaction between the machine and its surroundings. This section presents different mathematical tools for that purpose. For the control of robots, a kinematic and dynamic model is required. The kinematics allows relating the position and orientation of the terminal element of the robot with the values of its particular coordinates. The dynamics allows one to know the relationship between the movement of the robot and the forces that originate it. The prototype development also referred to the fundamental concepts of kinematics and dynamics of industrial manipulator robots.

The process of designing the universal automaton went through three fundamental phases:

i. Task analysis.
ii. Robot structure analysis and.
iii. Functional analysis of the robot.

Every one of these phases corresponds to a specific job. The analysis of the task and the respective production process consists of determining more specific tasks, methods and tools to be used in each of the stages of its realization. After this first phase, the analysis of the structure of the robot includes its functional specifications, the design and software and hardware detail. This phase results in documentation with all the information relevant to the manufacture, assembly, operation and maintenance of the robot. The conception and project phase ends with the functional analysis of the robot allowing to identify the functions and performance levels that can be automated, specifying the environment in which the task will be undertaken, that is, the experimental verification of the robot prototype.

However, if deficiencies are found in terms of quality, performance and potential costs, we must move on to a phase of improvement of robot performances, requiring the modification and variation of the planned tasks in order to make the performance more profitable.

The analysis and portraying the development process of a robot allow us to take the following considerations:

- There is a close relationship between the conception and design of a robot and the specific requirements of the task to be performed.
-

- The analysis of the task to be performed by the robot allows us to define some (non-standardized) parameters that are fundamental for increasing their functionality. To this end, we must take into account the characteristics of objects to be handled, transported or worked with.
- The conception and design of the robot has to be developed based on functional specifications, a process that is essentially intuitive and must be systematic.
- The requirements for the kinematic configuration of the robot are determined by the complexity of the task to be performed.
- For the determination of the geometric, kinematic and mechanics of the conception and design of a robot, the work systems must be automated, selected, observed and described.

15 Creating Prototype of an Automaton

As highlighted, automaton is a robot prototype with an ability to create robots for industrial use. Today, industrial manipulator robots are very advanced machines of great precision and repeatability. From a mechanical point of view, they are structures consisting of a kinematic chain of rigid bodies, interconnected by revolutionary or prismatic joints which constitute the degrees of mobility of a structure (usually six), having a fixed end (base of the robot) and another free to move (terminal element). The resulting movement of the structure is obtained by the composition of the elementary movements. As in a human arm, the industrial manipulator robots generally use the first joints to position the structure formed by the others, which are used to guide the terminal element. The joints used for positioning form the structure called the arm. The next joints form the fist, by analogy with the human arm.

The handle generally has two configurations: pitch–yaw–roll (YXZ) as the human handle or roll–pitch–roll (ZYZ) also called spherical wrist. The latter is most used in robotics manipulation, although its structure presents singular configurations. Robots also use a revolution arm of anthropomorphic structure and spherical pulse. The mobility of a manipulator robot is ensured by the presence of the joints. The articulation between two consecutive links can be prismatic or revolutionary in nature. A prismatic articulation performs a relative movement that is a translational relationship between two links, while an articulation of revolution performs relative rotational movement between two links. The industrial manipulator robots used in the various manufacturing tasks and assembly use one of the four basic categories of the definition of movement:

- Cartesian or rectangular coordinates (3 linear axes)—robot Cartesian;
- Cylindrical coordinates (2 linear axes and 1 rotation)—robot cylindrical;
- Spherical or polar coordinates (1 linear axis and 2 rotation axes)—polar robot;
- Articulated or revolution coordinates (3 axes of rotation)—robot revolution.

A manipulator robot uses the arm joints for the positioning and the knuckle joints for the orientation function. There are thus five main types of arms in manipulation robotics: Cartesian, cylindrical, polar, revolution and SCARA.

Cartesian robots use 3 prismatic joints in which the axes are orthogonal. They are widely used for handling tasks such as palletizing, storage and machining tasks such as jet and leisure cut in which the robot movements cover large surfaces. On the other hand, its axes can be organized and sized according to the tasks to be performed.

Cylindrical robots: coordinates of this system are x, y, θ angular. The cylindrical robot differs from the Cartesian because one of the prismatic joints is replaced by an articulation of revolution. The advantage of cylindrical systems is that the coordinate system is easy to view and calculate linear movements where they can be used.

Polar Robots: Coordinates of this system are x, $\theta 1$, $\theta 2$. These differ from the cylindrical one because one of the two prismatic joints is replaced by a joint of revolution. The advantages of spherical or polar systems are that they cover a large volume from a given central point. Their two rotational movements can be easily isolated, and they can also tilt downward to pick up objects.

Revolution Robots: The coordinates are 3 rotation angles: $\theta 1$, $\theta 2$ and $\theta 3$. The robot revolution consists of 3 articulations of revolution whose axes of the first articulation are orthogonal and the axes of the other two joints are parallel. The advantages of the revolution systems are that all connections are rotating and so it provides for the maximum flexibility since any location can be achieved. These are useful in dirty or corrosive environments, or even under water.

It is worth mentioning that the Selective Compliance Assembly Robot Arm (SCARA) robot is a subclass of cylindrical robots and has 3 revolution joints and 1 prismatic joint. Two of the revolution joints are positioned in the horizontal plane allowing the extension of the robot arm at any point on the horizontal plane. At the end of the robot arm, there is a vertical link which can be moved according to a prismatic joint. The tool placed at the end of the vertical connection can rotate around vertical axis of this connection (revolution joint), facilitating the control and orientation of the respective tool in the horizontal plane.

16 Use of Universal Automaton in Hospital Industry

The hospital sector is one of those that mobilize a greater number of economic resources and humans. It constitutes sector of great economic projection, in terms of both the number of companies involved and invoicing produced, and in terms of both quantity and diversity of the workforce employed. One of the main characteristics of this industry is the great weight on the cost of pandemics, since in the execution of the undertakings this cost is of about 50% of the total cost, especially in the times of emergency.

Universal automaton intention is to just replace the human nurse or healthcare specialists by the machines in only *risky manual work operations that are intensive and repetitive processes.* These also require precision and speed, as the hospital sector has aided field for application development. We will see, however, that this objective has very broad implications throughout the construction process or the robot (conception, project, planning and execution). This does not prevent the development of robotic systems that aim to automate some of the many tasks that are part of the **risky** hospital processes. Due to the precision, speed and diverse nature of risky manual operations, the object of these sections would be the presentation of a concrete application that develops a prototype of generic robot. This generic robot is captioned as "universal automaton" as this prototype would help in developing robots dedicated to a particular risky and manual hospital operation. Extensive use of 3D modeling and employing 3D printers to develop and create robotic parts are recommended and presented. These robotic parts can then be assembled and supplied to be used for a particular risky and manual hospital operation.

To improve current hospital processes, it is advantageous to apply the technology of robotics because the robots are of high precision and powerful for the execution of different types of tasks. However, it is necessary to integrate and adapt them to the hospitals. Thus, for the use of robots in hospital sector, it is important to characterize the working environment and the type of tasks carried out, as well as the nursing works during pandemics.

17 Characterization of the Areas

A careful analysis of the specific tasks of the hospital industry allows pointing out some possibilities for the use of robots in this sector. It is easy to verify that various hospital activities involve repetitive operations—measuring weight, temperature, general OPT chores like registering patients, patient verification process, assigning tickets and tokens, and later on even collection of blood samples and testing. Robots can immediately be put in use to substitute human nurses with precision, quality and speed for such homogeneous tasks. At the same time, nurses that were replaced by robots in these risky manual chores can devote their task in ensuring more complex works like assuring the quality of patient care, ensuring the oxygen and other supplies are in place and general hospital administration.

As highlighted earlier and as has been amply exemplified now during the time of pandemic spread, the hospital business is particularly perilous and continues to be, and one that surrounds higher number of work accidents, like countless nurses, healthcare workers and even doctors contracting the deadly disease. They contract the very disease they are treating as day in and day out they are put on duty with no respite. There is no "discharge" for them until the disease dies out. Alternatively, the robots can come to their rescue and provide them some necessary respite and a time to breath. Otherwise, the frequency and severity of the accidents are set to increase. This is so as, for one, lack of security and training deficit and tendency to commit an error on the required protection standards can cause serious harm to healthcare professional. For another, the high degree of risk inherent in tending dependents in highly contagious diseases may lead to lowering the standard of care due to some inevitable and unavoidable reasons. This will not be the case when robots are deployed as in no way a robot can contract the deadly disease caused by the biological germs.

18 Conclusion

In many cases, one may witness a certain disregard for basic personal safety standards on the part of the healthcare workers. Reluctance to use a PPE, masks or proper sanitizers to handle appropriate tasks at hand and committing an error to use gloves, goggles, breathing masks and protection against common risks are evident and can be inevitable. Workers may continue to fail to comply with safety standards in collective actions in order to make the work environment less dangerous, namely when applying proper sanitizers at the floors or properly disposing of the waste, maintaining protected openings and ventilations at workplaces and providing properly lit and illuminated areas. Also, the high degree of risk inherent to some tasks carried out on site is an opportunity to resort to the use of robots. Apart from the pandemics, there is always risk of chemicals (toxic) or radiation (exposure to high levels of radiations) is also the potential area where robots can be deployed in normal times.

The implementation of hospital robot in the process requires prior and detailed study of the cost (from its acquisition to its effective amortization), weighing the advantages and disadvantages of its introduction. If it is a fact that the economic justification for the use of robots determines their viability and profitability, it is also a fact that, in addition to the cost of acquisition, tools and equipment and installation of the robot in the factory, we have to consider the benefits that the use of the robot, or automation in terms of general. The bottom line is to create robots that can just replace the risky tasks, and not all tasks, in hospital operations. The created robots should be very cost effective and affordable to common hospitals in 3rd world countries. Furthermore, the robot itself must operate in risk-free manner and must be durable. Universal automaton will have the capability to construct such robots that are made of soft material, operate in a risk-free manner and highly affordable.

References

AHA (2021). Health care workers share harrowing and hopeful front-line stories. American health Association. Retrieved from https://www.aha.org/other-resources/2020-12-16-health-care-workers-share-harrowing-and-hopeful-front-line-stories

Amnesty International (2021). COVID-19: Health worker death toll rises to at least 17000 as organizations call for rapid vaccine rollout. Retrieved from https://www.amnesty.org/en/latest/news/2021/03/covid19-health-worker-death-toll-rises-to-at-least-17000-as-organizations-call-for-rapid-vaccine-rollout/

Balasubramanian, R., & Santos, V. J. (Eds.). (2014). The human hand as an inspiration for robot hand development (Vol. 95). Springer.

Broadbent, E., Kuo, I. H., Lee, Y. I., Rabindran, J., Kerse, N., Stafford, R., & MacDonald, B. A. (2010). Attitudes and reactions to a healthcare robot. *Telemedicine and e-Health, 16*(5), 608–613.

Kaiser, M. S., Al Mamun, S., Mahmud, M., & Tania, M. H. (2021). Healthcare robots to combat COVID-19. In *COVID-19: Prediction, decision-making, and its impacts* (pp. 83–97). Springer.

Katevas, N. (Ed.). (2001). Mobile robotics in healthcare (Vol. 7). IOS Press.

Karwowski, W., & Rahimi, M. (Eds.). (1992). *Human-robot interaction.* CRC Press.

Korn, O. (Ed.). (2019). *Social robots: Technological, societal and ethical aspects of human-robot interaction.* Springer.

Masceranhas, A. (2021). 15,877 healthcare workers contracted coronavirus across Maharashtra, 178 died: Health dept. data till Dec, 2020. Indian Express. Retrieved from https://indianexpress.com/article/india/15877-healthcare-workers-contracted-coronavirus-across-maharashtra-178-died-health-dept-data-till-dec-21-7119108/

Pickover, C. A. (2012). *The medical book: From witch doctors to robot surgeons: 250 milestones in the history of medicine*. Sterling Publishing

PTI (2021). 174 Doctors, 116 Nurses, 199 Health Workers Died Due To Covid: Centre. NDTV. Retrieved from https://www.ndtv.com/india-news/174-doctors-116-nurses-199-health-workers-died-due-to-covid-centre-2364200

Yogesh, S., Prasanna, B., Parthasarathi, S., & Ganesh, M. A. (2020, September). Open MV-micro python based DIY low cost service robot in quarantine facility of COVID-19 Patients. In *Congress on intelligent systems* (pp. 519–531). Springer.

Prevalence of Emotional and Financial Stress Among Management Students

Preksha Dassani and Deepak

Abstract Good health and a composed mind are a reflection of a person's well-being. Nowadays, stress has become an inevitable part of our daily lives. Sometimes, stress is beneficial as it pushes us to perform well while too much stress has its negative effects. An individual who is exposed to stress for a prolonged period often experiences exertion on physical and mental health. Students are the building blocks of a nation and the leaders of tomorrow. This chapter is an attempt to present the emotional and financial stress the students are exposed to during their college life. A study on 218 postgraduate management students shows that they experience emotional and financial stress from moderate to extreme levels. With the use of descriptive analysis and factor analysis, the findings and the possible way ahead have been presented. Based on the results, suitable suggestions have been put forth to mitigate the effect of stress on students. The chapter also links the benefits of emotional intelligence as a tool to combat stress. Higher emotional intelligence helps to improve understanding, communicate effectively and assist to manage one's emotions which relieves stress. Thus, reduced stress maintains good health and helps them to grow in their personal and professional domain.

Keywords Emotional stress · Financial stress · Management students · Emotional intelligence · Conflict management

1 Introduction

Stress has become an inevitable part of an individual's life. Pressure is felt in a family, at the workplace, in business, at study or in any social or financial action. In the context of students, particularly in India, students in the higher educational institution (HEI) need to deal with varied pressures, namely to maintain one's academic score assignment deadlines, discussions, project works, quizzes, other challenges when they

P. Dassani (✉)
Andhra University, Visakhapatnam, Andhra Pradesh, India

Deepak
Indira Gandhi National Open University (IGNOU), New Delhi, India

© The Author(s), under exclusive license to Springer Nature Singapore Pte Ltd. 2022
A. Chandani et al. (eds.), *Achieving $5 Trillion Economy of India*, Springer Proceedings in Business and Economics, https://doi.org/10.1007/978-981-16-7818-9_16

move away from home, i.e. setting into the new culture of the new place, homesickness, food habits, new relationships, travelling, and much more. The researchers conducted their study to examine the stress levels of students in private higher educational institution (HEI) and government higher educational institution (HEI). Their results showed that the former was exposed to higher levels of stress when compared to the latter set of students (Perwez, 2020). Undoubtedly, a controlled amount of stress is beneficial to reach goals, but a prolonged period of high stress is injurious to health. College students encounter stress due to the workload of classes, building new interpersonal relationships, preparations for new responsibilities, poor time management skills, erratic sleep, and eating habits. As one enters the postgraduation level, students enter with new hopes, dreams, and goals to achieve. The energy and enthusiasm to kick-start their career slowly become burdened with stress due to several reasons. As per the research published in the Asian Journal of Psychiatry, it was found that students in Indian universities suffered from moderate stress to extreme stress; i.e. 37.7%, 13.1%, and 2.4% of the students reported moderate, severe, and extreme severe, respectively. The universities barely have the infrastructure to address the mental grievances of students (Kunju, 2017). The purpose of this chapter is to present the existence of emotional and financial stress among postgraduate management students.

2 Review on Emotional and Financial Stress Among College Students

Several professional courses have burdened students to obtain loans for their education. The research on 87 college students enrolled for engineering and management programme in an institute in Uttar Pradesh presents the prevalence of stress among students. The loan aspect is a primary factor that triggers stress among students which is further exacerbated with uncertainty regarding their job placements, social expectation, and family pressure. Some students expressed their concerns regarding social rejection and isolation. They felt unrecognised by their faculty and claimed to be taken for granted by their peers. These incidents aggravate their socio-psychological issues (Agrawal & Chahar, 2007). The leading reasons which made college students suicidal were troubles in relationships, problems in the family, financial stress, depression, feelings of social isolation, hopelessness, and anxiety (Westefeld et al., 2005). Increased financial pressure, academic and family stress leads to severe stress. They authors put forth that reducing financial stress can reduce distress and ameliorate the performance of the students (Cadaret & Bennett, 2019).

The author conducted a study to find out the harmful effects of financial stress on the well-being of students. Access to credit cards, the status of the dependent, and financial knowledge were significant factors that burdened the students (Robb, 2017). The author investigated the sources of stress among 201 college students in Taiwan, and the results showed that the male students experienced more stress arising out of family issues like "lack of support from parents" (mean value = 3.57), "getting along with siblings" (mean value = 3.55), and "excessively high expectations of parents" (mean value = 3.33). It was also found that students who had taken a loan experienced more stress in aspects of emotional factors, physical/mental factors, and relationship (Kai-Wen, 2009).

A study on 219 students of a B-School was conducted in Ahmedabad where the results showed that a packed workload was found to be one of the highest sources of stress. Managing various roles such as an ideal son/daughter along with the competitive nature to shine out among peers makes the students feel stressed. Students were constantly under the pressure to fulfil the expectations of their family, teachers, peers, seniors, and acquaintances. This arduous task of meeting expectations and the inescapable situation of not disappointing anyone takes a toll on the health of the student and causes stress (Sinha, 2014). An inverse relation between emotional intelligence and academic stress was reported; i.e. students with low levels of emotional intelligence experienced a high level of academic stress (Kauts, 2016). Therefore, it can be inferred that higher emotional intelligence helps to improve understanding, communicate effectively and assist to manage one's emotions which relieves stress.

3 COVID-19 Pandemic and Stress on College Students

The COVID-19 pandemic has caused severe stress across the globe. Even the student community has been hit hard which has harmed their emotional, financial, and physical health. During the pandemic, the students who lived away from home faced severe distress and worry as they were forced to vacate hostels at a short notice. Students were under pressure to travel to and fro to attend examinations even during the most perilous situations. With massive lay-offs of employees and suspension in several domestic industries burdened with curfew and lockdown, the families are experiencing financial difficulties. Inability to purchase a laptop, lack of access to proper electronic devices, and poor Internet connectivity are the glitches students experienced while attending the online classes in this new era of digital learning. Several students went back to their villages, and in remote places, they are unable to manage a Wi-Fi or a stable Internet connection. Furthermore, sticking to the screen for a prolonged period has made them feel tired and aggravated their mental stress. Students are finding it difficult to adjust to the sudden shift from traditional classroom teaching to the online mode. Being glued to the screens for many hours has affected their mental and physical health. Students are unable to meet and interact with friends and teachers which are highly essential in terms of the development of their cognitive, mental, and social skills (Hindustan Times, (2020). A study on 450 students was undertaken to understand the stress among students during the pandemic, and the results revealed that the students were more stressed due to online classes and issues related to self-management. The students found themselves more vulnerable to stress and were unable to adjust to the e-learning platform. The female students were prone to more stress and worry about studies when compared to their male counterparts. The students were burdened with fear, worries regarding breach of guidelines, frequent technical issues, and severe pressure which have exacerbated their academic progress. These factors impact the psychological well-being of the students. The research also showed that continued online classes have caused stress among students as they are confined to their spaces for an extended period (Chhetri et al., 2021).

4 Emotional Intelligence

Findings proved that emotional intelligence is a strong trait in achieving success in one's career (Urquijo et al., 2019). A person with high EI functions better as she/he has the traits to be a good team player, knows how to work under pressure, and consequently contributes to the productivity of the organisation. Not only does it add an edge at the workplace but it is also advantageous to students in their pursuit of academic goals and career advancement. An emotionally intelligent person grows to be a versatile employee as they move into the working environment. This trait is more important for individuals in the teaching profession as they need to be adept in handling the classroom atmosphere as they educate the young generations. A study on 278 college students from diverse fields in Malaysia revealed that the students who were aware of their emotions could understand and anticipate the kind of emotion which would help them emerge in varied circumstances. It also prepared the students to handle pressure effectively to progress towards academic excellence in high learning institutions (Mohzan et al., 2013).

A renowned psychologist Daniel Goleman popularised the subject of emotional intelligence. He described emotional intelligence (EI) as an ability to be aware of one's emotions as well as understanding the emotions of others. This competency helps to handle interpersonal relationships and conflicts in a smooth manner. He claims that emotional aptitude aids to maintain relationships and good health and enhances success at work (Goleman, 1998). Emotional intelligence (EI) or emotional quotient (EQ) is an essential aspect that aids an individual's capacity to identify and manage one's emotions and others in a positive way to empathise, conduct effective communication, build good interpersonal relationships, manage conflicts, and stay motivated. Not only intelligent quotient (IQ) but having high EI benefits an individual to perceive things positively and subsequently acquires to de-stress oneself.

Proponents of emotional intelligence argue that in determining leadership success, EI stands to be more important than IQ. Daniel Goleman's EI model constituted of five components, i.e. "self-awareness, self-regulation, motivation, empathy, and social skills" (Sadri, 2012). Emphasis on the development of emotional intelligence in education is vital as it enhances the ability of the students to compete in life. The academic curriculum should be designed in a manner that not only develops credibility but also shapes the personality of the students. It can also introduce programmes to impart and inculcate decision-making skills among students (Hassan et al., 2009).

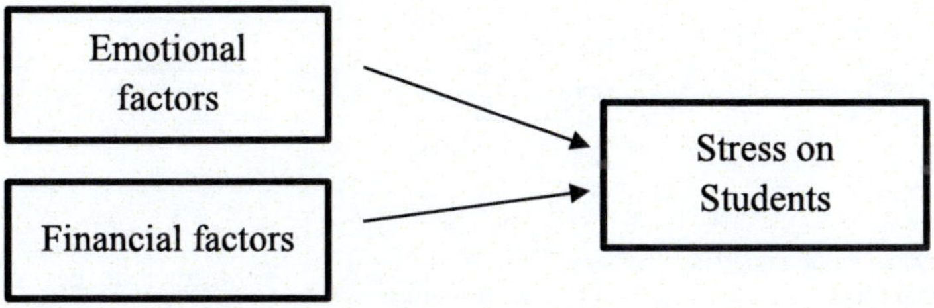

Fig. 1 Conceptual framework. *Source* Author's own work

These skills also help the students have a good work-life balance; i.e. high level of emotional intelligence is interlinked to employee engagement which is beneficial to the employee as well as the organisation.

The authors studied the influence of the emotional aspect as an element of employee engagement. They mentioned that emotional and psychological satisfactions are the key factors of employee engagement; i.e. the emotional connection which an employee feels towards the organisation is linked to their performance. Moreover, it was observed that individuals with a high level of employee engagement by default turn out to be high performers. Therefore, they stated that apart from the professional connection, it is necessary to build a strong emotional and psychological connection with employees to make them perform to their fullest capacity (Mehta et al., 2016).

5 Conceptual Framework

Apart from the demographic profile of the respondents, questions were designed on a five-point Likert scale to understand the level of emotional and financial stress prevailing among the students. Figure 1 shows the conceptual framework of the study.

6 Discussion

The data were collected using a questionnaire from 218 postgraduate management students of a reputed university in Andhra Pradesh. The analysis is presented using scale value analysis, frequency tables, and factor analysis in IBM SPSS version 20. The Cronbach alpha's value for the factors was observed as 0. 757. Since the value is above 0.70, the questionnaire's reliability is considered to be acceptable (Glen (n.d.)) (Table 1).

Out of 218 respondents, 51.8% were male students and 48.2% were female students, i.e. 113 and 105, respectively. All the respondents were aged between 20 and 30 years. About 31.1% of the respondents (68 respondents) were aged 22 years,

Table 1 Reliability statistics

Cronbach's alpha	No. of items
0.757	12

Source Primary data

Table 2 Scale value analysis of emotional factor

	Mean	Std. deviation	*N*
Conflict with teachers	2.87	1.177	218
Conflict with friends	2.67	1.095	218
Conflict with others	2.60	1.180	218
Conflicts with parents	2.78	1.139	218
Low self-esteem	2.72	1.121	218
Social media platforms	2.81	1.065	218
Loneliness	2.95	1.229	218
Paying college fees	2.85	1.174	218
Asking money from guardian	3.24	1.163	218
Sticking to budget	3.06	1.296	218
Spending pattern of friends	2.61	1.046	218

Source Primary data

23.8% of the respondents (52 respondents) were 23 years old, and 15.5% of the respondents (34 respondents) were 24 years old. Except for these ages, the remaining respondents also age within the 30 years' bracket.

The highest mean value (3.24) was observed for the response "asking money from guardian" which added to the respondents' financial stress (shown in Table 2). The respondents confessed that they feel hesitant to regularly ask for money for their expenses. A handful of the respondents were involved in a part-time source of work, while the rest were dependent on their guardians for their expenses. Lack of awareness to engage themselves in part-time jobs was a reason behind this stress. Students expressed their interest to work as their class was half day and they were willing to spend the remaining time fruitfully, but lack of proper guidance makes them remain idle. Some respondents had work experience and left their jobs to pursue a full-time course, so this financial constraint stressed them even more. The second highest mean value was found to be 3.06 for "sticking to budget"; i.e. students found difficulty in preparing a budget or/and sticking to it. It presents their inability or lack of skill in financial planning. Interactions with the students also revealed that they were impulsive in their buying behaviour which was stated as one of the common reasons for this lapse in financial management. Students also admitted that they were not good at saving money and did not keep a track of their expenses. This negligence on their part made them feel stressed and worried.

Frequent advertisements about credit cards with attractive rebates appeal to college students to use credit cards for their daily financial transactions like entertainment, gasoline, and food. The offers mask the intensity of the credit burdens. Students need to be taught the responsible use of credit cards along with techniques to tackle bait advertising which prompts them to adopt the use of such cards (Hayhoe et al., 2000).

In this era of digitalisation, it is uncomplicated to connect with friends and family. Despite the advancement in the various modes of communication, the students often experienced feelings of loneliness (Mean value 2.95). Among the emotional stress questions, this response showed the highest mean value. Nonetheless, the respondents were associated with numerous groups on WhatsApp, Facebook, Telegram, Instagram, Twitter, but it seemed like they did not connect with it in a real sense. This emotional stress was common in the respondents and exposes that technology has indeed disconnected people from hearts and has not brought them together. Many students had relocated themselves to pursue their higher education and made their attempts to be a part of a social group to comfort themselves, but whenever they failed in their attempts, they succumbed to a feeling of loneliness. Students also faced the problem of language barrier; i.e. they feel inferior to those who communicate better than them in the English language. This barrier makes them limit their social circle.

Such a feeling of belongingness was aptly put forth in Abraham Maslow's hierarchy of needs theory where he rightly mentions that as a human progresses, he feels the need to be loved and cared for. This American psychologist designed a model which elucidated the path to an individual's self-actualisation. The social needs include the human bonds (family, friendship, social groups) for belongingness (Corporate Finance Institute (n.d.)).

6.1 Analysis of Emotional Factors and Students' Stress

The questions were measured on a five-point scale, i.e. no stress (1), slightly stressful (2), moderately stressful (3), highly stressful (4), and extremely stressful (5). Table 3 presents the scale value analysis of the questions. Students were prone to stress ranging from slight to extreme stress when they encountered "conflicts with parents, teachers, friends, and others". In case of conflicts with parents, about 11.9% of the respondents felt extremely stressful and 14.7% felt high levels of stress. "Conflict/arguments with teachers" caused stress; i.e. 29.4% of the respondents felt high levels of stress. About 21.6% of the respondents felt more stressed when they had conflicts with friends/roommates, while 23.4% of the respondents felt highly stressed when they had arguments with others. This stress was expressed in terms of feeling anxiety, nervousness, and frequent emotional turmoil. "Fights between parents" is another issue faced by the students. When the environment at home is not congenial, students feel stressed and it affects their academic performance also. They feel disturbed and upset on regular basis. This leads to mood swings and forcibly makes them get into arguments. Approximately, 16.1% of the respondents felt extremely

Table 3 Crosstabulation using frequency between respondents' opinion and emotional factor

S. No.	Emotional factor	5	4	3	2	1
		ES	HS	MS	SS	NS
1	Conflict/arguments with parents	26	32	40	108	12
	100%	11.9	14.7	18.3	49.5	5.5
2	Conflict/argument with professors/teachers	27	37	55	79	20
	100%	12.4	17	25.2	36.2	9.2
3	Conflict with roommate or friend	22	25	45	111	15
	100%	10.1	11.5	20.6	50.9	6.9
4	Conflict with others	21	30	40	95	32
	100%	9.6	13.8	18.3	43.6	14.7
5	Fights between parents	35	28	35	84	36
	100%	16.1	12.8	16.1	38.5	16.5
6	Low self-esteem	21	34	47	96	20
	100%	9.6	15.6	21.6	44.0	9.2
7	Stress level when you use social media platforms and tend to compare your life with others	20	46	51	86	15
	100%	9.2	21.1	23.4	39.4	6.9
8	How stressful do you feel when you are lonely or out of the group?	34	48	33	88	15
	100%	15.6	22.0	15.1	40.4	6.9

Source Primary data, extremely stressful (ES), highly stressful (HS), moderately stressful (MS), slightly stressful (SS), and no stress (NS)

stressed and 12.8% of the respondents felt highly stressed when their parents had tiffs at home. Language barriers and the background of the respondent, i.e. place of prior education, were the major causes that made the respondents feel inferior or low self-esteem. Their desire to be recognised in college was an added factor. Over 25% of the respondents were largely stressed due to "low self-esteem", while 21.6% of the respondents felt moderate stress. The use of social media platforms has drastically impacted the lives of all and in particular the student community. The students relate their "likes", "positive comments", "number of followers" on the social media platform as a measure to gauge their social acceptance. Many students are keen to increase their friend list just to increase their likes and followers which adds to their stress. The craving to be liked has hit this generation which is harmful in the long run. The fear of missing out on updates and the constant urge to check their phones for new happenings have hampered their concentration power. Additionally, about 37.6% of the respondents felt lonely when they were left out of a group.

Table 4 Crosstabulation using frequency between respondents' opinion and financial factor

S. No.	Financial factor	5	4	3	2	1
		ES	HS	MS	SS	NS
1	How stressful do you feel while paying your college fees?	12	67	246	69	17
	100%	3	16	60	17	4
2	How stressed do you feel when you frequently have to ask for money from your guardians?	41	51	65	51	10
	100%	18.8	23.4	29.8	23.4	4.6
3	Rate the stress you feel in designing a budget and sticking to that	39	41	61	60	17
	100%	17.9	18.8	28.0	27.5	7.8
4	Mark the stress you feel when you happen to compare with the spending pattern of friends	16	29	45	113	15
	100%	7.3	13.3	20.6	51.8	6.9

Source Primary data, extremely stressful (ES), highly stressful (HS), moderately stressful (MS), slightly stressful (SS), and no stress (NS)

6.2 Analysis of Financial Factors and Students' Stress

The results shown in Table 4 present that 19% of the respondents felt more stressed in paying college fees while 60% felt moderate levels of stress. About 42.2% of the respondents were too stressed about asking for money from their guardians. They feel uneasy and hesitant to remain dependant on their guardians for financial support. More than 50% of the respondents were above 22 years and felt the urge to quickly make themselves employable. This worry about job placements and insecurity about the future often concerned them. The respondents were not good at preparing and following a budget. In this scenario, around 17.9% and 18.8% of the respondents experienced extreme and high stress, respectively. Over 25% of the respondents were moderately stressed in sticking to a budget and usually exceeded their budget. It is natural for students during their adolescence and early twenties to get attracted to branded products and services that are in vogue. Students feel more pressured when they find their peers spending well and leading a better lifestyle. Such a comparison and temptation to imitate is harmful to one's financial health. It was found that 7.3% of the respondents felt extremely stressed when they compared their spending pattern with their friends while 13.3% faced high levels of stress. Over 20.6% of the respondents encountered moderate stress.

6.3 Analysis of Factor Analysis

The use of factor analysis helps to group similar variables; i.e. this technique groups the variables into homogeneous subsets. The variables must be correlated to run

Table 5 KMO and Bartlett's test

KMO and Bartlett's test		
	Kaiser–Meyer–Olkin measure of Sampling Adequacy	0.762
Bartlett's test of sphericity	Approximately chi-square	996.340
	Df	66
	Sig.	0.000

Source Primary data

the test of factor analysis so that significant factors can be easily identified. Table 5 presents the KMO and Bartlett's test results; i.e. the KMO value is 0.762 which indicates that the sample is adequate to run the factor analysis, while Bartlett's test value of 0.000 (less than p-value 0.005) is significant at 0.05 level. This value rejects the null hypothesis at approximately chi-square value 996.340 with 66 degrees of freedom. The result of KMO is greater than 0.6 (0.762 > 0.6) which is a considerable value to proceed with further analysis.

The rotated component matrix (Table 7) is the main output of principal component analysis (PCA) that represents the factor loadings which are the simple correlations between the variables and the factor. The eigenvalue denotes the total variance (Table 6) explained by each factor. With the use of the varimax rotation method, the factor loadings are modified and sorted. The size of the loadings describes its significant contribution to the factor. The variables were extracted into two factors as designed, and on similar lines, 8 variables were named as "emotional factor" and 4 variables were labelled under the heading of "financial factor". The factors comprise 18.14% of data variance. All the variables/dimensions have values above 0.5 and are considered to have moderate to significant influence on the student's stress levels.

From Table 7, it can be observed that the variables were extracted into two factors, i.e. emotional and financial. The statement "designing a budget and sticking to that" was found to have the highest factor loading, i.e. 0.778 followed by 0.772 for the statement "paying college fees" and 0.747 for the statement "frequently asking for money from guardians". Out of all the statements, these statements significantly stressed the students. This shows the presence of financial stress among students. Apart from this, students expressed "low self-esteem" and conflict/arguments with parents to be highly stressful with the loading values as 0.727 and 0.721, respectively.

7 The Way Forward

This chapter presented the prevalence of emotional and financial stress among management students. Stress is unavoidable in every stage of life, but the budding citizens of the country need to be taught well to handle stress right from a young age. The analysis shows that the students are under stress and it needs to be addressed to help improve their well-being. The management stream includes concepts that

Table 6 Total variance explained

Component	Initial eigenvalues			Extraction sums of squared loadings			Rotation sums of squared loadings		
	Total	% of variance	Cumulative %	Total	% of variance	Cumulative %	Total	% of variance	Cumulative %
1	3.487	29.058	29.058	3.487	29.058	29.058	3.358	27.980	27.980
2	2.177	18.144	47.201	2.177	18.144	47.201	2.307	19.222	47.201
3	1.077	8.978	56.179						
4	0.818	6.816	62.995						
5	0.790	6.580	69.576						
6	0.761	6.340	75.916						
7	0.660	5.503	81.418						
8	0.608	5.068	86.486						
9	0.469	3.908	90.394						
10	0.448	3.735	94.129						
11	0.373	3.107	97.237						
12	0.332	2.763	100.000						

Source Primary data extraction

Table 7 Rotated component matrix

Factor	Variable	Factor loading
1	Conflict/arguments with parents	0.721
	Conflict/argument with professors/teachers	0.600
	Conflict with roommate or friend	0.692
	Conflict with others	0.647
	Fights between parents	0.664
	Low self-esteem	0.727
	Stress level when you use social media platforms and tend to compare your life with others	0.534
	How stressful do you feel when you are lonely or out of the group?	0.536
2	How stressful do you feel while paying your college fees?	0.772
	How stressed do you feel when you frequently have to ask for money from your guardians?	0.747
	Rate the stress you feel in designing a budget and sticking to that	0.778
	Mark the stress you feel when you happen to compare with the spending pattern of friends	0.580

Source Primary data

not only prepare the students to face the academic challenges but also gear them up to tackle the various challenges in life. Discipline and proper communication with teachers, friends, and roommates will help to reduce conflicts. Since conflicts highly influenced the students to feel stressed, both parties need to learn to compromise when needed and try to collaborate. The collaboration conflict resolution helps to find an amicable solution that will satisfy the respondent and the other party. This is a win–win situation for both and can ease stress in their lives. When the number of conflicts/arguments is reduced, the respondent can focus on more important things.

Students felt stressed about asking for money from guardians. To address this issue, students can take up paid internships. With the time in hand after regular classes, they can choose from the ample opportunities. Efforts need to be made from their side to grab the right opportunity. They can also invest time in learning about trading/investing in the stock market which is another way to invest and earn money. They must try to refrain from using credit cards as it increases debt and worry. The researchers recommend classes for managing personal finances as a management student must be taught the art of planning and controlling one's expenses and incomes.

At the classroom level, the teachers have the ability to mould and rightly shape the lives of the students. Apart from the regular curriculum, they can ensure that special attention is given to grooming the students in aspects like imparting emotional intelligence, regular budget management tips, and meditation programmes. As discussed, emotional intelligence will help students recognise and acknowledge their emotions which is the first step to handle or mitigate the negative impact of emotional stress. With the use of strength, weakness, opportunities, and threats (SWOT) analysis, every student must be aware of his/her strength and weakness. The peers and faculty must make efforts to recognise the talent and special skills of each student so that they feel a part of a group. This will help to reduce their feeling of loneliness. Patience and positive thinking are required to be imbibed among students. They need to be taught that one must learn to be content with what they have to that they learn to tackle their temptations and comparisons with the outside world. Students need to have a positive attitude to every situation so that they do not feel fearful in times of difficulty.

References

Agrawal, R. K., & Chahar, S. S. (2007). Examining role stress among technical students in India. *Social Psychology of Education, 10*(1), 77–91.

Cadaret, M. C., & Bennett, S. R. (2019). College students' reported financial stress and its relationship to psychological distress. *Journal of College Counseling, 22*(3), 225–239.

Chhetri, B., Goyal, L. M., Mittal, M., & Battineni, G. (2021). Estimating the prevalence of stress among Indian students during the COVID-19 pandemic: A cross-sectional study from India. *Journal of Taibah University Medical Sciences, 16*(2), 260–267.

Corporate Finance Institute. (n.d.). corporatefinanceinstitute.com. Retrieved 10th June, 2021 from corporatefinanceinstitute.com/resources: https://corporatefinanceinstitute.com/resources/knowledge/other/maslows-hierarchy-of-needs/

Glen, S. (n.d.). Retrieved June 10th, 2021, from https://www.statisticshowto.com/probability-and-statistics/statistics-definitions/cronbachs-alpha-spss/

Goleman, D. (1998, March). The emotionally competent leader. In *The Healthcare Forum Journal, 41*(2), 36–38.

Hassan, A., Sulaiman, T., & Ishak, R. (2009). Philosophy underlying emotional intelligence in relation to level of curiosity and academic achievement of rural area students. *Journal of Social Sciences, 5*(2), 95–103.

Hayhoe, C. R., Leach, L. J., Turner, P. R., Bruin, M. J., & Lawrence, F. C. (2000). Differences in spending habits and credit use of college students. *Journal of Consumer Affairs, 34*(1), 113–133.

Hindustan Times. (2020, November). hindustantimes.com. Retrieved from hindustantimes.com/jobs: With massive lay-offs of employees and suspension in several domestic industries burdened with curfew and lockdown, the families are experiencing financial difficulties.

Kai-Wen, C. (2009). A study of stress sources among college students in Taiwan. *Journal of Academic and Business Ethics, 2*, 1–8.

Kauts, D. S. (2016). Emotional intelligence and academic stress among college students. *Educational Quest, 7*(3), 149.

Kunju, S. S. (2017, April). ndtv.com. Retrieved 11th June, 2021 from ndtv.com/education. https://www.ndtv.com/education/world-health-day-2017-study-finds-37-per-cent-university-students-in-india-suffer-moderate-depressio-1679142

Mehta, M., Tewari, P., & Chandani, A. (2016). Employee engagement-review. *A Multidisciplinary Journal of Global Macro Trends, 5*(4), 81–97.

Mohzan, M. A. M., Hassan, N., & Abd Halil, N. (2013). The influence of emotional intelligence on academic achievement. *Procedia-Social and Behavioral Sciences, 90*, 303–312

Perwez, S. K. (2020). Stress among students studying in Higher Education Institutes (HEIS) in India. *Journal of Critical Review, 7*(14), 2020.

Robb, C. A. (2017). College student financial stress: Are the kids alright? *Journal of Family and Economic Issues, 38*(4), 514–527.

Sadri, G. (2012). Emotional intelligence and leadership development. *Public Personnel Management, 41*(3), 535–548.

Sinha, N. (2014). An assessment of role stress experienced by management students in India-Suggestive measures and strategies. *The International Journal of Indian Psychology, 1*(3), 147–160.

Urquijo, I., Extremera, N., & Azanza, G. (2019). The contribution of emotional intelligence to career success: Beyond personality traits. *International Journal of Environmental Research and Public Health, 16*(23), 4809.

Westefeld, J. S., Homaifar, B., Spotts, J., Furr, S., Range, L., & Werth, J. L. (2005). Perceptions concerning college student suicide: Data from four universities. *Suicide and Life-Threatening Behavior, 35*(6), 640–645.

A Study on Perception of Students Towards Online Classes in India

L. Lavanya

Abstract “eLearning doesn’t just “happen”! It requires careful planning and implementation” goes an anonymous quote. Unfortunately, the sudden shift to online teaching due to COVID-19 situation did not leave teachers and students a choice. The study was conducted in the wake of COVID-19 when colleges had to suddenly shift to online mode of teaching. Though teachers could get hold of teaching materials online, were the students comfortable to this shift? The call to shift gained more significance in some other aspects too—whether the students had the necessary accessories and connectivity to connect to the classes. Also, when they connected what were the challenges and how effective was the learning are some questions which opened up during these pandemic classes. The study was planned with this background, and the objectives of the study were:

1. To understand the purpose with which online classes started
2. To identify the understanding level of students
3. To bring out the issues felt by students
4. To analyse the differing requirements, if any, among different levels of study
5. To identify the preference of students towards online classes in future.

With this objective, data were collected from 123 students of UG and PG from arts and science colleges in Chennai. A structured questionnaire was prepared with 17 closed ended questions. Google Forms was used for data collection, and the students were reached through WhatsApp group and Email. Convenience and snowball sampling was used. A target of 100 students was planned, and by the cut-off date planned, 123 responses were received. As there were no missing data or information, all the samples collected were used for analysis with SPSS V.20. Frequency, chi-square, Friedman’s test, multiple response set, ANOVA and independent t-test have been used to analyse the data. The analysis revealed, inter alia, that

1. Majority of the respondents are girls and are in UG.
2. There is no association between demographic factors in the study and the variables of the study except gender.

L. Lavanya (✉)
Head Business Administration, Jeppiaar College of Arts and Science, Chennai, India

© The Author(s), under exclusive license to Springer Nature Singapore Pte Ltd. 2022

A. Chandani et al. (eds.), *Achieving $5 Trillion Economy of India*, Springer Proceedings in Business and Economics, https://doi.org/10.1007/978-981-16-7818-9_17

3. There is significant difference in certain aspects like need for more e-contents and class notes being shared among different levels of year of study.
4. More than 20% of the respondents had at least 3 issues related to taking up online classes.

It is important to note that though many studies have been conducted across the globe amidst pandemic with respect to students' perception towards online learning, it is significant that none of the studies focus on arts and science college students in Chennai, India. This study brings out the understanding of the problems faced by the students and the perception of the students to learn in a virtual environment. The scope of the study is limited to arts and science college students in Chennai and cannot be generalized to all streams of students. The data were collected in December 2020, and many changes in virtual platform have aroused interest in the mind of the researcher to do a follow-up study including the aspects of assessments, gamification in classroom and LMS which is not taken up in the present study. The practical implication of the study is that the college management should take into consideration the problems of the students and fine-tune the online classes accordingly.

Keywords Online classes · Students' perception · Virtual classroom · Preference · Online learning

1 Introduction and Background of the Study

"eLearning doesn't just "happen"! It requires careful planning and implementation" goes an anonymous quote. Unfortunately, the sudden shift to online teaching due to COVID-19 situation did not leave teachers and students a choice. The study was conducted in the wake of COVID-19 when colleges had to suddenly shift to online mode of teaching. Though teachers could get hold of teaching materials online, were the students comfortable to this shift? The call to shift gained more significance in some other aspects too—whether the students had the necessary gadgets and accessories and connectivity to connect to the classes. Also, when they connected what were the challenges and how effective was the learning are some questions which opened up during these pandemic classes.

While taking up these problems, the researcher went through a lot of existing theoretical and empirical researches which brought out that all the educational institutions adopted to this new method of teaching–learning process in a kind of overnight process, though it was present all along. It could be said that the circumstances forced the institutions to take this up which otherwise would have taken a really long time.

2 Literature Review and Research Gap

A surprisingly large review of the literature is available related to online classes, and some articles were many decades earlier in which researchers have tried to understand the perspectives of students in Web-based learning (Bennett & Bennett, 2002; Goodwin, 1993; Hara & Kling, 1999). Most research studies suggest that lack of immediate feedback is frustrating for the students in online learning.

Yang and Cornelius (2004) used qualitative methods to investigate the perceptions of students from two universities and one community college regarding the quality of online education based on their own online learning experiences. The study identified that lack of technical support from faculty, delayed feedback, monotonous instructional methods and poorly designed course content were the reasons for negative feelings of students in online classes.

Smart and Cappel (2006) examined students' perceptions of integrating online components in two undergraduate business courses where students completed online learning modules prior to class discussion. It was found that those who took up the course found it positive and those yet to opt found it marginally negative. It is concluded that instructors should be able to select and integrate online into classroom course where required.

Huss and Eastep (2013) in their study with 1085 college students (highest in any related research conducted till then) found that majority of the students opted online classes only when face-to-face was not an option. Preparedness for online classes by both teachers and students and the communication of work in clear terms were the major outcomes of the study.

Pasha and Gorya (2019) identified the use of integrated approach in online education. In their study in Hyderabad, they have found that the participants are aware of online learning methods and prefer online classes.

Though the above studies were conducted with the perspective of improvement in e-learning, the present study is about shifting to online due to pandemic. Interestingly, many researchers have contributed to this too.

Kulal and Nayak (2020) conducted a study that aims at analysing the perception of teachers and students about online classes. The study reveals that students are comfortable with online classes and are getting enough support from teachers, but they do not believe that online classes will replace traditional classroom teaching. It also finds that teachers are facing difficulties in conducting online classes due to a lack of proper training and development for doing online classes. Technical issues are the major problem for the effectiveness of the online classes.

Bączek et al. (2021) conducted a study among Polish medical students. The study brought out that the main advantages of online learning were the ability to stay at home, continuous access to online materials, learning at your own pace and comfortable surroundings. The study concluded stating that online teaching can be effective if more planned and active approach is taken up.

Muthuprasada et al. (2021) had studied student's perception and preference for online education. The participants were 307 agricultural graduates from different universities of National Agricultural Research System (NARS). It was found that curriculum pressure was the main reason for online classes. Technical competence of the faculty, interactivity and immediate feedback can make online classes effective.

Khan et al. (2021) in their study identified that online learning has emerged as the new way of learning for students. In their quantitative study of 184 university students in National Capital Territory of Delhi, it was found that students show a positive perception towards e-learning.

The above studies have sure touched on the topic related to student's perception on online learning. But, none of the studies have been conducted in understanding the perception of arts and science college students. The professional students and their colleges would have better infrastructure compared to arts and science students. So, this study aims to bridge the gap in the existing literature.

3 Objectives of the Study

The study was taken up in the above-mentioned background, and the objectives of the study were:

1. To understand the purpose with which online classes started
2. To identify the understanding level of students
3. To bring out the issues felt by students
4. To analyse the differing requirements, if any, among different levels of study
5. To identify the preference of students towards online classes in future.

4 Research Methodology

The study is descriptive research, and data were collected from 123 students of UG and PG from arts and science colleges in Chennai. A structured questionnaire was prepared with 17 closed ended questions.

The questionnaire had 3 parts—demographic and general information related to the study, perception of students towards online classes and problems in online classes. The questionnaire is provided as part of annexure at the end. The questions were keyed in on Google Forms and sent to students.

Google Forms was used for data collection, and the students were reached through WhatsApp group and Email. Convenience and snowball sampling was used. A target of 100 students was planned, and by the cut-off date planned, 123 responses were received. Google Forms is closed after the date to accept response. As there were no missing data or information, all the samples collected were used for analysis with SPSS V.20.

5 Scope of the Study

This study was done in the wake of COVID-19 when colleges had to suddenly shift to online mode of teaching. The data were collected among students studying in arts and science colleges in Chennai. The idea is that the students under arts and science stream do not have the technology access as equivalent to professional college students.

6 Reliability Test

Reliability test was done using Cronbach's alpha to understand the internal consistency between the items in the instrument to study the perception of students towards online classes.

Reliability statistics		
Cronbach's alpha	Cronbach's alpha based on standardized items	No. of items
0.882	0.899	6

Hotelling's *T*-squared test				
Hotelling's *T*-squared	*F*	*df*1	*df*2	Sig.
105.592	20.426	5	118	0.000

Going by the rule of George and Mallery (2003), Cronbach's alpha value of above 0.8 is good. Cronbach's alpha value for the questionnaire is 0.882 which indicates that the items have internal consistency. This also means that the perception of students towards online classes varies at 88% and that the statements in the instrument are understood at this level. Hotelling's *T*-squared is also found to be significant.

7 Analysis and Discussion

Analysis of the data is presented below. Part I of the analysis discusses the frequency analysis of demographic and other variables as mentioned below. Part II of the analysis brings out the independent *T*-test, ANOVA, chi-square and Friedman's test. Part III brings out the problems in online classes through multiple response set descriptives.

7.1 Part I

Part I of the analysis covers the demographic factors in the study like gender, level of course, year of study and also the other frequency tables related to:

1. Mode of online platform used
2. Objective of taking up online class
3. Preference towards audio or video classes
4. Preferred learning mode
5. Opening up to faculty in case of doubts/clarification (Tables 1, 2, 3, 4, 5, 6, 7, 8 and 9).

Table 1 Gender

		Frequency	Percent	Valid percent	Cumulative percent
Valid	Male	37	30.1	30.1	30.1
	Female	86	69.9	69.9	100.0
	Total	123	100.0	100.0	

Table 2 Level of course

		Frequency	Percent	Valid percent	Cumulative percent
Valid	UG	91	74.0	74.0	74.0
	PG	32	26.0	26.0	100.0
	Total	123	100.0	100.0	

Table 3 Year of study

		Frequency	Percent	Valid percent	Cumulative percent
Valid	I year	23	18.7	18.7	18.7
	II year	23	18.7	18.7	37.4
	III year	77	62.6	62.6	100.0
	Total	123	100.0	100.0	

Table 4 Mode of online platform attended

		Frequency	Percent	Valid percent	Cumulative percent
Valid	Webex	13	10.6	10.6	10.6
	Zoom	42	34.1	34.1	44.7
	Google Meet	57	46.3	46.3	91.1
	Other	11	8.9	8.9	100.0
	Total	123	100.0	100.0	

Table 5 What is the purpose of attending the online class?

		Frequency	Percent	Valid percent	Cumulative percent
Valid	Syllabus	31	25.2	25.2	25.2
	Doubt clarification	41	33.3	33.3	58.5
	Knowledge gaining	51	41.5	41.5	100.0
	Total	123	100.0	100.0	

Table 6 Do you prefer audio classes or video classes?

		Frequency	Percent	Valid percent	Cumulative percent
Valid	Audio classes	33	26.8	26.8	26.8
	Video classes	39	31.7	31.7	58.5
	Either	51	41.5	41.5	100.0
	Total	123	100.0	100.0	

Table 7 Do you feel any topic needed deeper explanation?

		Frequency	Percent	Valid percent	Cumulative percent
Valid	Yes	32	26.0	26.0	26.0
	No	35	28.5	28.5	54.5
	Maybe	56	45.5	45.5	100.0
	Total	123	100.0	100.0	

Table 8 If yes, did you provide your feedback to the faculty?

		Frequency	Percent	Valid percent	Cumulative percent
Valid	Yes	68	55.3	55.3	55.3
	No	55	44.7	44.7	100.0
	Total	123	100.0	100.0	

- Based on the frequency tables, it can be observed that around 70% of the respondents are female and around 30% are male students.

Table 9 Given a choice, what would be your preferred learning mode?

		Frequency	Percent	Valid percent	Cumulative percent
Valid	Virtual classroom	14	11.4	11.4	11.4
	Traditional classroom	65	52.8	52.8	64.2
	Blended classroom	44	35.8	35.8	100.0
	Total	123	100.0	100.0	

- Among the respondents, 74% are students pursuing UG and 26% are pursuing their PG course.
- 18.7% of the respondents are in I year and II year, and majority (62.6) of the students are in III year.
- 46.3% of the students are connecting through Google Meet, and the least used platform is Webex. Zoom is used by 34.1% of the respondents.
- The objective of attending online classes does vary among the students. Majority of the respondents (41.5%) attend online classes for gaining knowledge, whereas 33.3% attend for clarifying doubts and 25.2% feel it is for syllabus completion. This is in contrast to another research study Muthuprasada et al. (2021) which states majority of preferred online classes was for syllabus completion (cope with the curriculum).
- Majority (41.5%) of the respondents are comfortable with either audio or video classes. Around 26.8% of the students are not comfortable with turning on their video and prefer audio only mode during classes.
- 28.5% students feel that topics needed deeper explanation, and 55.3% of the students do not hesitate to ask their faculty if they need explanation.
- It is interesting to note that the majority of the respondents (52.8%) prefer to go back to traditional classroom, and 35.8% are in preference towards blended classroom.

7.2 *Part II*

Part II of the analysis brings out Friedman's independent *T*-test, ANOVA and chi-square test.

7.2.1 Student's Perception Towards Online Classes

Friedman Test

Friedman test was conducted to understand the presence of pattern in data and rank the variables related to the purpose of online class. The test statistics indicate that the test is highly significant ($p < 0.05$). The mean ranks reveal that usefulness of the sessions is the primary reason for attending online classes (Table 10). Additional e-contents and content clarity ranked second and third which shows that the students are ready to take classes in which their knowledge gaining can be enhanced. This can be correlated with Table 5 which shows that the main reason for attending online classes is knowledge gaining (Table 11).

Table 10 Ranks

	Mean rank
Objective of the sessions	3.63
Usefulness of the sessions	4.14
Content clarity	3.65
Sufficiency of notes shared	3.51
Additional e-contents shared	3.79
Preference to online class	2.28

Table 11 Test statistics[a]

N	123
Chi-square	131.380
d*f*	5
Asymp. Sig.	0.000

[a]Friedman Test

7.2.2 Testing Difference in Perception Among UG and PG Students

The difference in perception among UG and PG students is tested through independent *t*-test.

H0: There is no difference in the perception of UG and PG students towards e-content requirement, i.e. $\mu_{(UG)} = \mu_{(PG)}$ ("the two population means are equal").

H1: There is difference in the perception of UG and PG students towards e-content requirement, i.e. $\mu_{(UG)} \neq \mu_{(PG)}$ ("the two population means are not equal").

From Table 12, it is found that Leven's t-test is not significant. It can be concluded that there is no significant difference between the perceptions of UG and PG students with respect to:

(a) Sufficiency of notes shared in online class
(b) Additional e-contents being useful for enhancing knowledge

The mean values of UG students (3.84, 4.02) and PG students (3.78 and 3.91) indicate that they strongly agree towards sufficient notes being shared in class and the e-contents shared are useful for both the groups.

From Tables 13 and 14, it is found that Leven's t-test is significant. It can be concluded that there is a significant difference between the perceptions of male and female students. The meanwise comparison indicates mean value of male students is 3.35 and 3.81 which indicates moderate agreement to sufficiency of notes and e-contents provided. Mean value of female students' opinion is 4.02 and 4.07 which indicates strong agreement towards sufficiency of notes and e-contents provided.

Table 12 Independent sample test

		Levene's test for equality of variances		*T*-test for equality of means			
		F	Sig.	*t*	d*f*	Sig. (2-tailed)	Mean difference
Sufficiency of notes	Equal variances assumed	0.001	0.972	0.215	121	0.830	0.054
	Equal variances not assumed			0.216	54.777	0.830	0.054
Additional e-contents shared are useful for enhancing knowledge	Equal variances assumed	1.875	0.173	0.538	121	0.592	0.116
	Equal variances not assumed			0.475	44.622	0.637	0.116

Table 13 Independent sample test

		Levene's test for equality of variances		*T*-test for equality of means			
		F	Sig.	*t*	d*f*	Sig. (2-tailed)	Mean difference
Sufficiency of notes	Equal variances assumed	3.074	0.082	– 2.897	121	0.004	– 0.672
	Equal variances not assumed			– 2.660	57.060	0.010	– 0.672
Additional e-contents shared are useful for enhancing knowledge	Equal variances assumed	0.736	0.393	– 1.265	121	0.208	– 0.259
	Equal variances not assumed			– 1.192	60.077	0.238	– 0.259

Table 14 Group statistics

	Gender	*N*	Mean	Std. deviation	Std. error mean
Sufficiency of notes	Male	37	3.35	1.358	0.223
	Female	86	4.02	1.095	0.118
Additional e-contents shared are useful for enhancing knowledge	Male	37	3.81	1.151	0.189
	Female	86	4.07	0.992	0.107

Table 15 ANOVA

		Sum of squares	*df*	Mean square	*F*	Sig.
Sufficiency of notes	Between groups	0.765	2	0.382	0.347	0.707
	Within groups	132.227	120	1.102		
	Total	132.992	122			
Additional e-contents shared are useful for enhancing knowledge	Between groups	0.494	2	0.247	0.165	0.848
	Within groups	179.571	120	1.496		
	Total	180.065	122			

7.2.3 Testing Difference in Perception Based on year of Study

Testing difference in perception among first-, second- and third-year students with respect to e-content requirement was done using ANOVA.

H0: There is no significant difference between year of study and e-content requirement, i.e. $\mu_{(\text{I year})} = \mu_{(\text{II year})} = \mu_{(\text{III year})}$ (no difference among group means).

H1: There is significant difference between year of study and e-content requirement, i.e. $\mu_{(\text{I year})} \neq \mu_{(\text{II year})} \neq \mu_{(\text{III year})}$ (no difference among group means).

From Table 15, it is found that the students in different years of study—I year, II year and III year—do not have a difference in the e-content requirement and agree to the availability of class notes and the additional e-contents from their teacher.

7.2.4 Preferred Mode of Learning—Association Test

The association between preferred modes of learning with level of course, year of study and gender is done using chi-square test.

H01: There is no significant association between level of course and their preferred mode of learning (virtual, traditional, blended).

H02: There is no significant association between year of study and their preferred mode of learning (virtual, traditional, blended).

H03: There is no significant association between gender and their preferred mode of learning (virtual, traditional, blended).

From Tables 16, 17 and 18, it can be observed that Pearson chi-square is significant ($P < 0.05$) and hence the null hypotheses are rejected. It is revealed from the chi-square tests that the preferred mode of learning varies among students in:

(a) UG or PG.
(b) I year, II year or III year.
(c) Male or female.

So, it is important to understand these differences and plan virtual or traditional (face-to-face) or blended classroom going forward in future after the pandemic. A

Table 16 Level of course and learning mode

Crosstab—level of course * preferred learning mode

		Given a choice, what would be your preferred learning mode?			Total
		Virtual Classroom	Traditional Classroom	Blended Classroom	
Level of Course	UG	5	51	35	91
	PG	9	14	9	32
Total		14	65	44	123

Chi-square tests

	Value	*df*	AmoR-sig. (2-sided)
Pearson chi-square	12.037	2	002
Likelihood ratio	10.450	2	005
No. of valid cases	123		

Table 17 Year of study and learning mode

Crosstab—year of study * preferred learning mode

		Given a choice, what would be your preferred learning mode?			Total
		Virtual classroom	Traditional classroom	Blended classroom	
Year of study	I year	7	11	5	23
	II year	5	10	8	23
	III year	2	44	31	77
Total		14	65	44	123

Chi-square tests

	Value	*df*	AmoR-sig. (2-sided)
Pearson chi-square	17.190	4	002
Likelihood ratio	17.010	4	002
No. of valid cases	123		

similar finding was reported by Bączek et al. (2021) in a research among medical students.

7.3 *Part III*

Part III of the analysis brings out the problems faced by students in online classes. It is done with the help of multiple response set in SPSS.

Table 18 Level of course and learning mode

Cross tab—gender * preferred learning mode

		Given a choice, what would be learning mode?		your preferred	Total
		Virtual classroom	Traditional classroom	Blended classroom	
Gender	Male	11	19	7	37
	Female	3	46	37	86
Total		14	65	44	123

Chi-square tests

	Value	*df*	Asxim Sig. (2-sided)
Pearson chi-square	19.875	2	000
Likelihood ratio	18.789	2	000
No. of valid cases	123		

7.3.1 Challenges in Online Learning

The challenges in online learning had been collected as a multiple response option. So, data were cleaned and multiple response option was used for understanding issues faced by students.

Table 19 indicates 66.7% of the students face at least one of the issues during online classes and 2.4% of the students have about 4 issues. The exact issues chosen by the students are presented in the below table.

Table 19 Multiple response set

		Frequency	Percent	Valid percent	Cumulative percent
Valid	1.00	82	66.7	66.7	66.7
	2.00	29	23.6	23.6	90.2
	3.00	9	7.3	7.3	97.6
	4.00	3	2.4	2.4	100.0
	Total	123	100.0	100.0	

1—Number of students who chose one issue, 2—students who chose two issues, 3—students who chose 3 issues and 4—students who chose

$issues in online class frequencies				
		Responses		Percent of cases (%)
		N	Percent (%)	
Issues	1	63	35.2	51.2
	2	13	7.3	10.6
	3	36	20.1	29.3
	4	25	14.0	20.3
	5	16	8.9	13.0
	6	26	14.5	21.1
Total		179	100.0	145.5

1—Network issues. 2—Students talking parallelly. 3—Students not having access to laptop or smartphone. 4—Do not feel connected with the class. 5—Not comfortable with online tools. 6—Students not having Wi-Fi or data connection

This table provides that network issues are the top problem faced by the respondents. At least, 35.2% of the students are affected by this. 20% of students do not have access to laptop or smartphone which is another great setback to online classes. This shows that network and gadget issue need to be addressed on priority. Chakraborty et al. (2020) in their study concluded that Internet issue is the major thing to be addressed in the present-day context. Many other studies have also been highlighting the issue of digital divide in our country.

The least faced problem as observed from the data is students talking parallelly in the class (7.3%) and comfort level with online tools (8.9%). Yang and Cornelius (2004), in their study, highlight that monotonous classrooms cause negative opinion on online classes which is similar to our study which states that 14% of the students do not feel connected with online classes.

8 Findings and Suggestions

The major findings of the study are:

1. Majority of the respondents are women and are in UG.
2. It is interesting to note that the majority of the respondents (52.8%) prefer to go back to traditional classroom and 35.8% are in preference towards blended classroom.
3. Majority attend online classes for knowledge gaining.
4. Students give usefulness of classes as an important factor in attending online classes.
5. Level of study and e-content requirement did not have a significant difference, whereas it was significant for gender.
6. Using ANOVA, it was found that year of study and e-content requirement had a significant difference.

7. Using chi-square, it was identified that gender, year of study and level of study have an association with e-content requirement.
8. Multiple response analysis showed that network issues were a major hindrance for online classes.

The study identifies that the students are comfortable with online classes though there are issues in taking up them. Based on the findings, the following suggestions are proposed by the researcher for the colleges to take up:

1. There is a need to create awareness among PG students in gaining exposure towards additional e-contents and knowledge gaining activities.
2. The faculty has to provide varying levels of e-contents to the students in first, second and third year of study.
3. Students can be guided to options of getting recorded materials in case they miss classes due to network or other issues.
4. Faculty need to provide engaging activities online as many students have the feeling of not having a connect in the virtual classes.
5. Faculty need to be trained on quizzes and games so that they go beyond PPTs and Google Forms for teaching and assessment.

9 Limitations and Directions for Further Research

The scope of the study is limited to arts and science college students in Chennai and cannot be generalized to all streams of students. The data were collected in December 2020, and many changes in virtual platform have aroused interest in the mind of the researcher to do a follow-up study including the aspects of assessments, gamification in classroom and LMS which is not taken up in the present study.

10 Conclusion

In conclusion, it can be said that though the shift happened suddenly, despite constraints, students and teachers have started moving to this new method of teaching–learning. Considering the digital divide, it may take years to bridge the gap and have a fully oriented online learning. It is important to note that not only equipment, electricity and network coverage also to be completely provided for challenges free learning. The role of teachers cannot be ruled out. Blended learning is expected to be the way forward. Technology, in the hands of teachers, can really transform students.

Annexure I: A Study on Perception of Students Towards Online Classes in India

Dear Students,

Kindly fill this questionnaire based on your online classroom learning experience. This is for research purpose and will be strictly confidential.

Regards,

Dr. Lavanya L.

Part I General Information

1. Name
2. Gender

   1. Male 2. Female 3. Other

3. Level of Course

   1. UG 2. PG

4. Year of Study

   1.I year 2. II year 3. III year

5. Mode of online class attended

   1. Webex 2. Zoom 3. Google Meet 4. Other

6. Main purpose of attending online classes were for

   1. Syllabus 2. Doubt Clarification 3. Knowledge Gaining

7. Do you feel any topic needed deeper explanation?

   1. Yes 2. No 3. Maybe

8. If yes, did your provide your feedback to the faculty?

   1. Yes 2. No

Part II Perception Towards Online Classes

Statement	Strongly disagree	Disagree	Netural	Agree	Strongly agree
9. Was the objective of the sessions met?	1	2	3	4	5
10. Were the sessions useful?	1	2	3	4	5
11. Was the contents of the class clear?	1	2	3	4	5
12. Was the notes of the class shared sufficient?	1	2	3	4	5

(continued)

(continued)

Statement	Strongly disagree	Disagree	Netural	Agree	Strongly agree
13. Are additional e-contents shared by your teacher for enhancing knowledge?	1	2	3	4	5
14. Do you feel online classes are better than traditional classrooms?	1	2	3	4	5

Part III Problems in Online Classes

15. Did you face connection issues during the class?

    1. Yes 2. No 3. Sometimes

16. Do you prefer audio classes or video classes?

    1. Audio 2. Video 3. Either is OK

17. In your opinion, what are the main problems in online class? (you can choose more than one option)

S. No.	Statement	Please tick if applicable
1	Network issues	
2	Students talking parallely	
3	Students not having access to laptop or smartphone	
4	Don't feel connected with the class	
5	Not comfortable with online tools	
6	Students not having WiFi or data connection	

18. Given a choice, what would be your preferred learning mode?

    1. Traditional Classroom 2. Virtual Classroom 3. Blended

    Thank you for your time!

References

Bączek, M., Zagańczyk-Bączek, M., Szpringer, M., Jaroszyński, A., Wożakowska-Kapłon, B. (2021). Perception of online learning during the COVID-19 pandemic. *Medicine, 100*(7), e24821. https://doi.org/10.1097/MD.0000000000024821

Bennett, J. F., & Bennett, L. B. (2002). Assessing the quality of distance education programs: The faculty's perspective. *Journal of Computing in Higher Education, 13*(2), 71–86.

Chakraborty, P., Mittal, P., Gupta, M.S., Yadav, S., & Arora, A. (2020). Opinion of students on online education during the COVID-19 pandemic, First published: 17 December 2020. https://doi.org/10.1002/hbe2.240

George, D., & Mallery, P. (2003). *SPSS for windows step by step: A simple guide and reference. 11.0 update* (4th ed.). Allyn & Bacon.

Goodwin, B.N. (1993). A study of the perceptions and attitudes exhibited by distance education students and faculty at the University of Phoenix online programs, Unpublished doctoral dissertation, Colorado State University, (UMI No.9424186) cited from Yi Yanga and Linda (2004).

Hara, N., & Kling, R. (1999). Students' frustrations with a web-based distance education course. *First Monday*, *4*(12). https://doi.org/10.5210/fm.v4i12.710

Huss, J.A., Eastep, S. (2013). The perceptions of students toward online learning at a Midwestern University: What are students telling us and what are we doing about it? *Inquiry in Education, 4*(2), Article 5. Retrieved from https://digitalcommons.nl.edu/ie/vol4/iss2/5

Khan, M.A.; Vivek; Nabi, M.K.; Khojah, M.; Tahir, M (2021). Students' perception towards e-learning during COVID-19 pandemic in India: An empirical study. *Sustainability, 13*, 57.https://doi.org/10.3390/su13010057

Kulal & Nayak. (2020). A study on perception of teachers and students toward online classes in Dakshina Kannada and Udupi District. *Asian Association of Open Universities Journal, 15*(3).

Muthuprasada, T., Aiswarya, S., Adityaa, K.S., Jhaa, G.K. (2021). Students' perception and preference for online education in India during COVID-19 pandemic. *Social Sciences & Humanities Open, 3*(1), 100101.

Pasha, A., & Gorya, J. (2019). Student preference and perception towards online education in Hyderabad City. *International Journal of Trend in Scientific Research and Development (IJTSRD), 3*(3), 656–659. ISSN: 2456-6470. http://www.ijtsrd.com/papers/ijtsrd22876.pdf

Smart, K.L., & Cappel, J.J. (2006). Students' perceptions of online learning: A comparative study. *Journal of Information Technology Education, 5*.

Yang, Y., & Cornelius, L.F. (2004). Students' perceptions towards the quality of online education: A qualitative approach. https://eric.ed.gov/?id=ED485012. Retrieved June 10, 2021.

Indian Knowledge Tradition and Research

Sapna Sharma

Abstract India is not only a historic country but also a cremation ground. All the Rishi Munis took birth in India. If we talk about knowledge tradition, then the first word comes to our mind is '*Veda*'. And if the researcher wants to know about the history, then he quotes Vedas. Scholars of Indian scriptures have come into its grip and started to interpret *Sanatan* scriptures. Vedas include social order, policy, etc. The knowledge tradition has its own characteristics, its place of learning, its texts, and their classification. India has always been known about the knowledge tradition and a knowledge culture. Ancient civilizations are accepting India's debt in the field of knowledge. If we talk of knowledge, it is based on language, philosophy, inescapability of knowledge, folk, Sculptures. In India, there has been an unbroken series of *Acharyas, Rishis, Granthas,* etc., and teaching and learning took place through gurukul system. Students learnt about *Vedas, Vedangas, Smiritis and Stutis*. Education was imparted orally. There was a *guru–shishya* tradition. From the Vedic period, the knowledge tradition was high. Be it Taxila, Nalanda or *Vikramshila* University. But now this is more westward tilt. Indians are getting knowledge but just to get jobs in sake of earning money. But they are losing their culture, tradition, custom and ethic. So today, there is a need to find the treasure of this knowledge hidden in ancient text to groom it and use it for human welfare. There is need to research on these texts and let India to be connected to its origin.

Keywords Indian knowledge tradition · Research · Vedas · Yoga

1 Introduction

According to Wikipedia, 'Knowledge is the familiarity, awareness or understanding of someone or something such as facts, information, description, skills acquired through experience or education by perceiving, discovery or learning. It can be theoretical or learning'. The philosopher Plato defined knowledge as 'justify true belief'.

Sapna Sharma (✉)
Jayoti Vidyapeeth Women's University, Jharna, Jaipur, India

© The Author(s), under exclusive license to Springer Nature Singapore Pte Ltd. 2022
A. Chandani et al. (eds.), *Achieving $5 Trillion Economy of India*, Springer Proceedings in Business and Economics, https://doi.org/10.1007/978-981-16-7818-9_18

Knowledge is related to capacity of acknowledgment in human being (http://www.wikipedia.org/wiki/knowledge).

According to Wikipedia, 'Tradition is a belief or behavior (Folk custom) passed down within a group or society with symbolic meaning. Tradition has been derived from the Latin word '*tradere*' meaning to translate, to handover, to give for safe-keeping. Tradition can also be referred as belief or customs that are of prehistoric age, passed orally through poetic devices' (http://www.wikipedia.org/wiki/Tradition).

India has always known to be as 'knowledge society'. It is derived from the word VID which means to know 'Vedas as Shruti' which is considered as fountain head which can be known as knowledge tradition.

According to this, Rishi Munis composed the Vedic hymns, mantras. '*These hymns are and will be always there unchanging beyond our changing world*' according to N. Kazanas. So, Vedic mantras are called to be created by god or as '*Nitya*' and '*Apaurusheya*'.

What we call today modern knowledge has been mastered by our ancient scholar like 'Panini' (fourth century BCE) grammar. '*The Ashtadhyayi*' is the first completely developed grammar of any human language. In *etymology, Yaska's Nirukta (seventh century BCE)* was first serious work being *Yaska* the first scholar to treat etymology. Calculus was first discovered in Kerala School of Mathematics. If we take today's linguistic, the three disciplines are from Vedic knowledge, i.e., '*Shiksha, Nirukta, Vyakarna, Jyotisha, Chhanda and Kapla*' (http://www.indiatimes.com/theindicknowledgetradition).

According to linguistic and Indologist Kapil Kapoor, 'Indian thinkers were not hesitant in drawing information from all sectors of knowledge to build 'Knowable". It is a perception of unity of existence with relativism and truism, and it uses 'either/or both logic'.

He also stated that 'knowledge tradition of India are continuous and cumulative. They are tactual and exegetical traditions in different areas of thought and experience, philosophy, medicine, grammar, architecture, geography, literary theory, polity, etc. Concept and technical vocabulary of these tradition are still a part of thinking and language of modern India' (http://www.ancientscienceoflife.org/textbook).

2 Literature Review

If we talk about knowledge, three words come to our mind 'Darshan' (system) then the point of view which reads to 'Jnana' (knowledge) gathered in systematized in organized manner for reflection and pedagogy is called '*Vidya*' (discipline). Our entire body is divided into two sets '*Para Vidya*' and '*Apra Vidya*', the knowledge of ultimate principle, i.e., '*Paramatma*' or '*Brahma*'. The knowledge which is gained by eyes is '*Bahirmukhi*' directed toward outer world and the other, and the whole cognizing self is '*Antarmukhi*' (turned inward). To acquire '*Antarmukhi*' knowledge, the knower has to go through '*Sadhna*'.

As we all know, knowledge is constituted in minds, so there is requirement of oral culture. Which is transmitted in '*guru–shishya*' mode? In this, scholar has library in his mind and with high-speed processing. It also explains the puzzling requirement in scholastic tradition for a scholar to be master of fourteen disciplines.

The Indian tradition talks about 18 major *Vidyas* (theoretical) and 64 kalas applied. 18 Vidyas are 'four subsidiary Vedas, Puran, Nyaya, Mimasa, Dharma shastra, *Vedangas*, six auxiliary science, phonetics, grammar, meter, astronomy, rituals, philology'. Knowledge is classified into subset, i.e., 'Satvik Jnana' of non-difference, 'Raj Sika Jnana' of many existence, 'Tamsika Jnana' which clings to one body, to self and its trivial (http://www.iks.iitgn.ac.in/2016/01/kapilkapoor-indianknowledgesystem).

According to Professor Sharma, the Indian knowledge believes in religion, meaning, work and salvation. The rise and fall of culture is not its economic status but a knowledge tradition.

Swami Divyanand Tirth stated that ideology of Karl Marx and Simon Freud has consumed the whole world. One gives the importance to the other, but Indian philosophy has given importance to both. Artha is associated with religion, and Kama is associated with salvation. Indian knowledge considered religion, *Artha*, *Kama* and *Moksha* only. We cannot go to Bali temple wearing Western dresses.

In a lecture at Hindi Bhawan the president of philosophy department, Sagar University stated Indian knowledge tradition as it is not root but freedom to use discretion in the continuous migration (http://www.patrika.com/ampnews/indian-knowledgetradition).

According to space scientist Om Prakash Pandey, 'the Indian tradition of knowledge is one thousand year old'. He stated that we once again can become the world guru by studying the tradition of knowledge. There is a need to change the mind-set and adapt the Indianness input lives. We have insulted the ancient Indian tradition by presenting every subject from the perspective of west. There has been hundred of great men like '*Aryabatta, Charak Rishi, Nagaarjun, Harshvardhan,* Agastya Rishi, Bhardwaj Rishi' who have enriched the knowledge tradition of India. He stressed that youngster should try to understand the knowledge tradition of India by reading four Vedas and Upanishads, etc. (http://www.bhaskar.com).

According to Wikipedia, the Vedas are large body of religious text originating in ancient India. Vedas are also called Shruti (what is heard), literature distinguishing it from other religious text called Smirti (what is remember) (apte, 1965). The Vedic hymns assert themselves that they were created by rishis (Sages). In Hindu epic Mahabharata, the creation of Veda is credited to Brahma (Seer of fifth Veda; Krsna and DVaipayana Vyasa in the Mahabharata). There are four Vedas, i.e., 'Rigveda, Yajurveda, Samaveda and Atharvaveda' (Bloomfield, xxxx; Flood, 1996). Each Veda has been subclassified into four text types, i.e., 'Samhitas, Aranyakas, Brahmanas and Upanishads' (https://en.wikipedia.org/wiki/Vedas).

The Upanishads are ancient Sanskrit text of spiritual teaching and ideas of Hinduism. They are part of Vedas also called Vedantas, i.e., last chapter of Vedas. The concept of Brahman and Atman is central idea of all Upanishads (http://www.wikipedia.org/wiki/Upnishad).

3 Discussion

India has been the treasurer of intellectual activity during ancient and medieval times. This activity was related to various fields of study of text like Vedas, Upanishads, scriptures, science and art. India is a diverse country having multiplicity of thoughts, language, styles of livings with different artistic and scientific works done by the people. In ancient India, the rich knowledge tradition included branches of knowledge (Vedangas) and other discipline. Indians believe knowledge (Vidya) as the only real wealth. Ancient knowledge has been passed from generation to generation in the form of gurukuls where *guru–shishya* relationship flourishes. It was totally oral as only two organs were needed, i.e., *guru's* mouth and *shishya's* ear (http://google.com/mow-3rd-conference-sudha-gopalkrishna).

Every *Mantra* in *Veda* can be categorized into *Rik* (Mantra of divine conscientiousness), *Yajus* (Mantra of divine power), *Saman* (Mantra of divine Ananda) and *Athavana* (incantations) (http://google.com/hsbv.org/vedas).

Shankaracharya, an early eighth-century philosopher consolidated the doctrine of Advaita Vedanta which refers to idea that the soul or Atman is same as Brahman. He focused on Brahman, Atman, Vidya, Avidya, Maya, Karma, Moksha. His teachings and tradition were based on Smartism, founded four Mathas and influenced Santmat lineages (http://google.com/Wikipedia/adi-shankracharya).

According to Kapil Kapoor, 'The ancient Indian tradition is oral one but produce larger body of knowledge test. The sage sees with his eyes shut, and knowledge arises within. The creation, storage, dissemination and transmission of knowledge from one generation to other were through oral method' (http://youtube.com/oraltraditionsofindia-Drkapilkapoor).

Indian knowledge tradition also consists of Yoga Sutra. i.e., collection of 196 Sanskrit sutras on practice and theory related to Yoga. It was compiled by sage Patanjali in India who synthesized and organized knowledge tradition about Yoga. It relies on three Pranamas, i.e., Pratyaksha, Anumana and Shabda (http://wikipedia.org/yogasutraofpatanjali).

4 Impact of COVID-19 on Indian Knowledge Tradition

In modern age, we have accepted modern tradition and ignored ancient knowledge tradition. It's like we are ignoring the ideals of Gandhi but other countries like America, University of West Virginia, University of Hawaii have accepted them. We are ignoring our self-respect, national pride, our culture-rich heritage. This change is going to take us to decline. In ancient, youth have ideals, principles, ideas. Their thoughts and behavior were laced with Indian culture but now its not so (www.aaryalhd.blockspot.com).

Our original culture 'Vasudhev Kutumbhkam' is missing in today's culture. It is denoted by Mr Rajnath Singh (Former Defense Minister) that it is necessary to give values to children while imparting them knowledge. Only knowledge which is laced with values is beneficial for the society (http://www.outlookindia.com).

Several guidelines have been issued by NITI Aayog for the public or their safety against COVID-19 and suggested people to follow tradition and practice to help in boosting the body's defense system. He suggested to eat traditional food, use 'Mitti ke bartan, drinking water in tamba pot', etc., doing Yogasana, washing hands, leaving footwear outside the house which were practiced by our ancestors as a tradition (http://www.niti.gov.in/19-traditionandpracticestoboostimmuneagainstCovid19).

5 Conclusion

As we all know, modern science is based on knowledge tradition but it is up to its extinction, which was helpful to save ourselves from different problems. There is a need to revive knowledge tradition and establish it with research. Today, we are getting all education from outside so we are not able to move forward.

The scientific side of our knowledge tradition should be exposed to the people for their benefit. Various fields like agriculture, art, water, biodiversity should be linked with knowledge, suggestion and new scientific aspect should be searched.

In every field like maths, linguistic, logic, aesthetic, management, science, the Indian knowledge tradition insights are developed for its relevancy and valuableness. Many researchers are discovering new aspect due to their personal curiosity and dedication. Recent conferences played a vital role in raising awareness of the richness and necessity of knowledge tradition.

However, it is necessary to educate the younger generation in India's traditional knowledge at large scale and curbing their collective intellectual expertise for further research and innovation under the aegis of formal higher education.

So, it is time to rethink and review our ancient knowledge tradition and transfers it to our coming generation so that our youth should become responsible and cultured and try to change their attitude and behavior by teaching them various knowledge of tradition.

References

http://www.wikipedia.org/wiki/knowledge
http://www.wikipedia.org/wiki/Tradition
http://www.indiatimes.com/theindicknowledgetradition
http://www.ancientscienceoflife.org/textbook
http://www.iks.iitgn.ac.in/2016/01/kapilkapoor-indianknowledgesystem
http://www.patrika.com/ampnews/indian-knowledgetradition
http://www.bhaskar.com
apte. (1965). p. 887

Seer of fifth Veda; Krsna and DVaipayana Vyasa in the Mahabharata, Bruce M. Sullivan, 1999, Biograghy & Autobiography

Flood, G. (1996). *An introduction to Hinduism* (pp. 35–39). Cambridge University Press, ISBN 978–0521438780.

Bloomfield, M. *The Atharva Veda and Gopatha—Brahmana,1989 (Grundriss der indo-arischen philologies und Altertumskunde;2,i,b)*

https://en.wikipedia.org/wiki/Vedas

http://www.wikipedia.org/wiki/Upnishad

http://google.com/mow-3rd-conference-sudha-gopalkrishna

http://google.com/hsbv.org/vedas

http://google.com/Wikipedia/adi-shankracharya

http://youtube.com/oraltraditionsofindia-Drkapilkapoor

http://wikipedia.org/yogasutraofpatanjali

http://www.aaryalhd.blockspot.com/2018

http://www.outlookindia.com

http://www.niti.gov.in/19-traditionandpracticestoboostimmuneagainstCovid19

Vipassana Meditation: An Effective Way to Enhance Employee Contribution in Fostering Organizational Growth

Seema Pradhan

Abstract Very rapid and transforming changes are happening in all fields, thanks to the digital revolution in technology. This has created worldwide challenges as well as opportunities. However, in addition to technical knowledge and efficiency, psychological qualities like well-being, interpersonal skills, self-confidence, remain critically important. This empirical study attempts to measure the effect on employees' behavior, personality and psychological well-being by using Vipassana meditation as an intervention. For this purpose, 240 meditator and non-meditator employees were administered an instrument comprising of a psychological well-being scale and a specially designed behavior measure scale to study how mindfulness intervention affects personality and behavior. The data was analyzed using SPSS Ver. 20.0. The results indicated higher values for meditator employees on nine measures of behavior, personality and well-being. These scores indicated that they enjoyed higher self-confidence, interpersonal skills, equanimity, empathy, engagement and growth leading to better work ethic, teamwork and growth. It was not possible to adopt a "Before and After" study design due to the limitation of time available for completion of the study. The behavioral and personality changes that take place due to VM practice are subjective. In the future, it will be interesting to study these subjective changes in meditators by using a long-term study spanning over a few years.

Keywords Behavior · Employees · Personality · Psychological well-being · Vipassana meditation

1 Introduction

It is now widely accepted in business that workplace culture is a critical determinant of workplace productivity. The combination of behaviors and attitudes of people is what constitutes their culture and determines what they do and how they feel about what they do. The fast pace of technological innovations taking place resulting

S. Pradhan (✉)
Consultant Psychologist and Psychotherapist, Fortis Hospitals, Bangalore, India

© The Author(s), under exclusive license to Springer Nature Singapore Pte Ltd. 2022
A. Chandani et al. (eds.), *Achieving $5 Trillion Economy of India*, Springer Proceedings in Business and Economics, https://doi.org/10.1007/978-981-16-7818-9_19

in better workplace productivity is, however, mandating that people change their attitudes and habits as also their life styles if they are to accept and incorporate these technological innovations in their daily lives. Over time, this also impacts their culture and behavior.

The atmosphere at the workplace plays a significant role in shaping an individuals' life and well-being as well as that of the community (Harter et al., 2002). Spirituality at the workplace therefore influences human behavioral attributes such as personal development, honesty, job commitment, trusting others, finding meaning and joy at work thus enhancing employee well-being (Petchsawange & Duchon, 2012).

Recent scientific discoveries regarding brain development have confirmed that an individuals' early formative period plays a primary role in developing reactive patterns of behavior. Reactive patterns of behavior do not harness the complete capacity of human energy. Efficient and effective use of this energy is dependent on the choices we make from moment to moment. The productivity and safety in human endeavors are related to consciousness (Goleman, 1995). The important role that consciousness plays in human psyche that modern science is beginning to emphasize that was articulated by the Buddha 2500 years ago, in his teachings.

According to Ferguson (1981), meditation is a "technique to actualize and integrate the personality of human beings to fulfill states of personal integration". Maslow (1968) stated that self-actualization includes "increased acceptance of self, of others, and of nature's superior perception of reality" which is in tune with meditation objectives. Of late, significant research efforts are being done to study the benefits of Vipassana meditation (VM) in a workplace setting. Research on mindfulness, which stems from VM, has highlighted improvement in many aspects such as memory, resiliency, interpersonal relationships, enjoyment in addition to job performance and commitment (Glomb et al., 2011; Levy et al., 2012).

Buddha introduced the concept of "sangha" which espoused democratic principles of organization such as coexisting in harmony, sharing of knowledge and is similar to contemporary management principles. Buddha in his teachings emphasized the value of self-reliance to transform oneself (Gopalakrishna, 2006).

All these aspects suggested that we conduct a study which is empirical in nature to measure the effectiveness of VM with respect to behavior as well as psychological well-being of the employees. Coping with stress, emotional intelligence, interpersonal relationships and work place spirituality were the four constructs employed to design a questionnaire for this purpose (Pradhan & Ajithkumar, 2017a). In case of psychological well-being, a standardized questionnaire (Mehrotra et al., 2013) was administered. The findings were analyzed statistically, and conclusions were drawn which validate the research hypothesis put forth by us.

2 Literature Review

2.1 *Behavior and Personality*

Behavior is defined as "the way in which one acts or conducts oneself, especially toward others" (Merriam Webster's Dictionary, 2015). Ossorio (2006) observed that "all behavior is describable as an attempt on the part of an individual to bring about some state of affairs—either to effect a change from one state of affairs to another, or to maintain a currently existing one". In the course of their life, individuals attempt to improve or change their behavior in more desired ways through various methods. The interventions to alter behavior work best when they are directed toward the real causes of undesirable behavior while being focused on the removal of barriers that hinder the change.

Allport's (1961) view of personality is "… the dynamic organization within the person of the psychological and physical systems that underlie that person's patterns of actions, thoughts, and feelings". Personality is "individual differences in characteristic patterns of thinking, feeling and behaving. The study of personality focuses on two broad areas: One is understanding individual differences in particular personality characteristics, such as sociability or irritability. The other is understanding how the various parts of a person come together as a whole" (Kazdin, 2000).

Personalities are comprised of traits, which are the characteristics influencing our behavior across many situations. Introversion, friendliness, conscientiousness, honesty and helpfulness are important personality traits as they help us to understand consistencies in behavior.

The literature review resulted in the identification of four constructs which influence individual behavior and personality and have a bearing on their workplace productivity.

2.2 *Coping with Stress (CS)*

Stress is caused by facing up to unanticipated changing situations at home, in social situations as well as at work. It is at once a psychological as well as a physical body response, whereas when it comes to stressors, "stressors are external objective events that have the potential to create negative outcomes for individuals" (Lazarus & Folkman, 1984).

Controlling one's emotions when attempting to satisfy demands that are conflicting with each other is what coping with stress is all about. "Stress tolerance" defined by Bar-On, 1977 is "the ability to withstand adverse events and stressful situations without "falling apart" by actively and positively coping with stress".

Employee stress levels are modulated in a positive way by determining the sources of stress and then realizing how to manage the stress (Tagis, 2002). Employees prefer meditation as a tool to relieve stress (Nalawade & Pradhan, 2016). Mindfulness helps the individual to regulate the reaction to stress (Kadziolka et al., 2016). Practicing VM helps to reduce stress and enhances productivity, empathy and communication ability of the employees in the workplace (Hoge et al., 2017; Singh et al., 2017; Spadaro & Hunker, 2016).

2.3 Workplace Spirituality (WS)

Ashmos and Duchon (2000) stated that WS is "the recognition that employees have an inner life that nourishes and is nourished by meaningful work that takes place in the context of community".

Biberman and Whitty (1997) stated that "rekindling the spirit in work is not only good business, but also subconsciously sought after by workers and managers alike". Cheng (2016) put forth that organizational outcome can be positively affected by workplace spirituality. Employees perceive a sense of mutual respect and connectedness. This inspires them to promote changes and undertake beneficial activities leading to organizational development and transformation (Garg, 2017). Fulfillment in the workplace facilitates reduction in absenteeism, conflict and stress reduction leading to an enhanced work performance, a sense of well-being and improvement in quality of life (Afsar & Rehman, 2015; Lychnell, 2017; Marschke et al., 2011).

2.4 Emotional Intelligence (EI)

EI is "the ability to be self-disciplined, develop understanding and empathy for oneself and others and develop personal connection with others". As Goleman (1995) has stated, "emotional intelligence is a far more significant factor in personal performance than is IQ".

In a workplace context, harnessing emotional insight about oneself and colleagues and using it to understand and express feelings and emotions leads to enhanced cooperation and productivity. It is indicated that mindfulness facilitates EI and stress has adverse effect on EI (Baer et al., 2004, 2006; Brown & Ryan, 2003; Schutte & Malouf, 2011). Mindfulness is observed to mediate between stress and emotional intelligence (Oh & Koh, 2014). Subjective well-being (SWB) and life satisfaction are influenced by EI (Palmer et al., 2002). Further, EI has a positive effect on occupational stress (Bar-On et al., 2000), academic achievements (Van der Zee et al., 2002) and interpersonal relationships (Fitness, 2001). Improvement in well-being is observed due to increase in the level of EI brought about by mindfulness practice (Chu 2010; Sampaio et al., 2017).

2.5 Interpersonal Relationship (IR)

According to Bar-On (1997), IR is "the ability to establish and maintain mutually satisfying relationships that are characterized by intimacy and by giving and receiving affection".

Research indicates that satisfaction in relationships is influenced directly by the degree of mindfulness (Barnes et al., 2007; Michaels, 2007). Similarly, mindfulness practice enhances psychological well-being (Nyklicek & Kuijpers, 2008), emotional well-being (Weinstein et al., 2009), emotion regulation (Linehan, 1993) and empathy (Shapiro et al., 1998). Meditation also promotes the ability to respond adaptively in case of social conflict (Pepping et al., 2016), and this enhances day-to-day interpersonal functioning.

2.6 Psychological Well-Being (PWB)

By definition, PWB is "engagement with existential challenges of life" (Keyes et al., 2002). Ryff (1989), put forth PWB as "the striving for perfection that represents the realization of one's true potential". This is in tune with the Buddhist perspective where genuine well-being is, "realizing one's fullest potential in terms of wisdom, compassion and creativity" (Wallace & Shapiro, 2006).

Individual's goals for betterment and directions in life are, in themselves, an essential aspect of PWB. Moreover, achievement of one's purpose in life is an ardent task as it requires effort and discipline, which may mismatch with short-term happiness at times.

As reported by several studies, the focus of treatment programs related to mindfulness is reduction in indicators related to psychopathological issues (Reibel et al. 2001), stress (Kabat-Zinn, 1996) and betterment of well-being (Carmody & Baer, 2008). Buddhist view stresses that the basic quality of mindfulness is its ability to keep the mind in a tranquil state when facing trying situations or experiencing fear and pain (Goldstein & Kornfield, 2001).

Practicing VM enhances physiological as well as psychological well-being, triggering enhancement in cognitive and attentional abilities (Chambers et al., 2009; Moore & Malinowski, 2009). Hanley et al. (2017) showed a positive affect between selflessness, PWB and mindfulness. They further concluded that when self is more in tune with broader social and natural causes, there is a marked improvement in psychological well-being and mindfulness.

Meditation or yoga programs in prison demonstrated that inmates participating in these programs report greater PWB scores (Auty et al., 2015). Research has shown that those who enjoy supportive relationships develop a sense of well-being (Holt-Lunstad et al., 2010). Meditation helped students to achieve enhancement in PWB (Vijayaraghavan & Madhava Chandran, 2019).

2.7 *Vipassana Meditation*

Gautama Buddha rediscovered the technique of Vipassana meditation 2500 years ago. “Vipassana” in the ancient Pali language means, “to see things as they really are” in a special way, repeatedly in an iterative fashion.

Vipassana is also called as “insight” meditation, because it brings insight into the functioning of the human psyche. It helps to bring the attention to the physical and mental phenomenon as they are happening.

It is the practice of a “clear and single-minded awareness of what actually happens to us and in us, at the successive moments of perception” (Nyanaponika, 1973). This choice-less observation paves the way to observe and attend to all stimuli equally without any preference for any one of them. It helps the practitioner to develop non-judgment, and come out of interpretations, preferences and censorship of selection. Due to this, one’s mental patterns or processes no longer have control over his/her personality and behavior. This helps the individual, slowly but surely, come out of one’s uncontrolled and unaware psychic phenomenon, as the change happens at the experiential level (Nyanaponika, 1973).

Mindfulness appears to be linked to well-being as it helps to reduce ruminative thinking (Jain et al., 2007), disorders related to anxiety and mood swings (Goldin & Gross, 2010; Hofmann et al., 2010) and better emotion modulation (Arch & Craske, 2006). Modinos et al. (2010) have reported that non-meditators and meditator individuals’ ability to regulate emotional responses is governed by mindfulness. Brain studies undertaken by many researchers show case how meditation is facilitating long-term structural changes related to brain affect, positive affect and better immune system (Davidson et al., 2003; Hölzel et al., 2008; Luders et al., 2009); reduction in “amygdala response” related to emotional stimuli and increase in brain connectivity (Desbordes et al., 2012; Luders et al., 2011).

Banerjee (2012) documented that Vipassana meditator employees are more focused and composed. According to Avey et al. (2008), VM employees are more positive and optimistic due to being aware of their adverse thoughts, especially when, organizational change is taking place. Bhatnagar (2014) reported that VM facilitates productivity as anxiety in employees is reduced. According to Shiera and Graham (2011), Vipassana meditation has a positive effect on SWB. Marques and Satinder (2009) opine that VM practice enhances a feeling of well-being at work place paving the way for better productivity.

Also, it is observed that in addition to well-being, VM has a positive effect on psychological symptoms (Bowen et al., 2006; Chambers et al., 2008). The changes due to Vipassana were studied by self-report measures on well-being, cognitive flexibility and attentional abilities by Hartkamp and Thornton (2017). The studies showed that improved feelings of well-being are directly proportional to mindfulness level (Carmody & Baer, 2009; Chiesa & Serretti 2009; Wallace & Shapiro, 2006).

2.8 Mindfulness

Nyanaponika (1973) said mindfulness is "the clear and single-minded awareness of what actually happens to us and in us at the successive moments of perception". Hanh (1976) stated mindfulness is "keeping one's consciousness alive to the present reality".

Trait mindfulness could be developed as a skill and enhanced (Kabat-Zinn, 1996). Mindfulness practitioner can enjoy benefits in areas such as care giving (Shiera & Graham, 2011), health and well-being (Kabat-Zinn, 1982), personal growth (Ruedy & Schweitzer, 2010) and organizational environment (Avey et al., 2008).

Atkins and Parker (2012) documented that employee practicing mindfulness exhibited "compassionate organizational behavior". This indicates better psychological well-being as it is a demonstration of an individual's awareness and alertness in daily life situations.

Mindfulness awakens other mechanisms that positively impact PWB (Williams et al., 2000). Mindfulness also considerably decreases anxiety disorder (Hargus et al., 2010; Miller et al., 2012; Sharma et al., 2012).

Even brief mindfulness intervention indicated better emotional health and positive outlook toward life in participants (McCraty et al., 2003; Williams, 2006). Higher level of psychological well-being goes hand in hand with mindfulness and experience in meditation. Research has highlighted that mindfulness meditation practice is a useful intervention to enhance well-being (Bear, 2003; Segal et al., 2002; Wallace & Shapiro, 2006). Mindfulness-based stress reduction program (MBSR) showed considerable improvement in psychological well-being of participant patients who were suffering from rheumatoid arthritis (Pradhan et al., 2007). Non-clinical patients reported increase in mood and affect after practicing mindfulness, such as better mood and happiness even when the jobs were stressful (Davidson et al., 2003). The same findings were reported by employees working in healthcare sector (Galantino et al., 2005). Also, enhanced subjective well-being was observed in nonclinical patients (Orzech et al., 2009).

The literature review of the research conducted on psychological well-being indicates positive results when meditation techniques are used as an intervention. Mindfulness fosters positive relationships, increases PWB, creativity and performance related to task (Brown et al., 2007; Ryan & Deci, 2000). Penberthy et al. (2016) studied the effect of Tibetan Buddhist meditation on college students' PWB. The results suggest a positive outcome on the psychological well-being of participants and the mediating role played by mindfulness. Similar results are reported by other studies on college going students related to impact of mindfulness on PWB (Burns et al. 2011; Roberts-Wolfe et al. 2012).

Employees experience increase in engagement and productivity due to mindfulness practice. They also enjoy a sense of community and a greater team spirit which fosters a work ethic that delivers higher productivity (Krishna Kumar & Robinson, 2015).

3 Objectives of the Study

1. To study the effect of VM on the behavior and personality scores attained by meditators.
2. To study the effect of VM on the PWB scores attained by meditators.

4 Methodology

For this study, the research design used was After-Only with Control Design (Kothari & Garg, 2014).

The VM center selected for data collection was Bangalore Vipassana Meditation Center (Dhamma Pappula). Judgment sampling method was used for data collection. The subjects were employees from different organizations, coming to the center for a ten-day residential VM course. For administering the instrument, following two groups of employees were selected.

1. Control group = non-meditator employees; participating in their first VM course
2. Experimental group = Employee meditators who have completed minimum-3–10-day VM courses and have been practicing VM regularly

Participation in the study was voluntary. The questionnaire included clear instructions on filling it up and no personal details were captured. Participants had 3–4 h for completing the questionnaire. Questionnaire had a section for collecting demographic as well as information regarding Vipassana meditation practice being followed by the meditators. Before the start of the program, completed questionnaires were submitted by the participants (Pradhan et al., 2016). Total 240 responses were considered from each group after filtering out incomplete responses.

Aspects of employee's behavior and personality were measured by a specially designed Behavior Measure Scale (BMS) for this study. BMS was developed by incorporating four constructs identified through the literature review. These constructs were highly indicative of performance of the employee in the workplace. The constructs were interpersonal relationships, emotional intelligence, coping with stress and workplace spirituality.

The BMS scale was tested by conducting a pilot study. In the pilot study exploratory factor analysis (EFA) was conducted for a sample size of 395. Principal component analysis or PCA was employed by using varimax rotation to extract factors. The factors were validated by performing a confirmatory factor analysis or CFA for final 240 sample size, using *R* program for this purpose (Pradhan & Ajithkumar, 2017a).

A 5-point Likert scale was used. 1 = "Never or very rarely true" to 5 = "Very often or always true". The questionnaire had items like "*I like to challenge myself in a healthy and positive way*".

The research variables of interest were:

Table 1 Demographic composition of the two groups

Demographics	Control group %	Experimental group %
Mean age in years	38	39
Gender	Male proportion = 57	Male proportion = 57
Marital status	Married proportion = 63	Married proportion = 56
Education	Graduate and above = 90	Graduate and above = 91
Employment segment	Services and software = 57	Services and software = 62
Work position	Middle and senior = 54	Middle and senior = 55

- Equanimity
- Self confidence
- Self-awareness
- Interpersonal skills
- Empathy

To measure the psychological well-being (PWB) of the respondents, a standardized self-report scale modified by Mehrotra et al. (2013) was employed. This scale was originally developed by Ryff (1989) and is called the model of PWB scale (Ryff & Keyes, 1995).

This modified scale uses a 6-point Likert scale with: 1 = "Strongly disagree" to 6 = "Strongly agree" to measure four psychological factors. One of the items out of 20 items is *"I feel that I get a lot out of my friendships"*.

The four factors measured were

- Mastery and competence
- Positive relations
- Self-acceptance
- Engagement and growth

Higher scores meant higher levels of PWB (Pradhan & Ajithkumar, 2017b).

Care was taken to ensure that the two groups did not differ significantly on demographic parameters and a chi-square test was performed. The test confirmed that the two groups were independent of demographic factors as p values were greater than 0.05 for all demographic factors ($p > 0.05$).

The demographics of the group respondents are shown in Table 1.

4.1 Data Analysis

Quantitative data analysis was performed by employing SPSS Ver. 20.0. Analysis of the BMS data was carried out for determining the reliability and sampling adequacy for performing factor analysis using Cronbach Alpha and KMO test of sampling adequacy. The results for BMS indicated

Cronbach's Alpha = 0.846
KMO Measure = 0.846

Even though the PWB scale used was a standardized scale, the data collected was subjected to an EFA to confirm that the factor structure extracted was in line with the four-factor structure of PWB with the data sample collected. Reliability analysis was employed to test that the factors obtained were reliable. Kaiser–Meyer–Olkin (KMO) test was employed to test the sampling adequacy for running factor analysis. The values are shown below.

Cronbach's Alpha = 0.894
KMO Measure = 0.886

An independent sample *t*-Test for both the groups (240 respondents) indicated that meditator group secured higher mean scores on all five variables of BMS scale with $p < 0.05$ and four variables of the PWB scale with $p < 0.05$ (Pradhan & Ajith kumar, 2017b). Also, as shown in Table 2, all *t* values are negative. This shows that practicing Vipassana meditation makes a difference to all the nine scores achieved by the control group as compared to the experimental group, and the difference is statistically significant.

Table 2 Independent sample *t*-test for nine variables (BMS and PWB)

Factors	*t*-test (equality of means)				
	t	df	*p* value	Mean difference	Std. error difference
Interpersonal skills	−3.706	478	< 0.001	−0.955	0.258
Empathy	−4.465	478	< 0.001	−1.186	0.266
Self-awareness	−9.317	455.86	< 0.001	−2.391	0.257
Equanimity	−9.452	478	< 0.001	−2.688	0.284
Self-confidence	−4.604	462.55	< 0.001	−0.771	0.167
Self-acceptance	−5.079	474.42	< 0.001	−2.009	0.396
Mastery and competence	−5.733	478	< 0.001	−3.339	0.582
Positive relations	−2.597	478	< 0.010	−1.317	0.507
Engagement and growth	−4.689	474.51	< 0.001	−2.187	0.466

5 Discussion

The results on BMS and PWB met with the objective of the research and indicated that Vipassana meditation could be a useful intervention. As indicated in Table 2, above qualities like self-confidence, equanimity, interpersonal skills, empathy and self-awareness showed higher scores in meditator employees. The payoff for meditator employees was that they could remain equanimous and handle stressful situations better as well as were able to manage interpersonal relations in family and work arenas. This shows that meditator employees are able to deal with life situations with better awareness (Goenka, 2002). Also, with better interpersonal skills and empathy, the employees are better equipped to build teams and lead them well, leading to higher productivity by being focused on the goals, enabling organizations to become more productive. It becomes a win–win situation where the organization flourishes and the employees find that it is an ideal workplace.

When inner peace and calmness is experienced by the practitioner, he/she experiences greater clarity of thought, reduced self-delusion, self-control and is able understand others' point of view in an empathetic manner (Bockler et al., 2017). The increased self-awareness due to practicing VM gives a better sense of balance between mind and body resulting in reduction of automated non-adaptive reactions by induction of selective adaptive responses in the event of stressful life situations (Hart, 1987).

Equanimity helps the meditator to become resilient and handle stress situations well (Teasdale et al., 2000). Equanimous individuals are able to see that external events are transitory and will pass on their own. This gives them the ability to remain calm and becomes a natural stress relieving mechanism.

This research adds to the body of available literature. Experience in Vipassana meditation strengthens and enhances PWB (Lykins & Baer, 2009). Higher scores on PWB by meditators indicated development of abilities which helped them to maintain a harmonious environment and remain ethical in their dealings at work and life situations. Higher scores on "positive relations" and "engagement and growth" indicated that the meditator employees were able to form trusting and good relationships with others, are engaged in the task at hand and felt more positive and hopeful about themselves and life. They considered life as a process of learning and growth (Ryff & Keyes, 1995). They strive to attain mastery and competence in their field and show more responsibility and are more self-accepting. The higher PWB due to practicing meditation enables the practitioner to face and deal with work situations in a better and more effective manner. As PWB influences meaning in life, the results suggest that adopting meditation practice may help make life more meaningful.

These higher BMS and PWB scores would benefit employees in organizational scenarios because organizations predominantly comprise of teamwork, leadership, conflict management and they are essentially relational, focusing on social networking, effective communication, psychological safety and trust (Good et al.,

2016). The meditators with higher scores show that they can become better communicators through embracing the habit of listening with an open mind and be less judgmental of their peers, clients and superiors, resulting in better quality of relationship (Beach et al., 2013; Beckman et al., 2012).

The self-awareness brought about by practicing mindfulness is particularly relevant in the workplace (Creswell et. al., 2007; Lutz et al., 2016) as lack of self-control is the biggest block for successful leadership making it a useful key intervention in organizations (Doll et al., 2016; Marques, 2017). Mindfulness influences important attributes in organizations such as cognition, relationships and emotional control which are responsible for important aspects of workplace such as work performance and well-being (Good et al., 2016). At work, supervisory and managerial relations are very important as coordination and cooperation between them impacts performance (Dienesch & Liden, 1986; Mathieu, et al., 2000).

6 Limitations

"Before and After" study design was not implemented keeping in mind time considerations of the project.

7 Scope for Future Work

Changes occurring in an individual's personality due to VM practice are subjective. It would be interesting to study the changes in individual characteristics on a long-term basis stemming from the practice of Vipassana meditation.

8 Conclusion

The findings of this empirical research are in tune with existing literature. The findings showed higher scores on all nine behavior and personality research variables in case of meditator employees.

This study shows that there is a valid rationale to encourage employees in organizations to adopt and internalize Vipassana meditation as a part of their daily routine. Businesses attempt to employ various methods to enhance goal congruence in employees while reducing friction and enhancing team play. Adoption of VM can be an effective method to achieve these goals. This in turn can make the workplace a good place to be in and at the same time paving the way for commercial success.

References

Afsar, B., & Rehman, M. (2015). The relationship between workplace spirituality and innovative work behavior: The mediating role of perceived person–organization fit. *Journal of Management, Spirituality and Religion, 12*(4), 329–353.

Allport, G. W. (1961). *Pattern and growth in personality*. New York: Holt, Rinehart & Winston.

Arch, J. J., & Craske, M. G. (2006). Mechanisms of mindfulness: Emotion regulation following a focused breathing induction. *Behaviour Research and Therapy, 44*, 1849–1858.

Ashmos, D. P., & Duchon, D. (2000). Spirituality at work: A conceptualization and measure. *Journal of Management Inquiry, 9*(2), 134–144.

Atkins, P. W. B., & Parker, S. K. (2012). Understanding individual compassion in organizations: The role of appraisals and psychological flexibility. *Academy of Management Review, 37*(4), 524–546.

Auty, K. M., Cope, A., & Liebling, A. (2015). A systematic review and meta-analysis of yoga and mindfulness meditation in prison. Effects on psychological well-being and behavioural functioning. *International Journal of Offender Therapy and Comparative Criminology, 61*(6), 689–710. https://doi.org/10.1177/0306624X15602514

Avey, J. B., Wernsing, T. S., & Luthas, F. (2008). Can positive employees help positive organization change? *Journal of Applied Behavioural Science, 44*, 48–70.

Baer, R. A. (2003). Mindfulness training as a clinical intervention: A conceptual and empirical review. *Clinical Psychology: Science and Practice, 10*, 125–143. https://doi.org/10.1093/clipsy/bpg015

Baer, R. A., Smith, G. T., & Allen, K. B. (2004). Assessment of mindfulness by self-report: The Kentucky inventory of mindfulness skills. *Assessment, 11*, 191–206.

Baer, R. A., Smith, G. T., Hopkins, J., Krietemeyer, J., & Toney, L. (2006). Using self-report assessment methods to explore facets of mindfulness. *Assessment, 13*, 27–45.

Banerjee, S. (2012). A key to alleviate business related challenges: Crunching meditation science and its influence on brain and physiology. *International Journal of Management, 3*(2), 348–369.

Barnes, S., Brown, K. W., Krusemark, E., Campbell, W. K., & Rogge, R. D. (2007). The role of mindfulness in romantic relationship satisfaction and responses to relationship stress. *Journal of Marital and Family Therapy, 33*(4), 482–500.

Bar-On, R. (1997). *The emotional quotient inventory (EQ-I): Technical manual*. Toronto, Canada: Multi-Health Systems.

Bar-On, R., Brown, J. M., Kirkcaldy, B. D., & Thome, E. P. (2000). Emotional expression and implications for occupational stress; an application of the emotional quotient inventory (EQ-i). *Personality and Individual Differences, 28*, 1107–1118.

Beach, M. C., Roter, D., Korthuis, P. T., Epstein, R. M., Sharp, V., Ratanawongsa, N., Cohn, J., Eggly, S., Sankar, A., Moore, R. D., & Saha, S. (2013). A multicenter study of physician mindfulness and health care quality. *The Annals of Family Medicine, 11*, 421–428.

Beckman, H. B., Wendland, M., Mooney, C., Krasner, M. S., Quill, T. E., Suchman, A. L., & Epstein, R. M. (2012). The impact of a program in mindful communication on primary care physicians. *Academic Medicine, 87*, 815–819.

Bhatnagar, V. (2014). Stress management—a way to increase efficiency and effectiveness of employees: A study of Vipassana meditation. *International Journal of Application or Innovation in Engineering and Management (IJAIEM), 3*(1)

Biberman, J., & Whitty, M. (1997). A post-modern spiritual future at work. *Journal of Organizational Change Management, 10*, 130–138.

Böckler, A., Herrmann, L., Trautwein, F. M., Holmes, T., & Singer, T. (2017). Know thy selves: Learning to understand oneself increases the ability to understand others. *Journal of Cognitive Enhancement*. https://doi.org/10.1007/s41465-017-0023-6

Bowen, S., Witkiewitz, K., Dillworth, T. M., Chawala, N., Simpson, T. L., Ostafin, B. D., & Marlatt, G. (2006). Mindfulness meditation and substance use in an incarcerated population. *Psychology of Addictive Behaviours, 20*, 343–347.

Brown, K. W., & Ryan, K. M. (2003). The benefits of being present: Mindfulness and its role in psychological well-being. *Journal of Personality & Social Psychology, 84*(4), 822–848.

Brown, K. W., Ryan, R. M., & Creswell, J. D. (2007). Mindfulness: Theoretical foundations and evidence for its salutary effects. *Psychological Inquiry, 18*, 211–237.

Burns, R. A., Anstey, K. J., & Windsor, T. D. (2011). Subjective well-being mediates the effects of resilience and mastery on depression and anxiety in a large community sample of young and middle-aged adults. *The Australian and New Zealand Journal of Psychiatry, 45*(3), 240–248.

Carmody, J., & Baer, R. A. (2008). Relationships between mindfulness practice and levels of mindfulness, medical and psychological symptoms and well-being in a mindfulness-based stress reduction program. *Journal of Behavioral Medicine, 31*(1):23–33. https://doi.org/10.1007/s10865-007-9130-7

Carmody, J., & Baer, R. A. (2009). How long does a mindfulness-based stress reduction program need to be? A review of class contact hours and effect sizes for psychological distress. *Journal of Clinical Psychology, 65*(6), 627–638.

Chambers, R., Lo, B.C.Y. & Allen, N.B. (2008). The impact of intensive mindfulness training on attentional control, cognitive style, and affect. *Cognitive Therapy and Research, 32*, 303–322. https://doi.org/10.1007/s10608-007-9119-0

Chambers, R., Gullone, E., & Allen, N. B. (2009). Mindful emotion regulation: An integrative review. *Clinical Psychology Review, 29*, 560–572. https://doi.org/10.1016/j.cpr.2009.06.005

Cheng, F. K. (2016). What does meditation contribute to workplace? An integrative review. *Journal of Psychological Issues in Organizational Culture, 6*, 18–34. https://doi.org/10.1002/jpoc.211

Chiesa, A., & Serretti, A. (2009). Mindfulness-based stress reduction for stress management in healthy people: A review and meta-analysis. *Journal of Alternative and Complementary Medicine, 15*(5), 593–600.

Chu, L. C. (2010). The benefits of meditation vis-à-vis emotional intelligence, perceived stress and negative mental health. *Stress and Health, 26*, 169–180. https://doi.org/10.1002/smi.1289

Creswell, J. D., Way, B. M., Eisenberger, N. I., & Lieberman, M. D. (2007). Neural correlates of dispositional mindfulness during affect labeling. *Psychosomatic Medicine, 69*, 560–565.

Davidson, R. J., Kabat-Zinn, J., Schumacher, J., Rosencranz, M., Muller, D., Santorelli, S. F., et al. (2003). Alterations in brain and immune function produced by mindfulness meditation. *Psychosomatic Medicine, 65*, 564–570

Desbordes, G., Negi, L. T., Pace, T. W. W., Wallace, B. A., Raison, C. L., & Schwartz, E. L. (2012). Effects of mindful-attention and compassion meditation training on amygdala response to emotional stimuli in an ordinary, non-meditative state. *Frontiers in Human Neuroscience, 6*, 292. https://doi.org/10.3389/fnhum.2012.00292

Dienesch, R. M., & Liden, R. C. (1986). Leader–member exchange model of leadership: A critique and further development. *Academy of Management Review, 11*, 618–634.

Doll, A., Hölzel, B. K., Bratec, S. M., Boucard, C. C., Xie, X., Wohlschläger, A. F., & Sorg, C. (2016). Mindful attention to breath regulates emotions via increased amygdala–prefrontal cortex connectivity. *NeuroImage, 134*, 305–313.

Kazdin, A. E. (2000). Encyclopedia of Psychology. Washington, D.C: American Psychological Association, Oxford University Press. Oxford [Oxfordshire].

Ferguson, R. C. (1981). Vitalizing intimacy in marriage. *Family Process, 20*, 250–251.

Fitness, J. (2001). Emotional intelligence and intimate relationships. In J. Ciarrochi, J. P. Forgas, & J. D. Mayer (Eds.), *Emotional intelligence in everyday life: A scientific inquiry* (pp. 98–112). Philadelphia: Psychology Press.

Galantino, M., Baime, M., Maguire, M., Szapary, P. O., & Farrar, J. T. (2005). Association of psychological and physiological measures of stress in health-care professionals during an 8-week mindfulness meditation program: Mindfulness in practice. *Stress and Health: Journal of the International Society for the Investigation of Stress, 21*, 255–261.

Garg, N. (2017). Workplace spirituality and employee well-being: An empirical exploration. *Journal of Human Values, 23*(2), 129–147. https://doi.org/10.1177/0971685816689741

Glomb, T. M., Duffy, M. K., Bono, J. E., & Yang, T. (2011). Mindfulness at work. In J. Martocchio, H. Liao, & A. Joshi (Eds.), *Research in personnel and human resource management* (pp. 115–157). https://doi.org/10.1108/S0742-7301(2011)0000030005

Goenka, S. N. (2002). *Meditation now: Inner peace through inner wisdom.* Washington: Vipassana Research Publications.

Goldin, P. R., & Gross, J. J. (2010). Effects of mindfulness-based stress reduction (MBSR) on emotion regulation in social anxiety disorder. *Emotion, 10*, 83.

Goldstein, J. & Kornfield, J. (2001). *Seeking the heart of wisdom: The path of insight meditation.* Shambhala Publications, ISBN: 0834825252, 9780834825253

Goleman, D. (1995). *Emotional intelligence: Why it can matter more than IQ.* Bloomsbury.

Gopalakrishna, D. (2006). *Buddhism and Contemporary Management.* Kandy Sri Lanka: Buddhist Cultural Centre.

Good, D. J., Christopher, J., Lyddy, C. J., Glomb, T. M., Bono, J. E., Brown, K. W., Duffy, M. K., Baer, R. A., Brewer, J. A., & Lazar, S. W. (2016). Contemplating mindfulness at work: An integrative review. *Journal of Management, 42*(1), 114–142. https://doi.org/10.1177/0149206315617003

Hanh, T. N. (1976). *The miracle of mindfulness.* Boston: Beacon Press.

Hanley, A. W., Baker, A. K., & Garland, E. L. (2017). Self-interest may not be entirely in the interest of the self: Association between selflessness, dispositional mindfulness and psychological well-being. *Personality and Individual Differences, 117*, 166–171.

Hargus, E., Crane, C., Barnhofer, T., & Williams, J. M. G. (2010). Effects of mindfulness on meta-awareness and specificity of describing prodromal symptoms in suicidal depression. *Emotion, 1*, 34–42

Hart, W. (1987). *The art of living: Vipassana meditation as taught by S N Goenka.* New York: Harper & Row.

Harter, J. K., Schmidt, F. L., & Keyes, C. L. (2002). Business-unit level relationship between employee satisfaction, employee engagement and business outcomes: A meta data analysis. *Journal of Applied Psychology, 87*, 268–279.

Hartkamp, M., & Thornton, I. M. (2017). Meditation, cognitive flexibility and well-being. *Journal of Cognitive Enhancement, 1*, 182–196. https://doi.org/10.1007/s41465-017-0026-3

Hofmann, S. G., Sawyer, A. T., Witt, A. A., & Oh, D. (2010). The effect of mindfulness-based therapy on anxiety and depression: A meta-analytic review. *Journal of Consulting and Clinical Psychology, 78*, 169.

Hoge, E. A., Guidos, B. M., Mete, M., Bui, E., Pollack, M. H., Simon, N. M., & Dutton, M. (2017). Effects of mindfulness meditation on occupational functioning and health care utilization in individuals with anxiety. *Journal of Psychosomatic Research, 95*, 7–11.

Holt-Lunstad, J., Smith, T. B., & Layton, J. B. (2010). Social relationships and mortality risk: A meta-analytic review. *PLoS Medicine, 7*, e1000316. https://doi.org/10.1371/journal.pmed.1000316

Holzel, B. K., Ott, U., Gard, T., Hempel, H., Weygandt, M., Morgan, K., et al. (2008). Investigation of mindfulness meditation practitioners with voxel-based morphometry. *Social Cognitive and Affective Neuroscience, 3*, 55–61.

Jain, S., Shapiro, S. L., Swanick, S., Roesch, S. C., Mills, P. J., Bell, I., & Schwartz, G. R. (2007). A randomized controlled trial of mindfulness meditation versus relaxation training: Effects on distress, positive states of mind, rumination, and distraction. *Annals of Behavioral Medicine, 33*, 11–21.

Kabat-Zinn, J. (1982). An out-patient program in behavioral medicine for chronic pain patients based on mindfulness meditation: Theoretical considerations and preliminary results. *General Hospital Psychiatry, 4*, 33–42.

Kabat-Zinn, J. (1996). Mindfulness meditation: What it is, what it isn't, and its role in health care and medicine. In Y. Haruki, Y. Ishii, & M. Suzuki (Eds.), *Comparative and psychological study on meditation* (pp. 161–170). Netherlands: Eburon Publishers.

Kadziolka, M. J., Di Pierdomenico, E. A., & Miller, C. J. (2016). Trait-like mindfulness promotes healthy self-regulation of stress. *Mindfulness, 7*(1), 236–245. https://doi.org/10.1007/s12671-015-0437-0

Kothari, C. R., & Garg, G. (2014). *Research methodology*. New Age International Publishers.

Krishnakumar, S., & Robinson, M. D. (2015). Maintaining an even keel: An affect-mediated model of mindfulness and hostile work behavior. *Emotion, 15*(5), 579–589. https://doi.org/10.1037/emo0000060

Keyes, C. L. M., Shmotkin, D., & Ryff, C. D. (2002). Optimizing well-being: The empirical encounter of two traditions. *Journal of Personality and Social Psychology, 82*(6), 1007–1022.

Lazarus, R. S., & Folkman, S. (1984). *Stress, appraisal, and coping*. New York: Springer.

Levy, D. M., Wobbrock, J. O., Kaszniak, A. W., & Ostergren, M. (2012). The effects of mindfulness meditation training on multitasking in a high-stress information environment. In *Proceedings—Graphics Interface* (pp. 45–52).

Linehan, M. (1993). *Cognitive-behavioural treatment of borderline personality disorder*. New York: Guilford Press.

Luders, E., Toga, A. W., Lepore, N., & Gaser, C. (2009). The underlying anatomical correlates of long-term meditation: Larger hippocampal and frontal volumes of gray matter. *NeuroImage, 45*, 672–678.

Luders, E., Clark, K., Narr, K. L., & Toga, A. W. (2011). Enhanced brain connectivity in long-term meditation practitioners. *NeuroImage, 57*(4), 1308–1316.

Lutz, J., Brühl, A. B., Doerig, N., Scheerer, H., Achermann, R., Weibel, A., Herwig, U. (2016). Altered processing of self-related emotional stimuli in mindfulness meditators. *NeuroImage, 124*, 958–967. https://doi.org/10.1016/j.neuroimage.2015.09.057

Lychnell, L. (2017). When work becomes meditation: How managers use work as a tool for personal growth. *Journal of Management, Spirituality and Religion, 14*(3), 255–275.

Lykins, E. L. B., & Baer, R. A. (2009). Psychological functioning in a sample of individuals with long-term meditation experience. *Journal of Cognitive Psychotherapy, 23*, 226–241.

McCraty, R., Atkinson, M., & Tomasino, D. (2003). Impact of a workplace stress reduction program on blood pressure and emotional health in hypertensive employees. *The Journal of Alternative and Complementary Medicine, 9*(3), 355–369.

Marques, J. (2017). A mindful moral compass for twenty-first century leadership: The noble eightfold path. *The Journal of Values-Based Leadership, 10*(1), 7

Marques, J., & Satinder, D. (2009). Vipassana meditation as a path toward improved management practices. *Journal of Global Business Issues, 3*(2), 77–84.

Marschke, E., Preziosi, R., & Harrington, W. (2011). Professionals and executives support a relationship between organizational commitment and spirituality in the workplace. *Journal of Business and Economics Research, 7*(8), 33–48.

Maslow, A. H. (1968). *Toward a psychology of being*. New York: D. Van Nostrand Company.

Mathieu, J. E., Heffner, T. S., Goodwin, G. F., Salas, E., & Cannon-Bowers, J. A. (2000). The influence of shared mental models on team process and performance. *Journal of Applied Psychology, 85*, 273–283.

Mehrotra, S., Tripathi, R., & Banu, H. (2013). Psychological well-being: Reflections on an elusive construct and its assessment. *Journal of the Indian Academy of Applied Psychology, 39*(2)

Merriam-Webster Dictionary. (2015). *Encyclopædia Britannica Online*. Retrieved June 24, 2015

Michaels, J. B. (2007). *Mindfulness training and relationship satisfaction*. Pacific Graduate School of Psychology, ProQuest Dissertations Publishing.

Miller, C. K., Kristeller, J. L., Headings, A., Nagaraja, H., & Miser, W. F. (2012). Comparative effectiveness of a mindful eating intervention to a diabetes self-management intervention among adults with type 2 diabetes: A pilot study. *Journal of the Academy of Nutrition and Dietetics, 112*(11), 1835–1842. https://doi.org/10.1016/j.jand.2012.07.036

Modinos, G., Ormel, J., & Aleman, A. (2010). Individual differences in dispositional mindfulness and brain activity involved in reappraisal of emotion. *Social Cognitive and Affective Neuroscience, 5*, 369–377.

Moore, A., & Malinowski, P. (2009). Meditation, mindfulness and cognitive flexibility. *Consciousness and Cognition, 18*(1), 176–186. https://doi.org/10.1016/j.concog.2008.12.008

Nalawade, R. C., & Pradhan, S. (2016). Stress relieving techniques for organizational stressors. *International Journal of Research in Commerce & Management, 7*(3), 93–98. ISSN 0976–2183.

Nyanaponika, T. (1973). *The heart of Buddhist meditation: Satipatthna: A handbook of mental training based on the Buddha's way of mindfulness*. Weiser Books. 01-Jun-1973-Religion-223-pages

Nyklíček, I., & Kuipers, K. (2008). Effects of mindfulness-based stress reduction intervention on psychological well-being and quality of life: Is increased mindfulness indeed the mechanism? *Annals of Behavioral Medicine, 35*(3), 331–340.

Oh, J. K., & Koh, H. S. (2014). The mediating effect of mindfulness in the relationship between emotional intelligence and stress among clinical nurses. *The Korean Journal of Stress Research, 22*(3), 139–147.

Orzech, K. M., Shapiro, S. L., Brown, K. W., & McKay, M. (2009). Intensive mindfulness training-related changes in cognitive and emotional experience. *The Journal of Positive Psychology, 4*(3), 212–222.

Ossorio, P. G. (2006). *The behavior of persons*. Descriptive Psychology Press.

Palmer, B., Donaldson, C., & Stough, C. (2002). Emotional intelligence and life satisfaction. *Personality and Individual Differences, 33*(7), 1091–1100.

Penberthy, J. K., Williams, S., Hook, J. N., Le, N., Bloch, J., Forsyth, J., Schorling, J., et al. (2016). Impact of a Tibetan Buddhist meditation course and application of related modern contemplative practices on college students' psychological well-being: A pilot study. *Mindfulness, 8*(4). https://doi.org/10.1007/s12671-016-0665-y

Pepping, C. A., Walters, B., Davis, P. J., et al. (2016). Why do people practice mindfulness? An investigation into reasons for practicing mindfulness meditation. *Mindfulness, 7*(2), 542–547.

Petchsawanga, P., & Duchon, D. (2012). Workplace spirituality, meditation and work performance. *Journal of Management, Spirituality and Religion, 9*(2), 1–20.

Pradhan, E. K., Baumgarten, M., Langenberg, P., Handwerger, B., Gilpin, A. K., Magyari, T., Hockberg, M. C., & Berman, B. M. (2007). Effect of mindfulness-based stress reduction in rheumatoid arthritis patients. *Arthritis Care and Research, 57*, 1134–1142.

Pradhan, S., Ajithkumar, V. V., & Singh M. (2016). Effect of Vipassana meditation on mindfulness and life satisfaction of employees. *International Journal of Research in Commerce and Management (IJRCM), 7*(3), 11–16. ISSN 0976–2183.

Pradhan, S., & Ajithkumar, V. V. (2017a). Vipassana Meditation: An Effective Practice for Positive Changes in Employees. *Skyline Business Journal, XIII* (1), 45–59. (2017–2018). ISSN 1998–3425.

Pradhan, S., & Ajithkumar V. V. (2017b). The impact of Vipassana meditation practices on psychological wellbeing of employees. *International Journal of Applied Business and Economic Research, 15*(16) (Part-II). ISSN: 0972–7302. www.serialsjournals.com

Reibel, D. K., Greeson, J. M., Brainard, G. S., & Rosenzweig, S. (2001). Mindfulness-based stress reduction and health-related quality of life in a heterogeneous patient population. *General Hospital Psychiatry, 23*, 183–192.

Roberts-Wolfe, D., Sacchet, M. D., Hastings, E., Roth, H., & Britton, W. (2012). Mindfulness training alters emotional memory recall compared to active controls: Support for an emotional information processing model of mindfulness. *Frontiers in Human Neuroscience, 6*(15).

Ruedy, N., & Schweitzer, M. (2010). In the moment: The effect of mindfulness on ethical decision making. *Journal of Business Ethics, 95*, 73–87.

Ryan, R. M., & Deci, E. L. (2000). Self determination theory and the facilitation of intrinsic motivation, social development and well-being. *American Psychologist, 55*, 68–78.

Ryff, C. D. (1989). Happiness is everything, or is it? Explorations on the meaning of psychological well-being. *Journal of Personality and Social Psychology, 57*(6), 1069–1081. https://doi.org/10.1037/0022-3514.57.6.1069

Ryff, C. D., & Keyes, C. L. (1995). The structure of psychological well-being revisited. *Journal of Personality and Social Psychology, 69*(4), 719–727. https://doi.org/10.1037/0022-3514.69.4.719

Sampaio, C. V. S., Lima, M. G., & Ladeia, A. M. (2017). Meditation, health and scientific investigations: Review of the literature. *Journal of Religion and Health, 56*(2), 411–427.

Schutte, N. S., & Malouff, J. M. (2011). Emotional intelligence mediates the relationship between mindfulness and subjective well-being. *Personality and Individual Differences, 50*(7), 1116–1119.

Segal, Z. V., Williams, J. M. G., & Teasdale, J. D. (2002). *Mindfulness-based cognitive therapy for depression: A new approach to preventing relapse*. New York: Guilford Press.

Shapiro, S. L., Schwartz, G. E., & Bonner, G. (1998). Effects of mindfulness-based stress reduction on medical and premedical students. *Journal of Behavioral Medicine, 21*(6), 581–599. https://doi.org/10.1023/A:1018700829825

Sharma, M. P., Mao, A., & Paulomi, S. M. (2012). Mindfulness based cognitive behaviour therapy in patients with anxiety disorders: A case series. *Indian Journal of Psychological Medicine, 34*(3), 263–269.

Shiera, M. L., & Graham, J. R. (2011). Mindfulness, subjective well-being and social work: Insight into their interconnection from social work practitioners. *Journal of International Social Work, 30*(1), 29–31.

Singh, G., Maurya, A., & Jain, V. (2017). Spirituality in Indian organizations. In S. Nandram, & P. Bindlish (Eds.), *Managing VUCA through integrative self-management. Management for professionals.* Cham: Springer. https://doi.org/10.1007/978-3-319-52231-9_12

Spadaro, K. C., & Hunker, D. F. (2016). Exploring the effects of an online asynchronous mindfulness meditation intervention with nursing students on stress, mood, and cognition: A descriptive study. *Nurse Education Today, 39*, 163–169. https://doi.org/10.1016/j.nedt.2016.02.006

Taugis, J. (2002). Stress management for police special forces. *Journal of Applied Sport Psychology, 14*(4), 330–343. https://doi.org/10.1080/10413200290103590

Teasdale, J. D., Segal, Z. V., Williams, J. M. G., Ridgeway, V. A., Soulsby, J. M., & Lau, M. A. (2000). Prevention of relapse/recurrence in major depression by mindfulness-based cognitive therapy. *Journal of Consulting and Clinical Psychology, 68*(4), 615–623.

Van der Zee, K., Thijs, M., & Schakel, L. (2002). The relationship of emotional intelligence with academic intelligence and the big five. *European Journal of Personality, 16*(2), 103–125.

Vijayaraghavan, N. & Madhava Chandran, K. (2019). Effect of meditation on psychological well-being. *International Journal of Indian Psychology, 7*(2), 673–678. DIP 18.01.080/20190702. https://doi.org/10.25215/0702.080

Wallace, B. A., & Shapiro, S. L. (2006). Mental balance and well-being: Building bridges between Buddhism and western psychology. *American Psychologist, 61*(7), 690–701.

Weinstein, N., Brown, K. W., & Ryan, R. M. (2009). A multi-method examination of the effects of mindfulness on stress attribution, coping, and emotional well-being. *Journal of Research in Personality, 43*(3), 374–385. https://doi.org/10.1016/j.jrp.2008.12.00

Williams, K. (2006). Mindfulness-based stress reduction (MBSR) in a worksite wellness program. In R. A. Baer's (Ed.), *Mindfulness-based treatment approaches: Clinician's guide to evidence base and applications* (pp. 361–376). Burlington, MA: Academic Press

Williams, J. M. G., Teasdale, J. D., Segal, Z. V., & Soulsby, J. (2000). Mindfulness-based cognitive therapy reduces over general autobiographical memory in formerly depressed patients. *Journal of Abnormal Psychology, 109*, 150–155.